W9-BAU-001

A HISTORY OF AFRICA

South of the Sahara

A
HISTORY
OF AFRICA

South of the Sahara

by
DONALD L. WIEDNER

RANDOM  HOUSE

New York

TO

F. L. W.

AND THE MEMORY OF

G. G. W.

ACKNOWLEDGMENTS

THE AUTHOR of a historical work is deeply indebted to the scholars and chroniclers who have gone before. Whether he criticizes or accepts their theses, he recognizes that they have shaped his background and colored his own approach.

For specific criticism, advice and encouragement, the writer must turn to friends, colleagues and contemporary authorities. It is therefore a pleasure to acknowledge, with gratitude, the most helpful attention that each of the following people gave to portions of the manuscript:

Professor Gwendolen M. Carter, Smith College
Professor John Lobb, Mount Holyoke College
Dr. Robert I. Rotberg, Harvard University
Dr. Miriam Taylor Sajkovic, Mount Holyoke College

A word of appreciation is also extended to many others who have aided either in resolving single points or in discussing the general problems of interpreting African history.

D. L. W.

EDMONTON, ALBERTA

ACKNOWLEDGMENTS

CONTENTS

LIST OF MAPS

INTRODUCTION

1

PREFACE

DOES Africa have a history? In one sense history is made whenever and wherever man may live, and he has been as long in Africa as elsewhere. It used to be said that history exists only when we have enough coherent written records and archaeological remains to form a chronological pattern that can be interpreted. Egypt, the Nile Valley and North Africa have long been accepted as places with such a history, but south of those regions the traditional tools rarely uncover cohesive sources. Africa, it was believed, had no history except that which the Mediterranean and European explorers and colonists wrote in quite recent times; the African people had no history of their own until they came into contact with Europeans.

Modern methods and recent developments in attitude have substantially altered this perspective. Documents and archaeology are no longer the only sources of historical knowledge. Alternative methods have been yielding much valid material in recent years. In several cases the new methods have even led to the discovery of African documents or remains that might otherwise never have come to light.

Investigation that does not necessarily employ documents or archaeology began to develop extensively with the applica-

tion of scientific and psychological knowledge in the late nineteenth and early twentieth centuries. Its application to Africa,
in the form of anthropology and sociology, occurred relatively late, but it was discovered that Africans had preserved an
extensive tradition in both secular and religious legends. Many
of these are imaginary reconstructions or explanations of unknown phenomena. Usually the most credible legends emphasize lists of kings, battles, perhaps major migrations; the dating
of specific occurrences is often altered or compressed, and frequently the order of names and events is arbitrarily transposed.
Skeptics argue that the legends are no more accurate than a
game of chance, but there are several methods by which many
confused items can be corrected and valid legends separated
from fiction. If the oral tradition clearly records events that also
are described by European or Arab writers, many other details
in the tradition are likely to be accurate, and dates can be established. Archaeology sometimes helps to establish the authen-
ticity of a legend. At least once, an oral account included details
of a solar eclipse 250 years earlier; this corresponded exactly to
European astronomical calculations. In some cases land titles
are orally defined for centuries; the accuracy of these recollec-
tions is of such vital interest to every generation that major errors are almost impossible. Often the storyteller is heard and
corrected by other tribesmen who also know the tradition. The
legends of one tribe may resemble those of another group, but
this kind of evidence is inconclusive because of the possibility
of borrowing. Such legends, however, usually retain some impli-
cation of their origin, and their transmission—sometimes over
great distances or through intermediaries—is in itself a significant
historical phenomenon.

There are a number of extremely valuable written accounts
and chronicles—many by Arab travelers or scholars, a few by
Negro Africans in Arabic—that shed light on events in parts of
East and West Africa below the Sahara. In some cases, these
reach back more than ten centuries before the arrival of modern
Europeans.

Africa therefore has a history of its own. The chronicle can also be expanded and tested by using the reports of travelers, conquerors and traders from countries that had developed the art of record-keeping. From the unique combination of African historical sources there emerge several recurrent themes. Against a background of tribal organization and culture, the historian must consider indigenous political, economic, geographical, cultural and religious development. These societies, while continuing these processes, also begin to interact with European technological and institutional influences; then, as part of the modern world, Africans of both indigenous and European origin come increasingly into contact with one another and with the outside world, while both adapt their varied historical traditions to current environment and circumstance. There is neither more nor less homogeneity in Africa than in the European or American continents, and it should not be necessary to impose artificial unity in order to justify the study of a relatively large area. Variety as well as similarity can be explored by a general survey.

The Mediterranean littoral of Africa, centered on Egypt but extending with Islam westward to the Straits of Gibraltar, has long been a subject known to Western readers and historians. Sub-Saharan Africa was virtually unknown to any ancient or medieval Mediterranean civilization except the Arabic. Thus, there has rarely been much concern with regions below the Sahara, beyond the main course of the Nile River, south of the Highlands of Ethiopia. This part of Africa, rather than the entire geographical area, is therefore the most suitable unit to bring to modern attention.

2

BACKGROUND

BELOW the Sahara, Africa's vast northern desert, the dominant feature is neither mountain nor romantic jungle, but vast savannas consisting of grassland broken irregularly by trees and an occasional sluggish river. This grassland resembles the virgin American prairie between Texas and the Dakotas, but it is usually warmer and drier for most of the year. The rainfall in Africa is a particular problem because it is usually concentrated in one season of the year and often is insufficient to support the demands made upon the land. Only Australia has fewer mountains or highlands than Africa; both South America and south Asia have far more of the tropical rain forest popularly called "jungle."

Africa has an area of about 11,600,000 square miles, but almost 5,000,000 of those are in the Sahara and along the Mediterranean. Of the 6,600,000 square miles below the desert (twice the area of the United States) about 20 percent is tropical rain forest, where there is more rainfall and thicker vegetation than in the southeastern United States. The other 80 percent of sub-Saharan Africa has less annual rainfall than Miami, Florida. No part of Africa registers temperatures as high as those in the eastern United States, except in the Sahara itself, but only the South African mountains get as cool as a winter day in Washing-

TOPOGRAPHY OF AFRICA

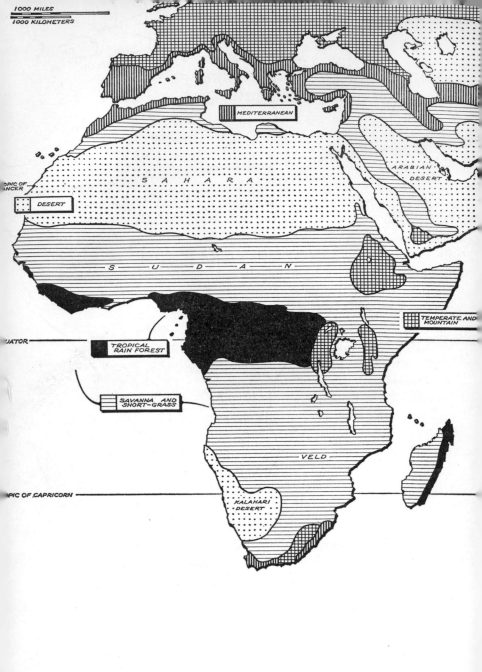

CLIMATE OF AFRICA

ton, D. C. Except for the rain forest, Africa's climatic range compares roughly to that of the area from Louisiana through Texas to New Mexico.

North Africa, bordering on the Mediterranean, has a semitropical to temperate climate, depending upon altitude, the most noticeable difference from the European shore of the Mediterranean being that it is slightly drier and, with the exception of Morocco and Algeria, yields rapidly to Saharan conditions. The Sahara is more inclined to be rocky than sandy, so there are several reliable, important waterholes or oases cropping out from its variegated 4,000,000 square miles. It is pierced at only one point in its width by any significant feature: the Nile River, which is largely navigable and constitutes a primary irrigation resource.

The beginnings of the savanna, where dry farming can be sustained, are found below the desert. Savanna grass increases in density and height until it yields abruptly to the line of the rain forest in the west and the middle; in the east, between the rain forest and the Ethiopian Highlands, the Nile forms dense papyrus swamps called the sudd. Farther upstream the Nile touches the eastern edge of the rain forest and brings a form of the savanna down to Equatorial Africa and the African Great Lakes. Westward, along the Congo River and the Atlantic coast, is the rain forest; on the east, the temperate Kenya Highlands and the savannas surrounding them; to the southwest, dry tropic scrubs. A ribbon of open country continues down through the center of the continent to South Africa where it broadens into the veld. This is another grassland, quite similar to the northern savanna. South Africa also has a series of coastal highlands beyond which there is an oceanside climate known as "Cape Mediterranean" because it is so similar to that of the Riviera. Marginal, limited deserts are found east of Kenya in the "Horn" of Somalia, and north of the Cape in Bechuanaland.

Although most of the sub-Saharan Africa has therefore a fairly uniform climate, there is a limited rain-forest area that has spectacular variations in both rainfall and vegetation. In three-quarters of this so-called "jungle," the annual rainfall is between 59.0 and 78.7 inches (Mobile, Alabama, averages 67.6 inches); the remaining quarter of the rain forest—about 5 percent of the land below the desert—ranges from 78.7 to almost 400 inches. Such heavy precipitation occurs in three areas: (1) parts of Guinea, Sierra Leone, Liberia and the Ivory Coast; (2) the central Congo basin; and (3) the Niger Delta and the Cameroons coast. The 200- to 400-inch belt is only found on the slopes of Mount Cameroon.

Rain-forest vegetation is dense. The nature of the undergrowth and the major trees varies considerably both in type and in tenacity, but these characteristics correspond quite logically to the amount of precipitation. Most of the Congo basin and the region immediately to its south would be rain forest, were there much rain; instead, there is "dry forest" with deciduous trees that shed their leaves onto a grassy savanna. Scattered areas of rain-forest vegetation are found along the southeast coast (Mozambique and Natal); this phenomenon is due to a steady year-round rainfall rather than to any spectacular amount of precipitation.

Except for the southeast coast, Africa has pronounced, predictable wet and dry months, and there is a consistent pattern of variation in these seasons from north to south. No general storm tracks are noticeable between the temperate Mediterranean and Cape areas, again except Mozambique, which is on the edge of a tropical storm belt.

Political boundaries are due less to geographical factors than to complex and frequently arbitrary historical factors, but geography did determine the routes of communication and commerce until European political and technological power made it possible to defy nature. Three major rivers (the Nile, the Niger and the Congo) are almost as important for communication as they used to be, but their utility for transport is limited by inconvenient falls, rapids, sandbars or seasonal fluctuation. Lesser rivers, such as the Shiré, Volta, Senegal and Gambia, were rarely used until modern times.

Human occupation extends over all of West, East, Central and South Africa; some is found scattered across the Sahara as well, but the thickest concentrations are along the West African Coast, between the Senegal River and the Cameroons (with particular density in the Niger Delta, northern Nigeria and the Ghana seaboard region); around the Great Lakes and along the Kenya-Uganda Railway (but most concentrated in Ruanda-Urundi); and in the eastern and southern parts of Southern Rhodesia and the Republic of South Africa. These more crowded areas compare roughly to the density variations within France, Ireland or Virginia, but the greater sub-Saharan area has a population about as scattered as that of northern Sweden or the American plains.

The widespread distribution of African population is quite a recent development, for about 500 years ago the densest occupation probably centered around the Niger River and the equatorial Great Lakes areas; the coasts and the southern parts of Africa seem to have been sparsely populated. In ancient times the southern and central Sahara were probably the most intensively peopled, with only a sparse distribution in the areas presently designated as savannas and forests. The earliest history is therefore found in the desert, after which interest shifts to the Niger savanna and the shores of Lake Victoria.

A number of recent discoveries indicate that the human species (Homo sapiens) may have originated in Africa. The earliest specimens seem to have been most similar, in both appearance and behavior, to the modern Bushmen, Pygmies and Australian aborigines. Scholars cannot agree whether modern Caucasians and Negroes are descended from these prototypes or developed in parallel.[1] However, it seems likely that the Bushmen types were scattered from South Africa through East Africa to Ethiopia, while Pygmies filtered from western Kenya through

[1] See the works of L. S. B. Leakey, especially *Adam's Ancestors* (4th ed.), London, 1953; the report of the Royal Anthropological Institute conference, *Early Human Remains in East Africa*, Cambridge, 1933; and *Proceedings of the 1st Pan-Africanist Congress on Pre-History*, Oxford, 1952.

the Congo and the coastal rain forests of West Africa; some of the Australoids were absorbed by the other two, but the rest migrated through Asia to Australia and Oceania.[2]

Caucasian types also began to appear in western Kenya. They are known variously as Capsian people, early Cushites or early Hamites, but there is no agreement whether this was an evolution from Bushman ancestry or another independent development. These people, it is believed, migrated northeastward into Arabia and western Asia as well as northwestward into Egypt and North Africa. Recent scholars (notably Joseph H. Greenberg)[3] have suggested that the term Cushite be applied to this parent Caucasian race, and that their basic language be called Afroasiatic (formerly Hamitic). Bushman would then be the name of another race, whose speech is called Khoïsan. Nothing definite is known about original Pygmy language, since this race adopted completely the languages of its later conquerors.

The origin of the Negroes has been the greatest enigma. A variation within the Cushites, or a combination of Cushites with either Bushmen or Pygmies, has been considered. Older theories, involving Negroes in India or Indonesia who mysteriously migrated but left no evidence on their way, are now discredited.

Dating of these prehistoric developments is necessarily approximate and relative, pending further research, but it appears that: (1) Cushites, Bushmen and Pygmies were quite distinct before 10,000 B.C., (2) Cushites who were developing Caucasian characteristics penetrated Egypt about 5,000 B.C., but (3) Negroes cannot be distinguished before about 6,000 B.C. (some suggest even as late as 4,000 B.C.). When they did appear, they were in the Sahara, well above the rain forest but not touching

---

[2] For discussion of the complexities of these and the following theories, see Sonia Cole, *The Prehistory of East Africa*, Harmondsworth, 1954; and Henriette Alimen (A. Broderick, transl.), *The Prehistory of Africa*, London, 1957.

[3] Joseph H. Greenberg, *Studies in African Linguistic Classification*, New Haven, 1955, pp. 54-55. The older summary by C. G. Seligman, *Races of Africa*, New York, 1930, is outdated.

the Mediterranean, and running from the Nile almost to the Atlantic Ocean. The best guess, supported only by slim evidence, seems to be that Negroes were a branch of Cushites on the upper Nile, quite close to Kenya, and that they spread rapidly westward. As far as scholars can tell, the initial occupation of the Sahara was by Negroid people who quickly dominated the whole area. Most of them spoke Niger-Congo (formerly called Negritic) languages.

Africa's four basic racial and linguistic groups therefore seem to have originated within a radius of 250 miles of Lake Victoria, although it is not known whether they had a common human ancestry. Quite clearly, the geographical distribution about 4,000 B.C. was approximately as follows: Bushmen in South and East Africa; Pygmies throughout the rain forest and most of the dry forest; groups of Caucasians along both the Asian-African shores of the Red Sea and across the North African littoral to the Atlantic Ocean (Morocco), with other Caucasian extensions from Arabia through Mesopotamia into Europe and central Asia; and Negroes in the Sahara and the savanna north of the rain forest. The language divisions seem to have been similar to the racial lines. Afroasiatic-speaking Caucasians developed five major linguistic subgroups: Semitic in Arabia and Mesopotamia, Berber along the northwest coast of Africa, Ancient Egyptian, Chadic in the Sahara, and the early Cushitic in Ethiopia. Niger-Congo divisions began to emerge, the major ones being Mande or Mandingo (western Sahara), Eastern-Negritic or Adamawa-Eastern (eastern Sahara), and Bantoid, also known as Central-Negritic or Semi-Bantu (southeastern Nigeria and the Cameroons Highlands). Negroes in the Nile Valley seem to have developed an entirely distinct language family, called Sudanic. This may have been based upon a conglomeration of Neolithic people's tongues, or an early break from the Negritic-language family. It is difficult to be more precise because speakers of Sudanic were buffeted repeatedly by the invasions of Ancient Egyptians, the Cushitic Ethiopians and Eastern-Negritic Negroes before 1000 A.D.; thereafter, Semitic Arabs, more Ne-

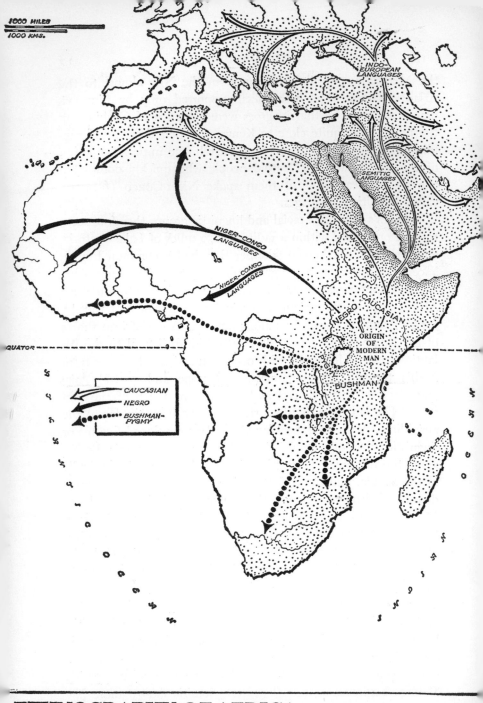

ETHNOGRAPHY OF AFRICA BEFORE 300 B.C. *(HYPOTHESIS)*

gritic speakers and various slave raiders have increased the confusion. Other language groups, which are neither widespread nor
well analyzed, are found in the eastern Sahara and the Nile
Valley, but the rest of Africa today is inhabited by people speaking Afroasiatic, Niger-Congo or Khoïsan tongues.

Between 8,000 and 4,000 B.C., four isolated groups of people throughout the world seem to have developed fixed agricultural methods. There is a considerable difference in time
among these early settlements, but no evidence of contact between any two. No other groups would have been capable of
transmitting this knowledge. Furthermore, the crops, methods
and social organization of each of these four preclude the existence of contact or transfer from one to the other. The four
distinct developments may have been (1) the Semitic branch of
Afroasiatic-speaking Caucasians in the Jordan or Tigris Valleys,
(2) the Mongoloid occupants of east Asia, (3) the American Indians between Mexico and Peru, and (4) the Mande Negroes
of the African savanna, along the upper reaches of the Niger
River between the rain forest and the Sahara. Ancient Egypt
probably learned about crop cultivation from Jordan and Iraq,
while the Negro methods gradually spread eastward from the
middle Niger to the upper Nile Valley. Egypt then merged the
cultures of the Fertile Crescent and of the Negroes—the first
contact of major cultures in human history—but, as a result, it
has been difficult to separate one culture's achievements from
the other. It used to be thought that the Negro achievement
was a result of the spread of Mesopotamian ideas through Egypt
and the Nile to the savanna Negroes, but carbon-dating and archaeological evidence now suggest separate beginnings (c. 5,000
in Jordan and before 4,000 in Africa) with contact between the
two not taking place in Egypt until a much later date.

The dating of these developments, and therefore the precise
location, relative importance and causal connection among
them, remain open to question. The strongest case for the
preceding theory has been built on anthropological and linguistic
grounds by George Peter Murdock, but Christopher Wrigley has

responded with a comparable argument that would reëmphasize the importance of Palestinian agriculture and place the first Negro cultivators along the Nile Valley. Arguing from the botanical viewpoint, Roland Portères would consider Africans to have invented agriculture quite independently, but would date its appearance as late as 1500 b.c. J. D. Fage, reviewing these interpretations from the historical viewpoint, favors Portères' dating and argues for coastal or middle-Niger Negroes other than the Mande.[4]

It is agreed that the Negroes, at some early date, developed several cereals (including the basic form of sorghum and several types of millet and rice), okra, certain forms of yams and groundnuts (peanuts), watermelons and gourds, kola, tamarind and sesame. Wrigley thinks many of these were borrowed or adapted early in African history, but both authorities agree that the most spectacular achievements were the cultivation of wild *Gossypium herbaceum* into the cotton plant and the adaptation of its fibers to textile manufacture, as well as the use of oil-producing plants (such as palms). Presumably, most of these were transmitted to the ancient Egyptians between 3,000 and 1,000 b.c., and thenceforth to Europe, India and the Orient. Major crops received from Mesopotamia and Egypt, via the Nile, were barley and wheat, peas and lentils, beets, onions, radishes, cabbages, grapes and melons, figs, garlic, olives and linen flax. Some time later, cucumbers, bananas, sugar cane, ginger and new forms of rice were introduced from east Asia. In Ethiopia, products such as coffee and cress were developed after agricultural methods had been learned from the Negroes and the Egyptians. European slave traders eventually introduced avocados, tobacco, maize

---

[4] See George Peter Murdock, *Africa: Its Peoples and Their Culture History*, New York, 1959, pp. 40-45, 64-70; Christopher Wrigley, "Speculation on the Economic Prehistory of Africa," *Journal of African History*, vol. I, no. 2, pp. 189-203; Roland Portères, "Vieilles agricultures de l'Afrique intertropicale," *L'Agronomie Tropicale*, vol. V, 1950, pp. 489-507; J. D. Fage, "Anthropology, Botany, and the History of Africa," *Journal of African History*, vol. II, no. 2, 1961, pp. 302-304.

(American corn), lima and string beans, pumpkins and toma-
toes.

For perhaps two or three thousand years the Negro maintained a substantial sedentary agricultural economy between
the forest and the desert. Much evidence exists to show that
the area now known as the Sahara was much more fertile in this
period, and that it could support extensive populations on herds
of cattle grazed there. Doubts about the Sahara's former fer-
tility were stilled by the work of the Lhote expedition[5] in 1956-
57, which produced evidence that agriculture without irrigation
was possible throughout most of the region until about 2,000
B.C., that cattle grazing was widespread until about 1,000 B.C.,
and that horses could be grazed extensively until Roman times.
About 46 B.C., when horses and oxen could no longer survive in
the desert, it was the Romans who solved the problem by introducing camels from central Asia. However, these "ships of
the desert" were not numerous or significant until the fourth
century after Christ.[6]

It is difficult to imagine that an area larger than the United
States, today a barren desert, could have been so fertile within
historic memory; however, the evidence of Henri Lhote, the reports of Roman traders, archaeological finds, and geological
analysis of the region all confirm this striking evolution. The
causes are difficult to ascertain, but erosion and lack of conservation by both the coastal Berbers and the inland Negroes
seem to have contributed. There are today points along the
fringe of the Sahara where desert conditions are penetrating arable land at the rate of five miles per year. Although this is unusual, it illustrates how two small patches of prehistoric desert
have grown into a divisive wasteland in about 3,000 years.

Because it was spreading, the Sahara is said to have been a

[5] Henri Lhote, *"Peintures préhistoriques du Sahara"* (catalogue of exhibition, Paris, 1958) and *La découverte des fresques du Tassili*, Paris, 1958.
[6] E. W. Bovill, *The Golden Trade of the Moors*, London, 1958, pp.
42, 48.

"living" desert which forced its human inhabitants to retreat—
Berbers to a thin, rather densely populated strip along the Mediterranean and Negroes into the savanna. A population pressure
began to develop below the desert in the first millennium B.C.
Fortunately a new ironworking technology and some new crops
for intensive cultivation appeared among the Negroes at this
time, making possible the development of alternative means of
support.

The earliest iron founders were probably the Hittites, about
2,000 B.C. This metal was not used in Egypt until almost a thousand years later, and became known to Carthage about 500 B.C.
Ironworking spread up the Nile from Egypt in the fifth century
B.C., where, at Meroë, a short distance north of modern Khartoum, iron production became a major industry. Meroë would
have been the logical source for Negro knowledge of iron, but
the Nile producers were very secretive. It is therefore quite likely
that Carthage taught the West Africans about metallurgy, for
horses still carried regular traders across the growing desert.
Clearly, Negroes were using iron about 300 B.C. in order to make
more efficient use of the dwindling savanna. Iron tools and arma-
ments also made possible the invasion and clearing of tropical
rain forests, where the expanding population could be accommo-
dated.

The role of agriculture in the invasion of the rain forests
has become a topic of discussion among recent scholars. Murdock
believes that the tropical forest was habitable only after sweet
potatoes and bananas had been introduced from Indonesia. He
therefore postulates the existence of an Indonesian settlement
before 100 B.C. on the East African coast, from which the new
crops were transmitted by a complex process along the southern
edge of the Sahara to the Niger basin.[7] Most of his colleagues
have quite convincingly replied: that Indonesian settlement
probably took place between 600 and 900 A.D., and then in
Madagascar, not East Africa; that any new crops could just as
easily have come along the well-known trade routes through

[7] Murdock, op. cit., pp. 207-211.

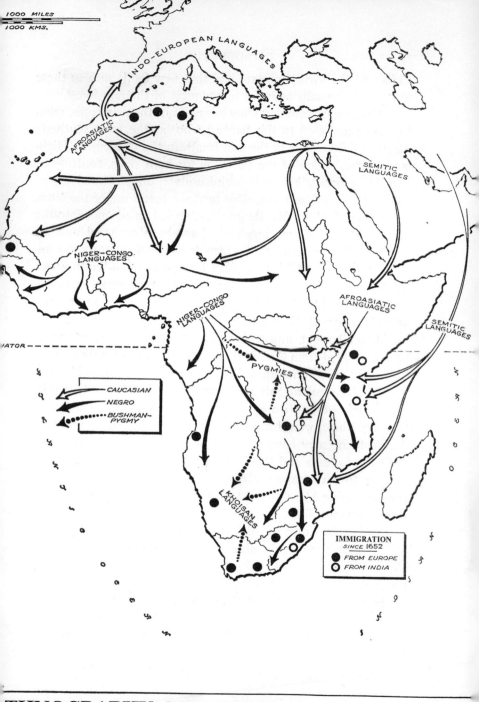

1000 MILES
1000 KMS.

INDO-EUROPEAN LANGUAGES

AFROASIATIC LANGUAGES

SEMITIC LANGUAGES

NIGER-CONGO LANGUAGES

NIGER-CONGO LANGUAGES

AFROASIATIC LANGUAGES

SEMITIC LANGUAGES

EQUATOR

PYGMIES

CAUCASIAN
NEGRO
BUSHMAN-PYGMY

KHOISAN LANGUAGES

IMMIGRATION
SINCE 1652
● FROM EUROPE
○ FROM INDIA

THNOGRAPHY OF AFRICA SINCE 300 B.C. *(MIGRATIONS)*

India and the Mediterranean; and that new foods such as these were not necessarily essential to conquest of the rain forest.

The new ironworking knowledge, if not the new crops, seem to have penetrated to the Bantu,[8] who, as the most southerly Negroes, lived closest to the rain forest, in the Cameroons Highlands. Introduction of the new skill, or both skills, contributed to a Bantu population explosion of unusual dimensions. Negroes to the north and west were able to make better use of the lands they already had, but the Bantu spearheaded an advance into the rain forest, which may previously have been occupied only by scattered Pygmy hunters. Spectacular population bursts are unusual, but ancient China, modern Europe and the Bantu about the time of Christ seem to share this phenomenon. The causes are always hard to pinpoint, but the Bantu occasion can be given as valid a hypothetical explanation as any of the others.

A similar but much less spectacular expansion seems to have emanated from Arabia through Ethiopia to the borders of Meroë in the centuries immediately preceding the birth of Christ. The Semitic-speaking Sabeans crossed from Yemen to the Ethiopian Highlands; Afroasiatic-speaking Cushites, previously established there, were forced to disperse thinly throughout East Africa. Some may have resettled as far away as Mozambique. Both the Sabeans and the Cushites seem to have known about iron, or to have learned about it during this period—probably from declining Meroë—and to have used iron tools to cut their distinctive monoliths.

It was the Bantu expansion, rather than the Cushitic, which was to make the greatest alteration in the human geography of Central, East and South Africa. During the early Christian centuries the Bantu had penetrated deeply into the Congo basin, bringing pastoral, agricultural and ironworking techniques and eliminating or subjugating the sparse Pygmy hunter groups. The pressure from the original centers in the Cameroon Highlands

---

[8] Properly, Bantu-speaking people, predominantly Negroid, who are customarily designated simply by the name of their language group.

apparently continued for some time, forcing the advance groups to press on gradually toward the east and south; as they expanded, conquered, and overran the Pygmies, the better-armed, better-fed Bantu seem to have developed increasingly strong military and political systems. When the pioneer spearheads discovered the fertile, open Great Lakes country, between 600 and 900 A.D., they were more efficiently organized and more viable units than the weak, autonomous clusters that were left behind in the Cameroons and in the rain forests. Once clear of the forest, Bantu-speaking vanguards spread rapidly southward to occupy the newly discovered savanna.

For example, the Batonga (modern Sotho)[9] group apparently penetrated by the tenth century as far as Southern Rhodesia, where they achieved a degree of unity stronger than any other Bantu migrants. Another series of Bantu moved more slowly toward the mouth of the Congo and Angola.

Ironworking was thus spread across the greater part of sub-Saharan Africa in the space of about 1200 years—between 300 B.C., among the Negroes in the Niger savanna, and 900 A.D. among the Batonga Bantu in Southern Rhodesia—but not all the credit can be theirs. Before the spearheads from the Cameroons reached the southern savanna, some of the Khoïsan peoples there had already learned about iron and cattle, probably from the small bands of Cushites who had brought this knowledge with them as far as the Zambezi basin at the time of Christ. Desmond Clark[10] has recently discovered that the Bantu arrived in this area 500 to 800 years after the Khoïsan people had begun to work with iron, but there was no effective production until the Bantu introduced advanced skills and organization. The well-developed Batonga spearhead also encountered the Caucasian Cushites, who had taught the Khoïsan ironworkers. The culture that resulted will be considered in the context of East Afri-

[9] Basil Davidson, *Old Africa Rediscovered*, London, 1960, p. 214.
[10] J. Desmond Clark, *The Prehistory of Southern Africa*, Harmondsworth, 1959, p. 283 ff.

can history after the tenth century. However, it was the Bantu occupation which was crucial in the development of history in southeastern Africa.

The Bantu units living along the Great Lakes chain, which provides a break in the rain forest, settled in well-organized societies and gradually accepted Cushitic influences. Others continued to penetrate from the lake districts toward the east coast, occupying sections of Tanganyika and Kenya between 1000 and 1500 A.D. East of the Great Lakes they encountered Bushmen, but these were either eliminated or reduced to isolated dependent colonies, just as the rain-forest Pygmies had been.

The third, or southwestern, group of Bantu encountered the dry forest and then the Bushmen as they pushed southward along the Atlantic coast. Their tribes near the Congo's mouth became particularly strong by the fifteenth century and had extensive contact with Portugal, while those moving on into Bushman territory were discouraged by increasing aridity. From the latter contact there arose two curious phenomena which have perplexed scholars. Both these problems involve people who, though speaking Khoïsan languages like the Bushmen, are quite different in appearance. One of these groups, composed of settled Negro farmers, is in all likelihood descended from Bantu warriors whose children were raised by enslaved or concubine Bushmen. The second question involves the Hottentots, formerly misclassified as a mixture of Ethiopian Cushites and Kenya Bushmen.[11] The Hottentots are now believed to be simply Bushmen who learned about cattle from the Bantu, thus improving their diet and becoming larger than other Bushmen, whom they otherwise resemble.[12]

Europeans used to believe that all African societies had the same kind of organization, but recent research has revealed many differences among tribal structures. It is probably true that the prehistoric tribes all traced individual rank and privilege through

[11] See C. Meinhof, *Der Sprachen der Hamiten,* Hamburg, 1912; Isaac Schapera, *The Khoïsan Peoples of South Africa,* London, 1930. See also comments by Murdock, *op. cit.,* pp. 52-53, 56-57.

[12] Greenberg, *op. cit.,* pp. 80-87.

the female line (matrilineal) rather than the male line (patri-lineal). The change from uniform matrilineal traditions to the contemporary complexity is sometimes attributed to military and agricultural influences over the last 4,000 years; for example, patri-lineal or male descent is characteristic of all Caucasians, as well as those Negroes who, like the southeastern Bantu, have been spearheads of semimilitaristic expansion, and of those whose economy has been sedentary, agricultural and commercial, such as the large tribes of the West African savanna. Matrilineal forms continue to prevail among people remaining in the Sahara, among Negroes in the West African rain forest, and among the Bantu in the dry forest of Central Africa behind the warrior spearheads. Whether or not their evolution is cor-rectly traced in theory, variations in social organization—in Africa as in Europe—have probably been haphazard and regional rather than consistent and universal.

There have been many speculations and contradictory theo-ries in the reconstruction of prehistoric Africa's human geog-raphy. Nevertheless, some consideration of the major hypoth-eses, such as those discussed in this chapter, furthers the un-derstanding of subsequent history.

BOOK ONE

OLD AFRICA

3

TRIBES AND EMPIRES

EARLY contact between the agricultural Negroes of West Africa and the ironworking Caucasians in Egypt and North Africa marked the beginning of a long period of cultural and commercial interchange. Carthage and the Roman Republic were both interested in the Negro trade. Ivory, gold and some slaves came northward; glass, salt, perhaps wine and wheat moved south from the Mediterranean borderlands. Desert communications were always difficult, especially when horses had to be abandoned, but the gradual introduction of the camel, early in the Christian era, revived trade and made possible some significant Berber migrations from the north to the southern side of the Sahara.

Salt is scarce in the Sudan area between the Sahara and the rain forest. The gradual recession of the desert had driven the Sudanic Negroes farther from the source of this coveted seasoning and preservative. Salt could be obtained below the Sahara only by the laborious distillation of grass or by carrying it through the treacherous rain forest from the tropical shores of the South Atlantic Ocean. Saharan salt was therefore of prime importance. Development of the saltpans in the north-central desert became a Berber responsibility, with salt being exchanged for gold and for Negro slaves to employ in the saltworks.

Trade, dependent upon the Berber camel, brought about the commercialization and political reorganization of the agricultural Negroes in the Sudan. The point of contact between Negroes and Berbers was usually along the Niger River, at the south edge of the desert across which the Berbers carried the salt. The Niger, an east-west artery for the Sudan, provided access both to the gold mines (probably near the source of the river, in modern French Guinea) and to the consumers of salt all along the river from Guinea to Nigeria. Among those who may have participated in this developing commerce were members of the Jewish trading communities in Roman Carthage and Cyrenaica—some of them may have been driven across the desert after a revolt in the second century A.D.—who settled along the Niger and Senegal rivers.

Tenth-century Arab travelers reported that, according to a Sudanic tradition, "white" conquerors organized and ruled the Niger Valley between the fifth and eighth centuries, after which a Soninke (Mande or Mandingo) Negro uprising installed an indigenous dynasty. Whether or not there was such a white dynasty, it is quite obvious that some kind of governmental organization and commercial centralization became necessary when the Mande farmers began to trade with camel caravans, exchanging salt for gold, between the second and fifth centuries.

No one knows what language was used in this Sudanic state—traditionally known as Ghana—but archaeologists have uncovered cities that were dependent upon extensive trade, and travelers document the existence of a strong monarchy, a system of established taxation and administration, and residences for both Berber traders and Negro subjects. Ghana acquired political control over the mid-Saharan salt mines, but the gold mines on her southern frontier remained in tribal hands. The Sudanic farmers controlled the crossroads, and the Berbers managed the saltpans and ran the caravans. Gold was obtained by a curious "silent trade." Tribal miners would leave gold ore on a riverbank; Ghanaian merchants piled salt

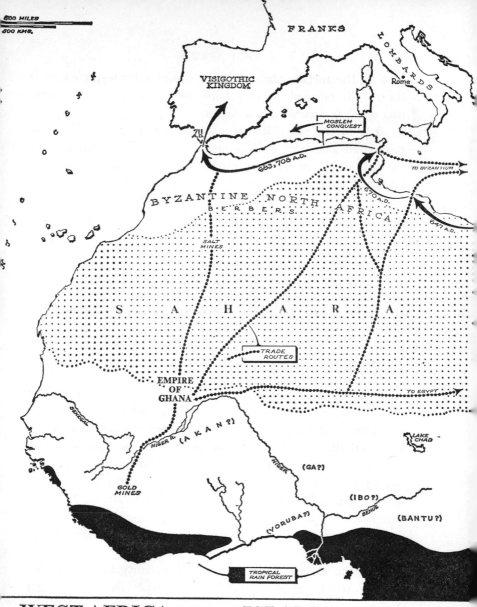

WEST AFRICA BEFORE ISLAM, 7th CENTURY

FRANKS

LOMBARDS

VISIGOTHIC
KINGDOM

Rome

MOSLEM
CONQUEST

711 A.D.

TO BYZANTIUM

BYZANTINE   NORTH   AFRICA

B E R B E R S

653, 708 A.D.

670 A.D.

647 A.D.

SALT
MINES

S A H A R A

TRADE
ROUTES

EMPIRE
OF
GHANA

TO EGYPT

SENEGAL

NIGER R.   (A K A N ?)

LAKE
CHAD

NIGER

(GA?)

GOLD
MINES

(IBO?)

BENUE

(BANTU?)

(YORUBA?)

TROPICAL
RAIN FOREST

next to the metals; the tribesmen would return—taking away the salt if satisfied, leaving both and starting the procedure over again if they wanted a bigger payment.

Far to the east, Caucasian people speaking a Semitic language had long been infiltrating into Africa. From the land of the Sabeans (Sheba), in southern Arabia, traders and migrants repeatedly crossed the Red Sea to the Abyssinian Highlands, in the first millennium B.C. Finally, the Sabean government also moved, and became, by the fourth century A.D., the Kingdom of Axum, or Ethiopia. Jews of the Diaspora, also Semitic-speaking, had likewise spread into Africa, but they were strongest in Egypt and tended to adopt Hellenistic civilization. Christianity followed the Jews of the Diaspora, and—as happened elsewhere in the Roman Empire—became the dominant religion of North Africa and the lower Nile Valley by the fourth century. Latin Christianity acquired a strong foothold around ancient Carthage, while Monophysite (Coptic) orthodox forms prevailed in Egypt and spread up the Nile to become dominant in Meroë (renamed Nubia by the Christians) and Axum. The core of the new religion was Palestinian and Eastern, but the converts in Africa were indigenous, not invaders. At least some of the Berber camel drivers and traders in the Sahara at this time accepted the Christian beliefs, but others may also have been refugees who chose the desert in order to continue their older religion. Christianity did therefore dominate in the east, but failed to penetrate the desert in the west. Non-Christian Berbers, many[1] believe, introduced Carthaginian religious ideas in Negro Ghana.

By the early seventh century Christianity had influenced all of Africa north of the rain forest, except Ghana, the Niger Valley and the Nile headwaters. However, Ethiopia was the only permanent convert. Islam, preached by the Prophet Mohammed in Arabia, rose steadily to the dominant position

[1] See especially Eva L.-R. Meyerowitz, *The Akan of Ghana*, London, 1958; also Basil Davidson, *Old Africa Rediscovered*, London, 1960, pp. 68-70; and Maurice Delafosse, *Haut-Sénégal-Niger*, 3 vols., Paris, 1912.

that it still holds north of the rain forest. Christianity lost most of its early footholds and did not reappear in Africa until the Europeans began to expand a thousand years later.

Mohammed led his followers from their hostile native Mecca to hospitable Medina, the first triumph and expansion, in the summer of 622. From this Hegira, Mohammedans—and most Africans in the savanna and Sahara today—measure the passage of time. Late in the year A.H. ("after Hegira") 10, or June of 632, the Prophet died, leaving behind a sacred scripture or Koran containing religious, social and political ordinances that made possible for the first time the organization of his nomadic converts on the basis of a universal religion rather than restrictive, divided, blood-related groupings. Divided tribes became one nation under the new religious law, but it took many months to enforce unity within the Arabian desert. Once thus organized, the Bedouins became eager to spread their faith to the rich Fertile Crescent.

On Easter Sunday of 634, less than two years after Mohammed's death, Bedouin marauders defeated the Byzantine Christians and besieged Damascus. Most of the Fertile Crescent, from Palestine to Persia, fell within three years, and Caliph Omar's armies passed through the Isthmus of Suez to cross the Nile near Cairo in the spring of 640. Four years later, Africa from Egypt to Carthage was paying tribute, but Christians continued to hold Nubia on the middle Nile and the Berber territory west of Carthage.

Byzantine counterattacks, the consolidation of gains, and a dynastic squabble after Omar's death combined to prevent further expansion for another generation, but between 670 and 683 the Arabs destroyed rebellious Carthage, ousted the Byzantines from present-day Algeria and reached the Atlantic. Berber uprisings forced the Arabs back to Egypt, but the Prophet's armies returned for permanent occupation a quarter of a century later. Conquering Berber converts, led by General Tarif, crossed to Europe in 711 at Jabal Tariq (Mount Tarif, or Gibraltar), occupied Spain and invaded France, where they were stopped twenty-one years later. The Moors—as the Berber and Arab mixture was known—consolidated their position south of the Pyrenees. At first, Moslem Spain was an outpost of the centralized Arab Caliphate at Damascus, but by 757 it had become virtually independent under the rule of a different dynasty.

The next 350 years were marked by dynastic quarrels and disputes among the Berber, Arab, and Spanish Moslems for privileged positions, but the divisions among the Christian guerrillas in the Pyrenees and the African administrators for the eastern caliph were just as great. Expansion was stopped and local independence increased throughout the Moslem world, including Africa; everywhere west of Suez a thin veneer of Arab warriors ruled through an unreliable body of indigenous converts over a heterogeneous unconverted population. Fighting disrupted irrigation and agriculture; forests were denuded to build ships for war and piracy; and the desert engulfed fertile land that was now being abused. For a while Berbers gained the upper hand, but in the eleventh century the central caliph—now a Fatimid at Baghdad—turned 200,-000 marauding Hilal Bedouins from Arabia loose upon North Africa. These Hilalians—the first large wave of Semitic-speaking settlers—ousted the Berbers from the coastlands, dominated the North African society, and transformed Islam from a religion of rulers to a mass faith.

Two consequences for Africa emerge from these events: the area of modern Libya and Tunisia became less fertile, so trans-Saharan traders developed new routes that favored the larger and less devastated Farthest West (modern Morocco); and some Berbers, rather than accept Arab domination and orthodox Islam, migrated across the desert to settle near the Atlantic coast, west of the Empire of Ghana. These Berbers gave their tribal name—Sanhaja, or Senegal—to the river along which they lived. Nominally they were Moslems, but zeal and conformity did not interest them.

Occasionally a Sanhaja Berber ruler would make the expected pilgrimage to Mecca. Early in the eleventh century Paramount Chief Yahia did this. He succumbed to the influence of a theologian on the way and brought back with him a fiery orthodox preacher named Ibn Yacin. Yahia's followers, not as enthusiastic as their chieftain, drove Ibn Yacin and his disciples onto an island in the Senegal River. These hermits (El Morabethin, or Almoravids) attracted curiosity, then converts, and returned to rule Sanhaja society. In 1042 their jihad for the purification of Islam began. Ibn Yacin's Almoravids brought the Berbers of the desert, who were lax Moslems, under his control; pagan, Negro Ghana was attacked in 1054, and the Arab caliphate in Morocco was annexed three years later.

In Spain Christian guerrilla organization had improved. The continued existence of quarreling Moslem rulers was threatened, so Yusuf—the successor to Ibn Yacin among the Almoravids—was asked to use his strong army to maintain order. Unity was restored to Moslem Spain and the Christians roundly defeated by 1086, leaving Yusuf the sole authority between northern Spain and the African rain forest. Such an incongruous empire was impossible to administer; it was soon realized that the Almoravids attacking Ghana (which fell in 1076) had become quite independent of Yusuf's main army in the north.

Almoravid power was almost as short-lived as Ibn Yacin's fervid reforms, but much was changed. The Spanish Christians were forced for the first time to unite in defense, with which unity they later took the offense; the commercial and political glory of Ghana was never fully restored. Intertribal feuds replaced true central government below the Sahara, with local independence predominating over the national interest. Ghana continued to exist until the thirteenth century, but only as a shadow of its former greatness.

Islam became the nominal religion of Ghana and most other Negro states throughout the western Sudan, but many preferred to emigrate rather than accept any part of the new faith. Among these were the Fulani cattle raisers who moved east into the area of modern northern Nigeria, and, perhaps, some who became the ruling class of the Akan tribes on the edge of the forest.

Early in the thirteenth century several short-lived tribal conquerors exercised control over part or all of Ghana, but the most orthodox Moslems, the Negroes of Mali, acquired a firm grasp on the area after 1235. Political order and commercial prosperity returned, still based upon the trans-Saharan gold-and-salt exchange; Mali for a time held sway from the Atlantic Ocean to the western edge of modern Nigeria. The existence of this empire was well known to Europeans of the fourteenth century, and the Mali ascendancy may have been the most active and advanced period in African history before the Europeans came. Mansa Musa, the Mali ruler who traveled to Mecca in 1324, was seen in Cairo by Venetian traders and created a legend of ostentatious wealth that survived in Egypt and Italy for some time. Medieval Arab travelers reported that Timbuktu, which had by 1100 replaced the tents and grass huts of Ghana City as the leading entrepôt of Africa, was now a center of brick buildings and Islamic education under Mansa Musa.

Ghana had not controlled the gold mines upon which its wealth depended; neither did the Almoravids or the empire of Mansa Musa. In all three cases wealth lay in the commerce which organized government made profitable. This very position, however, invited conquest by anyone who could provide either better organization or more direct access to the mines. Knowledge of Mansa Musa's wealth excited the desire of other Negroes, of Moroccan Arabs and eventually of the European Christians to take over or to by-pass the wealthy Mali trade monopoly.

One such people, the Negro Songhai—many of whom lived under and resented Mali's rule—arose and entered Timbuktu in 1468. Mali gradually crumbled before the interlopers. Few of them had accepted Islam, but in 1492 a Moslem coup

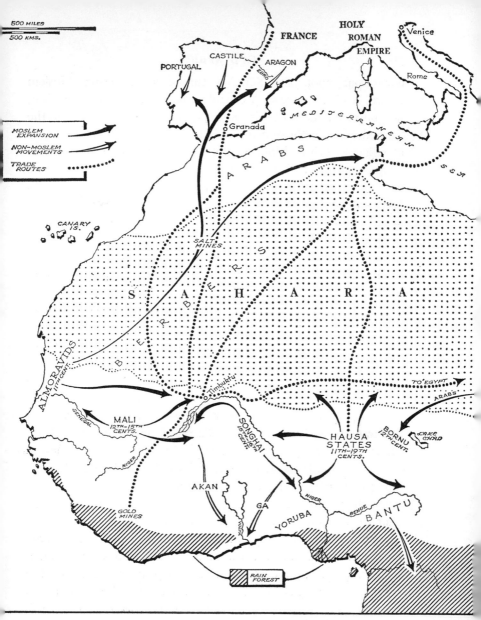

500 MILES

500 KMS.

MOSLEM
EXPANSION

NON-MOSLEM
MOVEMENTS

TRADE
ROUTES

HOLY
ROMAN
EMPIRE

FRANCE

Venice

PORTUGAL

CASTILE

ARAGON

Rome

EBRO

Granada

MEDITERRANEAN

ARABS

SEA

CANARY
IS.

SALT
MINES

S A H A R A

B E R B E R S

TO EGYPT

ALMORAVIDS
11TH CENT.

Timbuktu

ARABS

MALI
12th–15th
CENTS.

SONGHAI
15th CENT.

HAUSA
STATES
11th–19th
CENTS.

BORNU
12TH CENT.

LAKE
CHAD

SENEGAL

NIGER

AKAN

GA

NIGER

BENUE

BANTU

GOLD
MINES

YORUBA

RAIN
FOREST

WEST AFRICA UNDER ISLAM, 11th–16th CENTURIES

d'état put upon the Songhai throne a reforming Moslem Negro, Askia the Great. A capable intellectual and an organizer, he converted most of his subjects, gained the support of the learned Moslem theologians, and launched attacks in the name of religious revival. Much of both Mali and Hausa fell into his hands, but—as had happened with the Almoravids—the fire of reform degenerated into divisive quarrels for power, so Hausa, Mali and other areas gradually reëmerged as weak, despotic states in the sixteenth century. The economic prosperity of the Sudan seems not to have suffered from these quarrels, but the former strength of the area disappeared just at the time that the Europeans began to explore the West African coast.

The cupidity of people north of the Sahara also began to increase in the fifteenth and sixteenth centuries. The only trans-Saharan conquest since the Almoravid expansion was that of Morocco in the sixteenth century. El-Mansur, a young shereef who had decisively defeated a badly planned Portuguese invasion, tried to rally his quarreling followers by a dramatic expedition to seize the gold mines below the desert. In his position at the north end of the long trade route, he apparently did not know that the mines were beyond the southern edge of the Sudanic civilizations. Large quantities of cloth for desert tents, along with guns for his armies, were acquired from Elizabethan England, which seemed happy to arm a friendly customer so near to the queen's enemy in Spain. El-Mansur gained control of the Songhai salt mines in the northern desert, and in 1590 he dispatched a choice army across the Sahara with Judar, a Spanish eunuch, in command. Although three-fourths of the army died of thirst in a five-month march, Timbuktu was reached and Songhai overthrown in a series of dreary but valiant campaigns. Judar was made pasha, or viceroy, of the Sudan, but the Moroccans never advanced beyond the Niger basin and never reached the source of gold. Shereef El-Mansur, nearly bankrupt from the expense of the invasion, learned that the Sudan itself was a poor country and—worse yet—that trade and commerce had come to a virtual standstill. Apparently it was easier to trade through the Europeans who had arrived on the Guinea coast than it was to maintain the desert route amid such turmoil. El-Mansur was disappointed, faced with continued expense and rebellion both at home and in conquered Songhai, and suspicious of his Spanish commander. He replaced Judar, suppressed Timbuktu's schools and libraries, and gradually allowed the conquest to degenerate into despotic extortion.

Revolts on the periphery of the occupied territory created a number of petty, vengeful, disorganized, semitribal states. Morocco abandoned the project entirely in 1618, so the avaricious pashas took over as independent despots who spent most of the next century quarreling among themselves. Self-made pashas rose and fell in haphazard succession, trade and farming were thoroughly disrupted, and the once-thriving towns along the middle Niger fell to ruins, were swallowed into the desert, or became the ghost-capitals of local tyrants. The Moorish viceregal aristocracy at Timbuktu gradually weakened, intermarried, retreated and was finally overthrown by Negro tributaries about 1780.

The third would-be conqueror of the wealthy Sudan, Portugal, was also in the north, in Europe. Portugal originally had been part of Castile, one of the small Christian kingdoms in northern Spain. In the fight against Islam, and in the Christian reconquest after the collapse of the Almoravids in the twelfth century, Portugal was granted as a fief to French feudal nobility who had participated in the Spanish crusade. These French vassals in Portugal defied their Castilian overlord, established an independent monarchy with English assistance, and ousted all Moors from their own country two hundred years before Castile cleared her own territory. The next logical step, an extension of the crusade to Moorish Africa, absorbed Portugal's efforts for some time, culminating in an attack on Ceuta, Morocco, in 1415. Religious zeal was hardly more important than the acquisition of control over the Sudan gold trade, but the Moroccans had too strong a hold on this commerce. After withstanding a three-year siege, they forced the Portuguese to withdraw.

One of the Portuguese leaders, Prince Henry—younger son of the king—had considerable knowledge of geography and navigation derived from Arab libraries in the reconquered portions of Portugal and Castile. Often entitled "the Navigator," the visionary, hard-working and scholarly prince proposed to by-pass both the stubborn Moors and the forbidding desert to reach the gold mines by sea. It seems to be this idea—not the desire for slaves, and certainly not the notion of reaching India —that inspired Henry to establish a navigational institute at Sagres and to send out expeditions along the West African coast. There was a considerable element of chance involved— both in navigation and in uncertainty regarding the location of the gold mines—but Portuguese fishermen had already been at least 1,500 miles out from land in the Atlantic and Arab geographers had given some valuable evidence about the coastline as far south as Sierra Leone, at the northern edge of the rain forest. The first ships sailed in 1418; gold nuggets and Negro slaves were first bought from Berbers at Arguin (off the coast of modern Mauritania) in 1444; and the rain forest was reached before Henry the Navigator died in 1460. A profitable slave trade began, attracting for the first time European commercial interests, but exploration languished for a while, partly for want of Henry's guidance and perhaps also because the rain forest seemed unattractive. In the 1470's exploration revived. A break in the rain forest—where savanna grass came down to the sea—was found in modern Ghana; and the equator was crossed for the first time in European history. Gold and gold dust were found in abundance along the break in the rain forest, so the coast was named Mina—the mine, the "Gold Coast." A trading settlement called El Mina was established here during a later voyage in 1482. Christopher Columbus, the Genoese explorer who later discovered America, appears to have visited

the new fort a year or two later.[2] He had been in the Portuguese service since about 1477, first as a chart maker, then as
an officer gaining experience in oceanic navigation, and did not
seek backing for his famous westward voyage until 1486.

Communication and transportation by sea proved to be
both more reliable and more convenient than trans-Saharan
travel, so it was only a matter of time—as El-Mansur's Moroccans found out a century later—until the pattern of African
trade and development underwent a profound revolution. Actually the Portuguese gold supply probably did not come from
the sources that Ghana and Mali had long relied upon, but
from new mines in the rain forest lying immediately behind
the coastal savanna. The discovery of these mines, along with
the arrival of the Negro population on the coast, seems to have
occurred only a few years before the Portuguese arrival.

The religious and political turmoil in the Sudan from the
eleventh-century Almoravids to the Moroccan occupation encouraged some non-Moslem Negroes to move to areas outside
the pale of the strong empires. The same chaos probably contributed to the development of strong military-defense organizations among the tribes west and south of the prosperous
Niger Valley. Efficient tribal federations appeared among the
Akan people in modern Ghana, as non-Moslem Negroes in
large numbers began to penetrate the rain forest (where they
also discovered gold) and to settle along the Guinea coast.

Knowledge of precise developments along this coast is lacking, but it is possible to suggest some general outlines. Negroes
with considerable facility in ironworking apparently moved into
the area west of the Niger Delta over 2,000 years ago—just
about the time that Bantu-speaking Negroes, east of the Delta,
began to expand—and established a number of small, independent societies. A remarkable facility to carve miniature
human figures prevailed around Nok, in the southern savanna,

[2] For evidence and its evaluation, see Samuel Eliot Morison, *Admiral
of the Ocean Sea*, 2 vols., Boston, 1942, vol. I, pp. 53-54, and p. 59, *n.* 23.

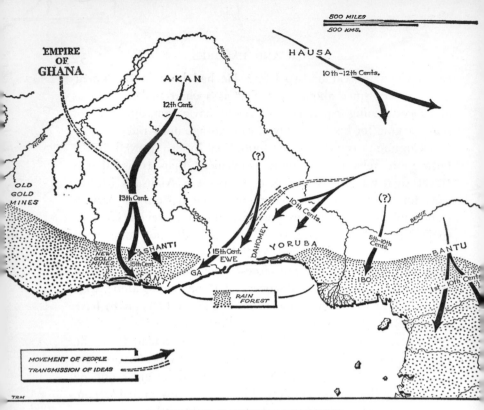

NEGRO MIGRATIONS
TOWARD THE GUINEA COAST *(CONJECTURE)*, 1st–15th CENTURIES

between 900 B.C. and 200 A.D. The Nok society represented a
transition from wood and stone to iron in West Africa, and its
motifs were the forerunners of art forms later adapted to terra
cotta and bronze media in central and southwestern Nigeria.
One of Nok's descendant cultures, that of Benin, developed
ironworking to a remarkable level about 1400. The Benin artisans produced some human and divine figures that are prized
for their aesthetic beauty rather than their utility. Other communities, especially the Yoruba and their vassals, the Dahomans, were particularly successful in fashioning tools; when
pressures from the turbulent Sudan about 1500 encouraged
their confederation for military defense, this art became one of
arms manufacture. The Benin culture declined in the sixteenth

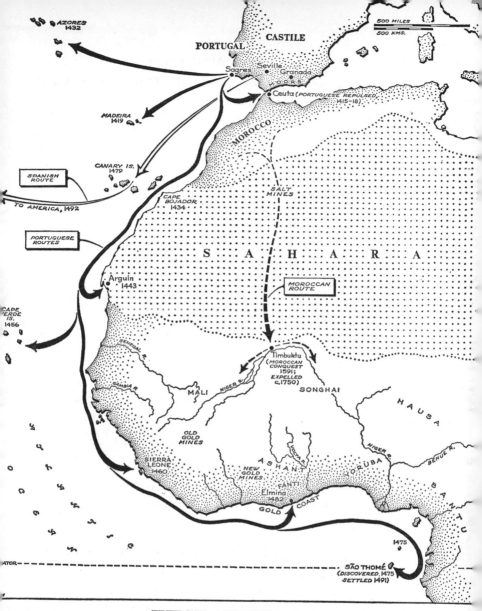

FOREIGN COMPETITION FOR WEST AFRICA, 15th AND 16th CENTURIES

century in the face of military pressure from the newly centralized Yoruba and cultural modifications from Portuguese traders and missionaries.

East and northeast of the Niger Delta, among Bantu and

other Negro people in and around the Cameroon Highlands, organization never developed extensively, although most of these people must have been in this area for several thousand years. In the savanna north of the Highlands, there has been Negro occupation since prehistoric times. The very early inhabitants may have been the Yoruba and Dahomans. They moved across the river to western Nigeria about the time of Christ. The next known occupants are the Hausa, who arrived about the tenth century. There probably were some Bantu in northern Nigeria—there are still scattered remnants—but most of the Bantu expansion was southward, not northward, from the Cameroons. It is possible that the Ga people, now living along the lower Volta River in modern Ghana, were here; their tradition seems to include a stay in northern Nigeria, from which they started to migrate about 900 years ago.

The Ga believe they arrived in the Volta area about 1300, while most traditions bring the Akan people from the southern edge of ancient Ghana or Mali to the north edge of the rain forest in modern Ghana between 1200 and 1400. Akan tribes penetrating the rain forest, calling themselves Ashanti, presumably discovered gold in the fifteenth century and began to form military confederations in the seventeenth and eighteenth centuries; other Akan, called Fanti, moved around the rain forest and settled the savanna strip in the Gold Coast, just west of the Ga. But how many of the traditions are acceptable? To what extent might one migrating tribe merge either with another or with earlier settlers of areas that were overrun?

Of the Hausa relatively little is known. Although they kept written records, most of these were destroyed in a Moslem uprising 150 years ago. They seem to have been Berber invaders —perhaps refugees from the Arab invasions—who established themselves over an indigenous Negro farming population. The Hausa were well-disciplined traders, organized into a series of sovereign city-states. An alliance between the kings and an entrenched bureaucracy helped to perpetuate the rule of a conquering minority over indigenous masses of people. This form of government was greatly influenced by Koranic regulations at a very early date, but Islam as a religion was only partially—and slowly—accepted, either by the rulers or by the masses. The Hausa specialized in fine cloth, leatherwork and slaves that were caught or bought east of the Niger Delta. The city-states traded across the desert, with the empires along the middle Niger, and with the Negroes of Yoruba and Ga. Were the Ga, then, refugees en masse from the Hausa conquerors who continued trading contacts but retained their independence?

It is hard to tell whether Negroes lived in significant numbers in the rain forest before the fourteenth or fifteenth century, but it is equally hard to believe that the Akan were refugees in large numbers from farther north. Their language corresponds too closely to that of their forest neighbors, and is too different from anything known in the Niger Valley from which they claim to come. This does not mean, however, that they necessarily have lived long in or south of the rain forest, and it does not mean that they received no influences from farther north.

The answer for both the Ga and the Akan may be that people speaking these languages have long lived on the southern edge of the savanna, above the rain forest and away from the coast, but that they more recently received an influx of traditions, organizational forms and even a ruling aristocracy from the places where they claim that they themselves originated. In turn, they have subsequently developed military prowess and have, since about 1300, retreated toward the coast and rain forest as a means of avoiding the increasing pressure of Islam and the turmoil of the Niger Valley.

Some parallel to this possibility, with slightly less complication, may be found in the indigenous rain-forest Negroes of the modern Ivory Coast, Liberia and Sierra Leone. In all of these areas forest penetration appears to have occurred in small numbers, relatively late, and by the groups least sympathetic either to central organization or to Islam. It would seem that they reluctantly left the savanna to escape Islam and strong government, but that they neither received the influence nor felt the pressures that forced the Akan to federate.

One group of people is found scattered across West Africa from the Senegal to the Hausa states. Called Fulani, they have been nomadic by tradition, seldom organizing a state of their own but living as a protected people in many societies of the southern and central savanna regions. They claim a white ancestry, which early scholars tried to justify through Berber connections, but recent opinion[3] has favored the view that they are basically Negroes who originated near the western tip of Africa. For centuries they resisted Islam; it may be that, or simply their pastoral inclination, that encouraged their gradual migration. Undoubtedly some of them were on the southern periphery of ancient Ghana when the Almoravids attacked that empire. Their dispersion seems to have increased about that time, for they were found as protected minorities in various savanna states from Senegal to Hausaland by the thirteenth century. During the chaos associated with the Moroccan conquests in the sixteenth and seventeenth centuries they began to play a significant role in the politics of the petty states that opposed the North African viceroys. Particularly large groups of them were found about that time in Futa Jallon (in the interior of recent French Guinea) and in Hausaland; in both territories they were still a pastoral, pagan minority, although a good percentage of those living among the Hausa were found in the cities where they intermarried and began to accept Islam. In most cases the Fulani cattle raisers lived in concord with the indigenous agriculturalists.

Except for the coastal people, it was three or four centuries before European exploration and expansion had a direct impact upon religious life. However, the indirect foreign influence, after about 1450, led to profound changes that substantially altered the course of West African history.

[3] See especially Joseph H. Greenberg, *Studies in African Linguistic Classification*, New Haven, 1955, pp. 24-32.

4

INTO SLAVERY

SLAVERY—the possession of human beings as personal property—has existed in Africa, as in other parts of the world, since prehistoric times. In its early stages it was a relatively minor, moderate and logical phenomenon: enslavement was a means of controlling and productively employing criminals, malcontents and war prisoners in a nomadic society that lacked both impersonal government and permanent prisons for law enforcement. For several reasons the total denial of humanness and personality usually associated with slavery was not present. For one thing, African societies did not have a strict concept of private-property rights, so the personal rights and general conditions of slaves were protected by the force of traditional law and communal responsibility. Also, slavery was usually for a specific period of time—commensurate with the nature of the crime or circumstances of capture—rather than being a perpetual condition, and it was also possible to earn freedom by good behavior or purchase. The owner was responsible for maintenance and protection. In return the slave performed an allotted amount of work without pay. However, in his free time, he could acquire movable property with which to buy his freedom and reënter society as a member in good standing.

These mitigating circumstances continued to prevail as
long as the slave was sold or traded only with neighboring societies that maintained a similar code. Difficulties and abuses
arose primarily when the slave was sold to a society that had a
concept of inviolable personal property and perpetual slavery.
Negroes sold to the ancient Mediterranean world encountered
such conditions, but even there good behavior and the accumu-
lation of personal property could be turned to account. A
somewhat harsher form of slavery arose with the spread of
Islam, for, although the Koran decreed humane treatment, it
did not provide for a communal check on conditions or protection of the rights of captives who were not monotheists in covenant with the true God. Castration, perpetual possession and
total denial of property rights were tolerated, so that enslavement was transformed into a radical negation of the victim's
humanness.

This type of total enslavement appeared in Moslem North
Africa and Egypt as early as the eleventh century, when Arab
settlers' control of the Mediterranean end of the Saharan trade
routes, and the spread of Islam into the savanna under the banner of the Almoravids, increased the volume of slave trading.
Most of the slaves were probably war prisoners and raiding victims taken by the savanna empires from the less-organized tribes
along the north edge of the forest. The largest source of supply, after the adoption of Islamic law in the Hausa states, seems
to have been the Negroes—especially the Bantu who did not
migrate into the Congo forest—who lived southeast of Hausaland; they consisted of numerous small tribes, lacking defensive
organization, and could be incited to war upon one another to
provide prisoners for the Moslem traders. Demands for slaves
increased in the trans-Saharan markets after the decline and fall
of the Byzantine Empire in the fourteenth and fifteenth centuries, because the Turkish conquerors needed dependent personnel to maintain their rule over the Christian population.
Several Negro slaves rose to key administrative positions under
the sultan at Constantinople, but castration was invariably re-

quired in order to prevent the rise of hereditary interests that might contest Turkish authority. The Hausa suppliers, to whom this policy guaranteed a permanent market, were particularly active in the preparation of these eunuchs for the trip to market.

Among the Bantu who migrated through the rain forest from the Cameroons throughout the Christian era, simple slavery was also practiced. Keen competition for occupation and domination of territory in the Congo watershed tended to create a series of relatively organized tribes, some of whom would succeed in overrunning their neighbors from time to time. Prisoners taken in such struggles might be enslaved, but the greatest source of chattel was probably a tribute in slaves exacted from subjugated tribes. There was no market or trade for these captives, but if they could be absorbed into the population of the victorious tribe, the power of the ruling chieftain could be enhanced both within that tribe and throughout the area.

Early Portuguese explorers and traders probably bought their first slave cargoes from Moslem traders on the coasts of Senegal and Mauretania in the middle of the fifteenth century. When Prince Henry the Navigator died in 1460, Negroes were being purchased from various Negro and Berber middlemen between the Senegal and Gambia Rivers; a few others were being seized by haphazard raids at the northwestern tip of the rain forest, but this was more expensive in European lives and money than peaceful exchange. After 1482, when the Portuguese were established at Elmina on the Gold Coast, the emphasis was on the acquisition of gold; enough slaves could be found nearer to Portugal, around Cape Verde, to satisfy the European demand. At Elmina treaties were made with the Fanti tribes along the coast that provided for the exchange of gold for salt, cloth, trinkets and tools. Relations were free and reasonably friendly so long as the Portuguese did not try to bypass these middleman tribes to operate mines or establish direct contact with the Ashanti producers inland.

Some missionaries and traders visited Benin, west of the

Niger Delta, but interest in this area was short-lived. Farther along the coast the Portuguese—now searching for the legendary Christian kingdom of Prester John and a route to India—came into contact with the Bantu people in the Congo. In 1483 the ruler of the Manicongo, which happened to be the ascendant tribe at that time, asked for help in maintaining his power, and expressed interest in Christianity. The Cape of Good Hope was discovered four years later, but Portuguese energy was diverted to the Manicongo before pushing on to the East. In the spring of 1491 missionaries, emissaries and technical advisers arrived in the Congo with tools and presents. Chief Nzinga Knuwu was baptized as King John I, an alliance of equal sovereigns arranged with John II of Portugal, and a tiny European colony established 125 miles inland at Mbanza, the tribal seat. Manicongo troops helped to put down a rebellion, but when John II became more interested in India, the Bantu kingdom began to backslide. The missionaries retreated to the coast with Crown Prince Mbemba-a-Nzinga, who, in ten years of exile, became an educated Portuguese, quite out of contact with Bantu ways.

During the exile deported Portuguese malcontents began to develop sugar on tropical, uninhabited São Thomé Island 600 miles northwest of the Congo. They first came to the mainland about 1500 to buy slave labor for their plantations, and found ready suppliers among the refugees from the Manicongo. When his father died, Mbemba-a-Nzinga took the name of Alfonso I, put down the pagan usurpers of his inheritance, and gave Mbanza, his capital, the name of São Salvador. More missionaries came out in 1508 to reinforce Alfonso's Europeanization program, but Alfonso was seldom remembered after that. Portuguese energy was diverted to the conquest of the Indian Ocean in 1509; the missionaries, concentrating more on concubines and slaves than on converts, gradually died off; and the chartered proprietor of the São Thomé plantations censored the protests and appeals that Alfonso sent to Lisbon. Emanuel, the new Portuguese king, issued model orders to rectify the situation, but could not enforce his will upon his own subjects.

The impetus for progress remained largely with Alfonso. Buildings of European design were raised in São Salvador. He sent chiefs' sons to study in Portugal—his own son took vows and became Bishop of the Congo, the only Negro so to do until modern times—but São Thomé enslaved many of the erstwhile students. Alfonso tried to strengthen the missions, but the traditional parade of tribute-enforcement wars continued to dominate his country. Prisoners taken in such campaigns were, of course, obvious candidates for transhipment to São Thomé; this did not particularly bother Alfonso. He was accustomed to slave raiding, and sincerely believed the Portuguese when they promised the benefits of conversion to these people.

New Portuguese traders and missionaries appeared in the Manicongo domains during the 1530's, but by their personal intrigues kept the kingdom in an artificial turmoil that no Congolese king could control. The Christian Bantu dynasty lingered on until the seventeenth century. The Bishop of the Congo—now a white Portuguese—was legally based upon the Portuguese-style cathedral in São Salvador until 1676, but he usually lived on the coast of Angola. Periodically new missions were sent to São Salvador—a college trained a few African priests there in the mid-seventeenth century, and the king was listed as a Christian—but the kingdom of the Congo paid tribute to Portugal after 1570, its people reverted to paganism by 1615, and the last vestiges of São Salvador and the Manicongo dynasty were gone before 1690. Portugal continued to recognize the country as a sovereign ally until 1883, but all that the Bantu remembered by that time was the name of Alfonso, the slave trade and a few mysterious amulets of Christian origin.

The experiment was remarkable, but neither Portugal nor the Manicongo kings resolved the conflict between European values and African tradition. On one hand, Alfonso and the Portuguese rulers wanted to create a cohesive, centralized political state with Christianity, bureaucracy, legal institutions and European culture; on the other, both continued to accept the decentralized Bantu system of tributary states that produced

slaves, encouraged factions and prevented lasting stability. Noble intentions at Lisbon notwithstanding, Portuguese traders
and missionaries preferred to encourage factions, the Bantu
tribute system, and the slave system thus created. It did not
even matter if the Manicongo were overrun by another Bantu
tribe; slaves could be bought from any victorious Bantu chieftain, and the supply was greatest when the situation was most
chaotic. Therefore, the only lasting consequence of the Congo
scheme was the slave trade.

Early in the sixteenth century, during the reign of Alfonso
and the brightest period of the Congo experiment, the slave
market was limited to the plantations of São Thomé Island.
Portugal and the Spanish in Santo Domingo were readily supplied from the tribes of Senegal and Gambia. After 1530, however, Spanish expansion to Cuba and the American mainland,
along with Portuguese settlement in underpopulated Brazil,
created new markets for African slaves, markets that could not
be satisfied solely from Senegambia. Before 1550 the gold
mines near Elmina began to give out, so the Fanti middlemen
turned to supplying slaves for the Americas. Slavers also drew
upon Benin, but placed their greatest demand upon the Manicongo where the economy's dependence on slavery soon obscured
the influence of European culture.

Portugal's interests, scattered by the middle of the century over the shores of three oceans, constituted a serious drain
upon her limited manpower. Trade monopolies, plantations and
missionaries were maintained in Brazil (sugar); Senegambia,
the Gold Coast and the Congo (slaves); East Africa, the Persian Gulf, India, Malaya, the East Indies, China and Japan
(spices and luxury goods). Portuguese ships also supplied
slaves to the Spanish American Empire, traders attempted to
dominate local trade in the Indian Ocean and east Asia, and
expensive military campaigns against the Moroccan Moors continued. Except in Brazil, it was necessary to abandon most attempts at mainland penetration, so increasing reliance was
placed upon offshore islands where the small Portuguese popu-

lation could be protected from attack and disease. On the Atlantic coast of Africa, Elmina was the only mainland station; the Congo, Benin and Senegambia missions and trading posts were officially discontinued. The emphasis shifted to the Cape Verde Islands and São Thomé. Both became corrals for slaves, but São Thomé also developed a lucrative sugar economy with a small number of luxuriously living European plantation owners. The island's demand for slaves continued, but the larger proprietary estates in Brazil became far more important.

The rigors of tropical climate had combined with fear of depopulating the mother country to prevent the emigration of European women, so preservation and extension of the Portuguese population depended upon miscegenation throughout the empire. Theoretically, half-caste colonial offspring inherited their fathers' status. In practice, their hereditary privileges were more noticeable than their European culture.

Although Portugal was unable and unwilling to involve herself deeply in Africa, some kind of control over and contact with the southern source of slave supply was necessary. The Manicongo used to claim control over the area south of São Salvador, known as Angola, but the waning of Bantu power had brought an end to the collection of human tribute there. In 1576 the court at Lisbon applied the proprietary charter system of São Thomé and Brazil to the unorganized coastal area, but, to prevent dissipation and confusion of effort, the king required direct rule over the divided Bantu tribes and the development of plantations. A strong coastal fortress with a slave depot was created at Luanda, and military units were freely used either to force chiefs to sell prisoners or to take slaves directly. Attempts to develop plantations usually failed because the slave trade was more profitable; the hope of finding valuable mines faded as the country was explored. Angola, under direct Portuguese domination, replaced the profitable but disorganized Congo area as the leading supplier of human cargo.

Reckless young King Sebastian I was killed fighting the Moroccans, so the Portuguese crown passed to Philip II of

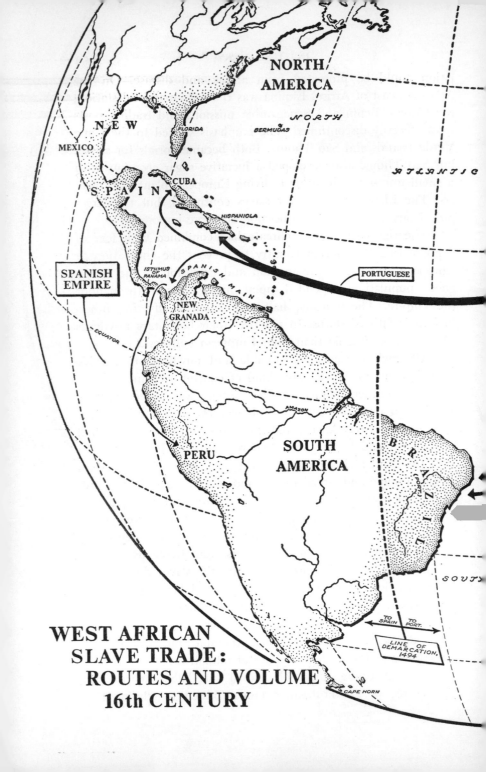

NORTH
AMERICA

NORTH

BERMUDAS

FLORIDA

NEW

MEXICO

SPAIN

CUBA

ATLANTIC

HISPANIOLA

SPANISH EMPIRE

ISTHMUS OF PANAMA

SPANISH MAIN

NEW GRANADA

PORTUGUESE

EQUATOR

AMAZON

B R A Z I L (PORT.)

PERU

SOUTH
AMERICA

SOUTH

TO SPAIN   TO PORT.

LINE OF DEMARCATION, 1494

WEST AFRICAN
SLAVE TRADE:
ROUTES AND VOLUME
16th CENTURY

CAPE HORN

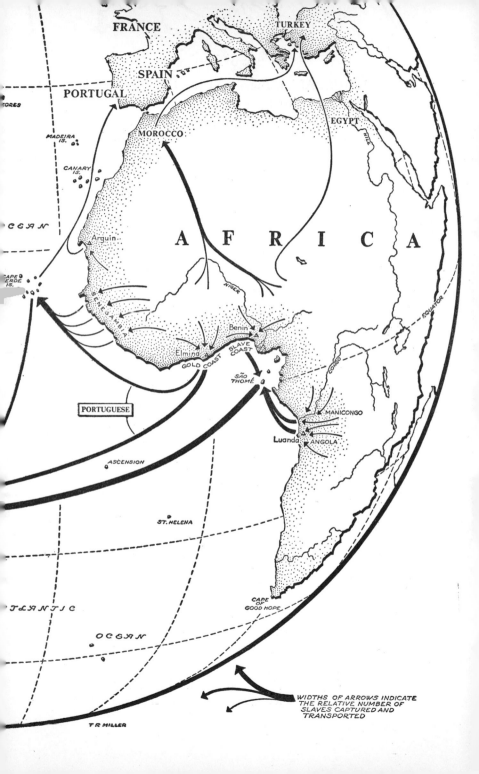

FRANCE

TURKEY

SPAIN

PORTUGAL

EGYPT

MOROCCO

AZORES

MADEIRA IS.

CANARY IS.

OCEAN

CAPE VERDE IS.

Arguin

A F R I C A

NIGER

EQUATOR

SENEGAMBIA

Benin

Elmina

SLAVE COAST

GOLD COAST

SÃO THOMÉ

PORTUGUESE

MANICONGO

CONGO

Luanda   ANGOLA

ASCENSION

ST. HELENA

ATLANTIC

OCEAN

CAPE OF GOOD HOPE

WIDTHS OF ARROWS INDICATE
THE RELATIVE NUMBER OF
SLAVES CAPTURED AND
TRANSPORTED

T R MILLER

Spain in 1580. Africa, Brazil and the East attracted less of his interest than Mexico and Peru. The Netherlands, shuffled to Philip when his father's Central European domains were divided, had adopted the Reformation and won virtual independence of Catholic Spain before the end of the century. Long accustomed to fishing upon and reclaiming land from the sea, the Dutch under Philip's rule had been the distributors to the North of the products that Portugal and Spain imported from overseas. The sovereign Dutch provinces rarely agreed on policy, but there was no hesitation about by-passing the hated Spanish middlemen to exploit the Orient, Africa and the Americas for themselves. Interlopers appeared in Portuguese Africa and India before 1600; soon the Portuguese were ousted or competing stations established.

Two companies, each more powerful in commerce and war than the divided home provinces, were given monopolies by charter; the Dutch East India Company, sovereign from the Cape of Good Hope to Japan, and the West India Company in the Atlantic Ocean. Dutch ships, built to a simple, standard design and economical to operate, were soon able to undercut the Portuguese monopoly without endangering the fantastic profits that could be earned. The West India Company preferred the Gold Coast to less populous Senegambia as a source for slaves. Treaties were made with the Fanti. New stations appeared there, and Portuguese forts were seized, but farther south, in Angola and the Congo, the Portuguese slavers disregarded Philip's orders and honored Dutch gold as readily as their own country's. Acquiring a foothold in northeastern Brazil and dominance over other Portuguese and Spanish consumers in the New World, the Dutch held a virtual monopoly on trans-Atlantic shipments until the 1670's. New markets were opened in the British and French West Indies, as well as in Virginia, and Dutch smugglers also penetrated the Spanish colonial market.

The Dutch consumed only a small portion of all that they shipped, so they relied largely upon foreign markets both for their slaves and for their Oriental products. England and France increasingly resented having to pay precious gold and silver for dependence upon Dutch services. Although they could not compete with the efficient Dutch shippers in free trade, they were able to erect tariff barriers and importation bans to encourage their own traders. Holland had more manpower and better efficiency than the Portuguese, but not enough resources to man both a merchant fleet and an effective navy, so England could enforce her regulations to break the Dutch position.

British and French privateers had been engaged in irregular slaving and smuggling since the late sixteenth century but did not have colonies of their own with which to practice monopoly trade until after the Dutch had overtaken the Spanish-Portuguese lead. By naval warfare and restrictive colonial legislation, England and France established mercantilist domination over their own territories, then gained control over both Eastern and Atlantic trade in general; Britain, being less involved in European affairs, was freer to concentrate on the sea and gained the upper hand by the end of the 1600's. Several slave-marketing Fanti tribes on the Gold Coast allied willingly with English intruders against the established Dutch, and contracts were made with emerging Yoruban and Dahoman Negro states that were named collectively the Slave Coast. Portuguese traders, who had continued to hold onto much of the Angola-Brazil trade, willingly added cargo to ships of their ancient British ally.

France acquired her slave prizes from the independent Negro states on the Slave Coast and along various shores (Senegambia, Gabon, etc.) that other nations neglected. After the establishment of rich plantations in Haiti, the Ancien Régime needed neither foreign slave markets nor additional territory to make her mercantile plans work.

Europeans had few qualms about the morality of slaving. Although the possession of human beings as private property was extremely unusual in medieval and Renaissance Europe,

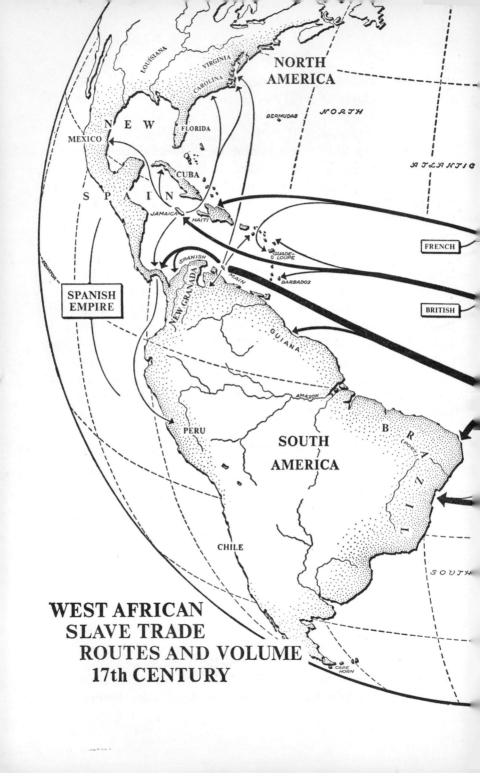

WEST AFRICAN
SLAVE TRADE
ROUTES AND VOLUME
17th CENTURY

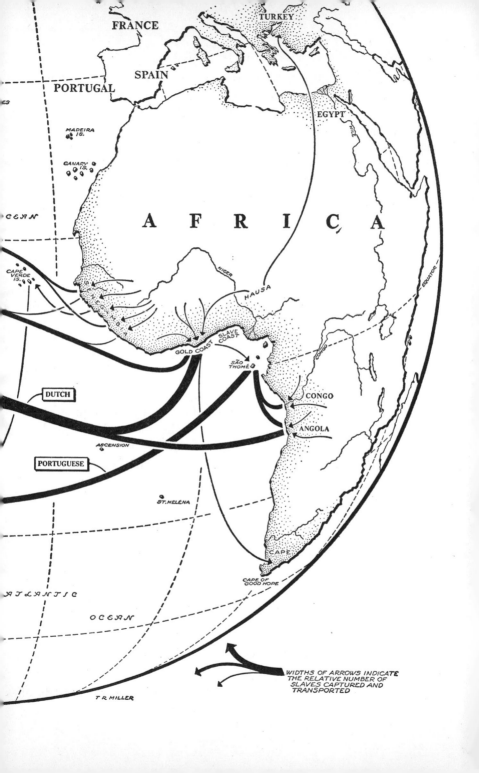

FRANCE

TURKEY

SPAIN

PORTUGAL

EGYPT

MADEIRA
IS.

CANARY
IS.

OCEAN

A F R I C A

CAPE
VERDE
IS.

NIGER

HAUSA

SENEGAL

GOLD COAST

SLAVE
COAST

SÃO
THOMÉ

CONGO

DUTCH

CONGO

ANGOLA

ASCENSION

PORTUGUESE

ST. HELENA

CAPE

CAPE OF
GOOD HOPE

ATLANTIC

OCEAN

WIDTHS OF ARROWS INDICATE
THE RELATIVE NUMBER OF
SLAVES CAPTURED AND
TRANSPORTED

T. R. MILLER

EQUATOR

it was not illegal. Most theologians, lawyers and responsible people accepted the slave traders' claim that Africans were better off under Christian supervision than they would have been under pagan or Moslem slaveowners. As long as slavery was "natural" among Africans, it was argued, the European only had to be sure that the African he bought was justly enslaved under African law. This, however, was very difficult to determine. Obviously the slave himself could not be trusted to tell the truth. Only on rare occasions did the Europeans know who had done the enslaving, let alone interview the captor; even less were the fine points of African traditional slave law understood. Middlemen and captors, of course, would claim the enslavement was justified—frequently customary law was tightened so that more slaves could be taken "legally." Competition among African groups for slave profit encouraged a marked increase in warfare, particularly in senseless and desperate warfare: no longer was war primarily for grievance or honor; no longer was it limited by mutual agreement or by religious codes. Warfare in Africa was transformed from a local, often ceremonial operation into a desperate struggle for senseless conquest, tribal wealth and ultimate decimation of the enemy. Honor and victory were no longer the goals of warfare. Even if defeated in battle, the tribe that took the largest number of captives made the greatest profit. The impact of this revolution in warfare was perhaps greater on West Africa, where both the slave supply routes and the pre-European trade development had been most complex, but in the Congo and Angola the impact upon the recently arrived Bantu farmers and herders was also profound.

Except for a few raids in Senegambia during the 1400's, the Europeans north of the Congo never had anything to do with the capture of the slaves. Operations in this area—from which perhaps two-thirds to three-fourths of the slaves came— were always through African middlemen. Several methods of exchange were used.

In Senegambia official stations moved from the coast to offshore islands before the end of the fifteenth century (Cape Verde Islands for Portugal; Gorée, near modern Dakar, for France and Britain); on the mainland a few half-castes who "went native" and the chiefs of coastal tribes took or bought cargoes for the Europeans who called intermittently. Along the Grain and Pepper Coasts (modern Liberia) the occasional trade was conducted between individual ship captains and the sparsely settled tribes. France usually traded in a similar manner along the Ivory Coast, although a permanent European depot was briefly used. In all of these cases the slaves were captured in raids or wars within about 500 miles of the coast, often in Futa Jallon or among the Mandingo tribes, before being sold to the coastal middlemen.

Along the Gold Coast, for about 150 miles on either side of the first Portuguese station at Elmina, the Europeans established a series of permanent trading depots, called variously forts, factories, stations, depots or colonies. In all cases these stations were commercial headquarters—armed only lightly—and every one of them was rented from the local tribe of the Fanti group of Akan Negroes. The treaties or contracts for each station were negotiated between European and Fanti officials with about as much duress as is found in any relations, then or now, among sovereign but unequal states; usually the agreement provided for a reciprocal military alliance, a payment in European goods as rental for the station, the hiring as needed of paid longshoremen, and a general trade agreement that included slaves. Portugal arranged for and built four stations (including Elmina) after 1482; a fifth was built a few miles inland in an attempt to revive gold production about 1623, but all were lost to the Dutch by 1642; a sixth station was tried but abandoned about 1683. Dutch traders built the first of ten stations in 1598 and held out until 1872. Britain came next, building thirteen forts between 1631 and 1787; her rule ended in 1957. Sweden built one in 1652, and another just before she was ousted in 1657 by Denmark, who added five more, some of which lasted until 1850. Brandenburg-Prussia built three after 1685 but

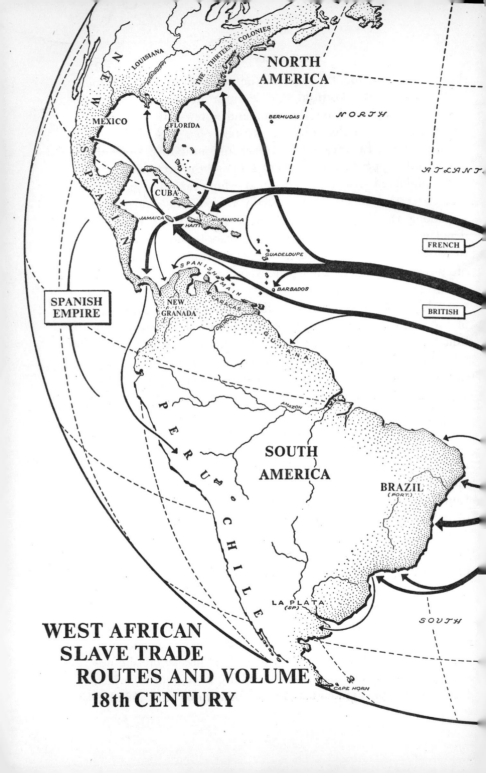

WEST AFRICAN
SLAVE TRADE
ROUTES AND VOLUME
18th CENTURY

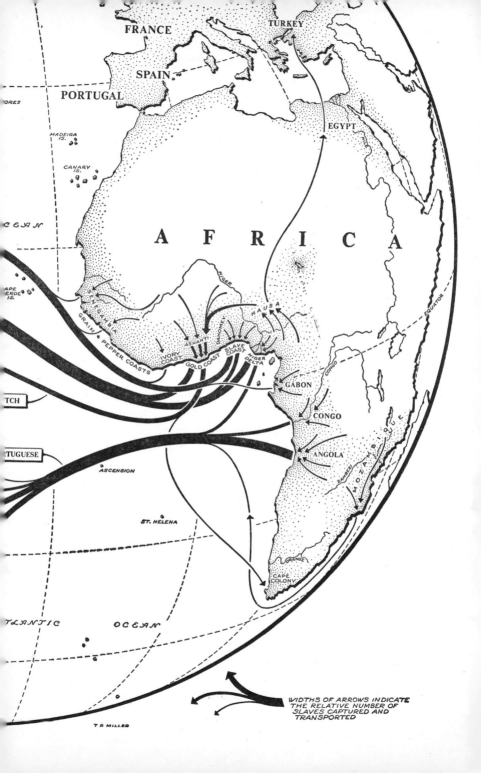

FRANCE

TURKEY

SPAIN

PORTUGAL

EGYPT

MADEIRA IS.

CANARY IS.

OCEAN

ORES

A F R I C A

APE ERDE IS.

NIGER

SENEGAMBIA

GRAIN + PEPPER COASTS

IVORY COAST

GOLD COAST

ASHANTI

DAHOMEY

SLAVE COAST

NIGER DELTA

HAUSA

EQUATOR

TCH

GABON

CONGO

CONGO

TUGUESE

ANGOLA

ASCENSION

ZAMBEZI

MOZAMBIQUE

ST. HELENA

ORANGE

CAPE COLONY

TLANTIC

OCEAN

WIDTHS OF ARROWS INDICATE
THE RELATIVE NUMBER OF
SLAVES CAPTURED AND
TRANSPORTED

T R MILLER

abandoned them fourteen years later. France tried one about 1688 but gave it up when her buyers rejected Gold Coast slaves. The last station was built by one of the Fanti tribes in 1798, but it failed because of the Napoleonic wars and the British ban on the slave trade during the following decade. Most of these changed hands several times by conquest, purchase or exchange. About 1800 eleven Dutch, eight British, five Danish and one Fanti fort were being used. By 1872 Britain held twelve and Holland eight active commercial depots.

Filling the slave quotas for the Gold Coast stations was often a cause for complex operations and keen competition. Wars were not infrequent among the Negro allies of competing forts. The Fanti, who acquired slaves either by direct warfare or by trading with the Ashanti, were the regular suppliers for every European power on the Gold Coast except the Dutch. Traders from the Netherlands usually bought directly from the Ashanti, with whom they alone had a commercial agreement, although they were often forced to outbid the Fanti. The Ashanti in turn obtained their captives either in upcountry wars or in trade with neighboring savanna tribes farther north, and, in later years, they may also have bought a few petty criminals and Bantu prisoners from the Hausa traders who traversed the interior.

Ashanti, as the entrepôt for most of the trade reaching the Gold Coast from the whole interior of West Africa, was in a position that was simultaneously privileged and precarious. Frequent warfare for the capture of slaves on one hand, and repeated defense against Fanti raids on the other, encouraged military development; trade with and protection against the savanna depended upon reliable organization of both trade and government. Before the end of the seventeenth century the Ashanti had changed from a peaceful, agricultural people into a military alliance that expanded first by conquest, then by threat and persuasion. By about 1701 the confederation of Ashanti allies had evolved into a cohesive nation under Okomfo Anokye, chief priest to the leader of the Kumasi tribe of Ashanti. Legend claims that Anokye, at a crucial conclave of alliance members, received from the sky a Golden Stool which embodied the spirit of the allied tribes. The kumasihene (chief of Kumasi) thereupon became the ashantihene (king of Ashanti).

Fanti quarrels gradually yielded to coöperation against the Ashanti Kingdom, which controlled the hinterland. Ashanti, however, was capable of maintaining a nearly invulnerable position because the savanna tribes were utterly dependent upon it for salt, tools and other European products that Ashanti, in turn, acquired from the Fanti. America's demand for slaves increased late in the eighteenth century, so Ashanti bought large quantities of arms and ammunition from the European traders. The new weapons facilitated conquests that swelled the volume of slaves coming from the interior. Slave records show a noticeable rise in the number of inland captives, eventually including—after 1800—many from the Moslem states such as Hausa. After 1805 Ashanti armies attempted to oust the Fanti from the coast in order to establish direct relations with the Europeans. They had some success with the Dutch, who had a more direct trade with the Ashanti before this, but the British defended the Fanti and led the other European stations in throwing back the conquerors.

East of the Fanti, trade was with the Ga people who moved toward the coast to make contact with the more easterly Portuguese stations. Ga settlers did not congregate around Accra until the middle of the seventeenth century, and they were never able to establish the efficient contacts with the interior that characterized the Ashanti-Fanti slave-salt trade. It is partly for this reason that the Danish, most of whose forts were in Ga country east of Accra, failed to receive as steady a stream of slaves as did the British and Dutch, who traded through the Fanti.

Farther east, Portuguese trade with Benin had contributed to the adulteration of the famous Benin and Ife bronze work, but imported firearms permitted Benin to carve a large empire from Lagos to the Niger Delta. Portugal's interest waned after

Benin had enslaved and sold most of the people she conquered; Benin degenerated during the sixteenth century from art, prosperity and effective state organization into random bloodletting, capricious militaristic rule and economic ruin. It no longer paid Europeans to risk the chaos, so slaves became victims of a new institution: ritual sacrifice, a symbolic sublimation of the military lust, cutthroat politics and unchecked rapacity that had been encouraged. Neighboring tribes were forced to unite for war or perish.

Behind Benin, near modern Ibadan in Nigeria, lay the Yoruba state of Oyo which had had an early flowering of stone carving, iron culture, then bronzeworking, about a thousand years ago. The Hausa may have introduced some advanced ideas of government. Ife was the early center and remained the religious center after the chief (alafin) moved to Oyo. Organization and defense became increasingly important as Songhai and Islam pressed from the north, then Benin from the south. This made military organization necessary by the end of the sixteenth century; it became the custom to send an army against some neighbor each year for glory, tribute and slaves. Yoruba colonies were set up in conquered territories, thus creating a large intertribal culture bloc centered on Oyo and Ife; more distant states, such as Dahomey on the west, were made into tributary buffers and undoubtedly learned a great deal about organization. The alafin reached the apex of his power in the eighteenth century, just after European slave merchants on the Gold Coast had begun to look for additional sources of supply; he traded freely with them through Lagos, a tributary state that was weaned away from decaying Benin, but rarely allowed a permanent European station to be erected.

The first European contacts east of the Gold Coast, except for the early Portuguese forays, were toward the end of the seventeenth century. A situation not unlike that on the Gold Coast appeared to exist: a series of small states along the coast, Ouidah (Whydah) especially, were quite willing to rent stations and open up a slave route from the interior. The difference was that the inland state, unlike early Ashanti, was already fairly well organized. This state, Yoruba-trained Dahomey, promptly began to conquer, capture and trade with a volume and a reliability that pleased the Europeans. The King of Dahomey realized that particular profit lay in control of the coastal area, and he succeeded—as the Ashanti did not—in conquering the coast. Then, between 1724 and 1729, he placed the little middleman-states under his viceroys and abrogated all the treaties. Dahomey could always provide prize slaves, promptly and reliably, so trade continued, but the Dahomans operated the stations themselves. Europeans came ashore purely as merchants, subject to Dahoman approval; the price was fixed from Abomey, the inland capital, but the arrangement saved the Europeans much expense and manpower because they had no administrative tasks to perform.

The king dominated the economy directly, enabling him to become an absolute ruler with a bureaucracy for administration and taxation that was often castrated to prevent the development of any interests that might contradict royal wishes. Every official, including the king, was theoretically subordinate to the queen mother, who was supposed to be the conscience and adviser but not the executive authority; a modification of this ceremonial supremacy extended even to the army. However, for slave raiding and major military engagements, the Dahomans preferred to employ an elite "Amazon" corps of virgin women; unlike the men, they were subordinate to nobody. Technically this despotic slave-taking machine remained tributary to the Alafin of Oyo, who proved to be undefeatable, but the Amazons marched west to meet the Ashanti, with whom a boundary line was drawn in 1750. Coastal states such as Whydah, Little Ardra and Popo (Pawpaw) repeatedly revolted—only, of course, to be enslaved—but Dahomey was never able to establish either trade connections or conquests among the Moslem states along the Niger, so the slave supply was smaller than that of the vast Gold Coast-Ashanti trade network.

In the Niger Delta, southeast of the Slave Coast, there

were no strong states with which to deal. Slaves from this area brought lower prices because they were less likely to be familiar with any skill but agriculture; they were not desired by small slaveholders, but were satisfactory for work on the great plantations in Brazil and the American cotton belt. After the invention of the cotton gin at the end of the eighteenth century, the production of cotton increased rapidly. Sea captains had begun to find, earlier in the century, that profit could be made even in transporting the cheaper, unskilled Niger Delta slaves, who were now in great demand. The Delta trade involved the payment of a small fee to one of the hundreds of sovereign chiefs, followed by the purchase of a few slaves that had been taken in the local wars endemic in this region. The ship would then move on a few miles upstream, start new negotiations and trade afresh. The cargo acquired might, in some cases, be the prisoners of opposing sides in a recent skirmish, or it might be a group of men whom a local chief bought or captured while the ship waited. Usually lacking depots or stations, often without any regular treaties or permanent agreements, slave traders customarily purchased slaves and stowed them away a few at a time until the ship was full. Sanitary conditions were often quite bad before a ship had even weighed anchor. This situation, plus the lack of preëmbarkation inspection such as Dahomey had provided, meant that the slaves who arrived in America were less healthy and useful than those of previous centuries.

During the late eighteenth century when Haiti became an insatiable market, French traders operated along the Gabon coasts using the same methods and finding Bantu cargo similar to that which British and Portuguese privateers found in the Niger Delta. Portugal continued to operate the Congo kingdom on an unofficial but lucrative basis, much as it did in the last days of the Manicongo experiment. The officially supervised trade from Angola probably provided a greater number of slaves than any other section except the Gold Coast, but the procedure was much more direct and simple than anywhere else. Portuguese half-caste scouts, and coerced or cajoled Bantu chieftains, provided a steady stream of real or artificial criminals, war prisoners and runaways that were sold freely to all comers, be they Dutch, British, French or Portuguese. The greatest proportion of Angolans went to Brazil, but they were dispersed liberally across all the slave-holding New World areas. The Portuguese trade eventually penetrated as much as 300 miles inland, tapping most of modern Angola and much of the lower Congo basin.

No reliable statistics exist on the number of Africans that were brought to America. Estimates run from a low of 3,000,000 to something over 20,000,000. Antislavery agitation may have contributed to the confusion because calculations kept inflating as the abolition movement grew during the nineteenth century. Many of the trading records have been lost or destroyed, but enough have survived to permit at least an estimate of the percentage of slaves who died during the rigorous ocean voyage: about 12 percent in French ships, contrasted to 17 percent in Dutch and British ships; Portuguese losses in the early centuries ran about 15 percent, but when the nineteenth-century abolitionist pressure forced the slave traders to take chances, the casualty rate rose to 25 or 30 percent.

In 1860, when most of the slave trade had ended, there were between seven and eight million people of African origin in North and South America. In areas for which reliable population statistics go back to the early part of the century, it appears that between one-third and one-half of this population resulted from natural increase. The number arriving from Africa must have been between 3.5 and 5.5 million; adding the number who died en route, it would seem that 4 to 6.5 million were embarked in Africa between 1441 and the end of trans-Atlantic slaving in the 1880's.

About 500,000 were sold in the thirteen colonies, half having first spent some time in the West Indies; approximately 1.5 to 2 million arrived in those islands, but the future United States and the Spanish repurchased about one-third of those. Brazil must have taken at least 1.5 but not more than 3 million, while

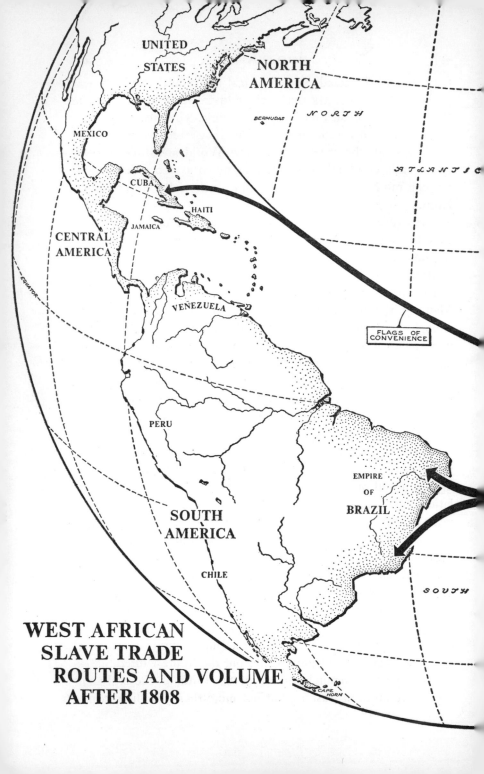

UNITED
STATES

NORTH
AMERICA

NORTH

BERMUDAS

ATLANTIC

MEXICO

CUBA

HAITI

JAMAICA

CENTRAL
AMERICA

VENEZUELA

FLAGS OF
CONVENIENCE

PERU

EMPIRE
OF
BRAZIL

SOUTH
AMERICA

CHILE

SOUTH

EQUATOR

CAPE
HORN

WEST AFRICAN
SLAVE TRADE
ROUTES AND VOLUME
AFTER 1808

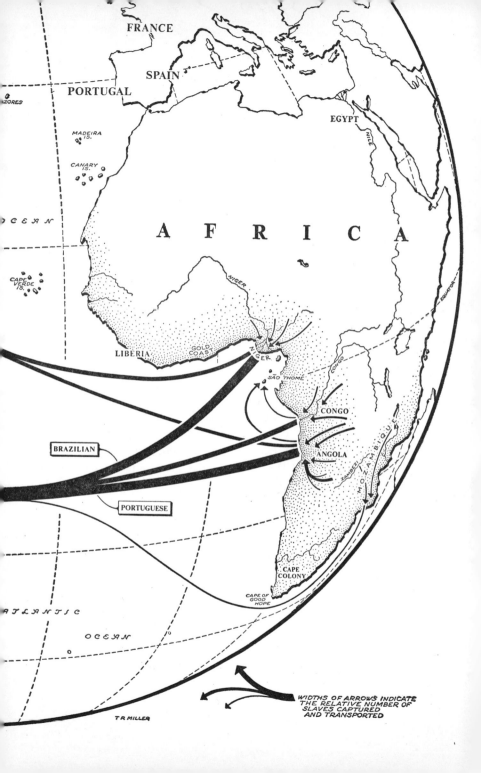

FRANCE

SPAIN

PORTUGAL

AZORES

MADEIRA IS.

CANARY IS.

OCEAN

CAPE VERDE IS.

EGYPT

NILE

A F R I C A

NIGER

EQUATOR

LIBERIA

GOLD COAST

NIGER

SÃO THOMÉ

CONGO

CONGO

BRAZILIAN

ANGOLA

ZAMBEZI

MOZAMBIQUE

PORTUGUESE

CAPE COLONY

CAPE OF GOOD HOPE

ATLANTIC

OCEAN

WIDTHS OF ARROWS INDICATE THE RELATIVE NUMBER OF SLAVES CAPTURED AND TRANSPORTED

T.R. MILLER

Europe, São Thomé, South Africa and other scattered settlements took another one-fourth to one-half million. This again indicates that 3.5 to 5.5 million arrived in foreign markets.

It is even more difficult to tell where in Africa the slaves came from, both because slavers rarely asked and because key records have been destroyed by the companies and governments involved. Perhaps two-thirds of the slaves came from the Gold Coast and Angola equally, but several areas had periods of popularity: Congo in the sixteenth and nineteenth centuries; Slave Coast, eighteenth; Niger Delta, nineteenth. Other areas provided slaves either sporadically or in a long trickle. Portugal dominated the fifteenth- and sixteenth-century trade, Holland three-fourths of the seventeenth century, and Britain the years 1672-1808; thereafter, Portuguese along with U.S., Brazilian, Spanish and French flags were dominant. Volume clearly varied widely from century to century, but in all, Britain and Portugal each carried about 32 or 33 percent of the cargo, the Netherlands about 18 percent, France about 12 percent and the United States (after 1783) about 5 percent.

By the end of the eighteenth century, protests against abuses and doubts concerning the morality of human slavery were being heard in every European country. The impact of these questions and the reforms that grew out of them created a new attitude toward Africa and a radical change in life within that continent.

5

THE DILEMMA OF JUSTICE

BEFORE the eighteenth century, Europeans believed that African customs should be judged by African standards. Slavery and slave trading had prevailed among African people since prehistoric times. Europeans who dealt in slaves felt only an obligation to follow African law, and, when possible, to spread Christianity. The gospel was not a program or standard of social action, but a message of salvation from this world. Thus, little popular indignation appeared in Europe during the first three centuries of overseas expansion. Indeed, few Europeans except slave traders and slaveowners ever saw a Negro bondman or understood what enslavement meant to the Africans involved.

Opposition to slavery was always present, however. Some of the Catholic hierarchy in Portugal repeatedly protested against the system during the whole 450-year trading period. Brave humanitarian voices spoke out from time to time in England and other countries, but very few of their listeners comprehended the problem they attacked.

Every European country tried to regulate the trade, or to insure that it was "justly" carried on. All slaves were supposed to be taken in accordance with established African law—that is, in "just" war, as proven criminals—and had to be purchased in legitimate fashion. Although African chiefs tended to increase the list of "crimes" and to launch unnecessary wars in order to get slaves, the Europeans had no effective way of distinguishing the justly from the unjustly enslaved. It was considered wrong to seize another man's country or to impose European cultural and legal standards upon alien societies. Thus treaties could be negotiated in good conscience with some friendly tribes, guaranteeing them protection from enslavement, and promising to buy the slaves that these tribes obtained by war or trade from their neighbors.

Of course, this attitude contributed directly to the development of the trade, because Europeans thought they would be doing the Africans—as well as themselves—a favor by buying slaves: Christian masters would be more just than pagan owners; a converted slave was assured full freedom and equality in afterlife; and Africans would learn the moral value of work while contributing to the prosperity of Christendom.

Spain, alone of all Christian powers, considered the slave trade illegal; her ships never were allowed to engage in slaving, and the law was quite strictly enforced. (Two exceptions were Christopher Columbus' enslavement of Indians—for which he was tried and imprisoned in 1500—and the nineteenth-century smugglers whom the Spanish navy was too weak to stop.) Slave-owning, however, was allowed—and even encouraged—on the grounds that it benefited both the Africans and the Spanish; but Portuguese, British and Dutch ships did the actual carrying from Africa.

The European attempt to respect and accept African custom was noble in theory but dangerous in practice because it served the European rather than the African economy. It was not traditional in Africa to enslave permanently, to consider slaves as unrestricted private property, or to make slaves a primary item of wholesale trade; it was not European custom to own humans or to use them for personal profit, but property owners traditionally had complete freedom to use or to dispose of their possessions. In this case the African custom of slavery was brought under the European system of absolute property rights. The merging of two traditional systems created confusion, distortions, and the danger of abuse and perversion.

Attacks on the institution of slavery increased throughout the eighteenth century because "Enlightenment" writers such as John Locke, Voltaire and Jean-Jacques Rousseau together claimed that there was only one universal code of law. What is immoral in one place is wrong everywhere, because all men are subject to the "rationale" of reason and possess the same natural rights. Reports of slave conditions circulated widely in the newly established popular newspapers. Religious reawakenings—especially mass movements such as the birth of Methodism in England—stressed humanitarianism. Traders and slaveowners, unable to convince anybody with their old arguments, were driven increasingly to stress property rights, commercial necessity and protection of investment. The more the materialistic argument was reiterated, the stronger the humanitarian reaction grew.

The Society of Friends, in 1727, was the first to condemn slavery; Quakers in both England and Pennsylvania began emancipating their Negroes. John Wesley's Methodist movement, emphasizing personal morality, influenced William Wilberforce, a British politician already well aware of Enlightenment thinking. The Anti-Slavery Society appeared in England in 1765, led by Wilberforce, and worked to convince Parliament that it was wrong to own a human being anywhere in the world. When in 1772 the Society convinced Lord Chief Justice Mansfield that the Common Law guaranteed freedom to all men, England became the first country to abolish slavery. The immediate result was merely that West Indian planters did not bring personal slaves to England. The ruling did not apply outside the home islands, so Parliament still had to be convinced that there was a uniform moral standard, even within the British Empire.

Slave trading in British waters and into or out of all British colonies was finally banned in the Act of 1807. The Royal Navy was responsible for the policing of British ships, but the wars against Napoleon prevented systematic enforcement for several years. Many British slave ships continued to operate—as before—with British crews, but would raise the American flag and claim immunity if challenged by a naval patrol. It was partly to stop this evasion under the cover of the Stars and Stripes that Britain began searching American ships. There was, of course, no sure way of telling whether an "American" ship was a legitimate merchantman or a renegade slaver manned by law-breaking Englishmen. Many of the legitimate ships were intercepted in the search either for slave traders or for other reasons. America protested, and the War of 1812 ensued. (The United States Constitution, written in 1787, required American ships to cease slaving after 1808, but this clause was not enforced until the Civil War.)

Even more vexatious to the British were two serious loopholes: the fact that once slaves reached British colonies their status was perfectly legal; and the continued legality of foreign slavers. The only way to prevent smuggling was to abolish the temptation. Thus, in 1834, Parliament freed all slaves in the empire, but—still quite conservative in its view toward property—appropriated £20,000,000 as compensation to their former owners. Among the foreign powers, Portugal had the greatest interest in slavery. After 1815 she agreed to operate no slavers north of the equator but broke her agreement in order to buy openly in the Niger Delta and to sell often in the West Indies. In 1818 Britain secured the right to search French ships and to detain any slavers, and Portugal was gradually forced to allow this also. Brazilian and Portuguese smugglers were still very active among the Yoruba in 1861, and the trade between Angola and Brazil continued, quite legal and virtually unlimited, until 1878. Illegal smuggling flourished for another decade; it died out only when Brazil, in 1888, became the last major country to abolish slavery. The British antislavery patrols operated—and occasionally caught smugglers—until 1901.

Some recent critics have accused the British of forcing other countries to abandon slave trading in order to destroy foreign economies, not because she was humanitarian. It is certainly true that Britain sought to dominate nineteenth-century commerce, but it is difficult to understand why Britain would have destroyed the very profitable slave trade—which she virtually monopolized—unless she was motivated by humanitarianism.

Humanitarians did not feel that their responsibility had ended when slave trading, and ultimately slaveownership, were banned. If universal standards of justice required these reforms, they also required Europeans to be concerned about emancipated Negroes in America and about slaving patterns within traditional African societies. Britain and the United States directed most of their early efforts toward American ex-slaves. The problem—the absorption or disposition of a new element in free, white, social and economic life—was not directly connected with Africa until philanthropists proposed returning the Negroes to their mother continent. Later on Europeans began to realize that the more pernicious and important problem was the contradiction between their own standards and those of African tradition. Consideration will be given to this complex issue after a review of the impact of abolition on Africa itself.

Britain faced the first extensive free-Negro problem in America at the end of the American Revolution. Slaves who had fled from the rebellious American colonies to Nova Scotia received freedom in return for their loyalty to the Crown; other Negroes, recognized as free but deported from the island of Jamaica after a massive slave revolt, increased the number of former slaves for whom British Canada was responsible. Negroes in England, freed by Lord Mansfield's ruling in 1772, and others who were seized by navy patrols from illegal slave ships in the Atlantic, added to the problem. The solution seemed to be "to return these Africans to their homeland."

Knowing relatively little about tribal differences within Africa, Europeans tended to think that all "Africans" were alike. Former slaves, it was thought, would be happier almost anywhere in "their own continent" than living among alien white societies. This opinion disregarded the fact that many of these Negroes had adopted European culture and European attitudes.

The first practical question, when "repatriation" of Negroes began, was where in Africa to send them. They could not be sent to the well-organized states, such as Dahomey, Yorubaland or Ashanti, where they would be either annihilated or enslaved as intruders. Areas such as the Niger Delta, Angola or the Congo, which Portuguese and tribal slave traders dominated, would not be satisfactory; allied African states such as the Fanti objected. Only the area between Senegal and the Ivory Coast was unorganized and sparsely populated; only in this area could land be acquired and enslavement of the settlers prevented. British and, later, American philanthropists chose portions of this area that are now known as Sierra Leone and Liberia.

The first Negro settlers from Nova Scotia and England arrived in Sierra Leone under British auspices in 1787. The idea was noble but no realistic plans had been made. The indigenous tribes refused to sell any land; they considered the colonists intruders who might, at best, rent a small zone. Thus, the Europeanized settlers had to take employment with slave traders and as port agents for West Indian slaving companies; their hopes were dashed first by disease and finally by an annihilating tribal attack in 1790.

The second colonization was organized in 1791 by the new Sierra Leone Company. In order to finance the transportation of new settlers from Nova Scotia, and to defray the cost of administration, the Company depended completely upon the capturing and selling of indigenous slaves. In order to stop this, Parliament in 1800 awarded the company a subsidy and granted it greater police power; eight years later the government took over the company and made Sierra Leone a British Crown Colony.

By tribal tradition, land in this part of Africa belonged to the descendants of the man who first farmed the soil. It could never be sold, so the settlers had to rent the sites for their towns and farms from the tribal owners. The Colonial Office vehemently opposed any contact between colonists and the tribes, failing to realize that unless treaties were negotiated the settlers would have to fight for land or face starvation. After fourteen years of debate, during which the settlers were totally dependent upon grants from philanthropists and Parliament, the negotiation of treaties and the rental of tribal land was allowed. None of the immigrants purchased any land until the end of the century, when English property-transfer law had replaced traditional law and technological developments made possible the cultivation of swampland that had never been used before. The imported Negroes always remained substantially European ("Creole") in culture, attitude and organization, quite distinct from the traditional indigenous society. Until the twentieth century, British influence was not extended beyond the narrow coastal strip that these settlers occupied.

United States interest in Liberia, which developed a generation later than the Sierra Leone plan, was entirely a private venture even though individuals in the Federal government were often interested. The American Colonization Society was chartered in 1816 in order to remove free Negroes from American society rather than as an antislavery device. Although some Southerners charged the Society with the creation of unrest by publicizing its interest in freedmen, the Society received as much support from slaveowners and Southern whites as it did from Northern humanitarians. The Society's report for 1819 captures the spirit of the only overseas colonization scheme that America produced in the early nineteenth century:

> "New forms of government, modelled after those which constitute the pride and boast of America, will attest the extent of their obligations to their former masters; and myriads of freemen, while they [cruise the banks] of the Congo . . . will sing, in the language which records the constitution, laws and history of America, hymns of praise to the Common Parent of mankind."

Land was bought south of Sierra Leone two years later. The initial settlement at Monrovia—named for President James Monroe—became the capital of "Monserrado County," and American naval vessels helped the colonists fight off native attacks.

The American Colonization Society gave Monserrado County a constitution four years later, while two other charities established their own settlements farther south along the coast: the Pennsylvania and Mississippi Colonization Society at Grand Bassa County, and the Maryland Society at "Maryland, Africa." Each society was distinct, so each colony—governed by its respective white sponsor—remained separate from its neighbors; among them, there were not more than 15,000 former slaves and about 5,000 Negroes liberated at sea (usually by the British navy).

Quite soon it was obvious that the limited resources of charity, and the refusal of most free Negroes to emigrate, would prevent "repatriation" from solving the American social problem. By 1834 the ACS had absorbed the Pennsylvania and Mississippi venture; the two colonies merged under the name "Liberia"; and the Harvard Law School prepared a model constitution. It provided for a Society governor, who was aided by "Council of Ten" settlers but retained the power of veto. Liberians rejected the plan until the ACS surrendered this privilege after five years of negotiation. The country received its first Negro governor in 1841, after which it had virtual self-government.

Liberia claimed its independence after 1847. The United States and the ACS did virtually nothing to counteract this, but formal recognition was withheld until the Civil War. During the interval American warships continued to defend the coastal settlers against attack. Maryland continued to be separate, under its small parent society, until annexed to Liberia by mutual agreement in 1857.

The government remained exclusively in the hands of the Americo-Liberians and their direct descendants. There was a veneer of civilization, largely an imitation of the Southern planter society in America, even at times to duplication of slave-ownership. No settlers dared to go inland, beyond the range of naval gunfire, until conflict with the indigenous tribes was resolved in the twentieth century.

Resettlement did not solve the Negro problem in the

United States or in British Jamaica. In Africa it only served to create a colonial problem because the settlers were too Europeanized to be absorbed by the indigenous people. In Sierra Leone Britain had to regulate two Negro societies that were almost as dissimilar as whites and Negroes in its multiracial possessions. American Liberia became not a "model" but a petty Europeanized power that alternately feared and dominated the Negroes in the interior.

Farther east, along the Gold, Slave and Niger Coasts, and in the savanna, where slaving was more extensive and population more concentrated, the impact of abolition created problems that European powers felt a responsibility to solve. Enslavement for the American market had converted a domestic system into a wholesale export race that drained population, encouraged wars and factionalism, and virtually destroyed established patterns of legitimate trade and agriculture. In return, the Europeans had imported virtually nothing except material goods. Christianity and education looked hypocritical, even to the tribes that allied with the Europeans. While Europe during the age of slavery experienced economic, social and intellectual changes that molded modern civilization, African abilities that might have proved fertile and sympathetic to these influences were directed toward a trade in which new or different ideas had no place. After almost 400 years, when the Europeans changed their viewpoint and banned slavery, many African states that had been built upon the slave trade resented the loss of markets. Smuggling, European pressure to stop enslavement, a new wave of desperate competitive wars, and a decline in the purchasing power of slave-centered economies contributed to a far-reaching convulsion inside Africa. It was increasingly obvious that if Europeans were to enforce the ban on trans-Atlantic slaving, they would have to stop slavery at its source because naval blockades could not prevent the continuation of profitable smuggling. In order to make slaving illegal in Africa, the new European concept of universal law would have to be made superior to African law.

On the Gold Coast, Europeans had the best opportunity to do this. Through the permanent forts or stations, which they held by treaty with the Fanti, they tried to introduce legitimate commerce to replace the slave trade. These treaties could not be abandoned, Europeans argued, because they involved a commitment to defend the Fanti against Ashanti threats from the interior; already, in 1806, the British had helped to repulse such an attack. When slaving stopped, the Ashanti—who had been powerful middlemen in that trade—renewed their onslaught against the coast. The British, Dutch and Danish forces were deeply committed in fighting that lasted from the slave-trade ban in 1807 to pacification nine years later. In the course of this war the Ashanti captured the treaties or "notes" from the Fanti; traditionally this meant that European rents should henceforth be paid to the Ashanti.

After the Peace of 1816, competition among the European powers for control of legitimate trade was nearly as keen as the contest between the Ashanti and the Fanti. It was soon obvious that Britain, the leading industrial power, had more to sell to Africa than others, so she became dominant on the Gold Coast. Britain, Denmark and the Netherlands then pitted their own Fanti allies against the others' allies. Each power tended increasingly to dictate behavior to the Fanti, especially in attempting to prohibit the Fanti from slave trading. This was probably illegal since the Europeans were only tenants in the country, but the manifest evil of slavery seemed to justify such intervention. Repeatedly the British indicated that they were going to quit the forts as soon as the Fanti had effectively banned slavery and made a firm peace with the Ashanti.

Another Ashanti war broke out in 1825, and the British had to remain in order to help their Fanti allies. However, instead of simply defeating the Ashanti and then being free to withdraw, the British captured the treaty "notes" from the enemy. In accordance with local laws, this made them the owners of their own forts. Denmark's notes, which were also captured, went to Copenhagen as a friendly gesture, but the Ashanti still

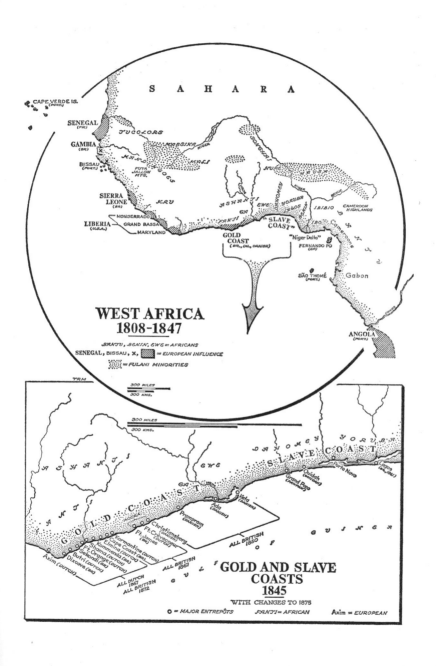

S A H A R A

CAPE VERDE IS.
(PORTS.)

SENEGAL
(FR.)

JUGOLORS

MOSSINCA

NIGER

SONGHAI

GAMBIA
(BR.)

BISSAU
(PORT.)

KRU-NDOOS

MALI

NUPE

FUTA
JALLON
MTS.

SIERRA
LEONE
(BR.)

KRU

ASHANTI

GA

EWE

DAHOMEY

YORUBA

BENUE

CAMEROON
HIGHLANDS

MONGERRADO

FANTI

LIBERIA
(U.S.A.)

GRAND BASSA

MARYLAND

GOLD
COAST
(BR., DU., DANISH)

"SLAVE
COAST"

LAGOS

I.B.I.B.I.O.

IBO

"Niger Delta"

FERNANDO PO
(SP.)

CAMEROONS

SÃO THOMÉ
(PORT.)

Gabon

C O N G O

WEST AFRICA
1808-1847

BANTU, BENIN, EWE = AFRICANS
SENEGAL, BISSAU, X, ▨ = EUROPEAN INFLUENCE
⣿ = FULANI MINORITIES

ANGOLA
(PORT.)

TRM

300 MILES
300 KMS.

300 MILES
300 KMS.

A S H A N T I

E W E

G A

DAHOMEY

S L A V E   C O A S T

YORUBA

Porto Novo

Lagos
(BR. 1861)

Ouidah
(WIDAH)

Grand Popo

G U I N E A

G O L D   C O A S T

Ada
(DANISH)

Prampram
(DANISH)

Vela
(DANISH)

Christiansborg
(DANISH)

Ft.Cr.(Crêvecœur)
(DUTCH)

Kormantine (DUTCH)

Ft. James
(BR.)

Cape Coast (BR.)

Elmina (DUTCH)

Kommenda (BR.)

St. George (DUTCH)

Butri (DUTCH)

Sekondi (BR.)

Dixcove (BR.)

Axim (DUTCH)

ALL DUTCH
1867

ALL BRITISH
1872

ALL BRITISH
1861

ALL BRITISH
1850

GOLD AND SLAVE
COASTS
1845
WITH CHANGES TO 1875

O = MAJOR ENTREPÔTS   *FANTI* = AFRICAN   Axim = EUROPEAN held the Dutch notes. Britain seemed to be involved more directly than ever, but her government reiterated its intention of abandoning the coast. Three years later the promise was fulfilled. The stations were turned over to a committee of London merchants and the official representatives withdrew.

Except for Sierra Leone, Liberia and a French agricultural settlement in Senegal, there were no other European interests north of the Congo. When slaving stopped, trade and official contact with Dahomey and Gabon was discontinued. Portugal confined her official contacts to Angola, where slave trading continued legally throughout most of the nineteenth century. Dahomey declined rapidly in wealth and importance, although the structure of her absolute monarchy, the thorough bureaucracy and the army remained strong. The Yoruba state broke down into a series of local units that vied bitterly among themselves for intermittent contact with Brazilian and Portuguese smugglers. Benin's empire dissolved. The sandy island of Lagos, controlling the one good harbor on the Slave Coast, was able to maintain her independence by playing one neighbor against another for access to slave smugglers or to imports of salt and coveted manufactures.

East of the Slave Coast, the Niger Delta had never had either European stations or well-organized African trading states. Therefore, when slavery was abolished, there was no territory to dispose of and no alliance treaty to be upheld. Trade in palm oil and ivory was encouraged in order to displace slaving, but the chief concern was the exclusion of smugglers. The tribal units were too small and too unpredictable to make antislavery treaties or concerted negotiation fruitful. Furthermore, it was firmly believed that the Niger Delta had no access to or connection with the interior. The river's many mouths were viewed not as a delta system but simply as a myriad of short creeks, known as the "Oil Rivers," all rising in a vast granite mountain range stretching across the country about one hundred miles inland.

The route and destination of the lower Niger River were unknown, even though European explorers had become quite familiar with the upper part that flowed through the savanna. The British government was trying to divest itself of interests on the coast, and was never directly involved in the "Oil Rivers," but considerable support was given to geographical exploration in the interior. Mungo Park had explored much of the upper and middle Niger; he died in a series of rapids, near Hausaland, in 1805. Heinrich Barth had been hired from Germany to cross the Sahara to report on geographical and political conditions shortly thereafter. In 1830 Clapperton and R. Lander also crossed the desert, launched a canoe into the Niger, and—to everyone's great astonishment—emerged in the "Oil Rivers," where they met British merchants. The government did not follow this up, but the traders began sailing well into the newly discovered river system; in so doing, they created violent enmity among the downriver tribes who had been by-passed, but also succeeded in reducing the supply of slaves to smugglers in the Delta (smugglers dared not penetrate restricted river waters, especially if British ships were sure to be there). Legitimate trade simply displaced slavery by competition and fortuitous circumstance; merchants had no special privileges and no depots, but after 1840 they and the river tribes had found the exchange of palm oil and ivory for European products to be mutually advantageous.

The effects of slave trading had spread northward from the rain forest, well inland from the coast. Political stability and economic prosperity had declined rapidly since the sixteenth century. Portuguese diversion of the gold-salt trade, followed by the rapacious Moroccan invasion and the reorientation of the forest tribes from savanna trade to coastal trade, had contributed to this. Of all savanna areas, Hausaland was the least disrupted. Her sophisticated governmental tradition was already one of decentralized autonomy, and unlike earlier savanna civilizations, which were dependent upon trade, she was a primary manufacturer (especially of cloth and steel).

Islam had entered Hausaland during the thirteenth and

fourteenth centuries, where it influenced considerably the structure of government and the development of Hausa literature, but its influence as a popular religion was superficial. Perhaps this laxity, perhaps simply the prosperity and stability of Hausaland attracted the anti-Moslem Fulani nomads about the same time. Islam continued to spread slowly in succeeding centuries, until it penetrated the itinerant, separatist Fulani as much as their ruling Hausa hosts.

Unlike most of his pastoral followers, the Fulani leader Usuman (Othman) dan Fodio had lived among the Hausa townsmen. When he returned from a pilgrimage to Mecca in 1802, Usuman dan Fodio was inspired to preach the purification of Islam. Under his command the subservient Fulani rose in jihad, or holy war, against the Hausa states. Between 1804 and 1810, one state after another, as well as parts of neighboring Yorubaland and a remnant of old Songhai, fell before the expansion of Usuman's Fulani Empire. Fighting was sharp. In a brief but violent terror generated by religious fanaticism, many non-Moslem vestiges in Hausa culture were destroyed, including most of the Hausa documents which are so sorely missed by modern scholars. The political system, since it was Koranic in origin, was still carefully preserved, although it was brought under a central sardauna, or emperor, at Sokoto. Usuman dan Fodio held that title, and he placed Fulani emirs, or district heads, over each Hausa state. In effect, then, the Empire was administered by a small coterie of Fulani organizers, who simply superimposed themselves upon the old Hausa system. Each Hausa state continued to function as it had for centuries; most laws, the large traditional bureaucracy and the daily administration of local affairs remained unchanged.

Islam was henceforth practiced in fairly orthodox fashion throughout what is now known as northern Nigeria, but the enthusiasm of the jihad soon degenerated into despotism and personal aggrandizement. Fulani conquerors turned increasingly to slave raiding, especially in the southeast, near the Cameroon Highlands, where Hausa states had traditionally acquired their slaves. Markets for these captives were slowly drying up—the Ashanti route, for example, was closed when Britain blocked the coastal trade; contact with smugglers at Lagos was impossible because the Yoruba state had broken into quarrelsome factions; sales to the Ottoman Turks continued, but European diplomats at Constantinople and fleets in the Mediterranean tried to prevent them. Fulani manpower was perhaps too small to dominate Hausaland indefinitely. When fanaticism declined, the new overlords became easier to corrupt. The emirs became increasingly sympathetic to their individual districts, the Hausa bureaucracy and legal traditions gradually defied Fulani authority, and the sardauna became a purely religious figurehead. By the last decades of the nineteenth century, autonomous states had, for all practical purposes, reëmerged.

Before the jihad of Usuman dan Fodio had disintegrated, however, his lieutenant, Ahmadu Lobo, had carried his enthusiasm to Fulani minorities scattered throughout the savanna regions. Aside from Hausaland, the strongest group was among the Mandingoes who lived between the Niger and Senegal Rivers, inland from French Senegal. Ahmadu Lobo imitated his master in overthrowing the hosts, but his own rule of the "Massina Empire" (1810-1844) was unimportant compared with the way in which his neighbors reacted to his religious and political ideas.

His two imitators were Omar, ruler of Futa Jallon after 1838, and Samory, a self-made Mandingo conqueror in the 1870's. These men put an end to chaos and isolation in the savanna—not by their own rule, but because their rapid expansion brought them into direct contact with Europeans who dominated the interior from then on.

As long as European powers felt that their responsibility extended only to allied states along the coast, they were not concerned with affairs in the interior and in states with which they did not trade. Indeed, as long as slaves were not traded under their very noses, the British—perhaps more firmly than anyone else—felt that government or military intervention was

unnecessary if not improper. Freedom for legitimate trade, it
was assumed, went hand in hand with progress for both the
buyer and the seller; protection of such commerce was the responsibility of the Foreign Office, but the government would
take no positive action aside from the suppression of slaving
ships. British traders were able to drive other Europeans out
peacefully, because England produced more and charged less.
Britain believed in free competition and found that it worked to
her advantage; the other powers accepted the idea also, but
lacked both the manufactures and the interest that were necessary to dislodge the British.

It was thus entirely logical for the British government to
withdraw from the Gold Coast in 1828, and to have no official
stake in the Niger Delta trade. Once peace had been established
along the coast, "natural laws" of economic necessity would lead
to conditions which would automatically satisfy both Africans
and Europeans. After the British quit the Gold Coast, their
diplomatic and commercial affairs were handled through officials
in Sierra Leone or referred all the way to London; traders occupied the stations in Fanti and handled their own affairs in the
Niger Delta.

Gold Coast commerce was handled by the private Committee of London Merchants. The traders chose George Maclean, a
forceful army officer, to negotiate a working peace with the restless Ashanti. In order to protect the Ashanti trade routes, which
were necessary for a successful commercial operation, he set
himself up as arbiter over all tribal disputes. The government
warned the Committee that this constituted a European administration, precisely what Britain wanted to avoid, but Maclean continued his policy because he and the Committee felt
that trade depended upon regulation of the tribes.

Maclean's exceptional firmness, impartial devotion and
endless patience brought an era of unprecedented tranquility
and coöperation to the Gold Coast. Africans trusted his judgment, which included an ability—unique at that time among
Europeans—to accept both the sharp words and the protracted

delays of traditional tribal negotiations. He was willing to travel in the interior without military escort, and, contrary to British government policy, he used European law only as a supplement to native custom. As a result, Maclean's authority spread rapidly and was greatly respected by both the Fanti and the Ashanti.

The government feared that Maclean and the London Merchants were committing Britain too deeply in native affairs, so it proceeded to oust the merchants in 1843. British officials then resumed direct rule over the forts and made plans for reducing the number of political obligations the merchants had contracted. In the course of his expansion in 1831 Maclean had worked out a truce between the Fanti and Ashanti that the government maintained until 1871, but on most other matters there was persistent indecision.

Since the Ashanti were pacified when direct rule was restored, the officials turned their attention to the petty disputes that divided the Fanti states. In order to pacify the coast, a "Bond" was worked out with the Fanti which provided for British arbitration and regulation of intertribal relations. The Bond of 1844 may have been made in order to strengthen English trade, or it might simply have been a plan to stabilize the area before the government withdrew. Parliamentary critics repeatedly called for withdrawal in order to save expense, but the tranquility after which that would take place never was achieved.

Paying for the administration of the colony constituted a continuing problem. British taxpayers resented the expense. Merchants, not the government, made the profits, but they could not be taxed or required to pay trade duties because this would permit the Dutch and Danish stations to undersell the British; moreover, such tariffs were contrary to free-trade policy. The only solution was acquisition of the foreign stations which incited Fanti disunity; then all the Fanti could be taxed directly. In 1850 Denmark willingly sold her interest. Britain took back the "notes" which established ownership, and the competitive turmoil was reduced. This meant more involvement, but peace and unity now seemed to be possible. The Fanti chiefs were then asked to collect taxes from their subjects. Using the Bond of 1844 as a lever to justify their actions, the British had a head-tax provision put on the Fanti lawbooks, but nothing was collected because the chiefs could not tax without the consent of their people.

Dutch stations were still interspersed among the British along the Gold Coast. Fanti tribes, allied with one power, still sought to destroy rivals that were allied with the other European country. Both powers agreed to exchange forts in 1867, so the western part of the coast became Dutch while the eastern sphere went to Britain. Now, it was hoped, peace and unity could prevail in each section. A small tariff to defray the cost of administration (but not for protective purposes) might even be possible.

A major misunderstanding prevented peace, however. The western Fanti felt that they were betrayed by their British allies when they were turned over to their Dutch enemies. Britain told all the Fanti—both in the east and in the west—that she was now withdrawing to her stations, and would no longer try either to defend the Fanti or to arbitrate their disputes. The Anglo-Dutch exchange of stations now seemed to be a withdrawal scheme rather than a realignment of traditional allies. The Fanti, quite logically, thought that this released them from the Bond of 1844; it is hard to tell what the British thought had happened to that agreement.

One Fanti chieftain proceeded as though the Bond were dead. Taking the title of King John Aggrey, he announced that British courts no longer had jurisdiction over his people and set about building an army. Other Fanti proceeded to confederate in order to protect themselves from the Dutch and their Ashanti allies on the west and north. The Fanti Confederacy agreed on a mature basic statute, the Mankesim Constitution of 1871, which provided for an elective king-president, a representative assembly, a permanent judiciary, and a system of public education. A copy of it was forwarded in proper diplomatic fashion to the British stations for their "information."

Horrified at the repercussions of their agreement with Holland, Britain reacted in a manner that astonished the Fanti. She demanded the right to veto the Mankesim Constitution, having apparently developed the notion that the Fanti were joining hands to oust the Europeans. It is now known that enmity between the Fanti and the Ashanti was increasing rapidly, but the Europeans, who understood very little of native affairs, became possessed with the notion that the Fanti were allying with the Ashanti. If Fanti self-government turned out to be chaotic— white men assumed that Negroes were too savage to organize —Britain would have to begin all over again to pacify the country. Furthermore, a Fanti bureaucracy would be much harder to deal with than autonomous traditional chiefs, so the peace that Britain wanted would be endangered by the Confederation. Britain therefore vetoed the Mankesim Constitution and revived the Bond of 1844.

The Netherlands was much more reluctant to use a strong hand against the Fanti. Dutch trade depended upon unfettered access to the Ashanti. Their trade was seriously disrupted by the strong Fanti reaction to the exchange of forts. Inasmuch as their trade had long been relatively light, the Dutch decided by 1872 that the wisest course was to sell their interest to the British. This would at first appear to have been a reasonable solution to many of the Gold Coast's problems, but it provoked a crisis of the first magnitude.

Since 1825 Britain and Denmark had owned their own forts because the "notes" or titles to them had been captured from the Ashanti. The Dutch notes, however, had not been captured, so their stations were still Ashanti property for which regular rent had to be paid. When the stations were exchanged with England in 1867, Holland continued to send presents to the ashantihene, but Britain did not understand this when she bought the Dutch interests five years later. The presents, England believed, were simply to encourage a dwindling trade. She should have known better by this time than to think such payments were unnecessary. Ashanti, considering the gifts a form of rent on which Britain had defaulted, registered a protest and finally attacked the coastal regions. Britain had thought that by reviving the Bond and acquiring jurisdiction over the entire coast, she could assure peace and stability without either inland penetration or great expense. Instead, she was to be drawn into the interior on an unprecedented scale. Such a new development caused a drastic revision of policy that will be given special consideration in Chapter 16.

Affairs in the Niger Delta were not affected by such a crisis. Free trading increased rapidly after the river was explored, so the Foreign Office provided a consul after 1849. He lived on Fernando Po, well offshore, but was available in normal diplomatic fashion to help traders in their negotiations with Delta chiefs. At times the lack of tribal organization created dangerous conditions. Time and again the merchants asked the consul to provide diplomatic support, but the Foreign Office steadfastly refused to intervene until 1872; thereafter the consul was allowed to arbitrate disputes over contracts and to organize punitive expeditions. Eventually he moved to Calabar on the coast, but affairs were still basically in the realm of foreign relations rather than political administration.

There were few regular British interests on the Slave Coast, but the navy continued to intercept a number of slave ships operating illegally from Lagos to Brazil. By 1851 competition for control of such smuggling had become keen among the tribes of the area. Powerful Dahomey tried to seize the port with a force of 18,000 of her invincible Amazons, but Lagos' soldiers, not as chivalrous as most Dahoman enemies, were willing to fight. They won, then cut off legitimate trade to the Dahomans and part of Yorubaland. A dynastic civil war ensued. Travelers' reports on the increasing chaos alarmed the British humanitarians. The port of Lagos, but no adjoining territory, was occupied in 1861. The Brazilian slavers fled, and the trade routes were reopened.

Britain alone was involved in West Africa to any significant degree during the first three-quarters of the nineteenth century. She had tried to restrict her interests, but found that antislavery humanitarianism and freedom of trade could not succeed without increasingly direct government intervention. By the mid-nineteenth century the foundations had been laid for subsequent imperial conquest, competitive partition and colonial rule in West Africa.

6

PUNT TO ZENJ

PYGMIES lived around the Great Lakes in protohistoric times, but Bushmen predominated elsewhere east and south. Pockets of both these people can still be found, but historical development begins with a series of alien infiltrations in a sequence that scholars have only begun to clarify. Apparently the first of these was a thin, scattering of Afroasiatic Cushites or Sidamo people who spread southward from the Ethiopian Highlands a few centuries before the birth of Christ. These agricultural settlers, archaeologists believe, introduced hillside terracing for the farmers, stone carving for construction, and a series of new crops. Near their settlements on Lake Victoria, they apparently wiped out the Pygmies. Farther south, however, they accepted the Khoïsan people and probably taught them the rudiments of ironworking. The Cushitic invaders had a considerable influence even though they were small in numbers and left few remains.

Ancient Egyptians occasionally mentioned the northeastern coast—calling it Punt—but Sabeans, from modern Yemen, were the earliest important people whose arrival on the coast has been concretely proved. Trade in Arabian, Indian and East African products began under their rule. There were a few settlements for trade and tropical agriculture in Roman times near

the Equator, but it is doubtful that there were many—if any—
Indian or Indonesian people among the colonists. Eastern ship-
building ideas and crops may have been used, but these could
well have been brought by the Sabeans in the course of their
trade.

No Negroes existed in East Africa until the Bantu-speaking vanguard began to emerge from the forest near the Great
Lakes between 500 and 800 A.D. Although they had been developing simple military organization during their forest trek
from the Cameroons, the Bantu must have struggled to overrun
the lake-side states that the stone-carving Cushite farmers had
built up. Ultimately the Negroes triumphed because they outnumbered the defenders and imitated their organization.

Kingdoms appeared on the lakes: Buganda on Lake Victoria, Bunyoro near Lake Albert, and Ruanda and Urundi north
of Lake Tanganyika. Bantu dialects dominated. Pygmies in Ruanda and Urundi, where the Sidamo Cushites had not eliminated
them, served as hunting and scavenging people. The Cushitic
patterns of organization, home building and agriculture were
adopted. Other Bantu Negroes—perhaps those who emerged a
little later from the Congo—continued into modern Tanganyika, then up to Kenya after the lake areas were occupied;
another Bantu wave followed the lake-shore corridor that broke
up the forest in order to reach the Rhodesias and Nyasaland.
Bushmen, unlike the pygmies, apparently fled southward in front
of these incoming waves or were annihilated.

Shortly before the time of Christ the Sabean traders decided to move from Yemen in arid Arabia to the more fertile
mountains of Ethiopia. Monophysite Christian missionaries
converted them in the fourth and fifth centuries A.D., but the
struggle with other claimants in the area prevented them from
continuing their seafaring and colonizing activities. Repercussions from the people they dislodged were felt eventually along
the Great Lakes, while Arabs and Persians replaced them in
coastal trade.

Sudanic Negroes living along the upper Nile were for many

centuries influenced by the Cushitic culture and language of neighboring Ethiopia. Cattle had come to the valley through this contact. When the Sabeans invaded the Highlands, many Cushites fled westward in order to find refuge among the Negroes. The resulting combination, the Nilotes, developed a fusion of Niger-Congo and Afroasiatic languages. Nilotic nomads subsequently began to expand toward the Great Lakes, where they encountered the developing Bantu kingdoms. Most of them finally settled in the Highlands of Kenya and Tanganyika, but two groups managed to make special arrangements in Buganda, Bunyoro and Ruanda-Urundi.

The tsetse fly, which carries a fatal cattle disease, does not exist along the lakes. Nilotic herds, a welcome addition to the Bantu economy, could therefore survive. Cattle-raising techniques were soon transmitted southward through the fly-free highland corridor to the Rhodesian and South African veld. The Nilotic cattlemen became a privileged class in Bunyoro and Buganda, the most northerly of the Lake kingdoms, but in Ruanda and Urundi they succeeded in parleying or fighting their way into actual control of the government. In these more southerly kingdoms the Nilotic Batutsi (Watutsi) constituted an exclusive aristocracy that governed the Bantu masses. They retained distinctive racial characteristics, including their great height, and had a reverence for both agility and leisure. One would expect to find these distinct qualities in an alien group that was ingrown, that remembered its military ability, and that developed abhorrence for peasant labor. In every case Bantu has replaced Nilotic speech, but the basis of the primary industry is cattle.

The prosperous Nilotes of Bunyoro and Buganda helped the Bantu chiefs, who gave them special privileges, to become nearly absolute kings. Extensive territories and large populations were governed by a permanent bureaucracy and a council that combined judicial and executive functions. Bunyoro expanded rapidly by military conquest during the eighteenth century. The territory was divided into districts that were placed under the administration of loyal chiefs. The king traveled frequently in order to supervise his scattered herds of cattle and the affairs of his district chiefs, so there was no permanent court and little finery. Buganda, however, was relatively insignificant until Bunyoro overextended itself. Early in the nineteenth century a revolt in Toro precipitated the disintegration of Bunyoro.

Buganda soon emerged as the dominant power on Lake Victoria. Cattle were less important in this state than the cultivation of millet, which prospered around the lake. There was little cause for such a society to expand, but—perhaps because Buganda was not aggressive—many surrounding tribes sought its protection and began to pay regular tribute. The king or kabaka had a permanent capital, into which the Nilotes had introduced much panoply and ritual, as well as an impressive array of warriors and several hundred war canoes to use either to defend his allies or to force them to pay overdue tribute. Although the kabaka rose, with Nilotic help, to a virtually absolute position, his subjects had long preferred settled agriculture to conquest. New tributaries usually became loyal subjects because they were ruled by trustworthy local chiefs instead of occupation troops or Baganda agents who might be resented.[1] The appointed chiefs received judicial authority and the power of taxation, so there was local autonomy as well as loyal service to the sovereign kabaka.

There was no conflict between the two states until 1869, when Bunyoro revived her expansionism and came into contact with the tributary network of Buganda. A conclusive struggle was forestalled by the arrival of Europeans in the following decade. At first, European observers believed the kabaka to be more sophisticated and pliable than his counterpart in Bunyoro. Travelers' reports emphasized the elaborate, settled character of the Buganda court, the importance of agriculture and the im-

---

[1] In Bantu languages, variations of a basic noun are indicated by prefixes: e.g., from the basic word *Ganda* are derived *Buganda* (land of Ganda), *Baganda* (people of Ganda), *Luganda* (language of Ganda); likewise, from *Nyoro* come *Bunyoro*, *Banyoro* and *Lunyoro*.

pressive discipline of the warriors and sailors. Bunyoro royal
residences seemed "filthy" and shoddy, but it is now known
that this poor façade was due largely to the transient nature of
the court. Behind it, there functioned a government that could
rule larger areas and depended less upon the exchange of
privileges than did the Buganda system.

Southwest of Buganda, Toro and Bunyoro lay the kingdoms
of Ruanda and Urundi (Ruandi). In many respects these five
states resembled one another; the differences are noteworthy,
but all were molded by the same Nilotic influences. Early Sidamo Cushites had relatively little impact on Ruanda and
Urundi, so the pygmies—whom they elsewhere killed—continued to survive. Furthermore, the Bantu in this area, not having Sidamo predecessors to imitate, were less well organized
when the Nilotes arrived from the northeast. As a result the invaders not only introduced Sidamo ideas to these Bantu, but
also became a privileged class with complete political and social
control. Their impact was therefore more sudden, more marked
and more revolutionary than it had been around Lake Victoria.

Neither Ruanda nor Urundi had fixed capital cities. The
ruling Batutsi maintained elaborate but mobile courts that
administered a form of feudalism. The Bantu-speaking Bahutu,
the older inhabitants, were reduced to the status of agricultural
peasants; they were allowed neither to fight nor to own land, so
they became virtual serfs. Title to the land and the right to
collect a percentage of its yield belonged to the Batutsi monarch, whose power was absolute. Pygmies (known in this area
as the Batwa) served as hunters, watchmen, pages and servants to the king and his aristocracy. Cattle raising was considered a privilege, so only the Batutsi—who were also the warriors
—could have herds. The ruling caste also controlled the judicial,
administrative and economic power in each country.

The Bantu tribes that moved eastward from the Great
Lakes learned about cattle raising from the Cushitic Galla people of southern Ethiopia and the Kenya Highlands. Bantu societies between the lakes and the Indian Ocean did not require

or receive complex organization, but they borrowed an extensive tradition of law and numerous ritual practices from their Cushitic, Sidamo and Nilotic neighbors.

By the early tenth century Bantu spearheads had followed the open country, along the Great Lakes, as far as the south shore of the Zambezi. They already were skilled ironworkers; to this, they added the art of stone cutting which they learned from the Cushites who were scattered thinly among the East African Bushmen. The Bantu also followed their usual custom of absorbing, driving off or annihilating the Bushmen who were in their way. Rich alluvial mineral deposits were found 200 miles on either side of the Zambezi River. Crops flourished, and a profitable trade with Arab merchants developed along the Indian Ocean coast before 1200 A.D.

The Cushites had done some mining and trading as early as the seventh century, but commerce did not flourish until the first Bantu, calling themselves Sotho, had settled in large numbers. After they had ruled for about 200 years, the Sotho were overwhelmed by Shona Bantu, who seem to have brought cattle through the disease-free corridor from the Great Lakes. By 1450 the Shona had created a kingdom, had given their ruler the title of "Monomotapa," and had begun the construction of stone-walled settlements.

The most intriguing and extensive of these is Zimbabwe. On this site, wood and mud villages had existed since the beginning of mining in the seventh century, and stone had long been used for ceremonial sites, but the stonework is now firmly dated in the Shona's fifteenth-century Monomotapa empire. The political system depended upon the collection of tribute from conquered neighbors. It may have been one of these tribes that, about 1600, overthrew the Monomotapa, occupied the stone cities, and added new buildings. After 1693 the Rozwi Bantu took over the area, rebuilt many of the original structures and spread stone building to other parts of Southern Rhodesia. In 1834 the Rozwi were destroyed by invading Zulus from the south; knowledge of stone building and the occupation of stone

cities came to an abrupt end. There is no doubt that Bantu
Negroes both conceived and executed the idea of Zimbabwe.
Bantu stone builders were observed as recently as the 1840's near
Victoria Falls and the 1820's in Transvaal. There is a similarity
to stonework in Ethiopia, indicating a Cushitic origin for the
art, but the specific decorative motifs have been traced to Bantu
in the Congo basin. The designs and functions of ceremonial
structures are the culmination of ideas that have been traced
back to the Cameroon Highlands.

Arab traders wrote reports on the development of Zimbabwe and other Monomotapa buildings; Portuguese missionaries, traders and emissaries visited them several times and left
clear accounts. Carbon-dating, examination of skulls and arti-
facts, and significant advances in Bantu studies have helped to
clarify the history of the stone cities. Confusion regarding Zimbabwe, which became a "mystery" of ridiculous proportions,
can be traced to three sources: none of the early explorers had
ever examined ruins before; research was hampered by the fact
that prospectors reached the ruins and desecrated them before
scholars could study them, so extensive excavation and great patience was necessary before a solution could be found; and most
untrained visitors invented a romantic theory which assumed
that Negroes were too "inferior" to be able to plan and build
in stone.

Much is uncertain, but an outline is clear. There is little
disagreement on major points among any trained authorities
who have investigated the site at Zimbabwe.[2]

The East African coast is a narrow, sandy strip. Forests and
highlands prevent easy access to the interior. Until the nineteenth century there was consequently very little penetration
beyond the coast. The ancient Sabeans of Arabia had developed

[2] The most authoritative works on Zimbabwe are: Gertrude Caton-
Thompson, *The Zimbabwe Culture: Ruins and Reactions*, London, 1931;
and the more recent observations of J. Desmond Clark, *The Prehistory of
Southern Africa*, Harmondsworth, 1959, pp. 289-313. An interesting sum-
mary of the controversy concerning Zimbabwe is Basil Davidson, *Old Africa
Rediscovered*, London, 1960, pp. 199-230.

a light trade with the scattered East African Cushites. This declined when the Sabeans concentrated upon the conquest of Ethiopia early in the Christian era. There may have been commercial settlements along the coast, but they did not have a lasting impact upon East Africa. Other Arabian people, who gradually replaced them along the coast, established an irregular trade with the Cushitic miners in the Zambezi Valley. Extensive development did not occur until the Bantu had arrived and Arab organization had coalesced.

Islam spread to all tribes in the Arabian desert during the seventh century, but political unification was difficult to achieve. The Bedouins in Oman, at the eastern tip of Arabia, remained independent because they looked to the sea rather than to the desert for their livelihood. Oman's one harbor, Muscat, dominated the tribes living in the interior. About 750 A.D. the spread of Moslem governmental theory made possible the development of a central ruler, entitled the Imam of Oman.

Omani desert tribes had few saleable products, but they found attractive profit in piracy and in carrying goods for others. Depots were established in India, Persia and East Africa. The basis of trade was the exchange of African gold and slaves for the cloth, utensils and trinkets that India and Persia produced. Sudanese Nilotes and Negroes, sometimes caught by the warlike Sabeans of Ethiopia, were sold in the Persian slave markets.

Religious disputes, dynastic quarrels and a slave uprising disrupted the peace and prosperity of ninth-century Persia. Turkish mercenaries usurped the power of the caliph. Persian nobles pressed for political control and a revision of Islamic teaching. Thousands died in the chaos; others sought refuge on Omani ships. They were transported to the East African coast, where Omani merchants and sailors helped them to establish permanent settlements. Oman was the protector and sponsor, but the cities were Persian in design and independent in politics.

The settlements from the Zambezi to modern Somalia were collectively known as Zenj (the Arabic word for Ethiopia), but

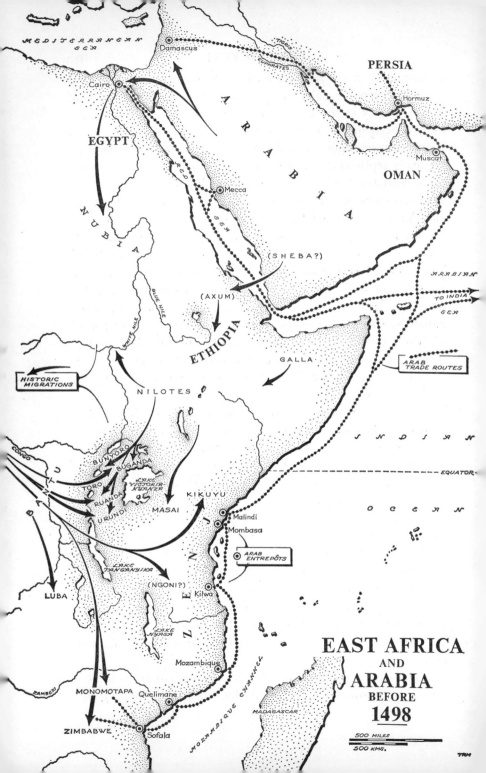

MEDITERRANEAN SEA

Damascus

PERSIA

Tigris

EUPHRATES

Cairo

Hormuz

EGYPT

A R A B I A

Muscat

OMAN

RED SEA

Mecca

NUBIA

(SHEBA?)

BLUE NILE

WHITE NILE

(AXUM)

ARABIAN

TO INDIA

ETHIOPIA

GALLA

SEA

HISTORIC MIGRATIONS

NILOTES

ARAB TRADE ROUTES

CONGO

BUNYORO

BUGANDA

TORO

LAKE VICTORIA NYANZA

RUANDA

URUNDI

MASAI

KIKUYU

EQUATOR

Malindi

Mombasa

I N D I A N

ARAB ENTREPÔTS

O C E A N

LAKE TANGANYIKA

(NGONI?)

LUBA

Z
E
N
J

Kilwa

LAKE NYASA

EAST AFRICA
AND
ARABIA
BEFORE
1498

Mozambique

MOZAMBIQUE CHANNEL

MADAGASCAR

MONOMOTAPA

Quelimane

ZAMBEZI

ZIMBABWE

Sofala

500 MILES

500 KMS.

TRH

there was no central organization. Each city-state was built on an island, safe from both attack and disease; except for trade, which began to develop as the Bantu arrived during the next century, there was little contact with the mainland. Plantations for the cultivation of palm oil developed, first on the islands, then on the narrow coastal strip. Slave labor for these plantations was easily obtained because the Bantu who reached the coast were weakly organized. As Zenj was settled and developed, trade increased rapidly. Entrepreneurs from India, finding the coast attractive, began to dominate the shipping, banking and farming activities; Omani and Persian Arabs became a leisure ruling class. Various seaboard populations—Bantu, Arabs and Indians (the last known as "banyans")—began to create the new Swahili cultural amalgam. As a language, Swahili mixed Bantu and Arabic vocabulary, but it was written with the Arabic alphabet. Trade and commerce dominated. The Moslem rulers and banyan entrepreneurs were often wealthy, but their culture was borrowed from Persia and Oman.

Most of the slaves were used on the East African coastal plantations, although a steady market also existed overseas. Negro servants were fashionable in Arabia, Persia and India; even China bought a few in later years. However, they were rarely used for extensive agricultural work, so the foreign demand was always limited. Not many Negroes are found today in these countries because the Zenj slavers exported only castrated males. This, of course, prevented racial inundation and helped domesticate the servant slaves. Zenj was also guaranteed a continuing market for replacements.

By the fifteenth century, ships occasionally came to the Zenj cities from Canton, but none of the Chinese stayed permanently. Arabs continued to control the politics and to collect the duties, but foreigners were allowed to dominate the commerce itself: Indians and Chinese on the sea, and Bantu in the interior of East Africa. Occasionally city-states such as Kilwa or Mombasa would impose tribute, disrupt trade or exert military influence in other ports, but each settlement remained essentially independent.

Indeed, the Zenj cities were quite different from one another. Malindi and Mombasa on the Kenya coast were important plantation states, with Mombasa dominating the export of slaves in that area. Kilwa, on the southern coast of modern Tanganyika, also specialized in slaves. The Zimbabwe gold trade passed through Sofala, at the mouth of the Zambezi. Mozambique City, having very little inland trade, depended primarily upon strategic domination of the Mozambique Channel and a few plantations for her prosperity. The fortunes of each state depended not only upon agricultural and military achievement but also upon the uncontrollable Bantu migrations in the interior. Slaving and the plantations would both decline if the Negroes either moved away or drove too hard a bargain.

Arab commercial and political ascendancy, strengthened by the flow of Bantu labor and mine products from the interior, was deeply rooted in the East African coast by the fifteenth century. At that time Vasco da Gama carried the Portuguese flag northward from the Cape of Good Hope, and the Europeans merely took over and operated the well-established Zenj system.

7

EMPIRES OF THE EAST
AFRICAN COAST

K ILWA dominated the southern Arab towns and Mombasa
the northern at the end of the fifteenth century. When Da
Gama's India fleet worked its way up the East African coast in
March, 1498, Mozambique was the first Zenj port to be dis-
covered. Initially the Arabs thought the fleet represented new
Moslem traders; the Portuguese believed they had discovered a
Christian kingdom, perhaps that of Prester John.

The illusions were quickly shattered. Vasco da Gama attacked and tricked one town after another, even though some
were friendly and others merely wary. It is not clear whether
his attitude was caused by religious zeal, by fear of Arab
strength, or by sheer depravity. Of all Zenj cities, only Malindi
could subsequently forget his behavior and call itself a Portuguese friend.

India and the East Indies were the main goal. In 1509-1510
a Portuguese military expedition, under Afonso d'Albuquerque,
systematically reduced all Arab, Indian and Malayan entrepôts
and gained control of the trade routes radiating from them.
Mozambique in Africa, Hormuz in Persia, Malacca on the Malay Straits, and Goa on the Indian subcontinent became the

cornerstones of empire. Portugal operated the main intercontinental trade routes with her own ships, but licensed Indian and Arab ships to serve the "country" or feeder trade along the African and Asian coasts. There was not enough Portuguese manpower to govern and trade everywhere, so the secondary country ports were regulated by intermittent tribute collections. From time to time most Zenj cities tried to evade both tribute payments and the trade restrictions. Mombasa was more defiant than any other tributary. Periodically Portugal had to send punitive expeditions to the East African ports in order to reinforce her authority.

Usually the Portuguese used the old Arab cities as their own. Swahili people continued to make up the population, but the Arabs were forced to take second place to the new conquerors. The Monomotapa gold trade, through the old Arab port of Sofala, continued without interruption; gold, slaves and ivory moved from East Africa in Portuguese ships to India and the Orient, where they were exchanged for Asian cloth, metal products and glasswork. Arab dhows continued to serve the "country" ports between Mozambique and Persia, but the cargoes had to be transferred to Portuguese bottoms for longer hauls. The monopoly was secure along most of the coast, but Portugal's only interior interests during the sixteenth century were in the Zambezi area between Mozambique and Sofala.

Monomotapa's mineral wealth grew in legend to fantastic proportions. Traders and missionaries tried repeatedly to penetrate to Zimbabwe (the "Zimboë" of Portuguese dreams). Plans were made for a Christian kingdom even more illustrious than the Congo experiment; perhaps there would be silver to rival the Spanish hoards in America. Antonio Caiado, who served for many years as the first of a long line of Portuguese representatives at the Monomotapa court, negotiated trade treaties and made arrangements for merchants and missionaries to visit the interior. The Bantu's mines were rarely seen, but "Zimboë" and other centers frequently received Portuguese visitors. Never, however, did the mines yield as much as the traders wanted.

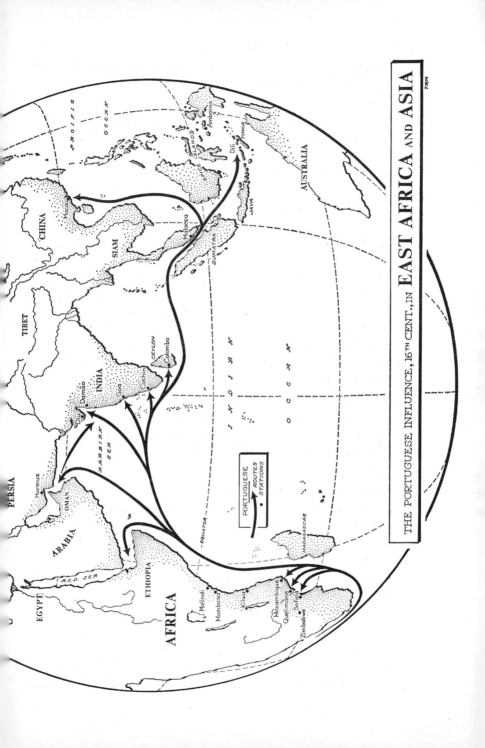

THE PORTUGUESE INFLUENCE, 16TH CENT., IN **EAST AFRICA** AND **ASIA**

PORTUGUESE
ROUTES
STATIONS

CHINA
TIBET
SIAM
PERSIA
ARABIA
OMAN
EGYPT
ETHIOPIA
AFRICA
INDIA
CEYLON
Macao
Hormuz
Damão
Diu
Goa
Cochin
Colombo
Malacca
SUMATRA
JAVA
SPICE ISLANDS
TIMOR
Dili
Amboina
AUSTRALIA
MADAGASCAR
Malindi
Mombasa
Kilwa
Mozambique
Quelimane
Sofala
Zimbabwe
RED SEA
ARABIAN SEA
EQUATOR
INDIAN OCEAN

Mission work was even less successful because Portugal could not provide enough priests to impress the power-conscious Monomotapa.

European women were rarely allowed to go out to the colonies, so the perpetuation of European rule depended upon the assimilation of native blood by intermarriage. Portuguese trade passed gradually into the hands of loyal half-castes during the sixteenth century. Hindu traders were still called "banyans," as they had been during the early Arab period, but Christianized and half-caste Indians were labeled "Goans." They usually came from Goa, Portugal's colonial headquarters on the Malabar Coast of India.

Interior penetration was always costly in both lives and money. The Monomotapa, despite Caiado's treaties, could not control their own Bantu tributaries. In order to maintain Portugal's hold on the promising interior, Goan and Portuguese adventurers were encouraged to settle along the upper reaches of the Zambezi. Vast plantations, like those that had been so successful in Brazil, were granted to these *prazeros*. In order to hold and develop these grants, the *prazeros* were allowed to acquire slaves both for labor and for private armies. Portuguese culture, white blood and obedience to the Crown rapidly disappeared, but the *prazeros*—fiercely proud of their feudal charters and European nationality—continued to dominate their large, semimilitarized, self-sufficient slave-labor estates.

Africa never was as important in the Portuguese scheme as Goa or the Spice Islands, except for the Sofala-Monomotapa gold trade. Goa became the main entrepôt and the gateway to Oriental wealth. East Africa was occupied in order to protect the shipping routes between India and the mother country, and to prevent other powers from threatening the Portuguese monopoly by gaining a foothold in the country trade.

Portugal had neither interest nor manpower for an effective occupation of all the Zambezi country. Only the force of Portuguese arms prevented a resurgence of rival Arab economic or political power farther north along the coast. Mombasa,

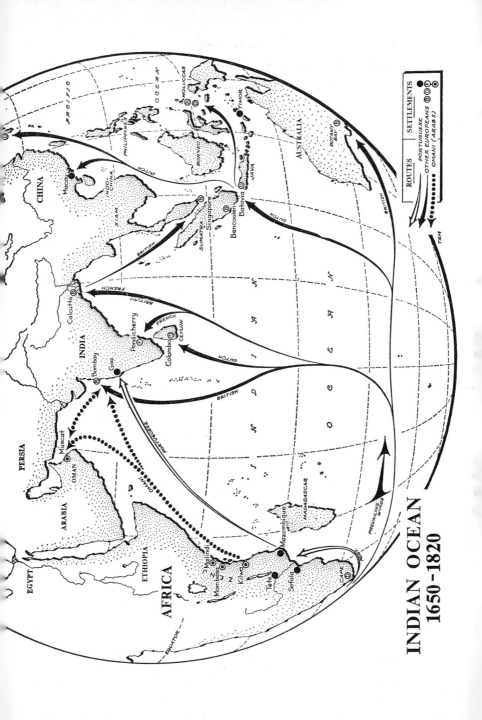

INDIAN OCEAN
1650–1820

ROUTES	SETTLEMENTS
PORTUGUESE	● ● Ⓟ
OTHER EUROPEANS	Ⓑ Ⓓ Ⓕ
OMANI (ARABS)	● OMANI (ARABS)

CHINA

Macao

PACIFIC OCEAN

MOLUCCAS

PHILIPPINES

BORNEO

DUTCH INDIA CHINA

SIAM

BRITISH

SUMATRA

Singapore

Bencoolen

Batavia

JAVA

TIMOR

AUSTRALIA

BOTANY BAY

BRITISH

INDIA

Calcutta

FRENCH

BRITISH

Pondicherry

FRENCH

Bombay

Goa

Colombo

CEYLON

DUTCH

PERSIA

Muscat

OMAN

ARABIA

ETHIOPIA

PORTUGUESE

OMANI

BRITISH

INDIAN OCEAN

EGYPT

AFRICA

Melindi

Mombasa

Kilwa

Tete

Sofala

Mozambique

MADAGASCAR

PREVAILING WINDS

CAPE

EQUATOR

TRM

Malindi and Kilwa, under their traditional Arab rulers, chafed at the enforced tributes and the choking restrictions that obliterated their former wealth.

Philip II of Spain inherited the Portuguese crown in 1580. Portugal immediately lost her chief customer, the Dutch, who had been trying for eight years to oust Philip from their own throne. Instead of trading with Portugal, or providing manpower for the Portuguese ventures, the Netherlands provinces now began to send their own fleets to India. Philip was more interested in American silver, the Dutch revolt and the Armada against England than he was in Portugal's imperial problems.

One after another, valuable eastern islands were lost. Stations in India fell or were by-passed. Princes and merchants who had dealt with Portugal turned instead to the newcomers. Even if they evaded the Dutch warships, Portuguese vessels found little left of the old trade connections. The Arab cities successfully repudiated the trade restrictions and tribute obligations that Portugal had imposed.

Throughout Europe, East Africa had acquired the reputation of being poor and unhealthy. The Dutch did not consider either its trade or its tribute worth bothering with. Moreover, Dutch navigators discovered new prevailing winds stronger and safer than those along the East African coast. By going due east from the Cape of Good Hope, they avoided the uncertain monsoons and the shoals of the Mozambique Channel. It was not always easy to estimate easterly travel in the open ocean—longitude was always a matter of shrewd guessing until good chronometers were introduced in the eighteenth century—but a good mariner could usually find India or Java, either of which meant certain profit. (Some Dutch navigators, misjudging the distance, discovered Australia and New Zealand before finding their way to the Spice Islands.) Britain and France, who succeeded the Dutch in the India trade, also avoided the East African coast.

At the time that Portugal started to decline, the Monomotapa realms were torn with strife. Ngoni tribes and Sotho groups passed successively through the mining areas on their way southward in 1590 and 1620, releasing many tribes from payment of tribute to the Monomotapa people and disrupting interior trade. Portugal intervened with Goan sepoys, recognized one of the rebellious tributaries as the new Monomotapa ruler, and even succeeded in converting his successor to Christianity. The situation was too complex, the Christian puppet-chief too weak, and Portugal's resources too limited; commercial prosperity and stability could not be restored. Even before the turmoil lessened in the 1620's, the Arabs were asserting themselves again. In 1693 the Monomotapa region was completely subjugated by Rozwi Bantu, who advanced from the area of Lake Tanganyika. European interest and activity in the gold mines and stone cities had already died out.

Oman, in Arabia, began in 1622 to help the East African Moslems to evict the Portuguese. By 1650 most of the coast was clearly Arab. The Portuguese were able, by concentrating forces, to hold only one or two points for a few more years. The Zenj cities reappeared as entrepôts of Arab slaving and agriculture. Oman, by virtue of her ability to fight the Portuguese, was able to hold Zenj allegiance much more effectively than she had before 1498. Repeatedly Portugal tried to recover the cities north of Mozambique—the last effort was at Mombasa in 1728-1730—but the balance of Omani and Portuguese power was finally reached at Cape Delgado, between Mozambique and Kilwa. To the south, the *prazeros*, a slave trade that had developed after 1645, and the practical limit of Omani power protected the Portuguese interest. Other powers let her alone, simply because they were not interested, although the British provided indirect support by virtue of the traditional Lisbon-London Alliance and a marriage treaty in 1661. Above Cape Delgado the Omani were welcome protectors in the Moslem coastal towns. By 1740 the imam had consolidated his Arabian landholdings so that he could direct his attention to Zenj.

India was the most reliable customer for Oman's East African slaves. The Princely States could afford to pay better

prices than either Persia or Arabia, and Indian cloth and utensils commanded high prices in Zenj. Oman was, therefore, the
middleman in a trade that European powers had neglected
since the decline of Portugal. As long as the Europeans quar-
reled over India, the Omani position remained secure. However, Britain dislodged the French in 1763, and, in 1799, Tipoo
Sahib, the last pro-French prince, was defeated. Britain now
controlled the trade routes between India and Oman, but she
did not occupy the Princely States. Therefore, Parliament's Act
of 1807, which prohibited slave trading, did not apply to
Oman's markets. The Arabs continued to defy the British ban,
but the Foreign Office put diplomatic pressure on Saïd, the
reigning Imam of Oman. By the Moresby Treaty of 1822 he
agreed to restrict slaving to his own empire, in Arabia and East
Africa, and allowed the British navy to police it. A considerable
amount of smuggling continued, but the Zenj ports began to
lose some of their former prosperity.

Mombasa, the strongest of these towns, revolted against
the sultan and asked Captain William Owen of the Royal Navy
to proclaim a protectorate. The Arabs believed that the India
trade could be revived if Mombasa were incorporated into the
empire. However, the British cabinet was as determined to stay
out of East Africa as it had been to get out of the Gold Coast.
After two years as "Owen's Protectorate," Mombasa was formally returned to Sultan Saïd in 1826.

However, Mombasa refused to consider rejoining the dwindling Omani empire. By 1835 Imam Saïd had subdued the defiant city—not by military force but by bribery, trickery and
fraud. In the course of the nine-year siege, the sultan had established advanced bases on Zanzibar, the cool, green Isle of Zenj.
After the fighting had ended, he returned to his capital at Muscat in Arabia. It was hot and dry. Zanzibar seemed safer and
more pleasant than the desert port, and it was a more convenient center from which to develop the wealth of East Africa.
Therefore, in 1840, the Omani sultan moved his capital from
Muscat to Zanzibar.

Saïd had gained power by murdering his rivals in 1806, subsequently maintaining and extending his authority by endless intrigue, but was always careful to ingratiate himself with well-placed European diplomats. He used his armies only as a last resort, after all manner of connivance had failed. The imam was frugal and the court unostentatious, despite a rapid increase in royal wealth, and Saïd's visitors believed that he was a benevolent, noble patriarch with genuine honesty and self-effacing devotion.

Soon after moving his capital to Zanzibar, Saïd initiated an extensive development program for his East African domains. The cultivation of cocoa and palm oil was increased. Clove trees from Indonesia were planted on Zanzibar. As the plans progressed more slaves were needed. Old slaving routes were worked to their limits. New paths to the interior were opened. Armed caravans set out on regular schedules for Lakes Nyasa and Tanganyika. Except for military and trading posts along the caravan routes, no territory was annexed and no new Bantu tribes came under Zenj rule. Only the Arabs had firearms. Many of the Bantu were enslaved by ambush, trickery or direct frontal assault; others were bought from tribes with whom the merchants were allied. One tribe was often paid to attack a neighbor.

The Arabs had remained near the coast for a thousand years, until 1840. Within eighteen years their caravans, armed posts and agents advanced as far as the upper Congo, halfway across Africa. The Zenj traders carried Swahili into the interior, making it the lingua franca of East and Central Africa, but they also generated an unprecedented series of ferocious tribal wars. Settled agriculture was disrupted. Entire Bantu villages were enslaved or massacred, and the population declined sharply. The Europeans, who later occupied East Africa, found some areas that were still chaotic in the twentieth century.

Zanzibar, under the absolute rule of Sultan Saïd, successfully dominated the coast from Mozambique to Somalia, as well as Oman and some ports in Persia and Baluchistan. Much

of the African interior was thrown into turmoil. By cultivating
the plantations systematically, Zanzibar was able to acquire the
world monopoly in cloves. The volume of Zenj's trade increased
tenfold in twenty years.

The Hammerton Treaty of 1847 forbade the exportation of
slaves from Africa. Oman therefore lost its source of labor, but
slave ships were still allowed to cruise the Zenj coast. British
patrols on the high seas were unable to differentiate between
legal slavers along the coast and the illegal slave smugglers. After
1861 slaves were not supposed to be carried by any ships, but
Omani dhow captains quickly learned to confuse the British
by insisting that their Negro cargoes were oarsmen rather than
slaves.

Saïd died in 1856. Oman, angry at the loss of its slave supply and at its relegation to a minor role in the Zenj empire, revolted five years later. Britain supported her demand for independence—hoping thereby to discourage violation of the
antislave treaties—and Majid, the new sultan at Zanzibar, had
to accept the partition. The Imam of Oman became a separate
office from that of the Zenj Sultan. However, slaving did not die,
so Britain sent Sir Bartle Frere in 1873 to negotiate an emancipation agreement. The slave market was closed, but emancipation did not follow until 1897 on Zanzibar itself, 1907 in Kenya,
and 1919 in Tanganyika.

During the expansion of the slave trade under Sultan Saïd,
branches of the caravan routes reached as far north as the southern borders of Buganda and the eastern edge of Ruanda-Urundi.
At the same time another series of slave traders was approaching
Buganda's northern boundary from bases in Egypt.

Nominally Egypt had for some centuries been under the
suzerainty of the Ottoman Turks at Constantinople. Since
ancient times slaves had been transported down the Nile.
The Moslem conquest of Egypt had isolated a series of Christian kingdoms in the middle Nile. Slavery continued to exist
but there was little trade. Between the eleventh and fifteenth
centuries these kingdoms were infiltrated and finally converted

OTTOMAN
EMPIRE
1820

PERSIA

Cairo

Hormuz

EGYPT
(AUTONOMOUS
BY 1820)

Muscat

ARABIA

OMAN
1820

Aswan

Mecca

RED

NUBIA

SEA

Dongola
1820

Suakin
1818

SOCOTRA I.

Omdurman
1820

Khartoum
(BEGUN 1830)

Massawa
1866

El Obeid
1821

El Fasher
1874

Sennar
(1821)

Gondar

ETHIOPIA
1820

Berbera
1875

Fashoda
1849

INDIAN

Addis
Ababa
(BEGUN, 1883)

ETHIOPIAN AND CONQUESTS 1881-1900

Gondokoro
1871

LAKE
RUDOLF

EQUATORIA

CONGO

ROUTES
EGYPTIAN & OMANI
ROUTES OF TRADE
AND EXPANSION
AFRICAN

BUNYORO

EQUATOR

TORO

BUGANDA

Mmengo

LAKE
VICTORIA-
NYANZA

RUANDA

SETTLEMENTS

OCEAN

URUNDI

Malindi

EGYPTIAN
OMANI / ZENJ
AFRICAN
EUROPEAN

SEYCHELLES
IS.

Mombasa

LAKE
TANGANYIKA

Tabora

Zanzibar

Ujiji

Bagamoyo

AMIRANTE
IS.

LUBA

Kilwa

NGONI
MARAUDERS
1834-35

LAKE
NYASA

EXPANSION
OF
EGYPT
AND
OMAN (ZENJ)
1820-1880

ZAMBEZI

Tete
(PORT.)

Mozambique
(PORT.)

Zimbabwe

Sofala
(PORT.)

MADAGASCAR

300 MILES

500 KMS.

TRM

by Islam. During the chaos the Nile states were too weak to conduct any major slaving raids.

Egypt began a systematic conquest of the Upper Nile in 1820. Mehemet Ali, an Ottoman general who had excited all Europe by his treatment of the Greek Christians, had become the khedive. He made Egypt a sovereign power, independent of the Ottoman Empire. Expansion brought glory and a revival of slave trading. Britain blocked the seaborne traffic, but Mehemet Ali developed a reliable inland trade route. Before his death Ethiopia had been by-passed and isolated, and the Egyptians were on the northern edge of equatorial Buganda. Farther south, Zanzibar's slaving caravans were wreaking their greatest havoc.

At this point European interest began to develop. Vivid reports from the interior pointed up the unsavory character of Egyptian and Zenj slaving. Naval patrols were obviously not an effective check on the abuses. When the Suez Canal was opened in 1869 Europeans became involved in Egyptian affairs, and there was a new, short route to Zenj. Britain, France and Germany soon developed an active concern with the East African interior.

8

THE INVASION OF SOUTH AFRICA

AFTER the Sotho and Ngoni marauders had ravaged the Monomotapa lands and disrupted Portuguese Mozambique between 1590 and 1620, they crossed the Limpopo River into South Africa. The scattered, weakly organized Khoïsan people, who since prehistoric times had been the country's only inhabitants, were quickly dispersed. The Bushmen were killed or they fled to the Kalahari Desert, west of the grassy highland veld. Many of the Hottentots moved toward the Cape of Good Hope, and others merged with the Bantu invaders.)

The Ngoni, who were the earlier and fiercer invaders, took the semitropical coastlands of modern Natal for themselves. As they came over the Drakensberg Mountains from Transvaal, they split into four groups to occupy the new country: Swazi the northeast, then Zulu, Pondo, Tembu and Xosa along the coast toward the Cape. When they reached the Kei River about 1700, their conquering urge was, for the time being, satisfied.

The Sotho remained in the interior, between the Drakensbergs and the Kalahari. The southern branch arrived during the seventeenth century in the modern Orange Free State; the Northern Sotho remained in the Transvaal.

By the seventeenth century the Khoïsan people had been pushed out of most of Africa except the Kalahari, modern South-

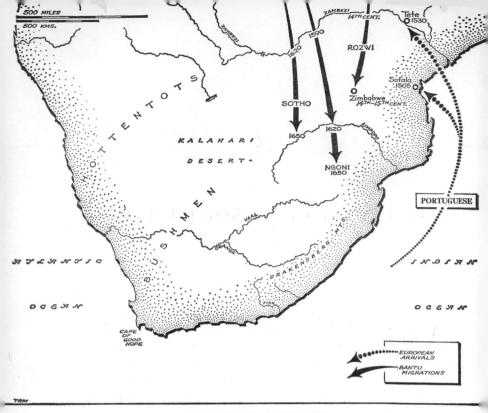

west Africa and the Cape Province. Bushmen lived by hunting
while the Hottentots were preëminently cattle herders. The lands
they still controlled were quite suitable for their occupations.

Portuguese Indiamen, en route between Europe and the
Orient in the sixteenth century, usually made two stops: in
Brazil or West Africa, and in Mozambique. The Cape of Good
Hope was not a convenient port-of-call in this system. Dutch
and English ships, replacing the Portuguese, preferred the
open route eastward from the Cape, so they had to find a new
revictualing point that would separate the long Atlantic and
Indian Ocean voyages. The Dutch East India Company occupied St. Helena between 1617 and 1645, while English ships

either called at the Dutch station or stopped alone in South Africa in search of water, meat, and perhaps some exercise for their crews.

St. Helena was not satisfactory, however. Properly it lay in the Netherlands West India Company sphere, which Dutch East Indiamen were supposed to avoid. The island was too small to provide all that was required, and it was often out of the way for a ship that was trying to find the best winds. After a crew that was shipwrecked near the Cape had successfully passed the winter of 1647-48 in South Africa, the East India Company directors decided to move the station to the mainland.

Three shiploads of settlers and supplies raised Table Bay on April 6, 1652. The next day Governor Jan van Riebeeck founded Capetown and started planning for gardens, cattle herds and a little mission work. The Cape of Good Hope station was not considered either a colonization settlement or a base for wilderness conquest; it was merely a service station appended to the vast development scheme centered in the East Indies.

The Dutch homeland was simply a confederation of sovereign states that had finally won complete independence from Spain four years earlier. The Estates-General of the United Netherlands was weak; it could take no action without unanimous consent of all member provinces. All of them did agree, however, to charter the Company in 1602 to act as their sovereign representative in East Indian trade, diplomacy and war. For 200 years the government of the Netherlands Confederation probably had less power than the East India Company, whose affairs were managed from Amsterdam by "The Seventeen" directors, or Heeren Majores, representing the major commercial provinces. Batavia, on the Island of Java, became the center of operations in the East. There were trading stations in Japan, India, Malaya, Formosa and Siam, as well as plantations in Indonesia and Ceylon. Capetown, which served the ships that connected these points with Europe, was also administered from Batavia.

No Europeans since the beginning of exploration had discovered people as strange and as pitiable as the Bushmen. They seemed to be incapable of understanding any social organization larger than the family, and they did not absorb the European religious or commercial ideas. The Bushmen and the Hottentots soon constituted a major problem. Fighting began within four days. None of the rather feeble attempts to Christianize the Khoïsan people made any headway. Tension developed from the beginning between them and the Europeans, whose background and reasons for being in South Africa seemed incomprehensible. Although Van Riebeeck was eager to acquire cattle, the Hottentots traded only sporadically. They could not be relied upon until several generations of association and racial mixing had given the Hottentots a permanent connection with Dutch society.

The Company had to develop herds of its own to supply the passing Indiamen. Crops did not grow as well as had been hoped. European soldiers, and the peasants who were brought out on indentured contract, were poor farmers. On its lands the Company tried to raise European products, but they were not suitable for the Cape climate. To correct the situation, free settlers were brought out in 1657 and slaves were introduced: Negroes from the Gold Coast, and "Malays" from Batavia.

Although the Company wanted to keep the colony small and compact, the free farmers (called "Boers" in Dutch) began to move inland in order to find better agricultural and grazing lands. The Company was afraid that such migrating or trekking would make the colony expensive, inefficient and indefensible. The trekkers disregarded the official regulations (placaats) because they preferred to meet their own needs rather than pay the Company's high duties and taxes. However, Capetown continued to be the main market for their products.

Trekking was easier and cheaper than capital development. It cost too much to transport garden crops from the interior, but cattle could be driven long distances to the port markets and they always commanded premium prices. Trekking was therefore profitable: frontier ranches could be started without much capital, and the Company's rigid rule could be avoided. Frontier expansion quickly became the custom.

A large proportion of the settlers even failed to understand the purpose of the colony. They were of course willing to trade where there was a demand for their products, but felt no obligation to stay within the Company's effective jurisdiction. The majority of settlers had come from the interior provinces of the Netherlands. Many of them were accustomed to being a Protestant minority in the rural, southern, predominantly Catholic areas. Few of them understood or cared about the Company's complex mercantile operations. They were accustomed to self-reliance, to the authority of their own minority rather than the check of official administrators, and to life away from trade or commerce. Some of them had been shanghaied or tricked into their emigration agreements. Many thought they had signed up to get to the Indies to make quick fortunes, so they resented being dropped off at the Cape of Good Hope where they had to depend upon a monopolistic commercial organization for any transaction they made. Trekking seemed to be the best salve for their disappointment.

The nature of their background combined with the necessities of Trekboer life to create a distinct people. Frontier living was self-reliant and not overly complex. The Boers developed their own institutions of government, quite apart from the Company machinery: in this system, the father headed the traditional family and selected the officials of the district or drosdty (landdrost, or civil magistrate; veld cornet, or leader for "commandos" of neighbors that could be called out by any family; and heemraden, or trustees, six of whom assisted the landdrost to rule the drosdty). Gradually the Company came to accept this system because it was efficient and economical.

Technically, all land—wherever trekkers went—was owned by the Company. Farmers could lease it (leeningsplaatsen) for about ten dollars a year, and the lease would become a perpetual, rent-free grant after five years. Usually about 6,000 acres (9.5 square miles) were taken because they would support all the cattle that a family could tend.

The Cape was only a minor outpost in a vast scheme, and trekking was officially discouraged, so clergymen (predikants) and teachers were seldom available. Rural Dutch dialects merged, received significant influences from passing sailors, and absorbed many new words from the Khoïsan natives and Malay slaves. A distinct Cape dialect, Taal, soon emerged but, without teachers and the stimulus of outside culture, the syntax and traditional spellings disappeared. Religion was family-centered. Every father had a family Bible, printed in High Dutch, but as the dialect changed and literacy declined, it became difficult for him to read it. Because there were no trained predikants in the interior, the popular view of Christian doctrine became increasingly simple and dogmatic. In seventeenth-century Europe the faith of any rural population was simple and rugged, but that of the Boers was unusually rigid even before they left the Netherlands. As a minority in their original provinces, they had been noticeably independent of new intellectual currents. They were Calvinists but tended toward a particular minority interpretation of that theology.

One part of this unique doctrine had its roots in the Arminian controversy in the Netherlands early in the seventeenth century. John Calvin, the founder of the Reformed faith, had warned against overconfidence in one's own salvation:

> "But if we are chosen in Christ we shall find no assurance
> of our election in ourselves, nor even in God the Father.
> . . . Let him that thinketh he standeth, take heed lest he
> fall." [1]

Jacob Arminius later claimed that all believers would be saved. The Synod of Dordt, which condemned his view in 1619, decided that a very limited number of Christians would be

[1] John Calvin, *Institutes of the Christian Religion*, 2 vols., Grand Rapids, 1949, vol. II, pp. 223, 225.

saved. This group, the Synod said, would know that it had been chosen. The Synod's doctrine was short-lived in Europe, but it became a permanent doctrine among the peasants who migrated to Capetown a few years later. In South Africa it was therefore believed that the "elect" were those who adhered to the traditional religion, the family and the Dutch Bible. Of course, this included virtually all the Boers, but it excluded the Bushmen and the Hottentots, who were so hard to convert.

Perhaps it is particularly unfortunate that contacts during the early, formative period were largely with Bushmen and Hottentots. The former were so clearly different, and the latter such listless traders, that there was little opportunity for cultural interchange and no cause for a modification of religious ideas. Hottentot cattle were an important source for the Cape meat supply, but the tribes often had to be forced to engage in trade. The Boers soon believed that the Europeans were predestined to remain separate from and superior to all "natives." However, such attitudes did not prevent the farmers from using the natives' products or labor.

Several racial origins were soon represented in South African society. Malay slaves served primarily as domestics. They were rarely taken far from Capetown, and they usually continued to practice Islam, which the Boers considered an inferior faith suitable for inferior people. The Malays have always remained distinct from all other groups in South Africa.

After a few years Negro slaves were almost as numerous as the Europeans. All of them were imported from the Gold Coast and Mozambique. A fair number were taken to the frontier, but most of the big slaveowners had enough capital to remain nearer Capetown. Bushmen and Hottentots, although the most alien groups, were still free people. Sexual contact with Europeans was frequent: there were many more men than women in the European community, and there was nothing shameful about abusing an allegedly inferior people. A considerable community of mixed-bloods therefore emerged, known in early years as Bastaards but later called Griquas or Colored. Usually they were the free-labor class at the Cape, but many later emigrated beyond the frontier to form their own semitribal governments.

In 1685 Louis XIV of France revoked the Edict of Nantes, which for eighty-seven years had protected the Reformed Protestant religion. Several thousand Huguenots, now persecuted in their own country, fled through Holland to the Cape. They came in search of freedom to practice their Calvinist faith, and to settle permanently. The Dutch East India Company did not want to hire them, but the Boers welcomed the addition of free white population. Religious fervor increased. The Huguenots' political acumen helped to undermine the Company's authority on the frontier, and they strengthened the feeling of uniqueness that the Boers were already manifesting. The Huguenots had cut the ties with their homeland. A sense of common identity against the nonwhites, the Company and the world brought the two groups together within a generation. Many Boers acquired Huguenot names, and all soon shared a sense of being South African rather than either Dutch or French in nationality.

As the Boers trekked eastward, scattering themselves across the interior east of Capetown, the Company turned to German employees for maintenance of supplies and commerce in the city. Such Rhenish Protestants brought music, art and a new elegance to the colony, but they too, feeling no allegiance to the Netherlands, contributed to the development of South African nationality. Frontiersmen still had to drive their cattle to Capetown, where necessary ammunition, coffee, clothes and other supplies could be obtained. The German merchants with whom the farmers dealt did nothing to counteract the Boers' isolationist views or their sense of separation from the Netherlands. Such trade was often the sole contact with the outside world, except for the nachtmaal at the nearest church on Christmas Eve. This was the only social gathering, and often the only contact with organized religion, during the year. All baptisms, marriages and holy communion had to be taken care of at that time,

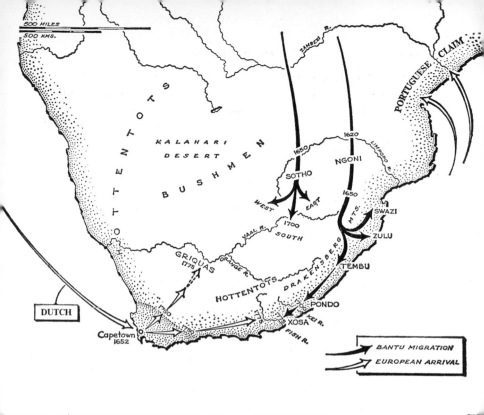

OCCUPATION OF **SOUTH AFRICA,** 1652-1775

so the influence of ideas from the outside world did not have
an opportunity to penetrate deeply.

  After the Huguenots had increased the Boers' numbers
and strengthened their ideas, the frontier population spread beyond the coastal mountains. Agricultural products could not be
transported for more than seventy or eighty miles, but cattle
could be marketed at a profit, so eighteenth-century trekkers
sought large areas for ranching: in 1700 all Europeans were
within fifty-five miles of Capetown; by 1750 some were as far
as 225 miles away; and a few by 1775 were scattered along the
Fish River, almost 500 miles to the east. Much of the newest
terrain—the inland Karoo Plateau—was too arid for anything

but grazing. It was not profitable to drive cattle to the Cape market from more distant points, so the frontier did not move again during the next half-century.

Landholders in the vast Karoo had labor problems that were unknown in the regions nearer Capetown. Slaves were well suited for agriculture, but they were not reliable enough for cattle driving in country as open as the frontier districts. However, laborers familiar with ranching were available among the Hottentots, whose tribal system was breaking down as the land was taken from them. Frontier Boers relied increasingly upon this source of trained, subservient labor, and the Hottentots became economically dependent upon the Europeans.

On the frontier a crisis in South African history was imminent. The interior veld, the coast of Natal and the eastern Cape had become the homeland of the well-organized Bantu Negroes who had entered South Africa early in the seventeenth century. Because of their superior organization, they had driven the Khoïsan-speaking Bushmen and Hottentots toward the Cape, where the Boers later landed. The Bantu tribes had technological abilities which made them more efficient farmers and fighters than the Khoïsan people. Their population grew rapidly, so their frontier gradually advanced toward that of the Boers during the eighteenth century.

Dutch hunters far in the interior had first encountered the Negroes in 1702, but contact between the two invading waves —Bantu from Rhodesia and Boer from Capetown—was not made until 1775, when the Xosa tribe and the white trekkers met on the Fish River. Both had been in South Africa for well over a century; both were now "native" to the country; both had cattle as the bases of their economies; and as they advanced, both had been chasing the Khoïsan people. The encounter was momentous because it brought two powerful, advancing frontiers into conflict with one another. Subsequent history is dominated by the manner in which they reacted to, and ultimately overlapped, one another.

9

BOER, BANTU AND BRITON

CONFLICT inevitably ensued when the Caucasian Boers and the Negro Xosa met on the Fish River in 1775. Both were cattle raisers, but each had contrasting, deeply rooted attitudes and customs. Each wanted to expand into the other's grazing lands. The Boers sought to consolidate and extend their pastures in order to satisfy the increasing demands of the Capetown market. The Bantu pressed for new land to accommodate an increasing population. Neither frontier could move without intruding upon the other. The Negroes, who began to trade cattle with the Dutch farmers, soon augmented the Cape meat supply. Other Boers began to move inland to the Karoo Plateau, even though this was poorer land.

The Bantu were more numerous, with traditions that assumed communal ownership of all but personal articles, but the Boers, who had superior weapons to compensate for their small numbers, continued to maintain the European tradition of individual property rights. Only the small Fish River separated these contrasting concepts of cattleownership. Clashes could not be avoided. Among the Xosa, cattle had great social as well as economic value: wealth was measured in animals, so that a prospective bridegroom was expected to demonstrate his status and good faith by depositing some of them with the

bride's family; this custom, called *lobola*, was a form of loan or
security, not a system of wife-buying or "bride-price" as Boers
and later missionaries sometimes thought.

Boers usually branded their cattle in order to establish individual ownership, then turned them loose to graze on the un-
fenced veld. Xosa, however, kept their herds in corrals or under
supervision while they were out to pasture. In their eyes un-
tended cattle were public property until someone captured and
corralled them. When Xosa applied this principle to Boer cattle
that wandered along the Fish River, they were accused of "stealing." As settlement on both the Boer and Xosa claims became
more intensive, the amount of "stealing" increased rapidly, until
the Boers organized punitive "commandos" under Adriaan van
Jaarsveld, the frontier veld cornet. Of course, the Xosa considered this to be warfare. The resulting skirmishes, in 1779,
were the first of the frequent "Kaffir Wars" that plagued
South Africa for a century. (Originally the Arabic term meaning
infidels, "Kaffir" was colloquially applied to Negroes by Christians as well as Moslems.) Van Jaarsveld, the plucky commando
leader, threw the Xosa regiments into confusion by trickery, and
acquired a hero's reputation by returning to the Boer frontier
with several thousand captured cattle.

The Dutchmen who had gone inland to the Karoo organized their own drosdty at Graaff-Reinet in 1786. The Dutch
East India Company provided no protection against Kaffir
"stealing." Nine years later the settlers took matters into their
own hands by proclaiming their independence. Van Jaarsveld,
the frontier hero, logically became their leader. The farmers
donned tricolor cockades similar to those worn by the French
Revolutionary armies. The heemraden became a national assembly, and the commandos a national army which set out after
the Kaffir thieves. In all, some 1400 adults, 1700 children and
600 slaves made up a republic that talked of Jacobinism and
"Liberty, Equality, Fraternity," but whose aim was simply frontier independence. The French influence went no deeper than
the slogans and a few trappings. The first trekker republic, born

of self-defense, was a revolt against authority. Capetown was still Dutch, but the Boers felt no allegiance to the old country.

In the same year, 1795, the French Revolution did come much more directly into South African affairs when the British occupied Capetown. France had conquered the Netherlands, and the Dutch East India Company had asked Great Britain to protect its colonies from the Revolutionary armies. A few settlers near the Cape tried to oppose the British, but the Company forces and the frontier did not.

Britain came in order to forestall a French invasion. She expected to administer the Cape in routine and orderly fashion while pursuing the enemy at sea. Young Graaff-Reinet promptly proposed to trade cattle for British arms, provided it was left alone on the frontier, but Britain intended to be a thorough administrator. The republic's Jacobin trappings alarmed her. In a series of skirmishes between 1797 and 1799, Graaff-Reinet was suppressed, its taxes collected and its leaders imprisoned.

For the first time extensive mission activity began among the nonwhites on the frontier. In Europe the secular Enlightenment and the religious revival which led to Methodism had created a new interest in the protection and conversion of alien races overseas. This evangelical movement happened to reach the Cape during the period of Britain's occupation. The connection between the two is largely coincidental, but the Boers believed that the idea had been deliberately invented and sponsored in order to subdue the rebellious frontier. The London Missionary Society decided to place its main station in Graaff-Reinet and to concentrate on the liberation of Hottentots, upon whom the Boers depended for labor. The Reverend Johannes van der Kemp, a Netherlander employed by the English evangelicals, took charge of the mission. He was morally lax—a man who had been converted in middle age but not tamed—and entertained ideas about the nobility of savages that were based upon a romanticized reading of Rousseau. He criticized the Boers' attitudes toward Hottentots and Bantu, and his fiery reports to the Society in England often included fabricated or overdramatized atrocity stories. The Boers quickly came to hate him, as much for the rebellious ideas he imparted to his converts as for the things he said and wrote, but the LMS used his reports to excite public opinion and to influence government policy. The Colonial Office usually tried to follow a neutral course, but it frequently had to rely upon Van der Kemp's information because official dispatches from the frontier were contradictory and irregular.

The British did not understand the peculiar origin and unique nature of Xosa-Boer relations on the frontier. They expected to administer behind a fixed boundary line, and were determined to avoid both the expense and responsibility of supervising the Bantu. In order to strengthen the hand of authority on the frontier, the governor decided to enlist Hottentots into the police corps. Those at Van der Kemp's mission were particularly suitable candidates, so they were duly armed and commissioned. The LMS was delighted at this decision, but the Boers protested vehemently. Until recently Hottentots had been dependent servants; the idea of submitting to armed non-white police recruited from the subversive missions was considered outrageous.

The Treaty of Amiens in 1803 brought a lull in the Napoleonic Wars. The Cape was given to the Batavian Republic, a Dutch government that was politically independent of France. However, much had changed: the Dutch East India Company was gone, the Batavian Republic had adopted much of the enthusiasm and liberalism of the French Revolution, and the new officials—direct representatives of the Amsterdam government —were determined to be thorough. The Hottentot police were maintained and increased. The missions were supported. Taxes were systematically collected. Batavia's reform administration was no more acceptable to the Boers than the alien British had been. Clearly there was a considerable difference in customs, attitudes and ideas between South Africa and the Netherlands. Only one Batavian reform took root on the frontier: the elevation of the veld cornets in the drosdties to a role resembling that of the Norman justices-of-the-peace, with authority over taxation, rough-and-ready justice, and community leadership.

Napoleon was not content with peace. War resumed in Europe, the Batavian Republic collapsed and Britain returned to the Cape Colony in 1806—this time to remain for more than a century.

Permanent British possession was confirmed in 1815, at the Congress of Vienna, but the military administration continued until 1823. The Boers had automatically become British colonial subjects. From the beginning the government's interests were obviously divergent from those of the decentralized frontiersmen. The missions continued to report Boer atrocities. English investigators found some factual basis for the complaints, but they also felt that the missionaries had encouraged the Hottentots to needle the Boers. In Britain the Boers were considered "inhuman," while the nonwhites seemed to be the "innocent and oppressed." Increasing numbers of Hottentots became armed policemen. The Boers considered them an insult and resented the threat to their labor supply. After 1807 Parliament's ban on slave trading aggravated the problem because it made the frontier completely dependent upon Hottentot labor. In 1809 a Cape ordinance, known as the "Magna Charta of the Hottentots," increased the tension by prohibiting debt contracts and guaranteeing the freedom of the laborers. However, it did try to prevent vagrancy by requiring the Hottentots to register and to carry passes.

The Xosa Kaffirs, pressed from the rear by Zulu expansion, were encouraged by the Hottentots' advances in the colony. They raided more frequently and more daringly across the Fish River. The frontier Boers sought permission to organize commandos, but the British denied the request. Instead, the settlers were ordered to congregate behind a line of forts west of the Fish River in order to prevent all contact with the Kaffirs.

Frontier settlement was profoundly affected by the Land Ordinance of 1812, which attempted to legalize this ban on intercourse. Most of the old Dutch land law was revoked. The new system, which would have increased Britain's direct authority, was supposed to be agricultural; there would be no cattle, so the Xosa would not be tempted to raid the frontier. The settlers would get only 1200 acres instead of the former Dutch leeningsplaatsen of 6000 acres. Under the old system the large estates had become freeholds after a ten-dollar annual rental had been paid for five years; the new, smaller plots were to require a perpetual quit-rent of about $100 per year, and were supposed to be subdivided among the heirs.

Boer reaction was quick and stubborn: the fees were too high; ranches should remain undivided, with heirs staking new claims; grazing was more profitable than agriculture. In practice, the old life-lease already was perpetual, so the British grants offered no advantages. The core of the controversy was of course the attempt to eliminate cattle raising, but the Boers knew that the eastern frontier was poorly suited for agriculture, that grazing was more profitable, and that resettlement would increase the alien influences upon their lives. For the most part the land law was disregarded. Settlers held onto their larger life-lease holdings, and continued to raise cattle for Capetown's insatiable demands. The British had failed to realize that cattle, not farm produce, sustained the eastern frontier economy, and that the western cities were dependent upon the Boer herds for food.

While this issue was being thrashed out, the missionaries began to encourage Hottentots to sue the frontiersmen for alleged maltreatment. The government appointed a special "Black Circuit" court to hear the charges. When accused, individual farmers were brought to it for trial. The London Missionary Society frequently provided attorneys for the plaintiffs. The Boers, who resented the equal treatment that the law gave to nonwhites, accused the LMS of "laxity" and "irresponsibility."

Some of the "Black Circuit" events have assumed the proportions of national legend in modern South Africa. One such case involved a charge of maltreatment which Booys, a Hottentot servant, brought against his employer, Frederick Bezuidenhout. Booys may have been coached by the LMS mission. Bezuidenhout, pleading illness, refused to answer the court summons, but he did send a series of patient depositions in answer to the charges. A posse of Hottentot police tried to bring him to court; he refused to let the nonwhites arrest him, fought the police and was killed.

Frederick's brother, Johannes Bezuidenhout, thereupon vowed revenge. A sympathetic neighbor, Hendrik Prinsloo, wrote to Gaika, chief of the Xosa, proposing an alliance, by which the tribe would be given land if it helped the Boers to set up an independent republic. British authorities intercepted the letter and arrested Prinsloo for sedition. The other farmers tried to rescue him, but failed to arouse enough active support to overthrow the military government. Johannes was killed in battle, but most of the rebellious farmers were arrested at Slachter's Nek and sentenced to death in 1815.

Their trials were held under the traditional Roman-Dutch law, the judges were all Dutch or Boer, and the evidence was conclusive. The uprising was certainly not unique in frontier history, and the movement had not attracted wide support among the farmers, but the peculiar circumstances surrounding the execution became the core of a major legend.

The families of the rebels were required to witness the hanging. The gallows collapsed—a distressing event which legend has interpreted as an "act of God" to save the condemned—so the authorities had to rerig and repeat the hanging. The British executioner, an unsupported legend says, had a reprieve in his pocket, but his failure to reveal it later haunted him to suicide. Slachter's Nek soon became symbolic of the frontier's grievances against the missions, the native policy, and British justice. The rebels became heroes who had defied arbitrary rule and misguided liberalism. Wood splinters—purported relics of the martyrs' gallows—have been sold in recent years. Although the actual events were minor, the legend built around them has had a major influence upon South African history.

Lord Charles Somerset, a self-confident, authoritarian officer, governed the colony for the rest of the second decade of the nineteenth century. His "anglicization" policy was supposed to integrate the white population, but it engendered much bitterness. The prevalent Dutch Reformed Church came under the government, which, although it was officially Anglican, usually sent Scottish Presbyterians to minister to the Cape settlers. Dutch congregations had to accept Scottish ministers for baptism, marriage and communion sacraments, but the Presbyterians were despised: they opposed the Boer view of predestination, they used the English language instead of Dutch, and they sympathized with the missionaries. In form, the Scots controlled the Boers' religion; in practice, a gulf developed between Boer ideas and the organized church. The depth of this division was apparent when, after 1828, English was mandatory in the churches but rarely heard in the homes.

Another kind of problem had begun to appear beyond the frontier, well inland and north of the Xosa. Between 1803 and 1813 the missionaries had encouraged large numbers of Bastaard or Colored mixed-bloods to leave the Cape Colony. They settled around mission stations along the Orange River and established a series of semitribal Griqua states that preyed upon Bushmen, wild game and stray cattle. The LMS prepared law codes, courts and advice for the Griqua "republics." Waterboer, one of the Colored chieftains, was able to impose a simple central government upon the scattered Griqua bands. Somerset extended a line of British control to the Griqua border, where a trade in hides and skins developed between Boer middlemen and Waterboer. In a vague way the Griquas were brought under the influence of British "residents," but the northeastern frontier was far from stable. In the long run, the Griquas and Boers were able to work out a border agreement that effectively forestalled conflict between them. In fact, the territories were too far from the Cape cattle markets and too arid to attract dense Boer settlement. Both sides benefited from trade and there were very few land disputes. Missionaries continued to be a bone of contention, but the pressing issues were still those farther south.

Deterioration had set in along the Fish River frontier. The

British plan of 1812 for resettlement and fortification was ineffectual. The Boers continued to maintain their original claims
and proceeded to defend themselves in commando fashion, so
the settlers and Kaffirs were engaged in a veritable free-for-all
beyond the jurisdiction of the blockhouses.

Xosa pressure increased markedly along the frontier in the
first quarter of the nineteenth century. Population growth increased the demand for land, but the immediate causes of conflict lay deeper in Bantu society. Like many southern Bantu
tribes, the Xosa tended to divide into separate subtribes upon
the death of a chieftain. Such a break, into East and West Xosa,
had caused the West Xosa to migrate toward the Fish River in
1775. Thereafter, there was no more vacant land, so the tribe
could not divide. Instead, tension built up within Xosa society
and contributed to the increase in frontier raiding.

Similar tendencies were found within other tribes, notably
the Zulu, who occupied the northern part of modern Natal. In
the 200 years since their arrival early in the seventeenth century,
the Zulu Ngoni had broken into a series of independent states.
They were surrounded by Swazi on the north, Sotho on the
west, and, on the south, the Tembu-Pondo-Xosa chain that extended toward the Cape frontier. In 1816 the chieftainship of
one Zulu group passed to Chaka, an exceptionally clever prince
with particular military ability. After he had parleyed and fought
his way to the post of great chief, in 1818, he launched a series
of wars against the neighboring Swazi. Chaka created an efficient field army composed of *impis*—self-sufficient, tightly organized regiments, armed with assegais, and operating as a tight
crescent (heavy in the center, with light, fleet-footed wings that
enveloped the enemy). All Zululand paid homage to the "Black
Napoleon." Swaziland was badly mauled. The repercussions,
which spread through Tembuland and Pondoland, pressed the
Xosa against the white colony west of the Fish River boundary.

Some of Chaka's generals refused to yield all glory to the
great chief. Zwide and Mzilikazi defied his absolute rule at the
end of the Swazi wars, but Chaka gave them no quarter. Zwide's

bands, known as the Ngoni refugees, fled northward into present-day Transvaal about 1820-1821. Here Zwide was succeeded
by his son, Zwangendaba, but the refugee *impis* remained strong.
Northern Sotho who inhabited the area were dispersed—the
remnants reorganized as Bapedi, Lovedu and Vendu tribes—and
the Ngoni soon resumed the northward march. About 1834 they
crossed the Limpopo into Southern Rhodesia, where they destroyed the Rozwi—the last of the people who knew the secret
of building Zimbabwe and other stone cities. A few Rozwi remnants tried to regroup and rebuild near Victoria Falls, but most
of the area, including Zimbabwe, remained deserted. Zwangendaba's Ngoni ranged northward almost to Lake Victoria before
returning to settle along Lake Nyasa. Certainly Zwangendaba
left a wake of destruction behind this long swath, and before his
people settled down they had also contributed much to the chaos
and instability that characterized East Africa at mid-century.
The ground was therefore prepared for the Arab slavers who
began their inland operations a few years later.

The other Zulu rebels, under Mzilikazi, crossed the Drakensbergs in 1823. By penetrating deeply into the Orange Free
State, far from Zululand, the rebellious *impis* escaped from
Chaka's dictatorship and his sphere of influence. Mzilikazi made
himself chief of a new tribe, the Ndebele. (The Sotho, Boers
and Griquas called them "Matabele.") Occasionally, Chaka
would attack and send the refugees scurrying across the veld,
but Mzilikazi was always able to defeat the Southern Sotho who
had occupied the area for two hundred years. Some Sotho remnants fled to the edge of the Kalahari, where they welcomed the
protection or advice of advancing LMS missionaries and organized a series of small tribes (Bechuana, Bamangwato, Barolong,
Bangwaketse, et al.) Other remnants found refuge in the Drakensbergs, but, lacking a traditional chief, they accepted instead
the domination of a militaristic commoner named Moshesh. He
organized defenses, created the new Basuto state out of the
disorganized melee, and managed to reoccupy a little of the
arable foothill country around his mountain fortresses. Most

of the veld between the Kalahari and the Drakensbergs remained empty because no one could organize an effective opposition to Mzilikazi's predatory Matabele nomads.

When the Bantu crisis in the interior spread to the Xosa in 1819, Britain's initial reaction was simple. In order to prevent contact and untoward incidents between Boers and Xosa, the whole west bank of the Fish River was made neutral territory. Boers were evicted, a no man's land was created, and military patrols were supposed to police the area. The pressures from Zululand were, of course, not understood. The policy was a failure: the Boers were furious and the Xosa streamed freely into the open country. Governor Somerset happened to be on leave in England when this policy was devised, but he reversed it when he returned the following year. The Fish River frontier, now empty of all but British troops, was given in 1820 to a group of new English immigrants.

These "Albany Bay" settlers were supposed to stabilize the frontier by giving it a dense population of loyal agriculturalists. However, few of them had ever farmed; the soil was poorly suited for anything but grazing; and those crops that did grow were destroyed by blight, flood or Xosa raiders for three consecutive years. Charity from India and Britain helped to sustain the bitter throng. Most of their support came, however, from the shrewd Boers farther inland who, though sometimes sympathetic, often made considerable fortunes by selling food and supplies to Albany Bay. Among the profiteers was Piet Retief, later a Boer political leader.

Like the Dutch before them, the English farmers also fought against Xosa raiders. They complained, as had the Boers, against the lack of government protection; the English protests and petitions of 1821-23 are more sophisticated but basically similar to the Dutch petitions of earlier decades. Somerset answered the grievances by banning political assembly, a move which angered frontiersmen of both nationalities. After their crops had failed three times, the immigrants abandoned farming in favor of trade and commerce. Some of the

English settlers moved to Capetown. Nearer the frontier, Port Elizabeth—and, later, East London—were established; they replaced Capetown as the markets and ports-of-call for the frontier areas. The Albany settlers became the middlemen, with the outside world on one hand and the Xosa or Boer cattle economies on the other.

The commercial revolution had a profound effect upon the frontier economy. The main restriction on Boer expansion had been the distance from the Capetown markets. It had not been profitable to expand beyond the Fish River, or as far as the Orange in the interior, because cattle would not survive the long drive to Capetown. After 1823, when the new entrepôts appeared around Albany Bay, a vast new area was brought within reach of profitable markets. Boers began to settle as far inland as the Orange River. The rainfall here was seasonal and sparse. The main settlements remained south of the river, but herds sometimes had to be taken to the north bank in order to graze. This country was not as fertile as the Fish River region, but it was vast and empty. The Griquas remained well to the northwest; the Xosa, of course, were farther south, near the coast. The veld was clear of all Bantu except for the predatory Matabele, who wisely retreated to the Vaal. As far as the Boers could see, there was no impediment to their expansion as long as the cattle markets could be reached. For that reason the settlements stopped abruptly at the Orange River and the frontiers of Griqualand West.

Between 1823 and 1825 Parliament ordered an extensive investigation and review of Cape affairs. Somerset was strongly criticized for his highhandedness, and the financial stability of the colony came under scrutiny. The governor was eventually relieved, a new Advisory Council of appointed officials took over many of the governor's executive and legislative duties, and the monetary system was reformed.

Dutch governments had issued paper money, backed by nothing but the word of the authorities, which had continued to circulate during the British occupation. Speculators could make a profit by discounting this paper, and farmers could pay taxes with it, but it could not be used to pay the military and administrative expenses for the colony. In order to finance his government, Somerset had therefore contracted heavy debts for which the investigating commission criticized him. As part of the reform, the Dutch paper money was redeemed at a greatly depreciated value. The frontiersmen usually bartered instead of using money, but they believed that demonetization was a deliberate attempt to destroy their prosperity. Moreover, the Dutch paper had become a symbol of Boer distinctiveness and separatist sentiment.

Far more serious were the reforms that were initiated in law, local government, Hottentot status and language. In most of these matters the crucial year was 1828, although the policies were not suddenly or systematically introduced.

The language question had arisen earlier in connection with the Dutch Reformed Church, which Scottish clergy had dominated since 1806. All government functions were gradually "anglicized" between 1823 and 1828. The Dutch language could no longer be used in the civil service, in the courts, or in the schools; as an arm of the government, the churches also had to adopt English for their services and synods. The consequences were certainly more severe than had been expected. Congregations became alienated from the modernizing influences and the theology of their churches; and two-thirds of the parents withdrew their children from the schools in order to avoid English-language instruction.

The Commissioners of Inquiry decided that the old Roman-Dutch judicial system was harsh and outdated. In its stead, British judges, a jury system, English law and the English language were to be introduced. However, the Boer frontiersmen found all these innovations to be obnoxious. In the long run, Roman-Dutch law remained for civil disputes, but criminal and commercial law became English. One of the problems as far as Roman-Dutch law was concerned was the lack of continuing tradition upon which to draw: Holland itself had adopted the Napoleonic Code during the French Revolution, and the Cape frontier lacked either a cohesive legislature or an authoritative judiciary that could modernize the old code.

Local government was completely abolished. Veld cornets were stripped of both their military and their ad hoc justice-of-the-peace powers. All effective authority was transferred to a network of district commissioners who were responsible only to the Advisory Council in Capetown.

The reforms in language, law and local government may have been efficient and progressive, but they defied a tradition of local responsibility and participation that had existed since the seventeenth century. The changes therefore disrupted the colony as much as they modernized it. Yet, alarming as these reforms were to the Boer settlers, they were overshadowed by the impact of the Hottentot reforms.

The London Missionary Society had extended its network throughout and beyond the frontier regions in the years after 1799, when Van der Kemp had established the first station. Missions were planted among the Hottentots in Graaff-Reinet, in the Colored settlements in Griqualand and the Orange River Valley, and eventually among the Sotho Bantu stretching northward from Griqualand along the edge of the Kalahari Desert. In 1818 Van der Kemp had been replaced by the Reverend Dr. John Philip, an advocate of equality and segregation of the races. His reports during the twenties had a great impact upon LMS thought and English public opinion. Parliament and the Colonial Office were influenced. Hottentots and Griquas, Philip claimed, could develop a civilization if there were missionary supervision, extensive land grants, and a ban on alcohol.

Philip did not advocate overthrowing or ousting white settlers, but he wanted to prevent them from exploiting nonwhite labor. To do this, he proposed to separate the races entirely. The different societies would trade with one another, but each group would own and work its own land. Much of his original intention was reasonable and progressive for that era, but the

attitude and behavior of the white settlers—English and Boer
—seems to have strained his judgment. Laws against stealing
and vagrancy, he said, were laws against free religion and human rights. He strongly attacked the pass laws, which prevented
landless Hottentots from running away from their employers.
Many South Africans felt that Philip had gone beyond humanitarianism and religious concerns; his emphasis seemed to them
to be a play for political action in England. His point ultimately prevailed when, in 1828, London ordered the Cape Governor to issue the controversial Ordinance 50.

Hottentots, Bushmen and Griquas could, for the first time,
own land. The pass laws were repealed; no longer could unemployed nonwhites who were found in settled areas be arrested
for vagrancy. Civil rights equal to those held by white citizens
were guaranteed, especially to the Colored in Griqualand.
White settlers began to protest bitterly about the danger of
uncontrollable marauders, and to complain that no Hottentots
or Colored would work for them; their labor system, and their
livelihood, had been destroyed, leaving only a relatively small
number of slaves to farm or to drive the cattle. Ordinance 50
was effective in the Cape Colony until 1910 and, for two more
generations, its guarantees for the Colored population were
included in the South African constitution.

Dr. Philip distributed plots of land and planned villages
for about one quarter of the liberated Hottentots, but most
of them abandoned his settlements after a few months. He
was accused of forging deeds for the land, a charge that an investigating commission later supported, but the case never
was concluded. Most of the Hottentots returned to their employers, but about 25 percent of them became marauders who
stole crops or became the uninvited "guests" of regularly employed relatives. Many frontiersmen suspected that Philip, the
Hottentots and the Kaffirs were in collusion to raise wages and
to harass them, but the LMS persuaded the Colonial Office
that there was no foundation for these rumors.

Slavery was abolished by Act of Parliament in 1834. Most

slaves in the British Empire were in the West Indies. The plantation landlords usually lived in London, where the compensation that Parliament had voted was paid. Few Boers owned slaves, but those who did were wealthy and influential. After the Hottentots had been emancipated, their slaves were the only reliable source of labor. In order to collect their compensation, the Boers had to rely on London agents who charged a commission equal to about two-thirds of the manumission payments. The loss of labor, the excessive commissions, and the Cape's monetary confusion increased Boer vexation.

Part of the emancipation problem was, of course, the disposition of the slaves. It was arranged that 39,000 ex-slaves should serve four years as apprentices, but within a month the Xosa opened a new frontier war that disrupted both the apprenticeship plan and the collection of manumission payments. This time the government provided some capable defense. Piet Retief also organized a commando, consisting of both Boers and English settlers. Many farmers contributed to the cost of fighting the two-year defensive war; they also lost two years' crops, their labor supply, and most of their emancipation money. Large numbers of them were forced into bankruptcy. Mortgages were foreclosed. The dispossessed could not go to another part of the colony; the government was auctioning all unclaimed land to the highest bidder instead of making it available for cheap homesteads.

Governor D'Urban, newly arrived from England, tried to resolve the Kaffir disputes by annexing parts of Xosaland. He hoped to make the Xosa chiefs responsible to him for the tribe's disruptive actions. However, the Boers interpreted the plan as an Anglo-Bantu alliance that threatened their security. Philanthropists and most missionaries protested D'Urban's scheme for taking over and controlling the Xosa. Within a year D'Urban was forced to withdraw to the earlier boundary along the Fish River. The Xosa were left once more to their own devices, and all frontier settlers were again without defense. Both the English and the Boer frontiersmen were furious and the Kaffirs resumed their relentless attacks.

Piet Retief commissioned three frontiersmen to look for new land in 1834. They reported that the veld beyond the Orange seemed fertile, empty and attractive. In the fall of 1835 about 150 Boer families decided to leave the area of British control. Parliament passed the Cape of Good Hope Punishment Act, which provided that all British subjects were liable to British law, even when they left the colony. Presumably the Act was a warning to anyone who naïvely thought that he could renounce British citizenship by going to unorganized territory. Piet Retief bluntly demanded that the government provide either security or independence, but his motives were increasingly suspect. In 1837 he and 2,000 others set out to cross the Orange River.

The Great Trek had begun. Louis Trigardt, in 1835, was the first to go; others straggled out during 1836, but the main body followed between February and September of 1837. Most of them reassembled outside the colony, deep in the empty veld beyond the Orange, at the campsite of Thaba Nchu. There they passed the winter of 1837 (April to October in the Southern Hemisphere).

Behind them, the frontier was either confused or deserted. D'Urban and the Colonial Office seemed to be dumbfounded and helpless. The Great Trek had carried the frontier beyond the British sphere; yet, in the final analysis, it did not solve any of the Cape's pressing problems: Xosa land, Hottentot rights, Griqua missions, law enforcement, or the attempt to balance expenditures with tax receipts.

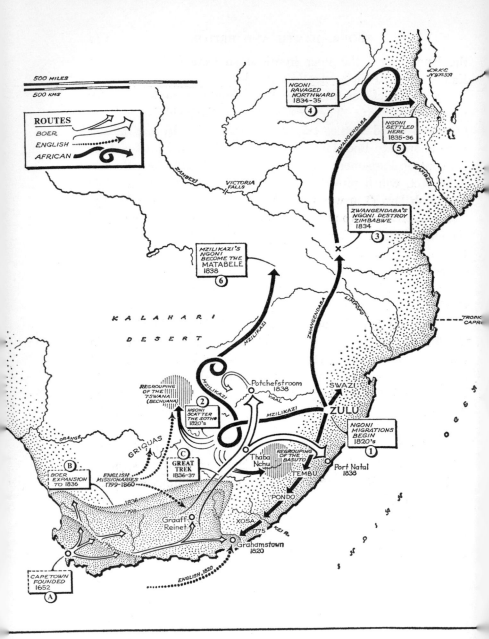

500 MILES
500 KMS

ROUTES
BOER
ENGLISH
AFRICAN

NGONI
RAVAGED
NORTHWARD
1834-35
④

NGONI
SETTLED
HERE
1835-36
⑤

LAKE
NYASA

ZWANGENDABA

ZWANGENDABA'S
NGONI DESTROY
ZIMBABWE
1834
③

ZAMBEZI

VICTORIA
FALLS

MZILIKAZI'S
NGONI
BECOME THE
MATABELE
1838
⑥

K A L A H A R I

D E S E R T

TROPIC
CAPRI—

ZWANGENDABA

LIMPOPO

MZILIKAZI

REGROUPING
OF THE
TSWANA
(BECHUANA)

MZILIKAZI

Potchefstroom
1838

SWAZI

VAAL

MZILIKAZI

ZULU

NGONI
SCATTER
THE SOTHO
1820's
②

ORANGE

GRIQUAS

ENGLISH
MISSIONARIES
1799-1860

GREAT
TREK
1836-37
Ⓒ

Thaba
Nchu

REGROUPING
OF THE
BASUTO

NGONI
MIGRATIONS
BEGIN
1820's
①

BOER
EXPANSION
TO 1836
Ⓑ

1836

TEMBU

Port Natal
1838

798

Graaff
Reinet

PONDO

XOSA
1775

KEI R.

CAPETOWN
FOUNDED
1652
Ⓐ

ENGLISH 1820

Grahamstown
1820

ENGLISH 1820

SOUTH AFRICA
NGONI MIGRATIONS AND THE START OF THE GREAT TREK

10

THE GREAT TREK AND
THE REPUBLICS

M OST Boers remained in the Cape Colony, but those who trekked in 1835-37 carried the spirit of frontier self-reliance, a sense of identity apart from Britain or the world, and the strongest set of grievances against the Scots-dominated church, the Bantu and the missionaries. The Boers believed that the veld was vacant, and did not realize that their trek would break down South Africa's clearcut divisions between white and nonwhite areas.

The true causes of the trek are not easily distinguished from the excuses that historians and mythologists have discovered in later years. Recent nationalists have implied that Britain was going to try to enforce miscegenation, that Hottentots would be given all the land, that the LMS had a scheme under way to suppress Boer language and religion, or that the government had begun to support the Kaffirs. Sir George Napier, in a report to the Colonial Office in 1838,[1] offered many explanations: the search for better soil, less taxes, and land for an expanding population; an "unprecedented" two year drought on

[1] Quoted in John Bird, *The Annals of Natal*, 2 vols., Pietermaritzburg, 1888, vol. II, p. 394.

the old frontier; the fact that people on a frontier are interdependent, so that if a few start to migrate the rest must follow; the bitterness over the slave-emancipation payments; the insecurity of the Dutch land titles under British law; the disgust with Kaffir raids; the apprehension about British policy toward the Xosa, and the belief that native treaties are ineffective. Trekker diaries[2] emphasized the desire to protect folk religion from the influence of modern theology, a fear that Roman Catholicism might be imposed by the government, and a resentment of British interference in the "proper relations between master and servant." This abhorrence of "ungodly equality" may have been a greater stimulus for the emigration movement than any other factor.

It is also clear that the frontier ranches beyond the Orange River would be too far from seaport markets. If new land was to be occupied, or British control of the markets avoided, the only answer was mass migration to territory that was close to unclaimed sections of the East African coast. There can be no doubt[3] that the trekkers aimed to by-pass the Xosa in order to establish their own ports in Natal and Delagoa Bay; ranches would then be established on a frontier radiating outward from the new outlets.

Two small groups that set out in 1835—before the main trek movement—had bad luck. Louis Trigardt and Jan van Rensberg crossed the Vaal together. Trigardt's party chose the northern Transvaal, but had to abandon it in order to seek Portuguese charity at Lourenço Marques; the Portuguese sent them to Natal in 1839. Jan van Rensberg disappeared completely in 1836; the bones and wagons of his group were found twelve years later in Mozambique, where the party had been massacred. The main body proceeded out of the Cape Colony a little later with more caution and greater organization.

[2] See the authoritative listing of Boer accounts in Eric A. Walker, *A History of Southern Africa* (3rd ed.), London, 1957, p. 197, *n.* 3, part (a).
[3] See S. Daniel Neumark, *The South African Frontier, 1652-1836: Economic Influences,* Stanford, 1957, pp. 168-170.

During 1836 Andries Hendrik Potgieter roamed widely through the veld, first crossing with and defeating the Matabele, then returning to Thaba Nchu to meet the later trekkers. The predatory Matabele, under Chief Mzilikazi, had been the only effective occupants of the Vaal basin; they fled northward to the newly emptied areas of Southern Rhodesia, an area known since as Matabeleland.

Victorious but dangerously weakened, Potgieter joined the Gerrit Maritz party at Thaba Nchu. Maritz and a six-man council were elected as an executive body for the general meeting of all trekkers. Piet Retief arrived early in 1837 and got himself elected to the governorship by playing Potgieter and Maritz against one another. During June, Jacobus and Piet Uys—the last of the leading figures—arrived. While the parties camped together for the winter, competition among the leaders increased. Each of them provided some unique quality that was indispensable to the others, but no one was prepared to subordinate himself to the others. Potgieter's particularly insatiable land-hunger had given him control of pastures that all wanted. Maritz had the most legal and administrative experience, and Retief had the greatest ability for practical political and ecclesiastical organization. The Uys brothers were apparently most jealous of their autonomy, though all groups maintained independence in military matters.

By October factionalism and impatience rose to the surface at Thaba Nchu. The Uys brothers proposed to set out for Natal but were slow to get started. Potgieter laid claim to all land beyond the Vaal, and, by the spring of 1838, he had established his followers in a republic centered at Potchefstroom. A dogged little group, the Jerusalemgangers, set out for the Promised Land; like Moses in the Exodus, they crossed the Nile (Nyl, a creek in Transvaal), but perished somewhere farther north. Retief meanwhile set out in advance of the main body to arrange for land in Natal.

While the trekkers struggled to bring their wagons and cattle across the Drakensbergs, Piet Retief entered into negotiations with Dingaan, the militant Zulu chief who had succeeded Chaka as the dominant power along the Natal coast. Dingaan bargained, and finally accepted a treaty, but he was really only delaying Retief until the *impis* could be organized. The emissaries were tricked and slain in December, 1838 (an event recalled by "Dingaan's Day" an annual memorial holiday in modern South Africa). Andries Pretorius took Retief's place as military commandant, but the Zulu *impis* managed to deal a severe blow to the main trekker corps as it descended from the Drakensbergs near Weenen. Pretorius reorganized, pressed on toward the coast and decisively defeated the Zulus, killing 3000 warriors and Chief Dingaan at Blood River nine days before Christmas. Natal was now a Boer state. The republic founded at Thaba Nchu had a permanent home, one in which Bantu tribes were for the first time directly controlled by Boer masters.

When the Natal republic was formally organized in 1839, an iron-fisted "native policy" placed all Zulus under Cetewayo, a puppet chieftain who was heir to Dingaan's paramountcy. This, of course, took care of the most urgent problem in the country, but a rudimentary parliamentary framework also emerged. Each veld cornet polled his constituents for nominations to the Volksraad; the twenty-four men most frequently listed automatically became representatives-at-large. Theoretically the representative Volksraad held all power, but it rarely met because Pretorius' decisions were popular while organized central government was distrusted.

Although there were good farmlands and the nearby port of Durban, thus making Natal a workable economic unit, the settlers were eager to find both markets apart from the Empire and allies who might discourage British occupation of the new country. A Dutch traveler, Smellekamp, posed as an agent of the Netherlands government and committed his king's "great power" to aid Natal. He was simply an opportunistic adventurer, but the Boers seem not to have realized this. Neither did they understand that the Netherlands was no longer a major world power.

Certainly, however, Natal had good reason to fear British encroachment. The queen's forces had been interested in the unclaimed Natal coast, although no formal claims had been made. Indeed, a small British contingent had been in Durban harbor when the trekkers arrived. It withdrew when the republic was organized, but the British "interest" was never fully renounced. There was, however, a more fundamental question that both the trek and the occupation of Natal raised: do people who move from an organized country to unclaimed territory forfeit their citizenship in the country they left? Can Boers who leave British territory set up an independent state, or do they remain British subjects until they become citizens of some other organized country? The issue, which was not really resolved, underlay many of South Africa's later quarrels. In the twentieth century it is possible to say that citizenship cannot be changed except by special permission, by successful revolution or by emigration to an organized foreign territory. There was, indeed, a law to this effect throughout the trek period (Cape of Good Hope Punishment Act of 1836, which provided that British subjects were subject to British law, even outside British territory), but this was not yet an accepted principle of international law. It was law in the empire, however, so that the Secretary of State in 1841 could argue that ". . . the Queen cannot acknowledge a portion of her own subjects as an independent republic."

A year later British occupation began in earnest. At first, the Boer republicans were able to besiege the invaders, but a Zulu uprising threw the balance in favor of Britain. Natal was formally annexed in 1843, and the Crown offered 6000 acres to any family that would remain, but most of the Boers refused to accept defeat. Again a trek was organized. Again the ox wagons crossed over the Drakensberg passes. Some went north of the Vaal River, near the Potchefstroom republic which had been founded five years earlier, and set up three more states: Lydenberg, Zoutpansberg and Utrecht. The rest stayed south of the Vaal in order to create the Winburg Republic under Andries

Wessel Pretorius, who had previously organized Boer Natal.

The annexation of Natal meant that Britain controlled the entire coast, upon which all Boers in the interior were dependent. There had been no decision on the status of the five inland republics; they claimed their independence, which Britain neither recognized nor suppressed.

Within three years Bantu unrest and disagreement between them and the Boers over land title caused Britain to move in troops. Winburg and the Bantu territory between the Vaal and Orange Rivers became the "Orange River Sovereignty," but the four straggling Transvaal republics remained isolated. In Winburg, A. W. Pretorius revolted against Britain, but he was defeated at Boomplaats and fled to Transvaal. Potchefstroom greeted him as a hero and promptly made him its president.

British control brought only a brief respite to the Sovereignty. By 1850 the Bantu in the Drakensbergs—between the Orange River and the eastern Cape Colony—had exploded. Fragments of Sotho tribes whom the Zulus had driven out of the veld early in the century had taken refuge in the mountains. Some Zulu renegades joined them, but all had lost both their tribal distinctions and their traditional leadership during the melee. At first, these disorganized remnants lived a primitive, frightened existence in their barren retreats, causing little trouble for any neighbors. However, about the time that Britain took over the Orange River Sovereignty, a wily Bantu organizer named Moshesh began to reunite the mountain fragments. Moshesh's new Basuto "tribe," held together by his harangues and promises, began to threaten both the newly annexed Sovereignty and the whole eastern Cape district.

In London the Parliamentary leaders, who were eager to reduce bureaucracy, expense and overseas involvement, began to demand that both areas be abandoned entirely. This attitude in large part prevented the application of a dynamic policy, but it was not so easy to back down from annexations and commitments that were already made. For two years Britain conducted a desultory Basuto War from her unwanted base in the Orange

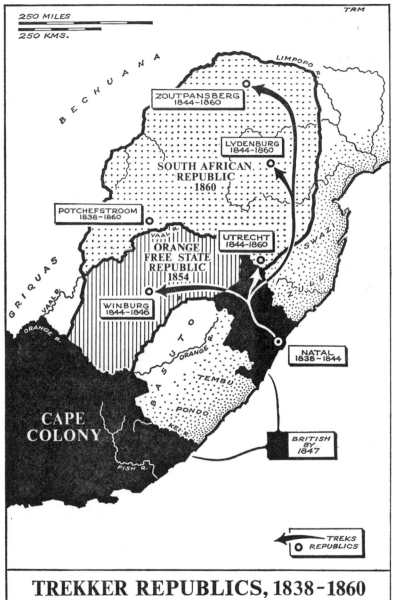

250 MILES

250 KMS.

TRM

BECHUANA

LIMPOPO R.

ZOUTPANSBERG
1844-1860

LYDENBURG
1844-1860

SOUTH AFRICAN
REPUBLIC
1860

POTCHEFSTROOM
1838-1860

VAAL R.

ORANGE
FREE STATE
REPUBLIC
1854

UTRECHT
1844-1860

SWAZI

ZULU

GRIQUAS

VAAL R.

WINBURG
1844-1846

ORANGE R.

BASUTO

ORANGE R.

TEMBU

NATAL
1838-1844

CAPE
COLONY

PONDO

KEI R.

FISH R.

BRITISH
BY
1847

TREKS
REPUBLICS

TREKKER REPUBLICS, 1838-1860

River Sovereignty. Moshesh, who gradually gained the upper hand, discredited British power quite thoroughly in the area. By 1852 the Colonial Office had decided that humanitarian intervention and actual occupation of the interior were impractical, expensive and generally unpopular. The best answer to Moshesh's advances would be coöperation with the Boers; if British withdrawal were complete, the animosity between London and the Boers might give way to a common policy toward the Bantu.

Accordingly, Britain met with representatives of the four Transvaal republics—including the recent enemy President A. W. Pretorius of Potchefstroom—to draw up the Sand River Convention of 1852. The independence of the four republics was formally recognized. Two years later, at Bloemfontein, the Orange River Sovereignty was transformed into the Orange Free State, and the queen agreed that the Boers would no longer be considered British subjects. However, the boundaries were poorly defined; for many years it was not unusual for some Boers to serve both a republic and the Crown—in other words, to change citizenship rather informally.

At the same time, Britain granted a measure of partial self-government to the loyal Cape Colony. The executive was still appointed from London, but the Cape Parliament henceforth was rarely overridden or contradicted. In many ways, however, this grant of self-government destroyed the good will that Britain hoped to develop by recognizing the republics. The Cape could set its own tariffs, so it promptly proceeded to impose high duties on goods in transit to or from the Boer territory; and, much to the disgust of the republics, the franchise was extended in 1853 to include the Cape Colored (mixed-blood) population. It was therefore virtually impossible to develop a mutual trust between the British and the Boers in approaching the native question, which grew more intense and became increasingly interwoven with white politics.

Within a year after the Sand River Convention, A. W. Pretorius died and was succeeded as president of Potchefstroom by his ambitious son, Marthinus Wessel Pretorius. M. W. Pretorius tried to unify all Transvaal. The other three republics rebuffed his proposals. Then, in 1857, he tried to annex the Orange Free State, but an ad hoc alliance between the O.F.S. and Zoutpansberg, Lydenberg, Utrecht and friends in the Cape Colony forced him to retreat. The Free State subsequently petitioned for British annexation and protection, but the Crown refused to accept the responsibility.

In this context the pressure of an increasing Bantu population became severe. In the past, tribes such as the Xosa had been able to solve this problem by expansion, by "stealing" or by warfare. White settlement, British military power and increases in both white and Bantu population had put an end to these traditional solutions. In 1857 the Xosa living east of the Cape Colony were swept by a desperate religious upheaval. Prophets called for the abandonment of traditional religion, the destruction of all crops and property, and the slaughter of all cattle (even those basic to the economy and the tribal social structure); then, they promised, a miracle would occur. A dramatic "whirlwind" would sweep both Britons and Boers into the sea, Xosa heroes of the past would rise from the dead, and all South Africa would turn fertile—filled with lush grain and herds of prime cattle!

The frenzy swept the crowded reserves. Property, crops and animals were destroyed. The Xosa sat down to wait for the miracle.

When the "day" came, nothing happened.

The British army, forewarned, rushed supplies across the frontier. There was no time to consult economy-minded London. Relief supplies were provided at the personal expense of Sir George Grey, Governor of the Cape. Thirty percent of the population was saved, but the toll of the "Xosa starvation" was staggering.

Never again did the Xosa emerge as a united tribe; the tribal economy never regained its former importance. The Bantu area between the Cape Colony and Natal became a vast

preserve dependent upon the European economy for its subsistence. The only salable commodity was labor, and the Xosa
—as well as their dependent neighbors—sought employment
among the Cape farmers, merchants and manufacturers; the
absorption of Bantu into the economy, and the preliminary outlines of modern racial interdependence, had begun.

Sir George Grey immediately instituted an investigation
that revealed the origins of the Xosa upheaval. King Moshesh
of the Basutos was planning a war to wipe out the Boers. In
order to divert British attention, he had sent agents into Xosaland to provoke crisis and a frontier war. Moshesh probably did
not expect the scheme to be so devastating to the Xosa economy, and he certainly did not anticipate Grey's ability to per-
ceive the situation.

Although his plan did not trap the British, Moshesh decided in 1858 to proceed with his attack upon the Orange Free
State. Boer resistance crumbled, but Grey interposed between
the two sides and, by mediation, was able to save the Free
State and to restore peace. At the same time, he attempted to
aid the development of the republic by creating a college in
Bloemfontein which he endowed with his personal library.

Nine years later the Free State—seeking revenge against
Moshesh and restitution for Basuto raids on the frontier—
seized the most fertile half of the Basuto lands. Again Britain
interposed. The new governor, who lacked Grey's patience and
understanding, was determined to end once and for all the
chain of native wars, unrest and confusion; all Bantu lands not
already under European control were annexed to the Crown
and placed under direct rule of the Colonial Office. This time
the Orange Free State felt that she was denied full victory. She
accused Britain of favoring and protecting the natives, of deliberately weakening the Boers, and of plotting with the Basuto
against the republics.

The four Transvaal republics had had very little contact
with the complex events arising out of the Basuto and Xosa
upheavals. Even Potchefstroom, the most important of the four,

had remained aloof from the developing economy and the extension of British influence. For the most part, trekkers to Transvaal were preoccupied with clearing the land—not of trees but of Bantu nomads.

Potchefstroom had been established by farmers who were almost totally lacking in ideas of political theory or the science of government. They wanted simply a pastoral, patriarchal, tax-free life. Rarely did any of them visit the little capital at Potchefstroom village, except at Christmas week. During the nachtmaal feast the annual market exchange took place, and the Christian sacraments (marriage, baptism, communion) were administered to the assembled nation; for the rest of the year, family patriarchs directed all religion in their scattered homes.

No regular predikants or clergy accompanied the trekkers, but there were itinerant preachers who gradually developed into a small, influential corps of local ministers. Several foreign missionaries were active among the neighboring Matabele, Zulu, Basuto and Griqua (Colored) tribes; one of these, the American Daniel Lindley, served for several years as the only ordained clergyman for all five republics in Transvaal and the Orange Free State. However, the other missionaries remained aloof from and extremely critical of the Boer congregations.

In large measure, the trek and the resulting republics represented a fragment of the seventeenth century that was fleeing from the more complex, industrial, enlightened forces of the nineteenth century. Much had happened in European intellectual, economic and political life between those centuries; little of this penetrated, and what did was unacceptable to Boer views. South African farmers from the beginning had represented an early, rural form of Dutch Protestantism; they had been isolated from the intellectual mainstream even before emigrating from the Netherlands. New ideas had been developing in Europe—especially, indeed, in Britain and urban Holland—from which the Boers had been insulated. The concept of tolerance, both racial and religious, as well as the development of eighteenth-century rationalism as a balance to religious dogma, had left little impression. Modern commercial and property laws and the increased fluidity of a monetary economy had had no perceptible effect.

The Boers were not inherently conservative; neither prohibitions nor negative impulses were as strong as a positive folk identity: the bulwark of society was the family—its father, its farm, its faith—based upon lineage, land and a rather awesome religion. Folk culture—in song and dance, legend and behavior, and the consumption of alcohol—was lively and unrestricted. In these secular respects the Boers frequently were in marked contrast to the missionaries who criticized them for both "libertine" social behavior and overly rigid religious dogma.

Through its impact on British public opinion, missionary criticism had an increasing influence on the Colonial Office attitude toward the republics. Missionaries accused the farmers of opposing Christian ideas and missions, of mass aggression upon the Bantu, and of restoring a form of slave trading. However, the Boers believed that missions disrupted God's predetermined hierarchy of superior and inferior beings. Proselytizing the servant was therefore misguided, because Bantu—as inferiors—were nomads who had to be regulated, apprenticed to work and treated like children in order to protect the superior community. Unlike frontiersmen in other countries, the Boers continued to disdain education, to disregard intellectual developments in the outside world, and to require large servant labor forces.

In no sphere is the contrast of opinion among various white groups more pronounced than in the field of religion. In 1843, shortly after the Great Trek had taken place, the British gave up all control over the Dutch Reformed Church. This made the Cape Church an independent, self-governing synod. To a noticeable degree, hostility to new ideas and to influences of Scottish clergy began to decline in the Cape Colony. The English language, a more moderate theology and, occasionally, a mission program acquired increasing importance. Some even

thought that homogeneity of the Boer and British settler populations was emerging. The trend of ecclesiastical organization
in the republics, however, ran counter to this.

Unification of the four Transvaal states was achieved in
1860 in the South African Republic. The country remained extremely poor and largely isolated, with religious controversies
dominating both the political and social lives of the Transvaalers. Issues such as Christ's divinity and the personality of
the Devil were widely debated.

In 1843 the regular Dutch Reformed Church broke into
three sovereign synods—the Transvaal, the Orange River country and the Cape. The last was independent of the colonial
government, but it continued to be suspect in the republics
because it accepted English and Scottish ministers. Some
Methodistic influence carried over to the two Dutch Reformed
synods in the republics, even though they were independent
and distrustful of the Cape synod. All three of these synods called themselves the Nederlands Gerefoormeerde Kerk
(NGK).

Many Transvaal communicants broke with the NGK in
1853 to form the Nederlands Hervoormde Kerk (NHK); their
viewpoint was conservative, antithetical to the Scottish influence and opposed both to the English language and to evangelical or Methodist tendencies. Dutch was the official church
language. This synod became the Transvaal state religion.

The NHK stand on racial distinction and an equivocal
stand on predestination continued to displease a significant
faction. These "Doppers" formed a third Calvinistic body in
1859 in order to stress apartheid (racial separation), the rigid
interpretation of predestination, and literal Biblical interpretation. They opposed the use of church music, Scottish ministers,
missions, the English language and the idea that Bantu had
souls. The NHK—whether in Holland, the Cape or the republics—was a heresy. Galileo was condemned; the world was
flat; the Boers were the chosen nation of Christ; the Bantu were
descendants of Ham, fit only to carry water and to hew wood.

The Dopper group was very small and exclusive, but it has produced an unusual number of significant leaders in the last one hundred years.

Both the NHK and the Doppers made their churches centers of virulent Christian cultural nationalism, putting particular stress upon language, nationalism and the distinctive character of Boer culture. As Dopper influence and leadership became dominant, both movements became more deliberately antiliberal. Firmly convinced that they were predestined to be the chosen and saved people, they saw both their history and their times in a distinctive light. It was therefore inevitable that they attack the former Dutch East India Company, the British, the Bantu, modern ideas of racial toleration or equality— in other words, anything which was economically, politically or socially "liberal." Conversely, liberalism itself was simply any movement or force that threatened Boer distinctiveness—that is, any threats to their God, to their church, to their folk identity.

Because Doppers dominated the NHK, and the NHK was the official religion, these two sects had a direct influence upon the government of the South African republic. There is no better example of this than Paul Kruger, a Dopper predikant whose presidency extended over more than half the lifetime of the republic.

Despite numerous British, Boer and Bantu efforts at some form of solution to the pressing cultural, land and policy problems in southern Africa, the divisive or destructive effects of indecision and isolation were chronic by the 1860's.

BOOK TWO

REMAKING AFRICA

11

THE LIBERAL MISSION

UNTIL the last third of the nineteenth century the European impact upon Africa was relatively superficial. Except for South Africa and a few scattered Portuguese plantations, there was no attempt at permanent settlement. Slavers had been replaced by private merchants who engaged in legitimate trade. Christian missions had set up a few isolated stations. However, both commerce and the missions were unofficial and frequently not permanent. They invested little capital, and almost always depended upon the coöperation or support of friendly African people.

Europeans had rarely penetrated beyond the coast, and their interest even in coastal lands had been restricted to a few more profitable areas. No real attempts had been made to influence, to control or even to understand the Africans' institutions and culture. Whenever the European settlements or interests were permanent, they were segregated from Africans—even when, as in South Africa, Europeans first penetrated the interior. The only notable exception was the Portuguese settlers; yet these, too, were invariably absorbed unless they became separated both racially and culturally from African life. Portugal had ruled certain Bantu areas, but white men did not begin to govern Africans extensively or effectively until the nineteenth

century. Only then did the Zulus come under the Boers, the
Xosa and Basutos under Britain, and Senegalese Moslems under the Second French Empire. Until the late 1860's Britain
thought in terms of abandoning all economic and political responsibility in both West and South Africa, although her policy
makers hoped to retain certain advantages. France, the United
States, the Netherlands and Scandinavia had lost most of the
little interest they had had earlier, and no foreign power, save
the Arabs, knew or cared about East Africa.

The liberal doctrines of free trade, laissez faire and
restricted governmental power, which spread widely through
Europe early in the nineteenth century, discouraged the application of any notions that might involve a government in political expansion, added expense, measures for economic control
and development, or military responsibility. The persistence of
this attitude prevented, for example, a permanent British decision with regard to control or responsibility on the Gold Coast,
and it precluded any decisive action toward either the Boers
or the Bantu in South Africa. It helped to prevent any power
from taking a real interest in either the interior or the east
coast, and it prohibited the development of permanent or
widespread interpenetration with any Africans. However, circumstances sometimes forced the Europeans to violate their
laissez-faire principles. Most noticeable were the efforts to
counteract the Boers, whose outlook was so different from that
of nineteenth-century liberal Europe.

Fundamental to liberalism was the belief that human economic, political and social relations were governed by immutable natural laws. As long as these "laws" were applied within
Europe itself, with the approval of a liberal-minded European
electorate, any contradictions and limitations of natural laws
could be either forgotten or explained away. Similarly the
standards of liberalism were applied to African politics: the
European government must reduce or even withdraw its influence, and, to a large extent, it clearly should be equally inactive
in the economic sphere.

However, natural law was theoretically applicable to all human beings regardless of race, culture or location. The greatest agitation on this point centered on the slave question, for—as liberals pointed out—if it is wrong to enslave Europeans, it is equally wrong to enslave Africans. In order to enforce this moral absolute, slavery had to be abolished. This meant, of course, that slavery was evil regardless of the culture pattern; no longer could the trade and use of human slaves be tolerated even if the slaves' own culture permitted it. Morality was not relative to individual culture.

The attack on slavery was the first wave of the liberal onslaught. After lengthy debate cultural relativism was duly condemned and slavery was abolished in all areas under the jurisdiction of the liberal-minded countries such as England, France, Scandinavia and the Netherlands. Inasmuch as slavery was an absolute wrong, it was not enough that one's own country ban it: less liberal countries promptly gained control of markets and African slave sources that liberal Britain had abjured; unscrupulous entrepreneurs flourished; and African middlemen whose strength and wealth depended upon slave trading either foundered or sought new outlets. The only solution was to put pressure upon tribes and nations that continued the practice, and to police the sea lanes that slavers frequented. Any such actions would, however, require the use of international diplomacy and of strong, expensive military forces. These two devices were the opposite of the liberal doctrines of economic laissez faire, governmental nonintervention and the reduction of government expenditure. Most liberal governments contented themselves with either quiet withdrawal or merely token enforcement, but Britain pressed firmly for a series of international antislavery agreements. Throughout the nineteenth century several British naval units were deployed among the slave routes in order to enforce both Britain's own laws and her foreign treaties.

Humanitarian considerations justified the use of diplomacy and naval power against all Europeans. Logically, the same humane obligation included the African tribes and trading states from whom slaves had long been bought. Therefore, it would be necessary to put down slavery among the Africans themselves, and to recast their lives and their economies in the liberal mold. This task became the liberal mission, but it took half a century to determine how much of this should be the government's responsibility. Also, there were some clear commitments in the trade and protection treaties that had been in effect with friendly tribes. At first the task in West Africa was largely delegated to the entrepreneurs, but they had a disturbing tendency either to assume new responsibilities or to be lax in discharging their obligations. In South Africa periodic military intervention seemed to be necessary to prevent the degeneration and dispersion of incompatible white and Bantu communities. It was not easy to withdraw the government, but the intention to do so was not entirely abandoned until the end of the 1860's.

Inevitably the liberals became concerned with the development of humanitarian efforts in Africa. To the European masses, the liberal mission and the humanitarian effort were not primarily philosophical. When combined with popular religious feelings and the mass desire to act rather than to theorize, it was perhaps inevitable that liberalism should spawn a revival of enthusiasm for Christian missions. Through this medium, individuals and volunteer groups—rather than a government—would endeavor to remold and to guide African people toward the universal liberal-Christian goals. Only isolated observers and intellectuals saw a real contradiction between secular liberalism and the Christian religion, or between laissez-faire ideals and the profound enthusiasm for the remaking of an alien culture.

Even before ideal and popular liberalism had begun to have a significant impact upon Africa, the rationalism of the eighteenth century had sparked a widespread scientific interest. For the first time, white adventurers penetrated extensively into the interior. Often they were not trained scientists, but they all shared a remarkable flair for sound reporting, a faith in the value and importance simply of knowing about distant places, and a determination to shed factual light on legends and rumors that for centuries had satisfied men's curiosity. Mungo Park and René Caillé penetrated the upper Niger in 1795-1806 and 1827-29, respectively; Clapperton, the two Lander brothers and Heinrich Barth searched the lower Niger and Hausaland between 1825 and 1856. A similar interest in South Africa during the same period led others to explore west and north of the Transvaal. Inevitably their monetary rewards were small and many commercial and political interests were even hostile to these dispassionate students. Their nationalities mattered very little at that time—many were known only to geographical scientists—but within that limited circle, the acclaim was international. Although these explorations were as much a product of the new scientific faith in universal order and knowledge as was liberalism, the two movements seldom coöperated in the African field.

During the first half of the nineteenth century, missionary movements tended to concentrate along the frontiers of the Cape Colony, or along the Gold and Slave Coasts where there was a deliberate effort to counteract the earlier slave-trader influence. South Africa's more scattered Bantu population, its open terrain, and the desire to counteract the influence of Boer expansion, all caused that mission field to expand more rapidly toward the interior near mid-century. It was here that science, religion and antislavery liberalism first came together in the person of David Livingstone (1813-1873).

Dr. Livingstone began his career in 1840 as a medical missionary on the South African frontier, in a long-established mission among the Sotho tribes just west of the Orange Free State. After repeated disagreements with the Boers, from whom he—as a scientist and Scottish churchman—was so different, Livingstone set out to explore the geography and the people of the interior.

Having a particular aptitude for scientific observations,

Livingstone contributed significantly to the knowledge of African natural history, geography and linguistics. His reports on culture or African personalities were somewhat less notable, but he was strongly motivated by a sense of justice and humanitarian zeal. On successive journeys between 1841 and 1853 he penetrated and proselytized into the Zambezi basin. By 1856 he had crisscrossed the territory between Angola and Mozambique, and discovered Victoria Falls. Three years later Livingstone established a major mission on the unclaimed shores of Lake Nyasa. His vividly written scientific and mission reports became best sellers among the nineteenth-century public both in Europe and the United States. A wave of enthusiasm—characteristic of the century's nearly unbounded popular confidence in both science and religion—culminated in a wave of vehement indignation when Livingstone sent out the first graphic and detailed reports of the Arab slave trade. Zenj traders had, he revealed, penetrated as deep as the Congo Basin. Many hitherto unknown aspects of the East African trade were described.

Dr. Livingstone's reports managed to encompass scientific, religious and romantic appeals that were immediately popularized, serialized and magnified in the sensationalist press. A new interest in both East and Central Africa emerged, in many ways quite distinct from either political or economic concern. In 1865 pressure from Arab slavers forced abandonment of the Scottish Nyasa mission. Dr. Livingstone set out on his third expedition—this time to find the source of the Congo River. World attention was at a fever pitch. Although Bantu runners brought occasional messages from his advance base on the east shore of Lake Tanganyika, the public in Europe and the United States was anxious and impatient when the expedition went into its fifth year during 1870. James Gordon Bennett, publisher of the sensationalist *New York Herald* decided to send a reporter to gather news throughout the eastern Mediterranean, India and the new area of interest in East Africa—including an interview with the famous missionary.

Bennett's choice for the assignment was John Rowlands, a

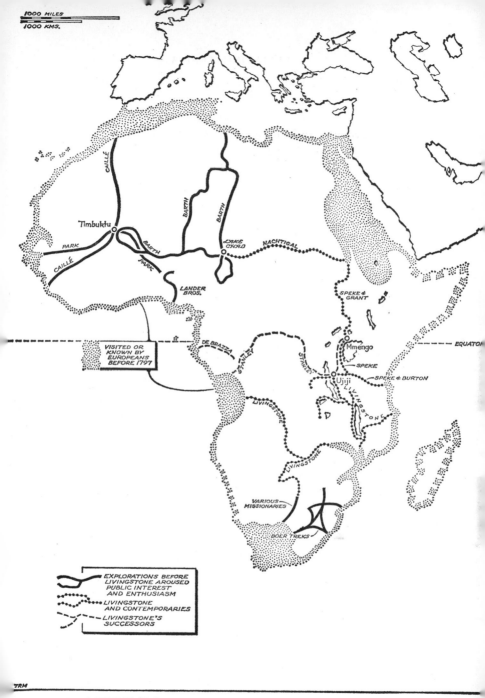

1000 MILES
1000 KMS.

CAILLÉ

CAILLÉ

BARTH

BARTH

Timbuktu

LAKE
CHAD

NACHTIGAL

PARK

CAILLÉ

BARTH

PARK

LANDER
BROS.

SPEKE &
GRANT

DE BRAZZA

VISITED OR
KNOWN BY
EUROPEANS
BEFORE 1797

Mmengo

EQUATOR

SPEKE

STANLEY

Ujiji

SPEKE & BURTON

LIVINGSTONE

LIVINGSTONE

LIVINGSTONE

D

LIVINGSTONE

LIVINGSTONE

VARIOUS
MISSIONARIES

BOER TREKS

EXPLORATIONS BEFORE
LIVINGSTONE AROUSED
PUBLIC INTEREST
AND ENTHUSIASM

LIVINGSTONE
AND CONTEMPORARIES

LIVINGSTONE'S
SUCCESSORS

TRM

AFRICA, EXPLORATION IN THE 19th CENTURY

Welshman who had stowed away to New Orleans and taken the name of his adopted father, Henry Morton Stanley. Never afraid to attack personalities, to hurt feelings or to romanticize a simple story, Stanley quickly acquired eminence in the flamboyant journalistic world of post-Civil War New York. His activities were well financed, noted for their sometimes reckless impatience, and usually executed in a dramatic manner. His reports from Africa deliberately appealed to the popular image of a "dark," savage and potentially wealthy continent. After several months' sojourn in the Near and Middle East, Stanley in 1871 proceeded to carry out the African portion of his assignment. He was barely thirty when he arrived at Zanzibar. Numerous expeditions had used this port, and the offices of the British consulate there, as a base during the preceding generation: Burton and Speke to Lake Tanganyika in 1854-55, Speke alone to Lake Victoria and the Nile headwaters in 1858, and Speke and Grant to trace the Nile into Egypt in 1860-63. All of these interior districts were by now well traveled and described, and all but the Nile area were also tapped by Arab slave routes radiating from Zanzibar. Stanley spent more money for porters and outfitting them than all his predecessors combined. In following Speke's route to Ujiji, where Dr. Livingstone was known to be, he depended upon Arab guides and caravaners. It is little wonder that the scientist-missionary, in receiving this unprecedented and motley array, was speechless until Stanley said, "Dr. Livingstone, I presume?"

Two years later, in 1873, Dr. Livingstone's porters brought first word of his death, then the body and his papers to the coast. He left an Africa whose central regions were no longer unknown or forgotten, and he had created a new atmosphere among the people of Europe that was to spawn keen political and economic competition and a forceful missionary endeavor. The result was a virulent nationalistic race among the great powers to carve vast blocks of interior territory. The liberal mission was turning into an imperial competition.

12

LEARNING TO THINK
IMPERIALISTICALLY

THROUGHOUT the 1860's and into the 1870's, European reformers expected increasingly effective action in the African interior. They wanted to suppress slavery, to reorient indigenous societies toward liberal Christian goals, and to develop economic and political institutions that would benefit both whites and Africans. Such a task was too great for small or individual groups; only organized governments could provide the necessary planning, protection and capital for such undertakings. This period is characterized by the gradual development and acceptance of direct governmental actions. The new attitude is a marked change from that of previous decades.

British government influence began to expand as early as 1861 on the Slave Coast and 1866 in South Africa, but these limited actions were reluctantly undertaken in order to regulate specific abuses in slaving or frontier quarreling. Deliberate extension of European power probably began with Emperor Napoleon III in 1861. He revived France's dormant interest in Senegal in order to enhance national glory and to generate a wave of popular loyalty at home. French settlement was encouraged, indigenous people in the newly annexed territory were brought into direct association with an imperial agricultural market, and (French political and social institutions were deliberately transplanted. Thus, the nationalist image of a growing, all-embracing culture was enhanced.

In Britain such nationalistic enthusiasm was slower to develop, partly because the contradictions in the liberal ideal were more clearly seen. (Rarely did all major political parties and public opinion agree on the necessity or desirability of acquiring any new land, responsibility or expense for the government. Liberals had come to assume that economic expansion benefited both Europe and Africa by increasing the velocity of production and exchange. By 1870 Europeans also believed that they were industrially mature; for further growth Europe needed overseas resources and markets. However, government action did not seem to be necessary until the notion developed that there was competition among European nations for domination. After 1871, when Germany united and began to industrialize, merchants realized that national political boundaries influenced trade patterns. The idea developed that the possibilities for economic expansion were limited. Britain was thus brought to recognize the nationalistic nature of overseas competition.

At the same time, universal manhood suffrage and the telegraph were being introduced. The Second Reform Bill of 1867 transformed Britain into a popular democracy. In preparation for the election of 1874, the Conservative (Tory) Party spent three years seeking popular support for prosperity and glory based upon expansion. New interests, such as South African diamonds, had given fresh economic impetus to the idea. The invention of the undersea telegraph cable brought a new awareness to the masses by permitting the presentation of fresh, detailed reports in a popular, cheap press. The Suez Canal, which was opened in 1869, made it possible to reach East Africa more rapidly and cheaply than ever before. In 1875 the government sought and acquired direct control of that vital political and economic waterway. This, in turn, made it even easier to reach

East Africa, to which Dr. Livingstone's popular reports had recently attracted both humanitarian and economic attention.

For some time the contradictory demands of liberal idealism and nationalistic necessity were apparent in British actions. British merchants and missionaries relied upon the Foreign Office consulates to protect them from foreign interlopers. Virtual spheres of influence developed. Sometimes attempts to stabilize an area or to exclude foreign competition culminated in sporadic political and military occupations. These were usually withdrawn because they involved expense or responsibility that the Parliamentary opposition and public opinion refused to tolerate. In another case, confused official efforts were made to induce a self-governing Anglo-Boer federation in South Africa that would be securely associated with Britain but would not increase her burden of responsibility.

Time after time such intermittent or auxiliary government intervention proved to be unsatisfactory. By the 1890's, permanent military and political participation, as well as direct expenditure, was needed in many areas in order to assure the success of humanitarian and economic goals. British administration became permanent in Nyasaland because the missions required continued protection from the attacks of Zanzibar slavers and the Bantu tribes, many of whom were recent Ngoni arrivals from Zululand, continually feared depredations from their neighbors and from the Arabs. Uganda required a continuous protectorate after factions of Moslem, Anglican and French Catholic converts engaged in civil war. After the diamond fields at Kimberley had been wrested from the Orange Free State, British prospectors had to be policed and included in the imperial customs zone. In cases such as the Niger Delta and the Rhodesias, government action was needed to restrain monopolistic commercial practices and to resolve contradictions in cession treaties that businessmen negotiated with indigenous tribes. In Kenya and the Gold Coast interior, only the government could maintain and protect the communication routes upon which commerce or missions depended.

The expansion of France's sphere of influence in Senegal came into conflict with the interests of the independent semi-militarized Moslem empires in the West African interior. Much of the last third of the nineteenth century was marked by a continuous struggle to find an effective boundary between the African and European authorities. No natural ethnic or geographical features separated Senegal from the inland states. The latter proved to be so extensive and so mobile that peace was impossible without total occupation. In the process, British commercial interests called upon their own government for protection both from French competition and from the Moslem defenders who moved across their territory. To some extent at least, French military leaders were driven to total conquest by the desire to demonstrate the power and glory of their forces despite the German victory before Paris in 1870. In addition, grandiose economic dreams with the vision of an extended French culture had considerable appeal to the electorate of the Third Republic.

At first, the newly unified German Empire seemed content to compete purely within the realm of free trade. Count Otto von Bismarck felt that internal unification, a diplomatic balance within Europe, and the avoidance of any political action irritating to Britain were the shrewdest courses to follow. Liberal German merchants were not satisfied with this lack of political assistance. Shortly after Bismarck was forced in the 1880's to turn to them for political support, he also began to authorize the establishment of German colonial possessions. He always tried to restrict these to unclaimed areas, or at least to reach a satisfactory understanding with England and France in each case. However, after the Iron Chancellor's forced resignation in 1890, Kaiser Wilhelm II was less astute.

Partitioning began from the coast of West Africa as early as 1884. Within ten years the outlines had been drawn at least 250 miles inland from the Gold and Slave Coasts, and up to 600 miles from Senegal. All the major divisions were completed by 1900. In South Africa the advance of European territory began from the Orange River in 1871. The Limpopo was reached in 1885. There was by then a sphere of British missionary and commercial influence in the Rhodesias and Nyasaland, but there was no political control for another fifteen years. No political penetration had yet occurred in either East or Central Africa. Five powers were interested in the area, and important unofficial expansion had already begun to take place in Uganda, along the coast facing Zanzibar, and at the Congo mouth.

The British consulate and some private German entrepreneurs had increased their activity along the Zanzibar coast, but European interest in the interior centered on Henry Morton Stanley. After he had visited Livingstone, many considered him the authority on Central and East Africa. When the missionary died, Stanley seemed to be the sole heir to the civilizing and exploring mission. In 1874, just a year after Livingstone's death, the New York press sent Stanley on a new equatorial expedition from Zanzibar, bound this time for Uganda, the unknown Congo and the Atlantic watershed. In Uganda he found Buganda emerging as the dominant power under the virtually absolute Kabaka Mutesa, but reported that Mutesa was gravely disturbed by the increasing Moslem pressure both from the north and from the coast. Specifically, Stanley added, the kabaka would like to have some missionaries in his well-organized kingdom to counteract this influence. The message was sent down the Nile and forwarded to England in 1875.

The Church Missionary Society, which responded enthusiastically, dispatched the Anglicans to Buganda two years later. France, inspired by nationalism and Cardinal Lavigerie's revival of the long-dormant Roman Catholic interest in Africa, soon sponsored a group of the newly organized White Fathers. Mutesa, however, wanted them not for religious purposes but as semimilitary shamans, so he kept all missionaries at the court, where they promptly became entangled in bitter internal politics.

Meanwhile Stanley had pressed across the rain forest to the Congo basin, which he proceeded to explore until 1877. Not being particularly familiar with either African conditions or indigenous tribal nuances, he relied heavily on the arms with which he had been liberally provided, and on the guidance of Tipoo Tib, an Arab slave-trade agent, as he fought and floated his way downstream. Many observers criticized his methods and predicted that severe difficulties had been created for later penetration. However, the public imagination of Europe and America was captured by the notion that Stanley had introduced civilization to the darkest, most terrifying part of the world.

Not the least impressed was Leopold II, King of the Belgians, who had begun during 1876 to organize a private International Association for the advancement of science, civilization and Christianity in Central Africa. At first Stanley paid little attention to the interest expressed by the Association's National Committees scattered in various countries, or to the money that Leopold was investing from his personal fortune. However, the Association persuaded Stanley to make a third exploration of the Congo region, entering this time from the Atlantic coast. The former access, through East Africa, involved a long overland march across territory that was now dominated by Britain, Germany and Zanzibar. Stanley's energy during five years of treaty making, surveying and road building was remarkable. On his return, in 1884, most of the river basin had become the province of the private Association rather than any of the great powers.

At the same time, France revived claims north of the Congo that were based upon the operations of her eighteenth-century slave-traders. By controlling the ports and by exploring inland from the South Atlantic shore, French military officers and commercial agents proceeded to convert their claims into effective occupation.

Since the end of the fifteenth century Portugal had claimed all of East Africa as well as the Congo and Zambezi basins. However, her explorers never made a documented transit of the continent, and most of the inland plantations had disappeared. All endeavors near both the Congo mouth and Zanzibar had been abandoned. In accordance with the principles of the

Treaty of London of 1600, other powers recognized Portuguese title only on the effectively occupied coasts of Angola and Mozambique.

Egypt became independent of the Ottoman Sultan in 1811. Mehemet Ali, a Turkish officer who led the revolt, began nine years later to revive the ancient Pharaohs' claims in the upper Nile basin. By the end of the 1860's, Mehemet Ali's successors had installed hired agents on the northern fringe of Uganda. Slave trading along the Egyptian-controlled Nile increased rapidly until Britain, through its control over Suez, was able to force a reversal of policy. Egypt then extended its interests during the 1870's, on the theory that she was putting down slavery. After Britain gained direct control of the bankrupt Cairo regime, Egyptian expansion continued, notably in the near-sovereign frontier province of Equatoria. The commander of Equatoria was an exceptional German scientist, Edward Schnitzer, who had become a Moslem and called himself Emin Pasha. Egyptian authorities quite justly considered him their most reliable agent in the Sudan and along the upper Nile, where he sincerely attempted to implement the unpopular antislavery policy. After 1881, most of this area turned to Mohammed Ahmed—the "Mahdi"—a xenophobic Moslem fanatic, who successfully isolated Emin Pasha and Equatoria from the outside world, destroyed the Egyptian imperial dream and blocked all Nile traffic.

The struggle over East and Central Africa had entered a decisive political phase by 1884. British commerce, supported by an active consul at Zanzibar, seemed to dominate that island and the coast facing it. The Foreign Office tried to destroy the remnants of slavery. Private German interests were also present. Both British and French missionaries operated in Buganda. Portugal pressed vague claims from the south on both coasts. French army elements and the International Association were opening up the banks of the Congo river itself.

At this point Bismarck asked the great powers to confer in order to prevent a major dispute.

When the Berlin Conference opened in November, 1884,

representatives were present from every interested government, including Britain, France, Germany, Spain, Portugal, Belgium and the United States. Britain had already recognized many of Portugal's extensive claims, especially those which conflicted with interests of France and the International Association. She was motivated, in part, by the hope of inducing Portugal to halt the Brazilian slave trade. However, the Conference decided not only to restate the old London doctrine of effective occupation, but also to require effective management as a test of title. The slave trade was again condemned. Britain was given title to the Niger River Delta, but freedom of trade on the river was guaranteed. Furthermore, France's claims north of the Congo were allowed. All the Congo watershed south of the river, plus a narrow access along both banks to an Atlantic port, was placed under an independent Congo Free State. This in turn was to be administered in trust by King Leopold and the International Association. All of the Congo basin and East Africa were declared free-trade areas, from which liquor was banned. This satisfied the United States, which had been the first power to recognize the Congo flag. All others followed suit. Spain received a minor reward near the equator, and restated her claim to a strip of the Sahara coast that nobody else wished to contest. In February, 1885 the Berlin Act was given its final form and accepted unanimously.

Within a few months German interests began to alarm the British in South Africa. The British South Africa Company hastily claimed semiofficial title to all land west and north of the Boer republics. Formal settlement did not take place until 1890, but direct contact between Germany and the Boers had been prevented, and British access from the Cape to the Congo headwaters was already assured.

After 1885 the East African scramble attracted the greatest attention. The Europeans were especially concerned with the competition among French, English and Moslem missionary factions in Uganda. A five-hundred-mile trek from Zanzibar was the only access to Uganda after the Mahdi had closed the Nile

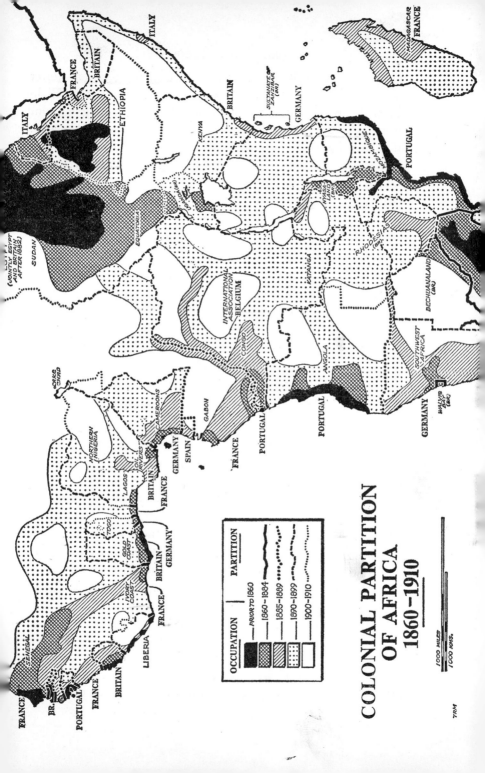

COLONIAL PARTITION
OF AFRICA
1860–1910

OCCUPATION	PARTITION	
		PRIOR TO 1860
		1860–1884
		1885–1889
		1890–1899
		1900–1910

1000 MILES
1000 KMS.

FRANCE
BR.
PORTUGAL
FRANCE
BRITAIN
LIBERIA
SENEGAL
IVORY COAST
GOLD COAST
TOGO
GERMANY
FRANCE
BRITAIN
GERMANY
FRANCE
BRITAIN
LAGOS
NORTHERN NIGERIA
OIL RIVERS
CAMEROONS
GERMANY
SPAIN
GABON
FRANCE
PORTUGAL
CONGO
INTERNATIONAL ASSOCIATION
BELGIUM
ANGOLA
PORTUGAL
KATANGA
SOUTHWEST AFRICA
GERMANY
WALVIS BAY (BR.)
BECHUANALAND (BR.)
RHODESIAS (BR.)
NYASA LAND (BR.)
MOZAMBIQUE
PORTUGAL
GERMANY
SULTANATE OF ZANZIBAR (BR.)
KENYA
UGANDA (BR.)
BRITAIN
ETHIOPIA
EQUATORIA
SUDAN
(JOINTLY EGYPT AND BRITAIN AFTER 1882)
ITALY
FRANCE
BRITAIN
ITALY
MADAGASCAR
FRANCE

TRM

route. However, British missionaries were trying to find a shorter route from Mombasa across the warrior-infested Kenya Highlands. A private German colonizing company, acting without Bismarck's approval, sent the explorer Karl Peters into the area. In 1886 Britain and Germany reached an agreement setting up two "spheres of influence" in the Zenj empire. Britain took a "primary interest" in Zanzibar Island and the northern Zenj coast, while Germany took the southerly coast.

A year later Stanley—now Governor-General of King Leopold's Congo Free State—started upriver from the Atlantic with the intention of bringing Emin Pasha under Leopold's jurisdiction. Indeed, this was intended to be a dramatic "relief expedition." The subsequent confusion and hardship were unusual for Stanley. Ultimately it was he who had to be saved—by Emin Pasha. Actually Emin Pasha, with loyal Egyptian soldiers, was fighting a fairly effective war against the Mahdi, and refused to surrender Equatoria in order to return to the Congo with Stanley. Meanwhile, in Europe, Stanley's "Emin Pasha Relief Expedition" had aroused much excitement and national pride. A German expedition, under Karl Peters, raced from Zanzibar and arrived in Equatoria before Stanley left. Emin Pasha was persuaded to join the German party. On the way back to Zanzibar, in 1890, he and Peters raised the German flag in Uganda.

Later they discovered that Bismarck and Lord Salisbury had reached quite a different decision in Europe at virtually the same time. Of course, the European decision—the Heligoland Treaty—was official; the action in Africa did not count. Britain received protectorate title to Uganda, Zanzibar Island and the Kenya coast with all land behind it. Germany acquired the Tanganyika coast with its hinterlands, plus Heligoland, a British island in the North Sea. The sultan was confined to Zanzibar alone, but he was promised an annual rent from the European powers on the East African mainland. Shortly afterward Germany and England agreed on the division of Southwest Africa.

After 1890 all of the continent had been partitioned except for a few areas of the Saharan fringe that were still contested.

French and British expeditions frequently competed with one
another for these regions. Some encounters, such as that at Fashoda on the upper Nile, became major diplomatic crises. However, the issues were resolved short of war by 1898. All European
claims had by then been established, but in some sections of
Africa precise surveys that would implement the agreements
were never completed.

In the same year that the Heligoland agreement was made,
a working conference of the colonial powers met at Brussels to
discuss ways of eliminating the persistent slave trade. East Africa
received special attention because Arab caravans, made up of
slaves, were still the only means of reaching the growing Uganda
Protectorate. The conferees recommended that railways, which
were the cheapest means of transportation, be built as rapidly
as possible. Slavery would then disappear because the caravans
would be driven out of business. No colonial power had ever
spent capital in the amounts that such railways required, but
over the next quarter-century Britain and Germany both im-
plemented the recommendations in East Africa by building two
lengthy and expensive lines connecting the coast and the interior.

By the end of the nineteenth century, commercial and mission enterprises had accepted or even demanded government intervention. This certainly protected the investments and assured
both peace and reliable communications, but sometimes it was
also a form of subsidy. Without political support, monopolies
were usually difficult or expensive to maintain. Governments
had money to spend for commercial services, and they could
often grant lucrative franchises. Frequently the colonies cost
the European taxpayer more than the entrepreneurs cleared in
profits. However, a profitable colonial enterprise might indirectly stimulate the mother country's entire economy. A few
colonies were established for humanitarian purposes, and most
of them had some such impact; the value of this cannot be balanced at all. For every profitable exploitation, there were many
ventures that floundered or went bankrupt. Everywhere, save in

South Africa, capital was chronically inadequate to the demand. Increasingly governments turned first to devices for the protection or encouragement of private capital, and eventually to direct government investment. By the end of the "laissez faire" nineteenth century, Africa probably had a greater proportion of government-supplied capital than any other continent. European interest in Africa had become inextricably associated with, and substantially dependent upon, governmental action.

13

CHRISTIANITY AND DARWINISM

B EFORE the Birth of Mohammed, Christianity had spread throughout North Africa, the Nile Valley and Ethiopia. West of Egypt the Latin variety had prevailed, but the Monophysite or Coptic doctrine—which early showed tendencies toward ritual emphasis—predominated farther east. Arab invaders had conquered the Mediterranean coast before the ninth century, and waves of Moslem settlers replaced all important Christian communities two hundred years later. The middle and upper Nile, along with Ethiopia, remained faithful although totally isolated from both the Byzantine and Roman communions.

Islam began to advance up the Nile during the eleventh century, but its victory in the valley was not assured until the sixteenth century. Ethiopia remained Christian because Portugal helped her to stem the Moslem tide at the foothills of the Abyssinian Highlands. Portuguese Christians then attempted to reintroduce Roman Catholicism to Africa. Particular efforts were made on the Senegambia, Gold, Slave, Congolese and East African coasts, but the missions did not have enough priests or enough experience to make many significant impressions. By 1600 Portugal's religious endeavor had been reduced to serving a small, scattered European and mixed population in Angola and Mozambique, and to a minor residual influence south of the

Gambia River. No Christians undertook any further efforts for almost two centuries, although Dutch settlers did bring Calvinism with them to South Africa.

Modern evangelism first began with Moravian Brethren and the London Missionary Society who, despite mounting Boer protest, preached to Hottentots in the Cape Colony during the Napoleonic wars. Wesleyans and the Church Missionary Society extended these efforts after 1804 to include both Bantu on the Cape frontier and the West Indian slaves who settled in Sierra Leone. However, no effective drive was made among either the tropical or the savanna tribes until 1828.

Before 1860 British and Swiss Protestants opened fields along the Gold and eastern Slave Coasts, where traders had concentrated since the abolition of slavery. They also made a small start near the old Portuguese stations on the Gambia River, and, in South Africa, special efforts had been attempted to reach the Bantu on both flanks of the Boer trekkers. Roman Catholic interests did not revive until the Holy Ghost Fathers entered French Senegal in 1846. Catholic missions in Gabon, near the old French slave stations, were opened two years later. However, the Roman church did not establish any other missions until the 1860's, after the British, Swiss and Germans had initiated Protestant work on both coasts of East and Central Africa. Both church groups thereafter worked with increasing fervor, save in the Moslem areas, where missions were always rare. Catholics concentrated upon the German and Congolese areas, and were almost exclusive in the French territories. Protestants were particularly active throughout the British and German possessions, and they developed a considerable interest in the Portuguese colonies. Christian influence was always greatest in the areas now known as South Africa, Southern Rhodesia, Nyasaland, Tanganyika, Uganda, southeastern Nigeria, Liberia, and the coast of Ghana. Prodigious efforts in the Congo basin, particularly after 1894, were dispersed across too large an area to have a comparable impact. Politics in almost every area has had an influence upon the character and denomination of missions,

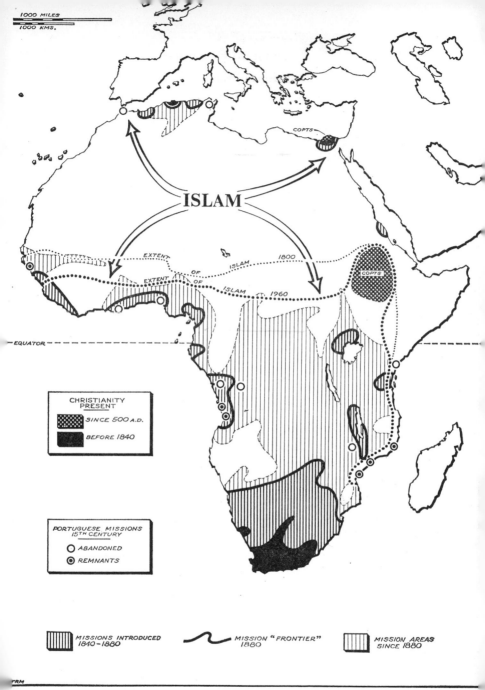

1000 MILES
1000 KMS.

ISLAM

COPTS

EXTENT OF ISLAM 1800
EXTENT OF ISLAM 1960

COPTS

EQUATOR

CHRISTIANITY
PRESENT

⊞ SINCE 500 A.D.

■ BEFORE 1840

PORTUGUESE MISSIONS
15TH CENTURY

○ ABANDONED

◉ REMNANTS

▥ MISSIONS INTRODUCED
1840-1880

〰 MISSION "FRONTIER"
1880

▥ MISSION AREAS
SINCE 1880

ADVANCE OF MISSIONS
EUROPEAN SETTLEMENTS NOT INCLUDED

but only in French sections of the West African savanna was the effect pronouncedly favorable to one church.

Christian churches often became the dominant architectural feature in the rural African landscape. Frequently the mission staff was far more numerous in an area than the European government or commercial population, although this has been less true in the twentieth century. Mission staffs usually had more direct contact with the mass of African people, and almost invariably they were less inclined to change their personnel. During the nineteenth century, mission groups were much more likely to include European families and children than were the official government establishments.

At the same time, missionaries tended to give many Africans the impression that they were apologists—or even agents—for political and cultural imperialism. The mere fact that churchmen were white people who spoke and behaved in the European manner was prima-facie evidence of association with foreign rule. Their educational programs usually included a European language—generally that of the ruling power—and the curriculum was increasingly one which the government dictated and helped to finance. Church organization always conformed to European political frontiers rather than the traditional tribal and cultural frontiers. Missionaries not only accepted the authority of colonial administrators, but it was known that they often influenced policy making itself. Furthermore, a missionary, however humble, had of necessity a standard of living and a variety of material possessions that were often noticed by far greater numbers of people than he might influence spiritually.

The obligation to preach a new spiritual idea was bound to have extensive repercussions throughout African society. Even if a missionary preferred example and service to direct proselytization, his behavior had to include a kind of self-assurance and authority that alien cultures easily mistook for arrogance or condescension. Christianity had numerous obstacles to surmount: it had a white Christ, white saints, and white missionaries. It was not satisfied with an amalgam or compromise with indig-

enous beliefs, but demanded a total acceptance. It required a
break with traditional religion. Thus, a convert was often forced
to isolate himself from the family, the tribe and the economic
system because these were inextricably associated with the traditional cultural faith. Therefore, there was an inherent tendency to demand cultural change as a part of Christian conversion.

In the context of nineteenth-century liberal attitudes, this
association of European culture and the Christian religion was
quite understandable. European culture, in which Christianity
had long flourished, seemed to present ethical standards and to
offer unbounded material and spiritual rewards such as no other
civilization had been able to produce. It alone seemed to have
eliminated superstition, ignorance, complete reliance upon manual labor, and group dependence, all of which prevented man
from achieving his ultimate spiritual potential. Its languages
contained knowledge and insight that Europeans—including
most missionaries—believed were unique in the world. The adoption of a Europeanized culture therefore seemed to be not only
the easiest but the necessary vehicle for the Christianization and
salvation of African souls.

Even in a sophisticated society, confusion or duplication
can result from the presence of numerous denominations that
emphasize different aspects of Christian thought. Within an
alien culture the impact can be even more negative. There is a
tendency to stress points which either are distinctive to one denomination or have popular appeal. Skepticism, even a light-
hearted attitude may then replace serious conversion, and there
is a persistent tendency to associate various denominations with
traditional social classes or political affiliations.

Occasionally such sectarian competition led to infighting
during which the African was either forgotten or used. However,
the usual consequence of such disputes was that none of the involved churches could acquire a stable congregation, a strong
program, or enough money to carry out its work.

Throughout Africa there also were many sincerely motivated

missionaries who were rejected by organized churches or who wished to work in an area not served by a regular group. These individuals operated entirely on their own. At times their poverty became so severe that they could give little effective service. However, their main shortcoming was usually a prolonged lack of contact with thought, medicine and education elsewhere in Africa or Europe. Of these unaffiliated missionaries, a few were renegades from Christian Europe, but they lacked the finances and the knowledge which were necessary if they were to have significant influence. On the other hand, a few of the individualists were among the most ingenious and effective contributors.

At the same time, the Protestant and Roman Catholic missions were pioneers of crucial importance in introducing education, some technology and the sense of national identity south of the Sahara. Every major African language was given a system of writing, almost always for the first time. Because the missions lacked funds and teaching personnel, their educational work rarely influenced more than 5 percent of the male population. Nevertheless, the missionary schools always preceded any government program, sometimes being more than a century earlier. Similar innovations took place in the teaching of European languages, basic skills and scientific subjects, although most missions tended until relatively recently to concentrate instead on less practical subjects, such as Christian literature and European culture. It should be pointed out, however, that the emphasis on classical rather than practical subjects was characteristic both of Europe itself and of the government-approved mission curricula, so the basis of this approach lay more in general European attitudes than in church policy.

Major competition to Christianity appeared in a renewed Moslem advance. Sometimes the organization and dispatch of missionaries was undertaken, including even medical and technological experts, in direct imitation of Christian methods. However, the influence usually came through neighbors or related families who had in turn been influenced from the savanna. The stress was always upon the fact that the missionaries, chiefs or other agents who carried the Koran were themselves African, and the claim was repeatedly made that Islam was an African religion particularly suitable for African society. Moslems demanded little—polygamy, tribal ritual, the traditional family structure were allowed—and a considerable amount of accretion was permitted. Islam, too, carried with it a system of writing, a considerable body of literature and a law code suitable both for small and large societies—all, of course, in Arabic—and, by its nature, the faith could confidently assure both salvation and continued social acceptance. Its philosophy was authoritative and very simple to understand, thus requiring far less active thought and much less belief in complex propositions than trinitarian Christianity. Throughout Africa since 1800 Islam has won about twice as many converts as the European denominations. This advance has been on a contiguous front southward from the grassy Sudan, immediately below the Sahara. Islam's progress has undoubtedly been helped by the fact that it is so united, and that it has emphasized the conversion of groups and districts rather than scattered individuals.

Before the end of the nineteenth century, Africans began to encounter Europeans who came not to preach, to trade or to govern, but simply to live among and study the people themselves. At first these anthropologists were the scientific vanguard of an interest that, in its popularized European version, was closely connected with the increasing speed of African conquest and colonial partition.

Charles Darwin's *Origin of Species*, written in 1859, had proposed the biological theory—based on his field work in the Pacific—that organisms produce more offspring than nature can support. Therefore, there is a continuous competitive struggle to acquire food. Those most suited to the environment will emerge victorious from the battle; the less fit will disappear. If there is some genetic mutation that improves a specimen's ability to survive, this individual will live and he will pass the mutation to his descendants. They, in turn, are better equipped for competition than the earlier form of that species, and they will replace it. Such a concept of "evolution" was not entirely new in scientific literature, but Darwin had been the first to test the idea by observations in the field.

In 1871 Darwin adapted this theory to human beings in *The Descent of Man.* This time there was no specific field work, but the book produced a storm of controversy that influenced both religious and secular thinking. An unusual popular interest, led by changes in secular thought, developed into a body of social and political ideas that were quite distinct from Darwin's scientific thesis. These popularizations had far more influence upon Africa than the relatively abstract religious disputes over the question of evolution.

Nationalistic writers and politicians proceeded on the assumption that Darwin's argument applied to cultural groups rather than to isolated specimens. By making the nation and the race the basic units in the struggle for survival, they had turned the scientific thesis into a theory that sanctioned competition between governments, even to the point of war; indeed, for some of the widely read writers, victory in war was the surest proof of national superiority. By similar logic these "social Darwinists" claimed that it was not only right but necessary for the "superior" Europeans to occupy and dominate the non-European countries. The white man needed the resources of Africa and Asia in order to survive. If he could seize them, he was entitled to keep them. However, most social Darwinists wrote from the context of one nation, or group of nations, so the masses who followed them tended to believe that the competition was among European nations as well as against alien races.

Such ideas were, of course, not at all compatible with Christian ideals, and they were hardly acceptable to the nineteenth-century liberals who believed in the freedom of man and universal equality. However, the liberals were divided in their views: some of them emphasized the universality of morals and the equality of opportunity for all men, but others stressed the importance of laissez faire. They said there must be no interference with the operation of natural forces. Since the "struggle for survival" was a natural law, the competition of nations and of races was desirable and necessary. At this point economic liberalism became (for a while) the handmaiden of social Darwinism. Opposed to them were the Christian humanists and the philosophic liberals. Both had a strong appeal to the voting masses, and to the university graduates who became colonial policy makers. Therefore, European attitudes by the end of the century were a mixture of nationalist expansionism and humanitarianism. This made it possible for democratic countries to pursue, with sincerity, two seemingly contradictory goals: commercial profit and political extension on one hand; and a program of missions, education and medical aid on the other. Both motives appealed to European voters, who did not understand the difficulties that were involved in combining the two philosophies. Of course, the humanitarian ideal was the Europeanization of the African people. However, there was no plan for African independence because everyone assumed that several centuries of "evolution" would be necessary. Evolution itself had now become a cultural concept rather than the biological theory that Darwin had discussed.

Darwin's scientific theses and the subsequent development of social Darwinism created two intellectual interests. The pure scientists measured and observed Africans in the field in order to find evidence for or against the Darwinian thesis of human evolution. In a rough sense this school was a forerunner of physical anthropology. The other group, which stressed culture, examined African societies in order either to demonstrate that a culture had deep roots or to document its inferiority to European concepts. These studies laid the groundwork for social and cultural anthropology.

In both schools of early anthropology, procedural techniques were necessarily tentative. For example, superficial similarities in cognate words, architectural concepts and social customs were given a great deal more weight than they currently receive. In the long run, social and scientific Darwinism were equally influential in both the physical and the socio-cultural approaches, but individual anthropologists varied greatly in their prejudices and their conclusions. Extreme caution is necessary in using the early works because their methods vary greatly and their interpretations represent two dominant schools of rigidly structured thought. These early field workers and theorists served a vital function, however, in that they experimented with many ideas and methods, recorded raw information in Africa that has since disappeared, and gave birth to general scholarly interest both in and among the African people. In the twentieth century their work—shorn of the earlier predispositions and known prejudices—has helped significantly in the making of government policy, the reassessment of mission functions and the development of mature knowledge in many fields of study.

After World War I, when anthropology had become more dispassionate and reliable, a number of far-reaching problems came to light that had not previously been recognized or understood. Among these problems were the breakdown of tribal authority and tradition (detribalization), the combination or fusion of one or more African cultures with European influences (acculturation), and the emergence of urban and industrial societies. In modern Africa each one of these has become a major historical factor, and each has had a significant influence upon political and social developments.

Darwinism and Christianity gave a new direction to the earlier liberal attitude toward Africa. In many respects the three perspectives were contradictory to one another. However, they tended to merge in the popular mind. Interest in Africa increased considerably, and there was a growing demand for direct European intervention south of the Sahara.

14

EQUATORIAL EXPANSION: I

DURING the late nineteenth century, migration, cultural upheaval, and policy innovation were more noticeable in East and Central Africa than in either the West or the South. The Ngoni, a rebellious fragment of the Zulu tribe, settled in 1835 on the shores of Lake Nyasa after cutting a destructive path from Natal across the Zambezi to the East African interior. The ambitious program of Sultan Seyyid Saïd, who transferred the Zenj capital from Oman to Zanzibar, led to an extensive development of cloves and sugar along the coast. By the 1840's the demand for slave labor had led Arab traders to dominate the interior as far as Lake Tanganyika and the upper Congo basin. In addition to slaves, they sought ivory, which Europeans were anxious to buy. The Arabs, in return, sold cheap European guns and industrial products. Before 1850 the Arabs had established and governed a chain of permanent commercial posts extending from Zanzibar to the Congo River. Selected Bantu tribal allies helped to protect the well-marked trade routes that connected the Moslem centers.

In Zanzibar the British had established a consulate in order to enforce the ban on slave trading. The consul also became the protector of English shippers who sold manufactured goods to the Arab merchants. After 1876 German industrial competition was increasingly evident along the east-coast market. Leopold II's International Association began to penetrate the Congo, but its base of operations was soon shifted from Zanzibar to the Atlantic coast gateway. Private interests predominated. European governments provided nothing more than rather extensive consular services) until the last decade of the century.

Before any European political or territorial expansion took place, East Africa had been extensively upset by the devastating Ngoni migrations, by relentless Arab slaving expeditions, and by a new concept of total war with modern arms which the Arabs had taught their Bantu allies. British, French and German missionaries, who entered the Great Lakes area in order to counteract these influences, worked either in conjunction with liberal merchants or in alliance with friendly Africans. Only in the last decade of the century did they turn to their respective governments for direct assistance.

The first white men to penetrate the equatorial interior were scientists searching for the source of the Nile. J. H. Speke, sometimes with either Sir Richard Burton or J. A. Grant, made three journeys from Zanzibar to Lakes Tanganyika and Victoria between 1857 and 1863, during which he discovered both the Arab slave routes and the developed Buganda kingdom. General public interest in the interior developed after Dr. David Livingstone's pioneer transcontinental journey in 1856. Three years later he opened up the River Shiré, discovered Lake Nyasa, and started the first mission in the Central African interior. He found that both Arab and half-caste Portuguese slave traders had penetrated the area before his arrival. The Arabs had recently opened a slave route from Lake Nyasa to Zanzibar. Livingstone believed that his small lake steamer would give the mission a military and commercial advantage that would put the slave traders out of business. However, the Arabs, who had converted the agrarian Yao tribe into a well-armed predatory ally, were unexpectedly stubborn. Other tribes so feared the slavers that they dared not associate with the missionaries. In fact, the latter had to abandon their work. The mission was not in a healthy location and its little steamboat was unseaworthy.'

Twelve years passed before Scottish missions reappeared in the Shiré-Nyasa country, and then another three, until the African Lakes Company was organized to develop communications and trade. The navigable mouth of the Shiré-Zambezi river system was not discovered until 1899, so communication de-- pended upon an overland connection through Quelimane, in Portuguese Mozambique. Peace depended upon agreement with Arab sheiks on the upper part of the lake. The company opened a trail to Lake Tanganyika, where a steamer was put into service. However, such expansion incited the Arab traders to break their truce in 1887. British consular service had been extended to the Nyasa area four years earlier, but the Portuguese began to demand duties, licenses and recognition of their own sovereignty. The Prime Minister, Lord Salisbury, eventually persuaded the Lisbon government to abandon these claims and to grant the right of free transit, but the African Lakes Company received no official aid in its expensive military campaign against the slavers. Captain Frederick Dealtry Lugard, on leave from the Indian army, directed the company's defense of missionary and trading stations during 1888 and 1889. Disgusted with Portuguese interference and the increasing chaos, he returned to England in order to revive official and private interest in Central Africa. Before he arrived in London, Harry Hamilton Johnston, who had both financial backing and territorial ambitions, had already left to take over the Nyasaland consulate.

Lugard and Johnston both combined qualities of imaginative perception, humanitarian motivation, practical ability and scholarly detachment that had been virtually unknown among their European commercial and administrative predecessors. Lugard was a courageous, disciplinarian soldier, with a genius for administrative organization and a rare capacity for human understanding, who first went to Africa in order to fight slavery while convalescing from the aftereffects of warfare and climate in Burma. On the other hand, Johnston's qualifications were rooted in the abstract belief that scientific evolution, a field in which he had an academic training and a scholarly reputation, ought to culminate in the spread of Christian ethics to backward people. His intellectualism was modified by gentleness toward subordinates, respect for seniority, a keen sense of humor and some weakness for exaggeration. An inveterate traveler and acute observer, Johnston throughout his lifetime wrote authoritatively and uninhibitedly about African society, politics, colonial policy, "cultural evolution," and natural history. His talents seemed to be particularly well suited to the pacification and organization of Nyasaland, whose problems Lugard had so well perceived.

Before the end of 1889 Johnston had been authorized to circulate among the lake tribes a standard treaty form—only the place, date and chief's mark had to be added—and, by declaring a formal political protectorate, he had stopped a Portuguese occupation force. Further developments were delayed by concentration on a treaty-making expedition toward the upper Congo. Johnston discovered that the International Association had already reached that area, but scattered agreements that he had made during the expedition gave Britain preëminence over the region now known as Northern Rhodesia.

Johnston's treaties and declarations were confirmed in the Anglo-Portuguese agreement of 1891. The west shore of Lake Nyasa, and most of the Shiré Valley, became the British Central African Protectorate. Britain wished simply to exclude all other Europeans; her parliament had no intention either of financing or of policing the territory. These responsibilities rested with the struggling African Lakes Company, which was reorganized as a subsidiary of Cecil Rhodes' wealthy British South Africa Company. The missions soon came to resent their dependence upon vast commercial organizations, while Rhodes' interests wanted both access to the north and the abolition of the unprofitable subsidiary. Johnston received the powers of a protectorate commissioner, and a direct government subsidy induced the Company to continue its noncommercial services. In 1893 the government accepted responsibility for all the mission lands. However, the boundary was drawn to include the least possible amount of territory and responsibility, while the Company took the greatest portion. Thus, the Nyasa region was deliberately created as a small, truncated, Christian protectorate, entirely separate from the vast neighboring area that later became Northern Rhodesia.

Arab slaving operations, supported by Yao military power, continued to disrupt both peace and communications. Both mission and government penetration were severely hampered by Arab propaganda, which effectively convinced the Ngoni and other tribes that the English were merely trying to get slaves that would be eaten in Europe. Abhorrent to traditional Bantu, who must have an entire body in afterlife, this tale was designed to make Arab slave labor appear the lesser of two evils. Johnston brought in a force of Sikh troops from India, conducted a series of short but sharp field campaigns, and finally subdued both the Yao and the Arabs near the end of 1895. Defeat at this point was hastened by the German influence in Tanganyika and the British power in Zanzibar itself after the coast was partitioned in 1890. However, it took both regulation of the shoreline and Johnston at the inland source to end the slave trade.

Not until 1904 did all tribes acknowledge the authority of the protectorate. Only then could the missions overcome the belief that Europeans ate slaves. During succeeding years Christianity made rapid progress. The protectorate, which was renamed Nyasaland in 1907, always remained important more for its mission work than for its economy. Nevertheless, tea and tobacco were developed in exportable quantities on large European-owned estates in the Highlands south of the lake.

Europeans who settled in Nyasaland created problems of land title. One of the protectorate government's first acts was the creation of law courts that could adjudicate conflicting claims. When Johnston arrived, planters were already buying

tribal land by dubious and extravagant means. The Crown
wished to reserve enough land to meet future African needs,
and to assure the tribes a fair price for land that they sold. At
the same time, the British also hoped to give secure titles to immigrants who would develop the country.

Much of the territory that the slavers had denuded was
located in the prime-quality Shiré Highlands. In this area Johnston let the chiefs sell their holdings, if he thought they understood the meaning of the transaction and received 3d ($.06)
per acre. Then he would issue an English-style freehold deed.
About 5 percent of the protectorate was sold to Europeans in
this manner. However, could a chieftain really sell land? He was
basically a trustee for property held in community by a tribe
that sometimes changed location. In every such case it was necessary either to ban Europeans altogether or to impose arbitrarily a European concept of perpetual tenure.

Johnston's experience with this problem gave him peculiar
qualifications for his extensive land program in Uganda at the
turn of the century. Although he undoubtedly considered himself experienced, the situation at the opposite end of the Great
Lakes chain was the product of a different history.

Speke, the first European to reach Uganda, reported in
glowing terms the existence of a viable, united and civilized
state on the shores of Lake Victoria. Lasting interest was not
aroused until 1875, when Kabaka Mutesa of Buganda asked for
missionaries. Stanley, who was in the area leading his second
expedition, received and immediately relayed the message to
Europe via the Nile trade routes. The kingdom of Buganda was
in a state of frenzy. Since 1840 Arab traders from Zanzibar had
been approaching from the south in increasing numbers, first to
trade, then to acquire slaves. Other Moslems, pressing through
the Egyptian Sudan, had now begun to arrive from the north.
Speke had come, then twelve years later Stanley himself. While
Stanley was there, a third explorer, Ernest Linant de Bellefonds,
arrived from France. Mutesa was afraid that the increasing
amount of contact was deterimental both to his power and to

the existence of his people. The kabaka therefore hoped that Christian missionaries could save the country from infiltration and division.

Stanley's dramatic message excited England. The Church Missionary Society promptly dispatched an Anglican staff to Buganda. When the Paris press reported on the British enthusiasm, French interest also developed and the White Fathers—recently organized in Algeria—were also sent. By 1877 both Protestants and Catholics had entered Buganda. Mutesa surprised them by using them to suit his own purpose. They were astonished when Mutesa promptly confined them to his court at Mmengo. He wanted to be sure that their priestly powers were used for his benefit. Thus, although Mutesa himself remained pagan, most of his family and the court were converted to one of the two faiths, which then became opposing factions.

Throughout most of the century Buganda had expanded and its central monarchy became stronger. However, the schism of *Fransa* Catholics and *Ingleza* Protestants after 1877 threatened the country's very existence. Chaos and civil war were probably prevented by the fact that Protestants and Catholics, Europeans or Baganda, could unite with the pagan kabaka against the Arabs and Egyptians who carried the Koran. Nevertheless, a number of Moslem converts were made in the frontier *ssazas* (roughly comparable to English counties) of Buganda.

Mutesa's fear of conquest increased when he found the missionary influence to be more disruptive than magical. Karl Peters' private German expedition skirted the southern edge of the kingdom. Agents of the International Association were reported to be in the Congo watershed, to the west. After 1881 most Egyptian interests to the north had been usurped by the active pressure of fanatical Mahdists. Only the eastern approach to Buganda remained clear of strangers, but this gave Mutesa some comfort. According to legend, Buganda could be conquered only from this quarter. When Mutesa died in 1885, he was replaced by Mwanga, who was equally aware of the legend. Although he had been raised by the *Ingleza* faction, the new

kabaka dismayed his Christian court by becoming a Moslem—
perhaps out of truculence, but more likely in order to preserve
his distinctive position.

Mwanga promptly made two disastrous moves. First, word
came that the new Anglican bishop, the Reverend James Han-
nington, was attempting to enter Uganda from the Kenya
Highlands in the east. Gripped either by traditional fear or by
anti-Christian design, the kabaka had him murdered. Then, a
year after his accession, Mwanga tried to slaughter the Christians in his country—especially the court retinue—but failed.
The inspiration to try this seems to have been religious, because
the kabaka's traditional position, even though he was a Moslem, was politically quite secure in a court that was divided into
two equal Christian factions.

It was at this time (1886) that Britain and Germany divided
the coast into two spheres of influence. Four years later, by the
Heligoland Treaty which similarly partitioned the East African interior, Uganda fell formally into the zone of British preëminence.

The British government, however, had never had any intention of accepting responsibility in East Africa. She did set
up the little Central African Protectorate around Lake Nyasa,
and the consul at Zanzibar was allowed to "advise" the Sultan,
but the other prerogatives were granted by charter for private
development. The Imperial British East Africa Company
(IBEA) was a combination of mission and steamship interests
that was authorized in 1888 to act in lieu of the government
under the Anglo-German agreements of 1886. The firm automatically acquired the additional privileges that Britain was
given in 1890. Nothing substantial was done until that happened, largely because the scope of responsibility was unclear
and a suitable leader not easy to find.

The central interest was of course Uganda. The little-
known, hostile Highland tribes and the infested coastal swamps
of Kenya were merely an annoying barrier, 400 miles wide, that
had to be crossed. The competent man was Lugard, formerly

associated with the African Lakes Company, whose well-known work on Lake Nyasa had now been taken over by Johnston and the government. By the end of 1890 his IBEA expedition had arrived in Mmengo, the capital of Buganda.

Civil war was raging on the shores of Lake Victoria. An alliance of Christian factions held Mwanga a virtual prisoner while they fought his Moslem supporters. Lugard joined the alliance, helped defeat the Moslems, and made a treaty with Mwanga that placed his kingdom under IBEA protection. However, Mwanga and the Catholic *Fransa* resented the British—each, undoubtedly, for his own religious reasons—and both wanted to ally with the Germans. Germany, even if she had been aware of Baganda feelings, was bound by treaty to recognize IBEA, so her would-be allies got no assistance. Once the Moslems had been dispersed in 1892, the Christians started to fight among themselves. The British, under Lugard, joined the Protestants in the three-month *Fransa-Ingleza* war; he and his escorts, who used the country's only machine gun, also won. Buganda was consequently partitioned into three zones: a small Moslem *ssaza* (county), another Catholic *ssaza,* and several dominant Protestant *ssazas.* The Moslem kabaka was now a Protestant puppet.

Such fighting forced the IBEA Company—which had done no trading at all—to the verge of bankruptcy. Lugard had planned to abandon the country, but the Church Missionary Society agreed to pay the Company's military bills for 1892-93. At the end of that year the government, yielding to missionary pressure and public opinion, established a protectorate and replaced the IBEA. Uganda thus became a landlocked possession because Kenya nominally continued to be Company domain. The latter region also became a government possession two years later, when Parliament appropriated money for the construction of the Uganda Railway. The Imperial British East Africa Company had operated for seven years, exercising the military, political and treaty-making powers of a government.

It never engaged in trade. In fact, it had been created simply as a funnel through which mission and steamship capital could be distributed.

Serious difficulties developed during the early years of the Uganda Protectorate. According to an ingenious plan for religious peace, each high Baganda office was given to two men— one Catholic, one Protestant (two Prime Ministers, two military commanders, etc.)—who were supposed to act in concert. The court, of course, continued to be divided along religious lines. Logically, therefore, the Baganda felt there should be two kabakas; but there was only one—a Moslem, prisoner of the Protestants and obviously subject to pressure from the British Commissioner. The confusion that resulted created a vacuum within which radical reforms were eventually introduced, but the protectorate government was far more concerned with peace than with any reform scheme at this time. The ideal policy was always to leave internal administration to each nation in the protectorate—especially Buganda, but also Bunyoro, Toro, Busoga, Acholi and a number of smaller ones—but the difference among these states made such a policy unrealistic. The kabaka and court in Buganda functioned fairly well on their own—except when dual posts for competing religions was tried —and Bunyoro could be artificially bolstered to do likewise, but it proved nearly impossible either to divide a chief's powers or to combine fragmented tribes in the other areas. In these circumstances, the protectorate government had to act as the direct administrator.

Kabaka Mwanga nominally returned to Christianity, but he continued to resent the British influence and their restriction upon his power. During July, 1897 he fled from Mmengo and attempted to organize an uprising. Quick military action put down the insurrection; Mwanga took refuge in German territory and was promptly deposed from his throne. The regency for his heir, the year-old Kabaka Daudi Chwa, fell to a triumvirate: the Protestant and Catholic Prime Ministers and a second appointed Protestant. The regency was surprisingly effective in its exercise of royal authority, but fighting continued inter-mittently for two years.

Equally disastrous for British prestige were two other re-volts. In 1897 mercenary Sudanese troops mutinied because their pay was overdue and because their traditional female cooks had been replaced by standard mess. Loyal Sikhs, sup-ported by the faithful Christians of Buganda, preserved the gov-ernment. The other crisis was provoked by Bunyoro's attacks, during 1894, upon smaller tribes with whom the Protectorate had signed treaties. Baganda troops provided important assist-ance, so both Protestants and Catholics were given extensive territorial awards and the Bunyoro chieftainship was forcibly reformed. Britain took two years to decide that Bunyoro should come under the protectorate, and six years before ruling that its people could continue to own land in the territory Buganda acquired. The government attitude is explained by its view that Bunyoro was conquered territory, whereas Buganda was a treaty acquisition.

At the same time, peaceful changes were being made. Christianity probably became the majority religion in Buganda during the 1890's; Protestant Baganda participated in govern-ing councils in 1884, and were ordained as early as 1896. The reli-gious issue receded after 1895, when the Pope placed Mill Hill Fathers from England in a position between the older French Catholics and the Anglicans. Buganda abolished slavery and instituted the rudiments of a tax-supported school system. Bet-ter communications with the coast, as the railway slowly ad-vanced from Mombasa, spurred the economy, but competitive world trade was not possible until 1901 when the line reached Kisumu, Kenya, where it connected with the Lake Victoria steamers from Uganda.

By 1899 something obviously had to be done to clarify the judicial and political functions that the protectorate govern-ment had begun to exercise. There was need for a regular method of taxation to support the government, a system of land tenure and sale that could be understood and enforced by British or African judiciary, a clear policy regarding immigrant land purchase, and a constitutional basis for the division of British and Baganda authority. Johnston (now Sir Harry), who qualified on the basis of his experience in British Central Africa, arrived in December, 1899 with broad powers of negotiation. Neither he nor the London and protectorate governments had a clear picture of Buganda's political structure and land system. His instructions emphasized the importance of increasing revenue, reducing expenditures, standardizing law and currency, abolishing slavery, and, in general, authorized him "to organize the administration of the Uganda Protectorate on lines which . . . will meet the requirements of the Protectorate on completion of the railway from Mombasa. . . ." Johnston made it clear before he left London that he would ". . . deal with [the land question] . . . much on the lines on which I dealt with . . . British Central Africa. . . . I would attempt to define existing boundaries of land in native occupation, and confirm the settled natives in possession of the soil they are cultivating. . . ."

Three days after his arrival he presented his program to the regents of Buganda. Although the British already there did not understand local conditions, and he had no time to study them, he proposed to set up a flat-rate tax on each hut or home, to put all foreigners under direct rule, to assert the right of appeal and review over Buganda's internal affairs, and to issue freehold title to established chiefs after reserving a large area for the Crown. He anticipated as ready an acquiescence as he had gotten in the Shiré country, but the Baganda turned out to be wily, literate diplomats who had long experience in European negotiation. It took nearly three months to reach agreement. At first, the regents and chiefs thought he intended to eliminate the kabaka and institute a fairly direct rule; it took Johnston some time to convince them that his phrase ("to govern themselves with a minimum of interference" meant that his jurisdiction would be limited to justice for foreigners, transport and communication, natural resources and the financial

structure. Discussion of these questions led to an extensive constitutional definition both of the Baganda government and of
its relationship to the British protectorate. Furthermore, land
title had always been an integral part of Buganda's political
constitution; when Johnston, who never understood this, insisted upon separating them in the British manner, the regents
and chiefs turned this misunderstanding to their own advantage. The result, which was far-reaching in its implications, is
the most noticeable feature of the final agreement.

In the traditional structure the kabaka was an absolute
legislative, executive and judicial power who, as effective sovereign, also held title to all lands. The realm was divided into
administrative *ssazas* (districts, or counties), over each of which
a member of the upper nobility (Bakungu) was given authority.
Each *ssaza* chief therefore received the responsibility for taxation, defense and local justice, as well as the right to assign land
to peasant tenants who were dependent upon him. Loyalty to
the central authority was guaranteed by the kabaka's power to
dismiss and replace the *ssaza* chiefs. Although such removals
were uncommon, the Bakungu would then lose title to the land
as well as their political powers. Control of land title was therefore the basic device by which the kabaka had customarily
checked disaffection and excessive local independence, even
when Buganda expanded rapidly in the early nineteenth century. The British government never understood this, and experienced missionaries, though they had some idea of it, did not see
the full implications.

Each *ssaza* chief would, in turn, subdelegate authority to
lesser chiefs (Batongole), who, in effect, constituted a minor
nobility and exercised a combination of landed and political
rights. The judicial and legislative process, before the protectorate began, was exercised exclusively by the kabaka, but he
could act only in the presence of the council (Lukiiko) of
Bakungu nobility. He was therefore both influenced and checked
by their freely expressed sentiment, though not by actual vote.

After 1893 protectorate officials sat with the kabaka facing the Lukiiko. There was still no Parliamentary voting, but with the Lukiiko and the chief ministers both divided along religious lines, the kabaka and his British escorts exerted uncertain and tenuous authority. Final decisions were made alternately by the Europeans and by the kabaka, sometimes without advance or formal agreement on the division of constitutional authority. If the Lukiiko had not been split into factions, the British inability to understand or to sense its feeling might have been serious. Authority was confused, the traditional devices for enforcing loyalty were replaced by a rather tenuous relationship based on the fact that the Lukiiko and the British were Christian while the kabaka's power lay first in the hands of a Moslem, then of an interim regency. Some kind of clarification certainly was desirable.

In accordance with British preconceptions of the problem, Sir Harry Hamilton Johnston enforced a separation of the constitutional and land issues from the outset. Once the Baganda chiefs realized that the kabaka and local autonomy were not to be eliminated, they accepted the political structure. The kabaka, as the native ruler, was to be assisted by three "native officers of state" and an advisory Lukiiko made up of the various *ssaza* chiefs. All these posts were to be filled by the kabaka, not by election, and were subject to British approval. The *ssaza* chiefs had to collect a tax of three rupees (4s6d, or about $1.10 at that time) from every hut and every gun owner in Buganda. This money had to be directly deposited with the British authorities. The British could dismiss any incompetent chief directly, but the kabaka could not fire a *ssaza* or Lukiiko official without British approval. The Lukiiko could initiate legislation, but the kabaka had to get British approval before signing any measures. However, it was not clear whether the kabaka could veto a measure, even if the British approved it. In short, the protectorate was committed to nothing that it had not already been doing, but the Baganda were clearly restricted. A major clause also added that the British could suspend the constitution and rule directly "should the kabaka, chiefs or people" be-

come "distinctly disloyal" to Her Majesty. However, the difference between stubbornness or disagreement and outright dis-
loyalty remained vague, especially in subtle matters separate
from the simple issues of political and financial relations.

Basically the agreement made Buganda a federal state
within a unitary central government. At first it seemed to afford
specific constitutional and treaty rights to the Baganda government, but, in 1926, the British Privy Council ruled that all
authority originated with the Protectorate government. Therefore, Buganda's powers, including those guaranteed in the agreement, existed only so long as the central (British) government
did not choose to use them. The 1900 Agreement meant, in effect, that the protectorate authority was complete throughout
greater Uganda. Buganda was allowed to exercise powers that
the British considered peripheral or optional, and she was permitted to reorganize her traditional institutions to carry out
these functions.

In introducing the land question during December, 1899,
Johnston had suggested that land be apportioned among the
kabaka, the royal family, the regents, the *ssaza* chiefs, the British Crown and the general population in various proportions;
Crown land was to be a reserve of forests and wastes, and a government board would administer the peasant holdings. During
the extended negotiations the Baganda chiefs succeeded in eliminating the general population and the British trusteeship plan
from the Agreement. The British were led to believe that the
chieftains were presently the owners of all land, and that peace
and prosperity were based upon their supervision of a traditional
tenantry. Johnston continued to worry about the peasantry, but
his aides and the missionaries persuaded him to preserve order
and enhance relations by yielding to the chiefs. The chiefs,
who were mostly high-ranking Bakungu from the Lukiiko, apparently knew perfectly well what they were doing: they succeeded in getting an English-style freehold, as Johnston wished,
but they convinced him that, on the basis of established tradition, their titles should be virtual provinces rather than indi-

vidually worked farms. This settlement was extremely favorable
to the Bakungu chiefs. It meant that their title was complete
and perpetual—no longer dependent upon their loyalty to the
kabaka—while, by retaining large estates, they kept control over
the peasants, who were changed from political subjects into simple tenants. This was not specified in the Agreement, of course,
but the British were persuaded that it would be wise to leave
the distribution of titles entirely to the Lukiiko. Grants were
specifically authorized for the kabaka and his family, the chief
ministers, and one thousand chiefs—a minimum of eight square
miles each—with the balance going to the Crown in trust. The
Lukiiko's decisions were subject to British approval, but the
protectorate officials preferred to allow considerable latitude
rather than interfere. In the end, grants of square-mile blocks,
known as *mailo*, were made to 3,700 chiefs—all the great
Bakungu chiefs and a substantial percentage of the more influential lesser Batongole chiefs—with each claimant receiving
area proportional to his rank or influence. The *mailo* allotments
were intended to match and to confirm existing holdings, according to the Agreement, but the Lukiiko gave first choice to
the higher ranks without regard to prior claims. The result was
a concentration of the biggest estates on the best, most convenient land, with secondary figures and smaller claimants scattered through poorer and less accessible land. There was no
provision for many of the lesser Batongole, who had to become
tenant peasants; likewise, the *bataka*, a special class that managed clan burial grounds and estates, were all but wiped out,
even though they had been the only hereditary landowners,
aside from the kabaka, in the entire Baganda system.

In the end, the *mailo* land settlement became a power
scramble that revolutionized both the structure and the function of Baganda political and economic life. Those who were
in the Lukiiko, or who held the chief posts, were men who happened by chance to have been the kabaka's most recent
appointments. Their economic position was at one stroke guaranteed forever; the kabaka lost both his primary device for en-

forcing loyalty and the only effective means for rewarding able public service. Henceforth it was virtually impossible for him to designate anyone but the established hereditary nobleman as chief of a *ssaza*. Chiefs, and the Lukiiko they controlled, felt more debt and more loyalty to the protectorate that had created their fortune than to the kabaka himself. Essentially, a dependent group that happened to be in political office at a particular moment was transformed into an independent, perpetual aristocracy.

For obvious reasons the new Baganda oligarchy became both enthusiastic about the 1900 Agreement and a loyal pro-British force within the Uganda Protectorate. Their support was well demonstrated when, between 1900 and 1907, a sleeping sickness epidemic required the British to move them away from the Lake Victoria shoreline. They understood and coöperated willingly with the medical program that was necessary. The British, who considered the oligarchy a burgeoning middle-class rather than an aristocracy, felt for many years that constitutionalism and the cultural interchange had been given a start in Buganda. The next step seemed to be an extension of the Agreement idea to other parts of the Protectorate; this was done in Toro during 1900 and Ankole in 1901. In both cases a traditional ruler was first recognized, then strengthened, so that he could be equal to the kabaka of Buganda. The land system was very different, however, because the Crown recognized no prior title or claim. Freehold gifts were made to the rulers and leading chiefs, but the general population became direct tenants-at-will under the queen. Similar settlements were imposed in the rest of the protectorate, where government rule over small tribes became virtually direct.

Telegraph service began in 1900, followed a year later by the railway to Kisumu, on the Kenya shore of Lake Victoria, about 200 miles by steamer from Buganda. The cost of imported manufactures and foodstuffs dropped rapidly, and an export trade became feasible. Indian merchants and a few European settlers arrived in advance of the railway, the former to

develop commerce and the latter to introduce extensive production of cotton. The Baganda astutely demanded high prices
from immigrants who wanted land. Kenya, after it was opened
to settlement in 1902, proved to be more attractive and accessible to most of them. Baganda peasants had taken over most
of the growing of cotton by 1907, and other provinces soon
joined in its production. Railway building, road construction
and capital-development projects attracted Indian, British and
indigenous capital for rapid development of the cotton crop and
cotton gins. Education, although left entirely to the missions
and the Lukiiko, without British government support, expanded
rapidly: by 1910 there were mission high schools, an intermedi-
ate school built by the kabaka, an industrial school under commercial sponsorship, and a teacher-training institute. Before
World War I Baganda clerks had replaced Indian and some of
the lower-ranking British clerks in government and business.
In 1909, when it was realized that the hut taxes were discouraging the construction of new homes in Buganda, a direct head
tax was substituted. As had now become customary, the reform
first introduced in Buganda was gradually extended to the other
provinces and tribes of the protectorate.

The territory east of Uganda, which the IBEA and the Foreign Office had both considered useless, came under government administration as the British East African Protectorate
(Kenya) in 1895. Work began on the Uganda Railway, connecting the Arab port and plantations of Mombasa with the interior, a year later; the five-year project, which cost £5,500,000
($26,000,000 at that time), was the largest capital project that
had ever been undertaken between South Africa and Suez. It
crossed deserts, tsetse-fly areas, and several precipitous ranges
of the Kenya Highlands. Its builders were attacked by lions, nomads stole rails to reinforce their forts, and telegraph lines were
turned into native bracelets. The railway was intended not only
to open a route to Uganda's missions and markets, but to assure British control of the upper Nile, upon which British Egypt
was totally dependent. Equally important was the desire to

exterminate slavery by undercutting it, as the Brussels Conference of 1890 had suggested; in this, the railway succeeded: Zanzibar, which supplied most of the slave porters necessary to reach the interior, abolished slavery in 1897. When the line reached Uganda, the cost of transporting a ton of goods from the coast had been cut 97 percent—from 7s6d ($1.80 then) to only 2½d ($.05).

In order to build the railway, laborers were imported from India. Many of these remained in East Africa, either as traders or as skilled laborers. Their role in the economy remained important, especially in the construction settlements that became settled cities, such as Nairobi. Their presence as the first settlers helped Europeans to realize, after the railway had already been built, that Kenya had value apart from the access to Uganda.

The land question has, if anything, been even more central in Kenya than in either Uganda or Nyasaland. Kikuyu tribes, which had settled east of Lake Victoria at least four centuries earlier, first began to occupy the fertile Highlands by 1800. The earlier, unknown inhabitants had either disappeared or been absorbed by the Bantu-speaking Kikuyu, who gradually became owners rather than tenants of the plateau's farms and forests. South of the Kikuyu, on the lower open plains that had been divided between British and German control by the 1890 Agreement, there roamed the warlike, cattle-rearing, Hamitic-speaking Masai tribes.

When the British government laid out the Uganda Railway, the route was brought through the Highlands because the Kikuyu, as settled farmers, were relatively peaceful and friendly. However, even before construction had gotten inland to their territory, the tribesmen fell prey to disease that the British and their Indian laborers had inadvertently introduced along the coast. First smallpox, then a wave of rinderpest—which destroyed the cattle—attacked the Highlands. Drought, a famine and finally locusts decimated the Kikuyu. Between 20 and 50 percent of them died, especially in the Highlands, so the reduced tribe withdrew temporarily from its prime land. Although the Kikuyu believed the land was still theirs, it appeared to be empty when the construction crews actually started to build the railway into the Highlands. At first the sole interest was in reaching Uganda, but after the railway was completed, Britain discovered that the soil and climate were favorable first for Indian, then for European settlement.

The first immigrants arrived in 1902 to stake out plantations on the vacant plateau. On the theory that all such land belonged automatically to the Crown, the British government freely granted 999-year leaseholds paralleling the railway, and valuable coffee plantations developed. Ultimately 20,000 Europeans established estates that occupied some 11,000 square miles of the best land in Kenya. However, those who could afford the £6,000 ($29,000 at the current exchange) that it cost to set up a workable plantation were precisely the people most needed in Europe itself, so Kenya was never a relief for so-called "overcrowding" at home.

Although the Kikuyu protested occupation of their property, they were forced by their economic distress to become laborers for the new plantation owners. At first, their status as tenants was a marked improvement over conditions in the lowland areas, but, as the number of tenants increased and contact with the tribal centers decreased, their position again declined.

Relations between the government and the traditional authorities became increasingly uncertain, largely because it was difficult to absorb the Kikuyu system into a larger government. Before 1902 there had been neither chiefs nor a central authority. Each *rugongo*—a mountain ridge or community—was ruled independently by a council of elders. Each *rugongo* council had a "spokesman," but he was simply a chairman or observer who had no individual authority. In affairs involving more than one *rugongo*, the councils concerned would meet and act together on the specific issue. When this happened, a merger of local sovereignties was implied, but such arrangements were always temporary. However, the British authorities were under the impression that all Africans had chieftains. The only Kikuyu who corresponded to chiefs seemed to be the *rugongo* spokesmen, so they were duly recognized and held responsible for all native affairs. In effect, the British had created chieftains who completely replaced the traditional councils. The true nature of the traditional "spokesmen" was not understood until the Highlands had already been distributed among the white immigrants. In some of the land disputes, the government tried to negotiate with and purchase claims from the traditional authorities; the spokesmen, who had no real power under Kikuyu law, either misunderstood the British or became overly ambitious.

Mission work among the interior tribes began after the European plantations had already begun to develop. Education, upon which churches in the twentieth century have put particular stress, was very appealing to the Kikuyu. However, any tribesman who attended school—even if he was not converted—adopted customs, attitudes and ambitions that automatically excluded him from participation in the traditional religious ceremonies. Since these, rather than political obedience, were the basic links among all Kikuyu, all European-educated people were ostracized. These people, cut off from their tradition, frequently were not yet Christian, but they had to depend upon European planters or urban employment for their existence. They were said to be detribalized, but only semi-Europeanized. By 1920 the Kikuyu and other Africans had become a large urban and tenant class, and only then was the severity of their problem fully recognized.

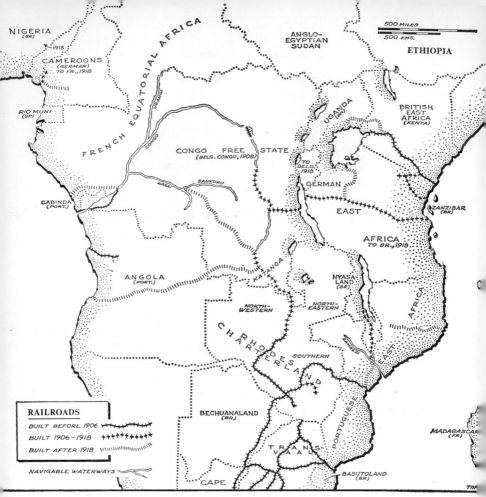

EAST AND CENTRAL AFRICA
DEVELOPMENT OF TRANSPORTATION, 1880-1940

15

EQUATORIAL EXPANSION: II

THE Heligoland Treaty of 1890 gave Britain preëminence in Kenya, but authority to the south went to the Germans. Even though Zanzibari sultans had long controlled both the coasts and trade routes, the contrast between Kenya and German East Africa soon became noticeable.

Kaiser Wilhelm II tried initially to emulate the British example of chartered company rule, which obviated both government expense and responsibility, but the German company went into bankruptcy within a year. The task of administering East Africa therefore fell to the Berlin government in 1891. The easiest and cheapest way to manage the colony seemed to be through the established Arab-Zanzibar system. Karl Peters, whose explorations and commercial efforts had led to the German claim, appeared particularly well qualified for the gubernatorial post. Assisting him were seventy German officers in the key positions. Local justice and administration for the 7,000,-000 new subjects depended almost exclusively upon the traditional Arab field agents. The government was concerned primarily with the suppression of slavery, often in conjunction with Johnston in British Central Africa, and in the extension of commerce.

German immigrants were encouraged to settle in the high

country near Mount Kilimanjaro, where 2,000,000 acres were granted in freehold. All other land, save the territory actually cultivated by various Bantu, Afroasiatic and a few Khoïsan-speaking tribes, went to the Crown. Except in the area allotted to settlers, a portion of Crown land equal to four times the current tribal farms was earmarked as a "trust" for "natives." However, the Kilimanjaro Highlands which were reserved for immigrants were also the lands upon which the tribes were most densely concentrated. It was impossible to find "trust" land in this area; indeed, in some cases, the immigrant grants even dispossessed established tribal farms. Governor Peters thought this pressure would be alleviated by the settlers' increasing demand for paid labor, but the Bantu-speaking farmers preferred to have their own holdings. Therefore, when the settlers needed laborers, the tribes had to be conscripted and forced. Discontent became serious. Large numbers of natives fled the area, starved, or rebelled openly: others were reduced to a landless laboring status.

The Arabs were an unsatisfactory foundation for the administration. Certainly they felt neither loyalty nor obligation to their alien masters. They tended to be weak or vindictive in their official tasks, and often tried to take unscrupulous or treacherous personal advantage of their power. Tribes with little German contact rebelled against the petty Arab officials, but the imperial army tended to crush this forcibly instead of correcting the abuses. Peters thereby acquired the reputation of "mkono-wa-damu"—the man with the blood-stained hands. He was indicted for cruelty in a German court, but not removed from office until 1897—five years later—when his corruption and misuse of power came to light.

Basic administrative policies were not revised until the colony had been torn by a violent uprising. The Maji-Maji revolt, which began during 1905, was a combination of several factors: resentment of the petty Arab despots, a reaction against the Arab and German inroads into tribal traditions, a protest against forced labor and taxation, and a pseudo-religious inspiration. Witches proceeded to distribute a potion that was supposed to deflect German bullets, and prophets promised a paradise to follow the destruction of the German forces. Most of the southern half of Tanganyika was involved in the insurrection, which ended only after the army burned the crops. About 120,000 tribesmen were slain, either by force or by starvation, during the course of two years.

Public opinion, as much within as outside Germany, drove the Reichstag to investigate and reform East Africa in 1907. The resulting law made native welfare the colony's fundamental concern. An ingenious codification struck a balance between German and tribal law. Every colonial official was required to attend a training school, German justices (*Bezirksamtmänner*) were stationed in each village, and a pioneer educational system was instituted. Local justice was returned to the jurisdiction of the traditional tribal councils, which were supposed to advise the *Bezirksamtman* as much as he advised them. Every adult male was guaranteed a minimum landholding of six acres; and, in order to accomplish this, money was appropriated for the repurchase or confiscation of alienated land. Forced labor could no longer be used on private estates. If conscripts were used for public works, they had to be paid. New programs for research in tropical medicine and agriculture made contributions that influenced all parts of Africa. In order to facilitate trade, communication and development, a railway was pushed from the coast to both Lakes Victoria and Tanganyika, but the work was so hastily done that complete reconstruction was necessary within a few years. Only a few of the reforms took full effect. In later years it was sometimes difficult to get the appropriations necessary to continue work already begun. It took time to recruit and to train the necessary personnel, and the territory was too large for the program, which benefited only sample areas. The outbreak of World War I thwarted most of the projects before they were far advanced, so they languished until revived or revised by postwar governments.

Not until the reform period did German influence penetrate as far inland as the strong Ruanda and Urundi kingdoms. These areas, which were both feudal and stable in structure, never were brought into the mainstream of German trade. For the most part, their established monarchs remained sovereign, except for the presence of a few advisers. They did not feel the influence of the Moslem faith of Arab traders or of Zanzibari culture.

By effectively occupying Kenya and Tanganyika after 1890, Britain and Germany had put an end to Portugal's claim to the Zenj coast. All ports north of Mozambique, jewels in the sixteenth-century Portuguese crown, had long since been lost to the Sultan of Zanzibar, from whom the new powers got them. Portuguese East Africa was thereby restricted to an area extending about 600 miles on either side of the Zambezi mouth. Only along this coast, and for about 400 miles up the river, had any remnant of Portuguese influence continued. The claim that Portuguese explorers had crossed from Angola to Mozambique via the Zambezi long before Livingstone's trek could not be proved; in any case, the territory had not been occupied, whereas the British were already moving into the interior. Only the coastal forts and the scattered half-castes' estates on the lower Zambezi qualified under international law as Portuguese territory. Nyasaland, the Rhodesias, and the coasts near Zanzibar all had gone to other European powers before the Portuguese government made any attempt either to occupy the remnants or to administer them effectively. Simple tribal authority, or the virtual sovereignty of isolated plantations, was the usual rule outside of Portugal's half-dozen crumbling forts. Between 1897 and 1902 most of the plantations were reconquered. Tribes near the British and German frontiers came under Lisbon's authority between 1896 and 1912, but parts of the coast were unoccupied until 1909. The last Arab sheiks surrendered to Portugal in 1910.

Commerce had all but ceased after the end of regular slaving in the 1850's. Arab smugglers operated into the nineties, and some slaves also went to the French planters on Réunion Island as late as the 1880's. Merchants from Goa and British India had conducted a desultory trinket trade for at least two hundred years, but only the Transvaal Railway in 1894, and the Rhodesian Railway three years later, brought capital. Even then, Mozambique's contribution was primarily one of transhipment at the port termini. There were dreams of wealth, but most of them were merely revivals of medieval legend that had borne no fruit since the sixteenth century. The colony produced barely enough basic foodstuffs for its own subsistence. The state provided a rudimentary primary education for about 0.01 percent of the population after 1870, a figure which foreign missionaries had raised to 0.04 percent by World War I. A civilian bureaucracy did not replace the military, which had ruled for four centuries, until the decade following 1900, and financial organization was postponed until the end of World War I. After 1902 Mozambique's economy and finances improved somewhat because African laborers, under contract to the Transvaal mines, paid Portuguese taxes and spent the balance of their wages in the colony.

Labor was the basic resource for both Mozambique and the Angola colony, which lay south of the Congo River on the Atlantic coast. The taking of slaves had been the main concern in both colonies until the nineteenth century. In Angola slaves were still the chief export as late as 1870. Agricultural and forest products eventually surpassed slaves in importance, primarily because slave markets were disappearing. There was no real increase in productivity, so the colony seemed to slumber. Angola, like Mozambique, became completely dependent upon Negro labor for its subsistence. The Holy Ghost Fathers began in 1865 to revive the Catholic mission work which Portugal had abandoned 250 years earlier, and Protestants first came in 1885. The religious endeavors eventually opened much of the interior, but educational achievements were hardly more noticeable in Angola than in Mozambique.

Traditionally Portugal had claimed that her policy included the civilization and absorption of Africans into the European population. The half-castes, who were supposed to be examples of such a transition, were actually much more likely to be absorbed into the African society. The government's education, mission and labor policies did nothing concrete to reverse this fact in either colony. The first significant white immigration since 1600 was the arrival of a Boer splinter-group in 1880, but these people remained in isolation until they returned to the Transvaal two generations later. Otherwise, no whites would come—despite persistent colonization propaganda—save the assigned administrators and a scattering of social renegades who quickly disappeared into African communities.

Even after British naval patrols prevented their exportation, slaves continued to be an important element in Portuguese Africa. Plantations in Mozambique used them freely; colonists, bureaucrats and the army relied on their services; sometimes there was smuggling, or the Arabs would be allowed to ply their brand of the trade. The pressure of foreign opinion and diplomacy had forced Portugal to abolish slavery in 1869, but, in practice, it merely continued under a new name. Former slaves were required to remain with their former masters, who were supposed to pay and protect them, until the "vagrancy" clause of a new Contract Service Law went into effect nine years later. Instead of buying a slave, the profiteer could buy only a "contract" for a chief's subjects. Sometimes the government would declare that all Africans in a particular district were "vagrants" unless they were under contract. In effect, this simply created an automatically renewable series of coercions: the state or an employer would seize all the paycheck to cover fines, overdue taxes or rent; when a "contract" expired, the African could either renew it or be sent back to work after an arrest for "vagrancy."

In 1899 the laws were amended to read: "All Portugal's overseas natives are morally and legally required to achieve subsistence and a betterment of their social condition by working." In order to be excused from this requirement, an African had to prove that he had either capital or a European cultural outlook. Both the government and private individuals, the law added, could "requisition" stubborn Africans. The substance of these laws was not modified until 1926.

Periodically rumors or reports of Portuguese labor conditions captured the mind of a foreign reporter. Sometimes the excitement was more fanciful or self-righteous than circumstances justified, but several protests were influential. The classic example is A Modern Slavery, which Henry Nevinson, a noted British correspondent, published in 1906. Angolans, he wrote, were forcibly drafted to work on the cocoa plantations of São Thomé Island. Both the methods of conscription and the working conditions were grimly painted. Other observers and business leaders who investigated confirmed the substance of his charges, and the Portuguese injured their own case by accusing the British of sentimental softness. Public opinion forced both European and American chocolate firms to cancel their cocoa contracts. The British Foreign Office, which gave the question particular attention for several years, reported a satisfactory improvement in conditions during the First World War.

Portugal's interest in the Congo River basin had become increasingly informal after the early contact with the Manicongo turned into slave raiding and chaos during the seventeenth century. Most later contact was directed toward the less organized Bantu-speaking people in the Angolan interior. By 1877, when Henry Morton Stanley first traversed the Congo, the Portuguese had no effective occupation and no continuing influence there. French interest in Gabon and the north bank of the Congo was revived by de Brazza's rapid treaty-making forays among the scattered Bantu-speaking tribes, but the heart of the river basin remained unclaimed. To some, it seemed forbidding or worthless; to most, it was—as the last neutral area —a region which so many wanted that none dared to touch. The great powers agreed at Berlin to let the seemingly neutral International Association into the vacuum. The only require-

ment was a guarantee of free trade along with a promise to perform the humanitarian and civilizing services to which all paid
lip service.

When Stanley returned in the year 1877 from his Congo
voyage, Leopold and the Belgian committee of the Association formed a special "Committee for Study of the Upper
Congo." Their scheme called for an international philanthropy
that would federate and civilize the Congo tribes by making
treaties with them. The Committee called it "a crusade worthy
of this century of progress." Stanley spent four years carrying
out the Committee's commission for mapping and treaty making. The results, and the philanthropic scheme, were the basis
for the Congo Free State, which was recognized at Berlin in
1885. Meanwhile the Committee had transformed itself into the
International Congo Association, a device which conveniently
separated the Belgian interests and King Leopold from the
old International Africa Association's committees in other countries.

Leopold immediately set about purchasing all the rights
which either Belgians or foreigners held in the old association.
He therefore emerged by 1886 as the sole owner of both the old
and the new associations, so he quietly abolished both the former
and its Belgian Committee. He had spent virtually all of his personal fortune, but the International Congo Association and the
Congo Free State were his private property, entirely divorced
from the Belgian government. There was, therefore, no constitutional or Parliamentary check upon his sovereignty.

The next step was active penetration, pacification and development of the Congo. Nearly all of the river is navigable year-
round, but obstacles occurred in such a manner that heavy investment was required before either goods or men could be
moved inland. Only 100 miles from the Atlantic, there begin
some 200 miles of treacherous rapids and precipitous cliffs that
block all movements to the interior. Beyond Kinshasa, which is
at the upper end of the rapids, the river is navigable for almost

1000 miles. Thereafter there are three more rapids that break the stretches of calm, safe water. In all, the river reaches 2200 miles inland, where it comes within 200 miles of Tanganyika and the Rhodesias. The river is navigable for 88 percent of its total length, but the impassable 12 percent, consisting of four widely separated series of rapids, is a major deterrent to development.

After purchasing all other interests, Leopold II had no money left for actual development in the Congo basin. The Berlin Act prohibited him from setting up a protective tariff, there were not yet any subjects to tax, and the Belgian Parliament would not give him any appropriations. The only way to raise capital or to develop the country was to grant attractive monopoly concessions. This was first done during 1886 in order to build the railway from the Atlantic around the lowest rapids inasmuch as all other development hinged upon this one ocean access. This line, from the port of Matadi to the new capital at Kinshasa (renamed Léopoldville), was not open for twelve years, but the concession system spread inland as soon as the railway plans were announced.

The usual procedure was to sell 50 percent of a monopoly's stock on the open market. Risk capital was attracted by a guaranteed monopoly over key products and by a freehold title to one-third of all land that the concessionaires could survey. Leopold automatically received a substantial franchise fee, plus the remaining 50 percent of the voting stock, as a personal gift. There were three types of concessions: the railways, the monopoly over specific products, and the inclusive regional monopoly.

In all, the Free State recognized three railways that built 395 miles of line: the main Matadi-Léopoldville line, running for 229 miles around the first rapids; a 78-mile route by-passing the second rapids, which are 1300 miles upstream; and a short branch to tap the coastal hardwood forests. Altogether, their land grants totaled 22,500,000 acres, or about eighty-eight square miles in freehold for every mile constructed. This was up to eighty times greater than similar railroad grants in the western United States.

Initially interest centered on rubber and ivory exploitation, which became a State monopoly in 1885. If Africans already occupied the forests and "continuously exploited" these resources, their rights could not be preëmpted, but an inquiry commission ruled that exploitation meant commercial sale prior to the Berlin Act. Since trade had then been confined to bartering for local use, no indigenous rights were actually recognized. All "native lands" and resources were therefore available for partition among the monopoly concessions. Companies then received by franchise the right to use, to exploit and to govern any land they could occupy. There is no way of knowing how much of the Congo Free State they actually exploited or occupied, but about 20 percent of the entire country was surveyed, and one-third of that became monopoly freeholds. The remainder technically belonged to Leopold, the owner of the Free State government.

The third form of concession included all economic and political power, as well as freehold title, to one-third of the chartered area, even if the land therein had not been surveyed. The largest such concession was the Katanga Company, which covered some 20 percent of the Congo. Without proper surveys, it was impossible to separate company freeholds from the Crown's possessions, so, after 1900, a Special Committee of the Katanga —four government members and two company—administered the politics and commerce of the area as a joint or pooled endeavor. By 1908 the concessions of all three types had acquired freehold over 11 percent of the country, surveyed about 35 percent, and exploited between 60 and 80 percent.

In addition, about 11 percent of the Congo, a continuous block near the center, was turned into the personal estate of King Leopold II. This property, which was as large as the British Isles, was in addition to his holdings as sovereign and owner of the government. Apologists called him an idealistic civilizer.[1] Critics found him vain, greedy and ruthlessly selfish.[2] One admirer,[3] admitting that Leopold was an opportunist without moral scruples, considered such qualities the mark of political greatness. In all, Leopold invested no more than $5,000,000 in Africa. Over the twenty-five-year period of his colonial rule, he received at least $20,000,000 in direct profits, 95 percent of which he spent on palaces, mistresses and propaganda in Europe. In 1908 he received an additional "gratitude fund" of $10,000,000 from the Belgian Parliament. Meanwhile Leopold also used other profits to establish the secret Neiderfulbach Foundation and other enterprises, which acquired $13,000,000 worth of speculative real estate in resort areas such as the Riviera, German spas, Belgian beaches and the French Midi. When he died in 1909, his will was probated at $80,000,000.[4] However, the precise nature of his dealings and profits is not known. His records, along with those of most concessions and of the Free State government, were destroyed before they could be investigated or audited, so the evaluation can only be indirect.

The African population was not willing to work for either the concessionaires or the king's private estate. They preferred to maintain their own farms and could not be tempted to exploit for pay the ivory and rubber resources which had been taken from them. Therefore, the Europeans said, it was their "civilizing mission" to teach Africans the value of work. "Native labor" was subsequently drafted to work for nominal wages. Inasmuch as each monopoly held both economic and political

[1] E.g., Henry Wellington Wack, *The Story of the Congo Free State*, New York, 1905.

[2] E. D. Morel, *Red Rubber*, London, 1906, passim; John Gunther, *Inside Africa*, New York, 1953, p. 655.

[3] Robert Stanley Thompson, *Fondation de l'État indépendant du Congo*, Brussels, 1933, p. 315.

[4] See: Harry H. Johnston, *George Grenfell and the Congo*, 2 vols., London, 1908, vol. I, pp. 451-452; F. Cattier, *Étude sur la situation de l'État indépendant du Congo*, (2d ed.), Brussels, 1906, pp. 216, 312, cited and analyzed by R. L. Buell, *The Native Problem in Africa*, 2 vols., New York, 1928, vol. II, pp. 432-450.

power, the labor drafts and the tax system were introduced simultaneously. Each African was required to supply goods and services in lieu of taxes. (It matters very little whether a man is paid, then taxed his full wage, or is simply drafted instead of being taxed.) Every year a typical village of about forty people had to donate four people full-time to "serve the government" —one of whom entered the military service—plus another ten people for public works or the collection of rubber and ivory. In addition, such a community had to provide a supplementary levy of five sheep, fifty chickens, 3000 pounds of corn, about 100 pounds of other vegetables, and 150 pounds of raw rubber. Villagers often had to take extra employment in order to be able to buy required items that were not produced locally. This was always true with rubber, which was a required payment even though the Europeans controlled all the rubber trees. Only after these requirements had been met could an African either tend his own farm or earn money for himself.

In the political and judicial administration of the tribal Free State, Leopold and the concessions refused to recognize the authority of any established chiefs. Every chieftain was deposed in favor of a *capità*. These were natives outside the traditional leadership clans who promised to be loyal to the Europeans. Frequently they harbored grievances against their former chiefs, and they were inevitably in competition with tradition. Since they received no European training, the *capitàs* usually had to rely upon physical terror to demonstrate their authority. The traditional tribal checks upon excessive taxation, corruption and abuse were gone. In a country without effective police or law courts, it was the *capità* who administered justice. Law was now his caprice instead of African tradition. Since tribal and social authority had been destroyed, his only effective means of enforcement was physical punishment. Murder, torture, cutting off fingers or hands, and branding were new concepts that the *capitàs* invented. Similar methods had rarely been known in Africa, where the entire body is sacred because it is needed in afterlife, and European law also forbade such ideas. The *capità* was inevitably an extremely disruptive and destructive element. He shattered the less cohesive tribes and disorganized the more stable or unified ones. Originally the *capità* idea was certainly European, but the brutality and detribalization developed because malcontents had been placed above the established customs that formerly restricted them.

In spite of the concession schemes and an unprecedented degree of exploitation, the Free State continued to have financial difficulties. The emphasis upon quick profit, rather than upon reinvestment, was a major factor. By 1891 Leopold had got permission from the Berlin powers to impose a high tariff. He tried to get money from the Belgian Parliament in 1889 by making them the beneficiaries in his will, but the Liberal government refused to make any appropriations. When by 1896 Belgian investment had become heavy, some grants-in-aid were made, but the mainstay of Congo finances continued to be concession fees and the tariff. Yields from the exploitation itself went directly to the companies or the king's private purse.

The Free State's first Governor-General was H. M. Stanley, but he resigned in 1887, shortly after the Berlin Act went into effect. Thereafter, as Leopold gained personal control of the entire International Congo Association and Free State, the mixed staff of British, Italians, Americans and others gave way to control by Belgian nationals. Zanzibar's influence continued to be strong on the upper part of the river. For many years Leopold's regional governor in that area was Tipoo Tib, formerly the manager of Arab slaving in the interior. He, his Moslem aides and their "arabized" tribal allies were more wily than willing. It was some time before slavery ceased or Europeans could penetrate the region. Tipoo Tib's followers openly defied their new masters as early as 1886, but the Congo army did not even try to oust them from control until their Great Uprising six years later.

Leopold tried to isolate the Free State and to discourage foreign travelers, but suspicion and criticism eventually developed. Sir Evelyn Baring (Lord Cromer), the proconsul of British Egypt, stimulated public concern when one of his reports discussed Belgian interests near the Nile. The Aborigines Protection Society, a liberal movement active in England since 1837, became concerned. It created a special Congo Reform Association, hired E. D. Morel to investigate, and gained support from the Liverpool Chamber of Commerce. Morel's reports, which began in 1897, attracted repeated attention in the British Parliament and in the press. Criticism and protest movements quickly appeared in the United States and on the European continent. Leopold usually disregarded the critics, though he did secure the support of loyal Belgian nationalists. Britain was accused of self-righteousness, hypocrisy and illegal interference in the internal affairs of the sovereign Free State. Some of the more sensational foreign reports were proved to be forgeries. Much of the criticism was based on abstract humanitarianism rather than fact, for the simple reason that nobody really knew what the African traditions and feelings were. However, the facts that could not be denied continued to inflame public opinion. Foreign groups justified protests on the grounds that the Berlin Act had to be enforced by the powers that signed it.

Reform agitation became strongest after Roger Casement, a British consul, made his critical report in 1903. The Foreign Office gave active diplomatic support to the demand for reform. A British Parliamentary resolution increased the pressure. Leopold appointed a commission of inquiry, whose report in 1905 failed to whitewash him. On October 18, 1908 the Belgian Parliament finally passed a law seizing the king's Free State and transforming it into the Belgian Congo.

The basic law of the new colony was embodied in the Colonial Charter. There was no objective of policy save correction of the abuses that caused the annexation to occur. The Congo was placed under Belgian sovereignty, but given a separate legal and administrative system. The charter stressed administrative machinery and economic development. Most political authority and about one-fourth of the freeholds were taken from the concessions, but their economic rights were not restricted because the colony's development depended upon continued attraction of private capital. Particular attention was given to railway extension because modern transport increased profits, reduced costs, opened new areas for development, and reduced the need for the forced porterage labor that foreigners had been criticizing. Within ten years the track mileage had nearly tripled; Lake Tanganyika, Northern Rhodesia and the newly opened Katanga mines had all been connected with the Congo steamers, and all the rapids had been by-passed. The Katanga concessions had been transformed into a government-regulated copper-mining monopoly, which established Elizabethville and several other cities. Indigenous people had worked the mines before the Europeans discovered and claimed them in 1891, but nobody developed them until the new colonial government sponsored railways and stabilized land titles in the Katanga.

Legally the Belgian Parliament was the supreme legislature. However, the colonial governor could make local ordinances that were valid for six months, and the king's ministers made permanent laws by decree. Parliament reviewed only major policy decisions, the annual colonial budget, and the granting of new concessions. After a few years the legislature ceased to bother with these matters. A Colonial Council, made up of experts rather than politicians, was created and given limited advisory powers. The unique Native Protection Commission, proposed and dominated by churchmen, existed only from 1908 to 1910.

Some of the Colonial Charter's strongest provisions concerned judicial procedure. Tribunals, with exclusive jurisdiction over all levels of justice, were to be administrated by professional lawyers totally separate from the colonial government. No tribes, parliaments, politicians or colonial executives had any authority. However, there were not nearly enough European professionals to administer both local and general law in the entire colony; Africans could not understand the concept involved; and, by 1923, law enforcement had become chaotic.

Development and stabilization were drastically disrupted by the First World War. Most of Belgium was under German rule. Foreign critics who had sparked the reform movement became Belgium's most sympathetic wartime supporters. Capital resources were cut off. All remaining energy was devoted to war production and to the assault upon German East Africa.

The aggressiveness of the Belgian development contrasted markedly with the French interests north of the Congo. French Equatorial Africa, the territory which de Brazza had secured northwest of Leopold's realm, was equally short of capital. Monopolistic forest concessions, which were also granted in this colony, created virtual anarchy and frequently disrupted both the land tenure and the life of Africans, but there were three ameliorating factors: there were forty relatively weak regional companies, rather than a powerful half dozen; the government rather than a private individual supervised them; and the original concession grants were slowly curtailed. Between 1912 and 1945, the freehold allowance was reduced to fifty acres and other monopoly activities were eventually brought under strict regulation.

In practice, relatively little consideration was given to indigenous Africans in either the French or the Belgian commercial schemes. Both powers assumed that economic development would benefit their colonial subjects. The prosperous Belgian system, ingeniously planned and highly centralized, influenced an increasing number of Africans and created an industrial complex without parallel in tropical Africa. On the other hand, the lives of French subjects, whose economic and social development was haphazard and poorly planned, were affected less regularly and less drastically.

16

THE LIBERAL JIHAD

EUROPEANS had abandoned the West African slave trade some time before 1850, but they continued to hold many of their old coastal depots. Britain, in particular, was promising to withdraw as soon as secure peace and some legitimate trade had come to the tribes with whom she had treaties. The French had abandoned most of their interests, except for a nominal control over the white settlers and associated tribes in Senegal. A few Dutch posts tried to maintain a legitimate trade, but the last of them were surrendered or sold by 1872. Denmark, Prussia, Sweden and Portugal had abandoned West Africa as soon as slaving stopped.

Neither the British nor the French were able to pursue consistent policies. Liberals did not want to assume colonial expenses and responsibilities, but they also believed in maintaining peace and free trade, honoring the obligations that tribal treaties imposed, and suppressing slavery. The European slave trade had created chaotic conditions in the interior, even though white men never penetrated beyond the coast. Rain-forest tribes who were in contact with the coastal stations had raided and traded in the savanna so effectively that the savanna's former stability, authority and prosperity had been destroyed. The sudden death of slave trading further disrupted and stifled the interior because legitimate trade was less profitable and slow to develop. The result was social upheaval, a wave of religious reform and a series of jihads or holy wars, led by despotic Moslem conquerors whose competitions for power and wealth reverberated upon the coasts. European powers began to think that they had to support their coastal allies and to pacify the trade routes by taking an active interest in the interior. Their expansion was in effect a jihad for liberalism.

France was the first power to develop direct, active and permanent inland contacts. There are several explanations for the initiative that she demonstrated after 1860: the only white settlers in West Africa were hers; the Senegal Valley produced marketable cotton which new French textile mills needed; Napoleon III deliberately sought glory and prestige to increase his popularity; and he appointed an exceptionally audacious, sagacious governor for Senegal. Moreover, only the French came face to face with the strongest savanna despots, so their hand was most directly forced.

The Fulani, who were cattle raisers dependent upon stronger societies throughout the savanna, started a social and religious revolt in 1802 that overthrew the traditional authorities in Hausaland. Eight years later the fanatic Ahmadu Lobo carried the movement westward and founded the Massina empire. Two established societies, either reacting against or imitating the Fulani, developed their own religious and political crusades. In 1838 the Tucolor Negroes on the eastern edge of Senegal had come under El Hadj Omar; by 1847 the Mandingoes, southeast of the French colony, were fighting for Samory, a Moslem commoner who had overthrown the aristocracy. Omar and his son, Ahmadu Lobo II, expanded their control rapidly toward both the Senegal and the Niger Valleys. Samory, who remained farther south, pressed against the Gambia basin and the interior. Both these empires attacked the Woloff tribes, who had treaties and traded actively with the French colonists. Napoleon III's governor, General Louis Faidherbe, proclaimed a policy of "power and powder" as soon as he arrived in 1854. Loyal Sene-

galese troops obeyed his command to defend France's Woloff
allies, upon whom the colony depended for peanut-oil production, cotton growing and a profitable trade. Faidherbe's primary concern was peaceful development within the colony and
the territory of its commercial allies, so the army tried simply
to keep Omar and Samory beyond a vague boundary. When
Faidherbe retired, his plans were well advanced, but the frontier
continued to be chaotic. By 1879 it was obvious that Samory
and Ahmadu Lobo II, Omar's successor as the Tucolor leader,
were not willing to recognize a fixed frontier. If the French did
not press the attack, the Moslem empires would soon counterattack. The French Army, chafing from the wounds of German
victory in the Franco-Prussian War eight years earlier, decided to
convert the desultory frontier wars into a conclusive victory.

Ahmadu and Samory could retreat through their territories,
which were almost 2000 miles deep, so the French spent
nineteen years and conquered most of the savanna before defeating them. Very often the Europeans were well received by
tribes whom they liberated from the predatory despots. The
long campaign was generally popular in France because it
seemed to be an excellent way of spreading culture, developing
trade and preparing for revenge against Germany—all without a
standing army to threaten the struggling civilian republic at
home. As large stretches of savanna became French, a passion
developed for railway schemes, dreams of mineral and agricultural wealth, and the prospect of a glorious Parisian civilization
stretching from Senegal across the Niger and Lake Chad to the
edge of the Nile basin.

France's advance influenced British policy and the location
of boundary lines in West Africa late in the century, but it
was not the primary cause of British expansion. Britain usually
avoided a political commitment until events forced her to make
a firm policy. Although the two powers often competed for influence, there were major differences in their problems, attitudes
and methods. For one thing, French activity was only one of
England's many concerns on the Slave and Gold Coasts.

In the latter region the only European competition had been Dutch, but their interest was sold to Britain in 1872. The Foreign Office still insisted that the government would retire as soon as trade and a stable peace had been established. However, the coastal tribes had not been allowed to form an effective confederacy and the interior Ashanti constituted a permanent threat. Ashanti expected rent for the old Dutch forts, but Britain insisted that none was due because they held title to the stations. Upon their accession, the British had misunderstood the basis for Dutch practice, including gifts and alliance help to the Ashanti. When the rent was not paid at the end of the first year, Ashanti armies moved against the British and their tribal allies, the Fanti.

The British were actively drawn into the interior during the intense fighting of 1873 and 1874. The Ashanti were defeated, but their country was not occupied. However, Her Majesty's government in 1874 decided to commit itself permanently to the defense and administration of the coastal strip, so the Gold Coast Crown Colony was created. The claim was justified by reference to the Bond of 1844, but there had been so much vacillation about it that a Royal Proclamation was also issued to resolve the legal confusion. The British had repeatedly failed to take advantage of good opportunities, such as the original Bond or the Fanti Confederacy, but had finally committed themselves to a policy that promised peace and order.

Shortly after the colony was established, the Colonial Office decided to emphasize uniformity rather than historical legality in order to administer the country. For the first time, the Fanti allies were treated like Rudyard Kipling's "lesser breeds without the law." All Africans within the colony were subject without distinction to the direct authority of Great Britain and her colonial law. However, this procedure could not be applied to the Ashanti because these former enemies remained sovereign.

Britain obviously did not understand the traditions of the Ashanti, and she was uncertain how to deal with the chiefs. The Ashanti were actually a free military federation, which small states had voluntarily entered during the eighteenth century. Without federation, Ashanti would have had either an arbitrary tyranny or a perennial civil war. Britain wanted the internal peace and commerce which federation made possible, but believed that the ashantihene (chief of the confederacy) was a conquering tyrant. The colonial authorities, who managed relations with Ashanti, thought it was their moral duty as well as military wisdom to break the federation's power. They were uncertain whether to deal with the ashantihene or to treat with each member state in order to undermine the union.

The consequences of misunderstanding are well illustrated by the issue of the Golden Stool, the symbol of confederation. The British thought it was the ashantihene's throne, similar in function to their own throne in Westminster Abbey. However, the Golden Stool symbolized the collected spirits of the Ashanti people and their ancestors. It was so sacred that the ashantihene himself would revere rather than sit upon it. It was impossible to separate the spirits collected in the Golden Stool, and equally impossible to defend the member states without the union it symbolized, so the ashantihene prepared to fight any state that tried to secede. When Britain tried to attract the weaker states into her orbit, the Ashanti repeatedly stressed the sacred and indissoluble character of their confederacy. The Golden Stool, which embodied this concept, continued to have crucial importance because the British time and again sought to destroy the union in order both to protect the coast and to reach the far interior.

An increasing number of English merchants had begun by 1890 to trade among the savanna tribes north of Ashanti. The British government had no intention of intervening in the Northern Territory, except to guarantee freedom of trade, inasmuch as the independent Ashanti straddled all the routes of communication. However, the Gold Coast army was sent north in 1895 because Samory, retreating from the French, was entering the free-trade zone. In order to prevent Samory's transit, and to forestall French conquest or loss of trade, the Northern Protectorate had to be proclaimed. The British then faced a peculiar situation: there was a coastal colony, and a government protectorate in the far interior; between them lay Ashanti, controlling all access. Every commitment that Britain made seemed to require new and more pressing policy decisions than the ones she had already made.

Within a few months Ashanti was surrounded by competing European powers. Britain's hold on the north and the coast was balanced by the French, who conquered the Ivory Coast on the western border. Finally the German government occupied the defenseless Ewe states which controlled the eastern frontier.

Germany's interest had begun with Bremen missions that were opened between the Gold Coast and the Dahoman slave stations in 1847. In 1884 the Kaiser formally annexed a forty-mile stretch of coast known as Togoland. Merchants, as well as missionaries seeking the Ewe tribes, pushed inland—much as the British were doing—and they too became apprehensive of the French advance. At first, the German government followed them more rapidly than the British had done with their merchants, so the Kaiser was able to acquire a strip behind the Gold Coast that was sixty miles wide, in addition to the extension of his original forty-mile coastal corridor. This interior annexation brought the Germans to the eastern borders of Ashanti during 1895.

Prempeh, the reigning ashantihene, became so alarmed at the annexations surrounding the confederacy that he tried to seal his frontiers. An Ashanti embassy then sailed for London to explain the ban on British transit to the north and to protest against British aid to secessionists in the confederacy. While the diplomats were still en route, the colonial governor sent an ultimatum to the ashantihene demanding (1) that the trade routes be reopened, (2) that human sacrifice be stopped, and (3) that the indemnity set in 1874 be paid. The ashantihene rejected the demands, pending the return of his London embassy; the embassy returned empty-handed; and the British army in 1896 marched to Kumasi, the Ashanti capital.

A perfunctory Treaty of Kumasi was dictated, renewing the demands for an indemnity of 50,000 ounces of gold (then equal to £205,000 or $1,000,000). The army looted the temples and shipped the ashantihene, his family and two chiefs to the coast as hostages for the indemnity. The governor's negotiators promised to accord them "due respect." A little later the British changed their minds, deposed Prempeh and forbade his return to Kumasi. Ashanti was horrified, and not a little confused. Why make the king a hostage, then depose and deport him before he could order the money to be paid?

Actually the colonial authorities had decided to break up the confederacy, to destroy the Ashanti monarchy, and to deal with the member states individually. As long as it was convenient for questions involving indemnity, trade routes and sacrifices, they treated Prempeh as though he had authority; thereafter he was no longer recognized. In effect, Britain was trying to get the advantages of a protectorate but none of the responsibilities.

In Kumasi and the other Ashanti states, the affairs of 1896 seemed to be an extortion scheme. Britain had in fact decided to solve the diplomatic question and to forestall the French or Germans by establishing her own paramountcy. Therefore, the governor was trying not to extort, but to force the Ashanti to default on the indemnity payments. He then would have an excuse for annexation.

For the next three years the British tried to find the Golden Stool so that Queen Victoria, the Protectress of Ashanti, could sit upon it. The colonial authorities failed to recognize the Stool's religious significance, but the Ashanti hid it in order to prevent such a sacrilege. In December of 1899 a small boy told Governor Sir Frederic Hodgson where it was. The British searched but failed to find it. Perhaps it had been moved, or perhaps the governor had been tricked. On a visit to the Ashanti during March, 1900, he again raised the issue.

In a public address, to the people of Kumasi, Hodgson began by revealing that the ashantihene had been deposed and exiled. Then he announced a labor-conscription program, and demanded an indemnity interest of £64,000 (then $310,000) annually—about 30 percent of the principal. Finally Governor Hodgson came to the point:

> "What must I do to the man, whoever he is, who has failed to give to the Queen, who is the paramount power in this country, the stool to which she is entitled? Where is the Golden Stool? Why am I not sitting on the Golden Stool at this moment? I am the representative of the paramount power; why have you relegated me to this chair? . . ."

The Ashanti were speechless. A war to revenge the insult to the symbol of their collective souls began three days later.

The governor and his party were besieged in the confederacy capital, but they broke out at the end of the eleventh week. Fighting continued into 1901. Prempeh, the Ashanti generals, and Yaa Asantewa (the queen-mother for whom the war is named) were transported for life to the Seychelles Islands, in the Indian Ocean. The indemnity and interest were commuted to a special tax, and the Ashanti kingdom became a crown colony, ruled directly by Great Britain after 1902.

The wave of expansion was complete. In a space of twenty-eight years British title had been established over three separate but contiguous areas: Gold Coast Colony, Ashanti Colony, and the Northern Territories Protectorate.

On the Slave Coast the European powers did not establish political authority until quite late in the nineteenth century. In Dahomey, just east of Togoland, France's former slave interests in Porto Novo and Abomey townships became a protectorate during 1882. The city of Lagos had been a British colony since 1861, and there was a Foreign Office consul among the Calabar missionaries, east of the Niger Delta, after 1882. Aside from these four points, of which the latter was not a title claim, the entire coast was a free-trade zone, under native sovereignty, until the Conference of Berlin began to function.

Commercial interest had been concentrated in the Niger Delta since 1854 because it provided a navigable access to the interior. Trade could be conducted directly from ships along the river channel and several Delta estuaries, so posts on land were not needed. When the traders did go ashore, they usually were trying to enforce their contracts and treaties with the tribes. Commercial agents and local chieftains formed a number of arbitration courts between 1854 and 1870, from Lagos through the Delta to Calabar and the Cameroons. In effect, this gave various commercial interests some degree of practical control over coastal affairs. The British consul on Fernando Po Island claimed judicial authority after 1872, but actual enforcement continued to depend upon the traders themselves. Frequently the competition among merchants from several European nations was so intense that none had the strength to defend himself or to enforce his contracts. There was inevitably an inclination toward monopolistic consolidation.

A new English merchant, G. Goldie Taubman (later Sir George Taubman Goldie), entered the Niger trade in 1877. A scion of the Isle of Man's leading family and always an outspoken atheist, he had abandoned a military career, first to live with an Arab girl on the upper Nile, then to be "compromised" into marriage by the family governess. Goldie began to manage his brother-in-law's small African trading firm, Holland Jacques and Company. Firmly convinced that material possession was the highest goal of civilization, he appears to have subordinated all social and political loyalties to the acquisition of monopoly and profit. Much of his personality and the details of his operations were hidden by his deliberate aloofness. He systematically destroyed all personal and commercial records before he died.

Within two years of his arrival in the Niger Delta, Goldie had amalgamated all major British and French enterprises into the United African Company. After he increased his strength by corporate manipulation in 1882, the enterprise became the National African Company, Ltd., but Premier Léon Gambetta of France had just begun to threaten this monopoly by investing his personal fortune in a French Equatorial Africa Company. Both companies wielded military as well as economic power, but Goldie succeeded in bankrupting and buying out Gambetta by October, 1884.

The intense struggle to build the British monopoly attracted world attention and made it easier for Germany to secure peripheral areas for herself. The British cabinet had decided as early as 1883 to establish a protectorate over the entire Niger and Cameroon coast, but insisted that the merchants, including Goldie, underwrite the expense. The National African Company was preoccupied with the destruction of its French competitor, so the government took no action. By April of 1884 the Colonial Office decided to assume the burden. E. H. Hewett left England, bearing the title of Consul at Calabar, in order to make treaties and to proclaim protectorates as he sailed along the West African coast. By July 12 he had got as far as the Niger Delta, where he was trying to annex the area before a French Consul arrived.

Hewett could not know that Count Otto von Bismarck had decided to enter the annexation race. German traders, led by a Hamburg firm, Adolph Woermann Gesellschaft, had long been active east of the delta, but they depended upon free-trade access which the monopoly-building now threatened. On May 19, 1884 Dr. Gustav Nachtigal left Europe—one month behind Hewett—with instructions to annex the West African areas that were already under German commercial influence. After a quick annexation ceremony on the short Togoland coast, he proceeded to by-pass Hewett. Originally a scientist and explorer of considerable repute, Nachtigal had now become a capable diplomatic middleman, determined to conclude with tact a protectorate agreement between Germany and King Bell's Douala tribe on the Cameroon coast. Woermann agents had already prepared the King when Nachtigal arrived on July 14. Bell had requested British annexation in 1877 but was turned down. Now he could not believe the report that a British Consul was finally coming. When Hewett did arrive on July 19, the German protectorate was already five days old. British missions, which had been in the area since 1845, and a British commercial court had to withdraw. The Consul was known henceforth as "Too Late" Hewett.

In the fall of the same year, the West African question came before the Berlin Conference. Besides partitioning the Congo, the powers gave their approval to the "effective" annexation treaties and called for free trade in the Niger-Cameroon regions. In 1885 the British Parliament ratified the Berlin Act and created the Oil Rivers Protectorate, centered at Calabar and controlling the Niger Delta. Goldie's company had made treaties with Sokoto, the leading emirate in Hausaland, and that also was recognized as part of the British sphere. In both cases the government title was nominal. Even at Calabar Mission, active administration did not begin for another six years, but Nana, chief of Jekris, was "licensed" to enforce British decrees.

Precise definition of the Anglo-German boundary was left to negotiation, which was delayed by the peculiar provision that Germany would get Mount Cameroon if Germany first bought a British mission in the foothills. The Reichstag would not spend the money, but the transfer was made in 1886 when the Basler evangelists purchased the English Baptist station. In return, Germany withdrew all claims and investments from the Niger basin.

Bismarck wanted not colonies but simply trade protection. The Cameroons therefore became a *Schutzgebiet* in which Germany maintained peace and dominated commerce. Dr. Nachtigal had specifically promised King Bell that the Doualans could continue to control interior trade, but the government had to circumvent the chieftain because the companies refused to send any agents unless they received a monopoly. Bell tried to defend Douala's position, but was defeated in a four-year war. In order to augment the revenue from tariffs, the government sold franchises for resource exploitation and for trade, but there was neither enough labor nor efficient transportation for profitable development. The monopolies were bankrupt by 1899.

Connections from the coast through the rain forest to the

interior savanna depended entirely upon Negro porters. Rubber, palm oil and cacao were developed, but they also depended upon indigenous labor. The population was scattered and the soil poorly used. There were never enough hands for the work that Germans wanted done. Negro laborers were rarely oppressed because they were scarce and indispensable. Scientific research led to hopes for agricultural and medical improvement, but little was accomplished because funds were scarce and the turnover of white personnel was too rapid.

When German mercantile expeditions reached the interior Adamawa region, about 1894, they found an agricultural Negro peasantry dependent upon Hausa rulers who were, in turn, subject to the Fulani. Nominally the entire hierarchy was obedient to Sokoto, but Britain did not attempt to stop the German advance. Islam had come to the Cameroons during the course of the Fulani uprisings in Hausaland, about 1810. Slaveownership was traditional, but the Kaiser's widely scattered agents worked to suppress it. However, their main effort was soon diverted toward the French advance which, as it moved northeastward from the Niger, began to agitate Britain and Germany as well as the Hausa in that area.

Britain's commercial domination quickly assured her political preëminence in the Delta, but the trade there depended upon free access to Hausaland. The National African Company received a monopoly charter in 1886 and became the Royal Niger Company, chartered and limited. Goldie immediately began to arrest all foreigners—a violation of the Berlin agreements. In 1889 the French navy attempted to force the Niger Delta, but was defeated by the Patani people, who were allies of the Company. The next year saw armies of the Third Republic descending the Niger, but Queen Victoria issued a Declaration of Support for Goldie's title. Two years later France decided to occupy in strength its protectorates on the Dahomey coast, and to link them with the expeditions coming down the Niger from Senegal. The isolationist Dahoman king protested the incursion, claimed sovereignty over the established protectorates, and demanded withdrawal. After more than a year of heavy fighting, during which the Dahomans used their female Amazon troops, the interior was subdued. The French armies joined hands in 1894, ready to move toward the domains of the Royal Niger Company.

Goldie sent urgently for Frederick Lugard, who had recently pacified Uganda, in order to negotiate a series of tribal treaties that would block the French invaders. The Royal Niger Company had begun to by-pass the Delta tribes, thus driving them out of business, by penetrating the middle Niger and the Benue valleys directly. Lugard's treaties successfully protected this monopoly, but the treaty-making race produced an unworkable interlacing of claims. France and Britain subsequently had to negotiate adjustments along the river in order to create reasonable boundaries. French interest turned northward to Hausaland, upon which the Goldie Company relied for trade. At the same time, Hausa slave traders periodically conducted raids or disrupted commerce along the river. During 1897 Lugard therefore led the Royal Niger Company's privately recruited army, which was in no way responsible to the British government, from the river into the grasslands of the Hausa emirates. The Moslem states were to be pacified and annexed. Some of the emirs refused to sign the Company's antislavery protectorate treaties, and the development of French interest in the area threatened to cause a war. An extensive military force seemed to be necessary. The British government joined the Company in supporting Lugard's new West African Frontier Force, which fought for both a private advantage and the balance of political power. The Frontier Force continued to receive subsidies from the imperial treasury, but the Company directed its activities without government supervision. However, when the Anglo-French agreement of 1898 established peace, the Company had to be brought under stricter regulation. Parliament and public opinion also demanded effective control and review over any forces or interests that received a government subsidy. The Royal Niger charter was therefore revoked in

1899, and a government protectorate took charge of the northern interior on January 1, 1900. The Company became a competitive enterprise known as the United Africa Company, with
Unilever being the parent holding company and Lever Brothers
the outlet for marketing palm-oil products.

The Oil Rivers Protectorate was established in 1885 to give
effect to British government claims in the Delta and on the
coast, but did not begin to function until 1891. Negro constables
and a police flotilla, subject to the Foreign Office, protected
peace and commerce. Two years later British control was extended to the interior in an effort to prevent attacks upon
friendly tribes. At the same time, the region was renamed the
Niger Coast Protectorate. Similar extension of the police power
occurred on the Benin River, some distance west of the Delta.
Traders continued to have intermittent contact with the Benin
kingdom, but in 1897 this state massacred a British embassy
mission. There were fresh reports of frequent and bloodthirsty
human sacrifices, which were a perversion of early Portuguese
slaving influences. The protectorate acted quickly to punish and
to pacify Benin, which was annexed, but the last Benin tyrants
were not caught and executed for another two years. On January 1, 1900 the coastal zones were transferred to the Colonial
Office, which renamed them "Southern Nigeria." The status of
the Lagos Colony, under direct control since 1861, was unchanged, but it was now completely surrounded by the two extensive British government protectorates.

Lake Chad was the only sector of West Africa still unclaimed at the beginning of the twentieth century. Britain,
Germany and France raced for the lake during 1900—France
from both the Niger and the Congo, the British from Nigeria,
and Germany from the Cameroonian hinterlands. All three
could then claim some of the shoreline, but Major François-
Joseph-Amédée Lamy managed, at the cost of his life, to stake
the largest share for France.

The basic outlines of the European spheres were therefore
clear by 1901. Several minor adjustments were made in later

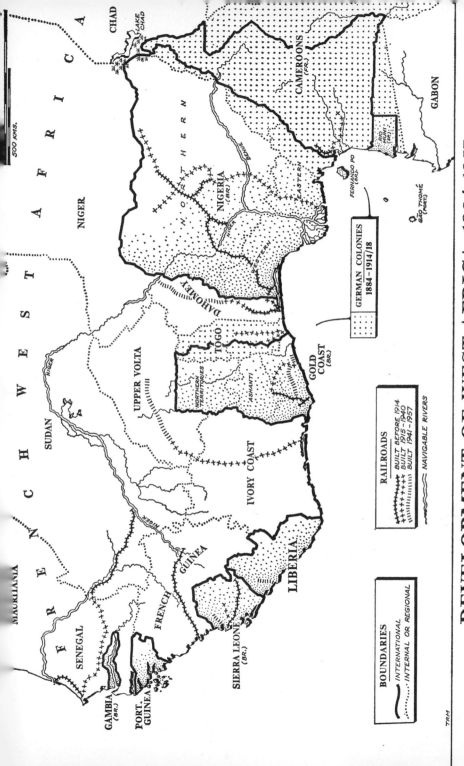

DEVELOPMENT OF WEST AFRICA, 1884-1957

CHAD

LAKE CHAD

CAMEROONS *(FR.)*

GABON

NIGER

F R E N C H

W E S T

A F R I C A

N O R T H E R N

NIGERIA *(BR.)*

EASTERN

BENUE

RIO MUNI *(SP.)*

FERNANDO PO *(SP.)*

SÃO THOMÉ *(PORT.)*

GERMAN COLONIES
1884 - 1914/18

DAHOMEY

TOGO

UPPER VOLTA

NIGER

SUDAN

NORTHERN TERRITORIES

ASHANTI

GOLD COAST *(BR.)*

MAURITANIA

IVORY COAST

GUINEA

LIBERIA

F R E N C H

SENEGAL

NIGER

SIERRA LEONE *(BR.)*

GAMBIA *(BR.)*

PORT. GUINEA

RAILROADS

+++++ *BUILT BEFORE 1914*
+++++ *BUILT 1915 - 1940*
‖‖‖‖ *BUILT 1941 - 1957*
〜〜〜 *NAVIGABLE RIVERS*

BOUNDARIES

——— *INTERNATIONAL*
········· *INTERNAL OR REGIONAL*

500 KMS.

TRM

years; some indigenous people did not come under European rule until the 1930's; but the primary concern, throughout West Africa after the turn of the century, was routine administration and peaceful development.

17

PEACE, PRESTIGE AND
THE POWERS

E UROPEAN political and economic influence predominated
throughout West Africa by the early years of the twentieth
century. Boundaries were dictated by the foreign powers' political, commercial and communication needs rather than by
ethnic or traditional factors. Tribal connections and indigenous
economic or political blocs were arbitrarily partitioned. For example, some Ewe were in British Ashanti, most in German Togo;
the Fulani-Hausa Confederacy, which was partitioned among
Germany, France and Britain, had its established trade patterns
and its social unity disrupted. New territorial divisions and six
types of European government were superimposed upon, and
enforced throughout, the area. The purpose of this chapter is to
outline the development of permanent, standardized administrative machineries in West Africa.

The administrative devices usually reflected the predilec-
tions of the respective European governments, with only an indirect relation to African conditions. French authority, which
was highly centralized, relied generally upon the tacit support
of Moslem leaders; it applied uniformly to Hausa cities, savanna
farmers and rain-forest tribes. German rule emphasized trade

protection, but tried to avoid extensive responsibilities and gave little attention to long-range theory or to local needs. Britain operated "indirectly" through the established states in the Northern Nigeria Protectorate—perhaps the most noticeable concession to tradition in all West Africa—but she ruled quite directly in her other protectorates and colonies. One exception to this was the Sierra Leone Colony, which was inhabited by the descendants of Westernized ex-slaves. Liberia was nominally independent; her approach was both unique and haphazard. Each of the six policies produced distinctive consequences.

France always intended—at least in theory—to have all colonial Africans become Frenchmen. In 1848 both the indigenous and white city-dwellers of Senegal had been given full citizenship, with representation in Paris. When other cities were conquered, similar arrangements were sometimes made. By 1895 the empire's growth caused fear that the mother country might be overwhelmed by the absorption and enfranchisement of Africans who had alien cultures and standards. The concept of "assimilation" was altered to one of "association." Those already *assimilé* retained their citizenship and passed it on to their heirs, but no new people were to be incorporated. However, an African could become "associated" if he were "*élite,*" that is, one who broke with his indigenous culture in order to meet the French educational, social and economic standards.

The separate military jurisdictions in West Africa were replaced in 1905 by a centralized civil government. The administrative ideal was a federation for unified economic and cultural development. Actually all decrees emanated from Paris to the Governor-General of French West Africa at Dakar. His direct and complete authority was executed through selected elements of the traditional African machinery; he was responsible for the protection of African landholdings from European buyers; and he directed the railway and agricultural development programs. France ruled directly, and used the colony to strengthen its own economy. The Africans were "subjects"—too "differentiated" for cultural assimilation—but the "associated" *élite* served as junior partners in continuing the transmission of culture and civilization. The theory envisioned an ultimate egalitarian identity, but in practice there was economic, social and political subordination.

In the French republic, power resided in the central government. Some of it was delegated to the Senegalese towns in 1848, where it was exercised by representative citizens' councils, though the Paris authorities retained the right of review or revocation. However, this council system was never extended beyond the assimilated townspeople until the middle of the twentieth century.

Associated and subject people had no representative institutions. French West Africa was divided into eight territories, each of which in turn contained up to twenty *cercles*. The boundaries deliberately dismembered tribes in order to discourage "separatist traditions." Each *cercle* was supervised by a French commandant and his advisory staff. They appointed the African chiefs, over whom they had direct authority, in graded ranks—at first, in three classes, but eventually in about twenty levels. Each was given a subdivision—province, canton or village—which usually was a French invention that defied the traditional tribal and cultural lines. Most of the appointees had formerly been tribal chiefs, but they found it difficult to administer the strange people and dismembered cultures that were assigned to them. In order to increase the chiefs' efficiency and effectiveness, without leaving the door open to abuse or tyranny, France reduced them to the status of virtual bureaucratic civil servants.

In the savanna the procedure was somewhat similar, although the French received strong support for their methods from the conservative Moslem theologians. European rule provided peace and order by suppressing the chaotic wars of upstart despots. After the association and differentiation policies became effective, there was no pressure to Europeanize the African subjects. France welcomed the theologians' Islamic law because it provided for territorial rather than tribal uniformity, and it commanded obedience to authority. The law made it possible for France to have peace, commerce and efficient administration; the conservative Moslems in turn were able to proselytize, and were allowed to maintain their dominion over customs and Koranic education. Christian missions were discouraged in the savanna because they displeased France's Moslem supporters and threatened social stability. Theorists have often praised the tolerance of French policy and the efficiency of the alliance with Moslem bureaucracy, theology and laws; they have described the empire as "the world's largest Moslem country." However, the alliance was a direct contradiction of the French cultural mission, and frequently served as a device for combined Franco-Moslem expansion.

France's economic ambitions were not fulfilled. The nineteenth-century investors dreamed of wealth and opportunity, but, for the most part, the savanna was dry, underpopulated, and not rich in natural resources. One plan, discussed for several years, called for an ocean channel across Tunisia. The Sahara would then be flooded, canals dug to the Niger and Congo basins, and French steamers could pass through sheltered waters from the Mediterranean to the equator. When an Italian geologist proved that the desert was above sea level, the scheme turned into a railway project. There was a protracted debate between those who wanted to survey the route and the advocates of "exploration by railway." The "explorers" would lay rails as they advanced, thus being supplied and protected without difficulty; the cost of building across unexpected obstacles would be less than the expense of a separate expedition. However, the more cautious minds prevailed, and a surveying party was sent out, only to be savagely slain by Berber warriors. When the savanna turned out to be poor country, all interest in the trans-Saharan project vanished. The tracks were never laid.

After 1900 the French government required each territory to meet its own budget. The budget was set by the *cercle* commandants and the French territorial heads. There was some difficulty in taxing the rain-forest people, but the Moslem authorities in the savanna were coöperative. Appointed chiefs received a small commission in addition to their civil-service salaries. Nominally there was an educational system—chiefs had to pass examinations in French before they could be appointed —but the local languages were forbidden. However, schools were expensive to build and staff, and they competed with the traditional Koranic centers, so few were actually built.

It has been said, perhaps justly, that racial segregation or discrimination are unknown in French Africa. Effective separation was achieved by distinctions based on territorial and cultural standards: citizens of Senegalese towns were socially and politically different from the associated or subject Africans, and the Gallicized *élite* stood apart from the indigenous culture of the masses. The French regime was in practice more concerned with efficiency than theory, and it tended to work through a selection of indigenous institutions that were adapted for direct rule.

German methods, in Togo and the Cameroons, were quite different: however, the administration was still in the development stage when the territories were lost during World War I. Count Otto von Bismarck had committed the Kaiser's government to the protection and pacification of territory acquired by German merchants, but he had consistently refused to authorize any deliberate official conquests. Togo and the Cameroons were *Schutzgebieten*—protected zones—but the initiative was left in private hands. Powerful monopoly companies were chartered to operate in and develop each protectorate, but the Togo and Cameroons companies never acquired enough capital or organization for effective activity. In retrospect, it is now obvious that nearly sovereign chartered companies had become outdated. They could not compete against powerful, organized governments, such as those of France and Britain, in the territory surrounding the German protectorates, and they were unable to provide the unity, authority and efficiency that a modern possession required. As early as 1891 Bismarck had reluctantly permitted the establishment of a native Cameroonian police corps, which was composed of Dahoman, Hausa, and Liberian Kru mercenaries. Togo and Sudanese recruits were added later, but the force was inadequate and mutinous. Units of light African militia (*Schutztruppe*) were created in 1895 to maintain order, but the German territories were only lightly protected and policed.

Germany's most persistent efforts were directed toward control of the lucrative trade between the coast and the Cameroonian interior. Doualan tribesmen had long been the intermediaries between European coastal vessels and the Fulani-Hausa entrepôt at Yaoundé (Jaunde), which lay about 125 miles inland. In the treaty which Dr. Gustav Nachtigal had made with King Bell of Douala in 1884, Germany promised to respect and protect the tribe's position. However, Bismarck's policy had given a free hand to the Hamburg merchants, who proceeded to usurp the Doualan position. Between 1891 and 1895 there was open warfare which threatened to disrupt all commercial activity. The government was forced to use its new police and militia forces in order to restore peace. Thereafter German merchants dominated the trade routes to Yaoundé.

Once the Doualans had been suppressed, the crucial problem was transportation. Caravans of African porters were essential because all transport animals succumbed to the tsetse fly. However, labor too was scarce in the underpopulated Cameroons. A railway was planned as early as 1901. Construction did not begin until 1911, and the line was not important until the French Mandate regime completed the work in 1927. Meanwhile, Yaoundé was reached by a primitive automobile road in 1913. France agreed in 1911 to allow German ships and ports on the Congo, a route which would have provided easier access to Yaoundé, but the Kaiser and his merchants had neither time nor money with which to develop this concession before the outbreak of World War I.

Labor therefore commanded a premium throughout the German period. Manpower was also in demand for the plantations which European settlers had founded on the slopes of

Mount Cameroon, northwest of Douala. Cotton could not be grown, in part because large numbers of unskilled laborers were needed for tending and harvesting. Pests frustrated the experiments with coffee. Tobacco was more successful because, though it required careful tending, its premium price attracted trained and highly paid laborers.

Plantations, like commerce, were more concerned with economic advantage than with native welfare. There was very little German propaganda concerning the "white man's burden," but the African population was carefully protected because it was scarce and valuable. Head taxes and forced labor were used, much as they were in the neighboring French territories, in order to encourage Africans to work. The most immediate consequences of German occupation were the conflicts between African tribal ideas of land tenure and the European concepts of fixed land ownership. For many years African tradition applied, but Europeans and their land claims were adjudicated in accordance with German law. The conflict was largely resolved by the creation in 1903-1907 of a uniform legal code, drawn both from African and German precedents, and applicable to all inhabitants regardless of origin.

Full political power, even on the local level, was in the hands of German colonial authorities after the chartered companies failed in 1886. Local authority was vested in the hands of those African chiefs whom the government and merchants believed to be trustworthy. German military commandants in the interior were not replaced by civilian magistrates until 1905, but two years earlier the governor had been given an Advisory Council (*Gouvernementsrat*). It was composed of Europeans —planters, missionaries, traders and colonial officials—whose influence was often considerable, but never binding. Members of the German Reichstag expressed the fear that the Council was a move toward self-government, which many of them thought should not be granted only to white settlers. There was a strong feeling in Berlin that colonial governments should be self-supporting. The Reichstag rarely granted subsidies, except on those occasions, such as East Africa in 1907, when public opinion demanded action to stamp out abuses. The colonies therefore depended for revenue upon head taxes, import duties and the sale of commercial franchises, so they were usually not able to finance extensive reforms. Development and revenue were further hampered by the fact that the mother country continued to levy duties upon the products of the African protectorates, which were legally foreign soil.

Nevertheless, the colonial governments made noticeable progress in agricultural research. In order to increase the efficiency of African labor, an educational program was instituted; indeed, the Cameroons were in 1910 the first African territory to have a compulsory attendance law. However, the emphasis was on the German language and there were not enough schools to accommodate all children.

Before war broke out in 1914, Germany showed many signs of developing a new attitude toward her colonies. There was some interest in a long-range program leading to self-government, which was countered by proposals to give the colonies some form of direct representation in the Berlin Reichstag. Education and transportation problems showed signs of being soluble. The government had become increasingly concerned with African welfare, and the Reichstag seemed somewhat more willing to authorize subsidies and public development projects. However, there were also indications of greater interest in competitive exploitation and in the direct conquest of British, French and Portuguese colonies. The prospects were thwarted in World War I by Germany's enemies, who conquered Togo and the Cameroons as well as the East and Southwest Africa protectorates.

During the first fourteen years of the twentieth century Britain's experience and administration in West Africa were distinguished by complexity, rapid changes and unique problems. There were three blocks of continuous territory but eight separate systems of government: Sierra Leone, a colony of freed slaves and a protectorate of indigenous Africans; the Gold

Coast Colony, with the Ashanti Colony and the Northern Territories Protectorate to its north; and the Niger River territories—Lagos Colony, Niger Coast Protectorate, and Northern Nigeria Protectorate. Each of these merits separate consideration.

Modern Nigeria began to emerge in 1900. On January 1 of that year the treaty rights and politico-military powers of the Royal Niger Company were transferred to the British Crown. Sir Frederick Dealtry Lugard, formerly the leading Company agent, became High Commissioner for the new protectorate. His friendship with Flora Shaw, which had begun with an exchange of news and opinions when she became colonial editor of *The Times* in 1893, soon became a romance, although they were not married until 1902. Meanwhile, in writing about her fiancé's new domains, she coined the name "Nigeria," which Parliament officially accepted as "Northern Nigeria" in order to make it clear that Lugard's authority included only a portion of Britain's interests in the Niger basin. Lady Lugard subsequently resigned her editorship in order to work with her husband in Nigeria. Poor health prevented her from remaining long in the protectorate, but she continued to advise him and began work on the first major scholarly history of the area.[1]

The annexation of Nigeria had given Britain power over more people than any single act since the conquests in India early in the nineteenth century. Lugard's task was great—perhaps, because of the proximity of foreign competition, it was unique—and it included the pacification and administration of a number of well-organized, stable savanna societies, as well as nomads and a variety of rain-forest tribes. The government's authority was based upon a number of treaties which had been inherited from the Company. Most of them conformed to a standard pattern, prepared in advance and hastily presented to the chiefs for signature when the Company had raced against

[1] *A Tropical Dependency: An Outline of the Ancient History of the Western Soudan with an Account of the Modern Settlement of Northern Nigeria*, London, 1906.

the advancing French armies to acquire spheres of influence. Some treaties were vague about boundaries. Some conflicted with treaties that France had made or with other tribal agreements that the Company had made. A number of them were not suited to the peculiarities of local political or geographical conditions. In some cases the African signatories chose simply to overlook or to discount the British altogether. A message stating that Lugard was now an agent for the government, instead of the Company, was for example completely disregarded by the Sultan of Sokoto, who was the dominant Fulani authority over the powerful Hausa states. Emirs and chieftains near the river accepted the transfer, but those who had not been under extended Company influence usually did not. Lugard could do little until 1901, when the troops who were fighting Ashanti were transferred to his command.

The first operations were aimed at the slave raiders of Kontagora and Yola. This trade was stubborn—"Na-Gwamachi," the Emir of Kontagora, defied his English captors: "Can you stop a cat from mousing? When I die I shall be found with a slave in my mouth." As late as 1904 Cameroonian prisoners were so plentiful in the Northern Nigerian slave markets that they could be bought for 1s6d to 2s (then $.36 to $.48) per head. Virtually all trading had been stopped by 1907.

Lugard's second move, during 1902, sought to secure the protectorate's frontiers against French incursions. Small states on the middle Niger welcomed the British, who released them from the tyranny of Sokoto and the Emir of Nupe, but in the Lake Chad region, a military force was needed to break the centralized, pro-French slave-trading power of Arab-ruled Bornu.

The third problem was to overcome the strong city-states that defied the British government. Some of the lesser or subordinate Hausa states welcomed the protection that Britain offered against the Fulani overlords and the inveterate slave raiders, but the Sultan of Sokoto became increasingly hostile. "Between us and you," he wrote to Lugard, "there are no dealings except as between Mussulmans and Unbelievers, War, as God Almighty has enjoined on us." The British were therefore threatened with a new jihad. However, the Hausa subjects refused to follow the Fulani into battle. Thus, Lugard's light forces were able to establish control over the northern emirates during 1903.

The British had only limited financial and manpower resources with which to administer the vast, well-organized Northern population. Most of the area was far from the Niger River, where there was transportation and where the Company had previously ruled. Lugard drew upon his experience with the protectorate machinery of Nyasaland and Uganda, which was based upon a liaison between British officials and the established African bureaucracy, but modified and elaborated upon the idea to make it more suitable for the extensive Fulani-Hausa system that already existed. The result was labeled "indirect rule." Fulani superiority was maintained, as were the Hausa language, bureaucracy, laws and judiciary. British "Residents" were placed in an advisory capacity alongside the key African emirs and administrators. By 1906 the system was functioning well enough to gain the support of the Fulani Sultan at Sokoto, who during that year augmented the British army in completing the conquest of the protectorate.

Indirect rule was designed to preserve African customary rule and to keep British responsibility at a minimum. In essence, the system merely placed Europeans alongside a revitalized Fulani aristocracy that, in turn, administered the ancient Hausa governments. High Commissioner Lugard restricted the British advisers to four fairly specific concerns:

1) Maintenance of peace. Internecine war, military raids and brigandage were forbidden, and the chief or emir of each district had to provide an adequate internal police force.

2) Reduction of tyranny and corruption. Laws were to be enforced uniformly and humanely. British residents could not intervene in internal affairs except to prevent abuse, caprice and misappropriation of funds. The established tax system was

retained, although it was subject to simplification, standardization and audit; each chief or emir paid one-fourth (later, one-
half) of the total receipts to the high commissioner, who provided modern health, transportation and public works services.

3) Reduction of trade with the neighboring French possessions. Northern Nigeria's commerce and contact had traditionally been with the savanna regions and Fulani-Hausa states
that had fallen under French rule. European partition had divided this region and erected new political and tariff barriers,
but Lugard proposed to compensate for this by opening up new
routes between the North and the outside world through the
Niger coast. The Hausa entrepôt at Kano was linked by rail
to Baro, a Niger River port, in 1911. An extension from Lagos
had already entered the Northern Protectorate a few months
earlier.

4) Suppression of the slave trade. Under the terms of indirect rule, the British army (whose Nigerian contingents were
too small for any major campaign) could not legally intervene
in internal affairs. Lugard therefore decided to kill slavery by
subtle devices that would not lead to social upheaval, economic
chaos or military action. Slavery itself was not abolished, but
slave raiding, slave trading and child enslavement were forbidden. No person born after April 1, 1901 could be enslaved;
no slaves could be bought or sold; a slave could buy his own
freedom at a fixed, moderate price; and slave-labor conditions
were rigidly regulated. Active intervention to prevent raiding
was necessary, especially in the southeast, until 1907, exactly
one hundred years after Parliament had originally forbidden
the trade; thenceforth slavery was doomed and it rapidly diminished in importance. In more recent years there were still
slaves in Nigeria, but the vestiges all but disappeared in the
progressive nationalistic fervor of the late 1950's.

Southern Nigeria in 1900 was in a position considerably
different from that of the North. Lagos had been a British colony since 1861, and portions of the delta a protectorate since
1885. Between 1891 and 1896 the Lagos Colony had acquired

a chain of formal protectorates in Yorubaland. East of Lagos the Niger Coast Protectorate was transferred on January 1, 1900 from the Foreign Office to the Colonial Office, which renamed it Southern Nigeria. The administering consul-general became a high commissioner. Concentrated efforts put an end to slaving by 1902 and established a semblance of peace by 1906. Pacification was particularly difficult east of the Niger Delta because it was necessary to deal with about five hundred sovereign Ibo villages, plus another two or three hundred autonomous communities who belonged to a dozen different language families. The British never did locate or conclude treaties with all seven or eight hundred groups, but they succeeded in reducing some of the competitive hostility and suspicion that set them one against another.

All political institutions in the colony and both coastal protectorates were under British control. Lagos Colony acquired a Legislative Council in 1862, but it was purely advisory, composed of Europeans, most of whom were colonial officials. Governors tended to obey the Council's opinion on most matters, so by 1914 their actions were subject to the "advice and consent" of the legislature. However, the Legislative Council was strictly forbidden to exercise any influence over affairs in the Lagos Protectorate. There were no advisory or legislative bodies in either that protectorate or Southern Nigeria, but the Governor of Lagos and the High Commissioner of Southern Nigeria both had officials who advised them (Executive Council). The African chiefs were responsible directly to the British chief executives. Administration through such chiefs was fairly effective in the Lagos Protectorate, but frequently chaotic in disunited Southern Nigeria. In the latter case the high commissioner tried to remedy the situation by creating two peculiar institutions: house rule (an attempt to strengthen the authority of traditional leaders), and warrant chiefs (British-appointed leaders in areas that had no effective chiefs). Neither device was as adaptable to African tradition as the government had hoped.

The Colony and Protectorate of Lagos was merged with the Southern Nigeria Protectorate on May 1, 1906. The chief executive, entitled the governor, resided in Lagos; the Legislative Council continued as before in the colony, but the new protectorate (both Yorubaland and the Delta) was administered without representative institutions. Transportation and communication were emphasized by the newly centralized administration. Lagos harbor was deepened, and a railway toward the north planned.

Both the government and private individuals became increasingly concerned about the lack of common policy in Nigerian administration. The Lagos Railway entered the Northern Protectorates at one point; the Northern authorities tried to ruin it by building their own line to a river port from which ships could sail without touching Southern Nigerian ports. Finances, public works and general services in the North and South tended to compete or to duplicate one another. Instead of aiding interdependence, each region was diverging from and contradicting the efforts of the other. E. D. Morel, a journalist and reform advocate, pointed out the limitations and dangers that might result. The Colonial Office in 1910 recommended an amalgamation of North and South, and recalled Lugard from the governorship of Hong Kong to put the plan into effect.

In 1912 Sir Frederick became the governor of both the Northern Protectorate and the Southern Protectorate and Colony. During the following year he proceeded to amalgamate the railway and to create a tariff union. On January 1, 1914 the federated Colony and Protectorate of Nigeria came into existence, with Lugard occupying the position of governor-general. The colony, which was still restricted to the city of Lagos, continued to have its Legislative Council, made up of officials (the majority), private Europeans (two), and now Africans (two). In addition, the governor-general was advised on the federal level by a Nigerian Council, which consisted of the two lieutenant-governors (one of whom administered each protectorate), officials from the Executive Council, and a minority group composed of seven British businessmen and six African chiefs. The council system did not function as effectively as its inventors had hoped, but the economic development of Nigeria was noticeably assisted by the unification plan. The plan's success was in large measure due to the personality, prestige and foresight of the governor-general. His reward was elevation during 1928 to the peerage as Baron Lugard of Abinger.

There were in Nigeria three practices that deserve mention. All African authorities, including those of the North, derived their legal authority from British royal patents rather than from native customary law. The protectorate government therefore had the right to adjudicate all disputes regarding administrative jurisdiction, and to require loyalty from the local emirates. Secondly, Europeans were barred from land ownership. Therefore, there was neither a settler class nor any fundamental change in the African customs regarding land title and sale. Finally, the responsibility for education remained with the traditional Koranic schools in the North and private Christian missions in the South.

The Gold Coast region was tranquil after the annexation of Ashanti in 1901. All three sections—Gold Coast Colony, Ashanti Colony and the Northern Territories Protectorate— were administered by one governor and an official Executive Council that sat in Accra. The first of these regions had had an advisory Legislative Council since 1850, though colonial officials continued to occupy a majority of the seats in it. The Gold Coast Colony was entirely separate from Sierra Leone after 1874, and from Lagos after 1886. One Fanti merchant had been appointed to the Legislative body in 1888. However, he was not supposed to be an "African representative." No other African appointment was made until 1925. Inasmuch as the governor was not accountable to the Legislative Council, the British believed that it should have spokesmen for every interested element rather than representatives for a cross section of public opinion. Popular feeling was usually voiced through the

private Aborigines' Rights Protection Society. Fanti chiefs and
the general population used it as their vehicle for expression,
and the government treated it as a semiofficial representative
body from 1897 to 1925. In addition, the towns of Accra,
Sekondi and Cape Coast were given Town Councils between
1896 and 1905. Half the membership of each council was
chosen in a general election; the other half was appointed
by the government.

The Ashanti Colony contrasted markedly with the Gold
Coast Colony. Since it had been conquered, instead of being
ceded by treaty, the region was administered directly in semimilitary fashion without the advice of any legislative or private
councils. British district officers were superior to and held complete authority over the indigenous chieftains. The third sector
under the jurisdiction of Accra was the Northern Territories Protectorate, wherein chiefs retained local authority but were subject to rather more check and stronger advice than was the case
in Northern Nigeria. Nevertheless, it was customary to label
the Northern Territories as an area subject to indirect instead
of direct rule. Only in the Fanti-occupied Gold Coast Colony
were there any unofficial advisory bodies; only in the North
did Britain recognize any chiefs' prerogatives.

Sierra Leone, a British possession on the Senegalese coast
nearly nine hundred miles northwest of Accra, has had a peculiar history because it was founded in the eighteenth century
by freed slaves. Negroes liberated by Lord Mansfield's decision in
England, by the American Revolution, by a West Indian uprising,
and the British antislave patrol, began to arrive in 1787. These
settlers, whom the indigenous tribes of course resented, constituted a distinct society known as the "Creoles." At first, there
was virtual self-rule: the settlers were sponsored not by the
government, but by a philanthropic company, and they elected
their own governor and magistrates. By 1808 the settlement at
Freetown had become a government colony because of three
major miscalculations in the original plans: unexpected, persistent armed resistance by the indigenous tribes; the lack of any

provision in indigenous law for the sale of land to outsiders; and the failure to realize that the presence of lush rain-forest vegetation did not guarantee success for cultivated crops. The colony was poverty-stricken, difficult to defend, and, in accordance with the custom of the time, not provided with any representative institutions. After 1811 one private Creole was regularly appointed to sit on the official Advisory Council. In 1863 this peculiar combination was broken down into the system of executive and legislative councils that one usually found in other colonies. Membership continued to be determined by appointment, rather than election, until 1924, but it always included Creoles alongside the customary official majority.

The government restricted the colony to a series of small lowland peninsulas and islands, and attempted to prevent contact with or extension into the mainland tribal areas. Smuggling, land squatting and illicit slaving were common. Not until France began to expand from Senegal into Futa Jallon did the government take an interest in the interior. By 1895, however, commercial and strategic concerns had led to a series of preference treaties which brought the indigenous chiefs into a formal protectorate. The attempt to collect a hut tax caused a general revolt three years later, but a British military victory opened the way for three major innovations in the Sierra Leone Colony and Protectorate: English land law replaced the traditional code, making it possible for Creoles to purchase and develop permanent farms; a light railway, built into the interior after 1906, increased Freetown's commercial importance and opened up productive diamond mines; and—a procedure unique in British Africa—British officials in the Protectorate were seated on the colony's Legislative Council, which acquired some degree of competence over both portions of Sierra Leone.

Creoles continued to follow European social and economic customs rather than the African, but they developed unique dialects of the English language and a distinct sense of cultural identity. Christian missions continued to be an important element, one which culminated in the establishment during 1827

of the "Christian Institution," a theological seminary in Freetown. It became Fourah Bay College in 1845, but was still a
small institution emphasizing basic classical curricula when it
was affiliated with the University of Durham thirty-one years
later. Nevertheless, it attracted students from both the Gold
and Niger coasts until 1948, when each of those areas acquired
its own university.

Although Liberia, which adjoins Sierra Leone, also originated with the resettlement of liberated slaves, its development
has contrasted considerably. Descendants of the immigrants are
known as Americo-Liberians instead of Creoles; they tended to
seek domination of the interior rather than isolation from it;
they soon acquired nominal independence instead of colonial
status; and their institutions were adaptations from the American ante-bellum South in lieu of the British models.

By 1900 there were about 10,000 descendants of the original American slaves. Outwardly they appeared to be imitations
of the Confederate planters—vast estates, traditional Protestant affiliations, and social isolation from the laboring masses
(which, in this case, were drawn from the tribal areas). Many
of their houses were reminiscent of American cotton-belt ar-
chitecture. There were about twenty indigenous tribes whom
the Americo-Liberians periodically dominated by cajolery or
force. Theoretically the government was a popular democracy
with a separation of judicial, legislative and executive powers;
in practice, a few thousand Europeanized voters governed
through a single-party "True Whig" oligarchy. Education was
entrusted to missionaries, and there was no real intelligentsia.
Capital did not exist in such a plantation society, and the Liberians were afraid to accept foreign investments. In large part
the country was able to maintain the independence it acquired
in 1847 simply by balancing one foreign power against another.
Britain granted a loan in 1871, on which Liberia later defaulted; France offered protection against the creditors, but the
United States protested. Great Britain then suggested a joint
Anglo-American protectorate, but the American isolationists

rejected the proposal. A British development company granted
another loan in 1906, and acquired control of the customs and
the "Frontier Forces." Liberia requested American aid, which
the U.S. Congress approved but the State Department rejected.
Germany, Britain, France and the United States in 1912 formed
a consortium to collect the customs duties. However, the power
bloc broke up when World War I began two years later.

Meanwhile, the four powers had long been demanding
internal reforms. Each ultimatum was answered by promises,
each financial crisis forestalled by loans from competing powers,
and each military threat thwarted by an American naval "visit."
The threat was sometimes French, sometimes tribal, and, in
1914, the *U.S.S. Chester* actually helped the Americo-Liberians
by transporting troops, munitions and supplies which were necessary to suppress a Kru revolt. Between 1917 and 1919 United
States officers commanded the Liberian army against another
uprising, and a $5,000,000 grant restored temporarily a measure
of stability. Tropical Africa's one independent nation owed its
existence more to power politics than to any nationalism, economic strength or diplomatic wisdom of her own. She was therefore as much a product of the European colonial partitions as
any of the conquered or ceded territories; indeed, her own government was less African than foreign in structure and attitude.

All of West Africa, from the Sahara to the equator, had
nominally been brought under the influence of European
powers by the beginning of the twentieth century. In the years
preceding World War I each enclave had been pacified—either
by force or by the pressure of European prestige—and the African population became part of the economic and military
reserve upon which each mother country could depend. No
longer open to free competition, West Africa had become a
series of European colonial appendages, each of them receiving
a widespread, stable and rather impersonal administrative system.

18

POVERTY AND PROSPERITY

S OUTH AFRICA in the early 1860's did not seem to be destined for rapid development or increasing prosperity. The established Cape settlements had been allowed to have a representative government, and the newer Natal colony had similarly loosened its dependence upon Great Britain. In the interior veld, two Boer republics were virtually independent, though their economies were simply agricultural and barely self-sufficient. The Suez Canal, under construction in Egypt, promised to eliminate South Africa's importance as a depot on the water route between Europe and Asia.

The Colonial Office was determined both to reduce expenses and to prevent any extension of its responsibilities. The London Missionary Society began to abandon its work on the northern Cape frontier among the Griquas, who were already protected by Ordinance 50 and would soon be eligible for individual land grants. Evangelicals and traders had transferred their attention to the Tswana or to other Bantu in Bechuanaland, beyond the British sphere, and the most intrepid Europeans had made contacts in the Zambezi basin. One LMS missionary had even established tenuous relations with the predatory Matabele, a Zulu offshoot that had crossed the Limpopo in order to avoid the Transvaal Boers. Penetrations toward Zambezia, along a route that Livingstone had blazed between the Boer republics and the Kalahari Desert, created a Missionaries'-and-Traders' Route, later known as the Great North Road.

In 1868 the South African Republic laid claim to the road and made arrangements with Portugal for free transit to Mozambique. Although Britain denied having any expansionist intentions, she insisted upon banning any other interests on the Great North Road and upon preserving the Cape-Natal monopoly over Boer trade routes. Both the republic and the Portuguese were forced to yield. Clearly Britain was still the paramount power in South Africa even though she had no desire to accept direct responsibility.

There were faint hopes of counteracting the depression which the opening of the Suez Canal was expected to cause in Southern Africa. Matabeleland and Natal were, in turn, particularly attractive to dreamers, developers and speculators.

Mzilikazi, founder and leader of the Matabele, had been succeeded by his son Lobengula. He combined effective tribal leadership with remarkable diplomatic acumen, having acquired tact and wisdom during contacts with the LMS, and seemed to have perceived that European expansion could be forestalled but not prevented.

Natal did not become a separate crown colony until 1856. Britain occupied the colony in order to thwart the trek, to protect the Bantu, and to preserve the British monopoly on South African commerce. The bureaucracy controlling Bantu and judicial affairs was distinct from the Cape's government. A few Mauritius planters straggled in, but the white population rapidly declined as the Boers trekked once more, this time toward the Transvaal. Most Boer farms fell into the hands of real-estate speculators, many of them Capetown merchants and minor officials, who in turn depended upon agents in Britain to recruit emigrant buyers.

The most ingenious of these recruiters was John Charles Byrne, the most garrulous of a long line of Irish cattle dealers, who came into contact with Cape speculators in the course of a business trip to the Australian ranches. After returning to London in 1847 he persuaded a number of shipping firms, most of them active in the Australian emigrant schemes that flourished in this period, to present his own scheme to the government's emigration board. In 1849 Byrne received a license permitting him to recruit, to select and to sell Crown land to British settlers bound for Natal. Some of the people whom he selected did not meet the government requirements for emigrant land grants, and others found that the land was not suitable for subdivision into small yeoman farms. He lost his license and speculators in Natal undersold him. When his own settlers failed to cultivate according to plan, Byrne was forced to forfeit the bonds he had posted with the colonial authorities. Bankrupted by 1851, Byrne thenceforth limited himself to Dublin cattle and the Liverpool Stock Exchange. However, he had in two years sent to Natal nearly two-thirds of its future English-speaking plantation-owning population. These settlers were quite well established by 1856, when they acquired a representative Legislative Council.

Natal's economy during the forties had been based upon wild game, ivory and some Zulu trade. The settlers of 1849-51 had hoped to produce cotton for the mills of Manchester, England, but labor problems, pestilence and lack of capital prevented development. Moreover, production costs were excessive and the fibers of Natal cotton were not suitable for the English machines. John William Colenso, who was appointed to the Anglican Bishopric of Natal in 1854, tried unsuccessfully to teach the Zulus to raise the crop. During the American Civil War, when the chief source of cotton was blockaded, Manchester was willing to adjust its mills and raise its price in order to encourage Natal's exports. However, the colony's economy was nearly destroyed when American production resumed in 1865.

Other crops were tried: coffee, which was ruined by improper soil, dry autumn winds, excessively moist summers, winter frosts, and uncontrollable borer pests; indigo, which could not compete with recently invented synthetic dyestuffs; arrowroot, for which there was very little market; and limited amounts of tobacco, fruit and flax. Sugar was overlooked for several years because it grew less rapidly in Natal than in Mauritius or Jamaica. However, the South African cane seemed to be sweeter and the soil required less fertilizer. The first small sample crop was harvested in 1849. Regular cane cultivation began in 1854, and modern processing a year later. The settlers, who had been familiar with mechanized farming in Europe, realized that similar methods could be used in the rock-free soil of Natal. Thus, their large, mechanized estates could produce as cheaply as the older island colonies that relied upon manual labor.

Although the Natal planters found that sugar, and later tea, were suitable and profitable, full development was hampered by continued marketing and labor problems. Cuba, which began centralized sugar growing in the late sixties, seized the European market. Natal's product could compete only in nearby Capetown, whose demands were limited. The inland republics became an important market in the 1880's, but they were not yet densely populated. Furthermore, the Natal railway, which was begun in 1860, did not carry beyond the coast until 1875. For wider export markets, production had to be greater, more regular and cheaper. Thus began the search for masses of cheap labor.

Neighboring Bantu, such as the Zulus, would seem to have been a logical source for hired help. However, two important factors made Bantu labor unsuitable. First, they did not understand the precise terms of a labor contract, the necessity for intensive work at harvest time, or the operation of agricultural machinery. All these qualities were essential for Natal plantation development. Furthermore, the British government since the annexation in 1843 had attempted to isolate the Bantu in order to prevent them from overrunning the Europeans. In 1846 Theophilus Shepstone (later Sir Theophilus), the Diplomatic Agent of Natal, had organized a series of Bantu reservations wherein customary law rather than European precedent would prevail. A system of magistrates, schools and agricultural development was planned for the reserves, but funds were never available. Shepstone in 1852 became Secretary for Native Affairs, a post which included supreme judicial and legislative power over all Bantu chiefs and elders. His plan preceded Lugard's system of indirect rule by fifty-four years, but it did not include the latter's important provision for native treasuries that could finance development and commerce. The Natal settlers resented the reservations, which, they believed, created a direct military threat and deprived the colony of dependent labor. The Zulus, who were not included in Shepstone's system, remained sovereign though isolated until 1897. In fact, the colony's inability to attract or to use Bantu labor was probably due to the preservation of tribal unity and the separation of Bantu institutions from European control. The tribesman was most concerned with his own lands, his own crops and family. Wage labor, at best, was only a supplemental, temporary adjunct, but the settlers needed a permanent labor force. There appears to have been an irreconcilable conflict of purpose: on one hand, protection of the Europeans and of Bantu institutions required separation; on the other, progressive Bantu development and an efficient labor supply required integration. Nevertheless, integration for labor purposes would not necessarily have aided Bantu development. In point of fact, Shepstone's reservation and separation policy remained unaltered until 1906. Labor for the sugar plantations therefore had to be found elsewhere.

Nobody had defended the Zulus more vehemently than Bishop Colenso. For such opinions and for his unusual surplice, the settlers resented him. He was also a scholar who was condemned a heretic by the Convocation of the Province of Canterbury because of his liberal writings. Colenso denied the Archbishop's authority, protested to the civil courts and won the decision in 1863. The churches in all British colonies were thereby disestablished, no longer state but rather private institutions, and the Bishop became in Natal a hero, a champion of colonial rights. Curiously, though Colenso spoke often on the Bantu behalf, he seems to have given no opinion on the importation of foreign non-European labor. Such, of course, was the only alternative to coercing Bantu, which Colenso opposed.

Individual planters in Natal had already experimented with Malayan, Chinese, Mauritian Creole and Malagasy labor. Indentured Indian labor had been used on Mauritius and in the West Indies since 1842. In earlier centuries similar people had been important in the development of Arab Zenj, the Netherlands East Indies, and southeast Asia. Natal newspapers proposed an Indian indenture system as early as 1855, and the Legislative Council approved the idea four years later. The queen, through the Cabinet in London, also assented, but the Governor-General of India ruled that the scheme was contrary to Indian public interest. The Indian government acquiesced only when Natal increased the minimum pay scale and guaranteed to give the laborers freedom after five years of bonded service and five years of free labor, plus a small land grant or return transportation.

There was supposed to be one woman for every four men indentured, but women had to be recruited among the lowest classes and the Natal planters did not want to take them. Indian labor was skilled, reliable and dependent upon the plantations. The Indian government eventually decided that indentured emigration would relieve Asia's population pressure, so it was happy to have the laborers stay in Natal. The planters had not given serious consideration to the social problems that would follow. The laborers themselves seemed unwilling to return to India, even though they were subject in Natal to racial prejudice and social upheaval. There is, moreover, good reason to believe that they would never have dared to return to the Indian cultural environment. During the outward voyage they had been crowded together and fed without regard to caste. In Natal the men were thrown together with outcaste women whom they had of necessity shared with or seduced from others. There was no marriage law for them. Often they had had to eat meat or to perform duties forbidden to their caste. Some—but not all—found Natal's free-labor wages attractive; others invested their meager savings in commerce which tied them to the new country. Most of them had abandoned or modified their religious practices; a few had become Christians. When the ten-year contracts expired most Indians elected to remain in Africa instead of returning home to an outcaste status.

Bantu labor virtually disappeared from the plantation labor force. Frequently an Indian peddler became the intermediary between Bantu reserves and the European wholesaler. Sugar cultivation gradually attracted the more sagacious or fortunate Indian farmers, though their landholdings never were as extensive in size or in number as the British estates. The Indians acquired a monopoly in the growing and ginning of cotton because English speculators, whose overhead was greater, could not compete against them. Producers in Alabama and in central India could also undersell any European planter. The white man's fortunes in Natal seemed by 1869 to be declining.

Economic depression, the LMS withdrawal, the opening of the Suez Canal (which reduced South Africa's strategic importance), Britain's reluctance to act, and Boer independence all seemed to presage the disintegration of South Africa. Gold was found at Tati, in Matabeleland, but it did not develop into a major resource. However, this discovery revived Portugal's long-dormant cupidity and increased Britain's foreign policy problems. The Griqua states, which the LMS was abandoning, were becoming not individual landholdings, as had been hoped, but a league of semitribal states under one Nicholas Waterboer. His territories clearly lay outside the British Cape Colony, but the boundary with the Orange Free State remained undemarcated. The question of sovereignty was particularly confusing along the east bank of the lower Vaal River, in Griqualand

West, inasmuch as Britain, the OFS and Waterboer had all issued title deeds in the area.

David Arnot, an attorney and self-styled empire builder, had decided in 1862 to develop and subdivide the Vaal basin, as a prelude to possible British expansion along the Great North Road. He attracted a few settlers from the eastern districts of the Cape, but the Boer and British governments alike considered him a mere nuisance. In 1867, near Hopetown in Griqualand West, a farmer's child was found playing with a diamond. Within two years several stones—one of fabulous proportions—had been found on Arnot's and Waterboer's lands. Tati gold was overshadowed and forgotten. The Orange Free State made claims reaching into Griqualand West as far as the Vaal. President M. W. Pretorius of the South African Republic blocked the Great North Road and claimed the upper Vaal basin. Waterboer and Arnot joined forces to protect their claims. Britain, however, remained powerless and silent—partly because the High Commissioner at Capetown had just retired and his replacement, Sir Henry Barkly, had not yet arrived. Furthermore, Britain had promised in the Bloemfontein Convention of 1854 that she would never make treaties or take territory in areas, such as Griqualand West, that lay beyond the Orange River.

Now there was no doubt that South Africa was destined for economic prosperity. The question was which South Africans would benefit. The SAR and Waterboer based their claims on treaties, including some which were questionable. The OFS could claim intermittent occupation. Great Britain had neither treaties nor official occupation, but her economic interest plus her policy of neutralizing the Great North Road were at stake.

If Britain had not signed the Bloemfontein Convention and abandoned the Orange River Sovereignty, there would have been no problem. If the Orange Free State claim had been recognized, English prospectors probably would have outnumbered the Boer settlers and gained control of the country. Basically Britain felt that she must either withdraw completely or take over directly—to do otherwise would invite anarchy, confusion or the intervention of another European power. British prospectors, who had already set up a Diggers' Republic in 1870 at Klipdrift on the Vaal, threatened to involve Britain and the Boers in a violent confrontation. With this in mind High Commissioner Barkly and William Keate, Lieutenant-Governor of Natal, proceeded to arrange an arbitration settlement.

Charles C. Hay, Lieutenant-Governor and acting High Commissioner at the Cape, destroyed Britain's impartial position only a few days before Barkly arrived. He did not proceed with the arbitration plans, but sent a colonial magistrate, John Campbell, to take charge of the Diggers' Republic. At Klipdrift, the Diggers' President, Safford Parker, received Campbell and recognized his authority. British policy and precedent in Griqualand had been changed, not by London or a proper High Commissioner, but by the unilateral decisions of a subordinate officer. Waterboer followed Parker in obeying Campbell, but President Sir Jan Hendrik Brand of the Free State designated his own landdrosts for the area. Barkly arrived in February, 1871, made Richard Southey his Secretary-Agent in Griqualand, and put his arbitration plan before Presidents Pretorius and Brand.

Lieutenant-Governor Keate would be the arbitrator, a proposal which pleased Pretorius because Keate had recently given the Transvaal a favorable judgment in its dispute with the Zulus. Brand would have preferred arbitration by a Continental power, but his protests were drowned when Southey suddenly proclaimed a definite British annexation. Meanwhile vast diggings were discovered well east of the Vaal, at Kopje and Vooruitzigt, during 1871. Barkly revealed his intentions by telling the Earl of Kimberley, who was Colonial Secretary in London, that peace, wealth and British paramountcy depended upon British ownership. Kopje and Vooruitzigt were already occupied, and given the name of Kimberley, when the Keate

Award was made. The republics were excluded from all the land that Arnot had staked out. The Cape Colony refused to annex Griqualand, as Kimberley had expected it to do; Capetown controlled the profitable trade routes, but did not want the administrative expense and responsibility for Griqualand West. Britain therefore assumed direct control of the diamond fields, but many Anglophobes interpreted this as evidence that the Keate Award had been engineered by London interests.

Brand, who continued to demand foreign arbitration, emerged as the Boer hero. Pretorius, in the Transvaal, was impeached from office after his Volksraad learned that he had thanked Keate for his services. In the Cape, tax and customs revenues increased rapidly as the immigrant prospectors imported machinery and supplies. By 1872 the colony had a responsible executive and a full treasury. Prosperity came indirectly to the Free State, which provided food for the dense population that settled in the semi-arid diamond country, but the Free State government did not have to worry about the serious administrative and judicial problems that Britain faced in the mining towns. The Transvaal, however, remained isolated from the new industrial complex: Keate had denied her any mines, and her farms were too far from the lucrative Kimberley market. Nevertheless, the SAR's new President, the Reverend Thomas François Burgers, was relatively liberal: he sponsored prospectors, tried to develop a railway system, reformed the currency and traveled in Europe. None of these projects was popular at home, and none of them had much effect. Burgers tried to repudiate the Keate Award, to occupy once again portions of the Great North Road and to establish authority over the Swazi tribe. Barkly thwarted or denied every such move.

Many of the Natal planters, discouraged by the long depression and pressing labor problems of the late sixties, were attracted to the diamond diggings. Those who remained in the coastal colony were able to consolidate their landholdings, to increase the importation of indentured Indians, and to become more efficient sugar producers. Natal settlers who moved to Kimberley had an advantage over other immigrants direct from Europe: they were familiar with Capetown merchants, they understood Bantu labor problems and they knew how to handle the Boer republicans. One of the prospectors from Natal, Cecil John Rhodes, systematically gained possession of all the diamond diggings and eventually acquired political as well as economic influence over most of Southern Africa. Rhodes was eighteen years old when, in 1871, he left England for Natal in order to preserve his health. Cotton growing was not profitable enough to satisfy his ambitions, which already included economic empire building, and before the end of his first year in Africa he had moved to the Griqualand diggings.

A weak heart, for which Rhodes had gone to South Africa, also caused him to seize each opportunity as though it were his last. A maniacal impatience to achieve decisively, lest death strike, gave his imaginative thoughts and bold actions a monolithic, unswervingly grandiose character that evoked the extremes of love or hate, devotion or scorn, from the men around him. Unquestionably endowed with entrepreneurial genius, Rhodes acquired the absolute loyalty of his subordinates and the respect of even his competing peers. As certain as any social Darwinist could be about the destiny of Anglo-Saxons in Africa, he waited for neither governments nor laws, but built economic and political empires which, though theoretically British, were actually his own. Rhodes' enterprises, the sole passion of his life, began to emerge from the early chaos of the Kimberley mines.

The diamond fields had been subdivided into individual claims. The separate pits were too small for efficient digging, and few prospectors could afford to buy machinery. Rhodes, who acquired capital by retailing food and equipment to the miners, began to buy up and consolidate the small claims. Although he spent part of every year at Oxford reading for his B.A., he had amalgamated most of the diggings by 1880. In partnership with Alfred Beit, another speculator, he created the old De Beers Company. A railway line from Capetown, financed by Rhodes, reached Kimberley in 1880, and an extension was begun along the Great North Road, toward the Transvaal, the Limpopo Valley, and the unchartered interior.

Meanwhile Rhodes had also entered the Cape Colony Parliament. Griqualand West and the diamond fields were transferred from the Crown to the self-governing colony in 1880. Dutch settlers within the Cape Colony benefited from and participated in the prosperity that trade, mining and railway development created. Cape-Dutch voices, led by the moderate Jan Hofmeyer, were frequently influential in policy making and Parliamentary lawmaking. Hofmeyer's followers, in closer contact with the world and more coöperative with the British than the Trekboers in the republics, became known as Afrikaners. Rhodes and Hofmeyer together seemed to be creating a society that amalgamated and built upon both the Afrikaner and the British backgrounds.

Afrikaners realized that the new attitude of political coöperation gave them freedom, pride and the incentive to develop. Hofmeyer and the Dutch Reformed Church sponsored a revival of Dutch linguistic and religious education in 1882. Six years earlier, S. J. DuToit had proposed to replace High Dutch grammar with a new written language that corresponded more closely to the Taal (dialect) that Afrikaners spoke. DuToit's language, later known as Afrikaans, offended many advocates of High Dutch, but cultural pride and political pressure brought the factions together in a Taalbond, or language league, during 1890. Hofmeyer, the church, DuToit and the High Dutch scholars had united in a movement to introduce Afrikaans in the schools. In most areas Dutch usage had so faded that children had to begin from English to learn the dialect their ancestors had spoken. Afrikaans, which was based upon the spoken dialect and had a syntax simpler than Dutch, was therefore the logical language for Afrikaners to study.

Anglo-Dutch coöperation was also evident in the diamond fields. The Free State had been denied its claim to Kimberley, but the diggers and industrialists soon became a profitable market for farm produce. Both the miners and the Boers wanted cheap labor, and both believed that the Bantu on the Zulu and the Xosa reserves were "sinfully idle." Africans were therefore brought to Kimberley in order to do the heavy tasks; presumably they would then learn the moral value of hard work. In order to prevent them from escaping or disturbing the peace of Kimberley, the recruits were required to carry special passes. Diamond smuggling and illicit diamond buying ("I.D.B.")— crimes particularly tempting to poorly paid laborers—were punishable by death. The industrialists and the Boers both believed that the regulation of "natives" was the foundation of Kimberley's reputation for order.

At the same time the introduction of large-scale mining operations created radical changes in South African life. Industrialization made the British Cape Colony more powerful than, and increasingly different from, the agricultural Boer republics. Urbanized, English-speaking immigrants outnumbered the long-established Afrikaners in the colony. The center of population shifted from the commercial ports to the interior mines. The Griqua states disappeared, and the semitribal, semi-independent Colored mixed-bloods became skilled workers in the growing Cape cities. The Bantu reserves were soon transformed from frontier problems into sources of unskilled labor for a complex economy. The African was subordinate to the white man, but British industry and Boer agriculture were competing for his manual services. The farmer wanted cheap, seasonal labor that would not live permanently in his midst, but usually could not compete with the long contracts, centralized administration and fixed resettlement that industrial labor involved. Boer ideas were markedly different from the needs of modern industry.

Formerly the British had been satisfied with the domination of trade and the strategic ports, leaving the Trekboers free upon the veld. The diamond discoveries, however, had for the first time brought the Crown into direct competition with the republics for control of the interior. Such rivalry would only increase the divisions that separated the Boers and the British. The dangers of such bitterness became obvious in 1876, when the Zulus, led by Cetewayo, revived their tribal war machine. Lord Carnarvon, the new Colonial Secretary, felt that the only solution lay in an Anglo-Boer federation that could coördinate and combine all white interests. His idea was part of a broader British dream for imperial federation of colonial possessions around the globe, but Carnarvon's greatest hopes and efforts were concentrated upon South Africa. Undoubtedly he believed that Britain could withdraw with honor from an unsavory position if the colonies and the republics became a self-governing federation.

The federation movement, sometimes described as the "Imperial Factor," had strong support among the diamond-field administrators and the English settlers in the eastern part of the Cape Colony. Natal, although seriously endangered by the Zulu uprising, appears to have been neutral. The Cape Parliament, jealous of its self-government and dependent upon the support of Afrikaner voters, was as opposed to union as the two independent republics. Federation advocates hoped for a unified South African policy toward nonwhites and toward commerce, but the three strongest governments refused to yield any prerogatives.

Carnarvon then turned to more direct methods. Colonial officials were given a majority of the seats in Natal's legislature. The Free State was given £90,000 in order to assuage the bitterness resulting from her loss of the diamond fields. By reversing decisions of the Natal courts and acts of the Cape Parliament, Carnarvon seemed to be threatening the colonies' self-governing powers. During 1876 he also sent James Anthony Froude, a loquacious historian, to propagandize both the colonies and the republics. Froude tried to turn public opinion against the Cape government and organized a Federation Conference. Carnarvon nominated the delegates to the conference, which met in London. Natal was the only state with adequate representation. Federation was not even discussed, but Carnarvon decided that his scheme could still succeed if the Transvaal were united with Natal.

President Burgers had lost the support of the Transvaal Boers. The Doppers and farmers had ceased to participate in the government; many had stopped paying taxes, and others had trekked to Angola or Bechuanaland. Burgers' plans for a railway to Portuguese Mozambique had brought him into conflict with Sekukuni, chief of the Bapedi tribe, which controlled the proposed right-of-way. Fighting ensued; the Boer commandos refused to fight for Burgers' commercial schemes; and the republic seemed near to anarchy. The British were afraid that the Bapedi would call upon the Zulus, so Theophilus Shepstone, the Native Affairs Secretary of Natal, was sent to investigate. English prospectors in the Transvaal welcomed him. Burgers accepted a secret agreement, and in April, 1877 Shepstone proclaimed the annexation of the Transvaal. Carnarvon now believed that the Zulu threat could be reduced and the confederation plan applied. Accordingly he and Shepstone both promised eventual self-government for the Transvaal. Conservative Boers soon began to chafe at the delay, which was caused primarily by the continuing Zulu threat.

Cetewayo was told to disband his *impis* by January, 1879. He disregarded the ultimatum, so a British punitive expedition departed for Zululand. While the Transvaalers met at Wonderfontein to draw up an independence covenant, the British camped at Isandhlwana, near Cetewayo's kraal. The Zulus attacked on January 22, 1879, annihilating one regiment and decimating three others.

The repercussions from Isandhlwana were extensive. The Zulu War changed from a quick police action into a protracted campaign. Logistic problems were aggravated by Natal's inability to support a permanent standing army. The colony, now defenseless, was probably saved because the overconfident Cetewayo lost both time and advantage by celebrating the victory and burying his own dead. By recommending moderation, Bishop

Colenso, whom Cetewayo usually trusted, may also have helped to forestall a Zulu massacre.

Contrary to the Boers' advice, the British dissipated both morale and manpower in subsequent skirmishes with the Zulus. Britain's most noted casualty in one foray was the French Prince Imperial ("Napoleon IV"), last of the Bonaparte line, who had taken a commission in the queen's forces. Benjamin Disraeli, then Prime Minister, remarked that the Zulus were "a very remarkable people. . . . They defeat our generals; they convert our bishops; and they have settled the fate of a great European dynasty."

After six months of cautious advance, the British captured Cetewayo and crushed the Zulus. Once Cetewayo had been imprisoned, the Boers became restless. Their primary complaint was Britain's failure to grant self-government rather than the annexation itself, but they were content to let England subdue the Zulus first. Then, with only Britain to handle, the Boers believed they could fight even better than Cetewayo had.

The Zulu War had engendered a strong reaction that helped to drive Disraeli from office. Public opinion in Britain turned against expansion, against the federation scheme, and against the Transvaal annexation. In April, 1880 William E. Gladstone came to Downing Street with an electoral mandate to withdraw British forces from both Zulu and Boer territory. However, he did not wish to give the impression of retreating before a hostile army.

A new uprising, this time among the Basutos, increased Britain's problems in South Africa. The Cape government took charge of the counterattack. Although the revolt disrupted Gladstone's plans, he did not dare to interfere with the colony's autonomy. The Boers continued to wait, but when, in December, the Basutos began to weaken, the Transvaalers assembled at Paardekraal and revived the Potchefstroom Republic. Paul Kruger, a Dopper predikant, successful rancher and veteran of every trek since 1835, led the Boers' military triumvirate. The British, who were involved in scattered skirmishes against the tribes and weakened by desertions, quickly vanished from the Transvaal. Kruger proposed an armistice, which Gladstone approved, but the British commander wanted a victory with which to strengthen his hand in negotiation. The imperial troops took Majuba Hill, overlooking the Boer camps, but Kruger's commandos stormed the heights and regained the initiative on February 27, 1881. The Transvaal's victory at Majuba Hill was later interpreted in the republics as the decisive battle in a War of Independence.

At the subsequent Convention in Pretoria Kruger pressed his advantage. He wanted full independence; his country—renamed the Transvaal State—received "complete self-government, subject to the suzerainty of Her Majesty." Britain retained control over foreign relations, and the right to restrict encroachment upon native lands. The full meaning of "suzerainty," a European feudal term ill suited to South African conditions, remained undefined. Federation and annexation were both dead issues, but the former presaged imperial expansion and the latter contributed to Boer nationalism. Subsequent history would demonstrate that South Africa could not accommodate both ambitions.

Dissident and dissatisfied factions in the Transvaal continued to trek beyond the frontier in search of new land. Religious, economic and political feelings lay behind these movements, which were particularly frequent during 1882. New republics grew up along the Great North Road—Stellaland and Goshen were the strongest of many—and there was talk of expansion toward the Zambezi and across the Kalahari. At the same time Rhodes' railway was being extended northward from Kimberley. The Cape and British governments, noticing an increase in German activity in Southwest Africa, became concerned about their access route from the diamond fields to Zambezia and Central Africa. The Transvaal, by erecting tariff barriers, threatened to disrupt South Africa's economic interdependence, upon which British paramountcy depended. President Kruger was negotiating an alliance with Stellaland and

Goshen, and openly expressed his hope of removing the limitations on his independence that were contained in the Pretoria Convention.

Anglo-Transvaal discussions opened in London early in 1884. The Earl of Derby, as Secretary of State for the Colonies, acquired Kruger's promise to eliminate the tariffs, and, by getting recognition of Britain's claim to control of the Great North Road, he thwarted the Transvaal's expansion and prevented Kruger from joining hands with the German interests. However, the price was dear. The queen could no longer veto native legislation in the Transvaal, and the country became once more the South African Republic. "Suzerainty" was omitted from the London Convention, so Kruger believed that he had acquired control of his own foreign policy.

The Boers had apparently won their War for Independence. Britain prohibited them from expanding toward the Kalahari, an area that later came under the Crown, but the Transvaal seemed to be sovereign in virtually every respect. South Africa had been effectively split, and federation was a forgotten dream.

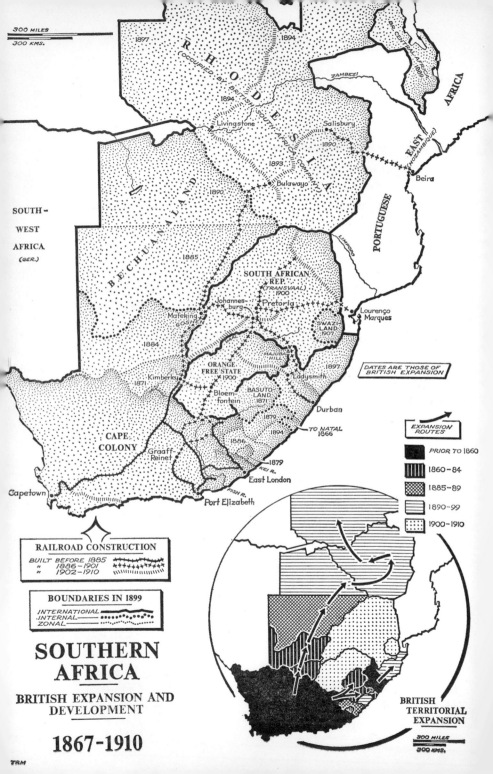

300 MILES
300 KMS.

1897

R H O D E S I A
(OCCUPIED BY BRITISH SOUTH AFRICA COMPANY)

1894

BR. CENTRAL AFRICA (1895)

EAST

AFRICA

ZAMBEZI

1894

Livingstone

Salisbury
1890

1893

Bulawayo

1890

PORTUGUESE

EAST
(MOZAMBIQUE)

Beira

SOUTH-

WEST

AFRICA

(GER.)

B E C H U A N A L A N D

1885

SOUTH AFRICAN
REP.
(TRANSVAAL)
1900

Johannes-
burg   Pretoria

Mafeking
GOSHEN

LIMPOPO

Lourenço
Marques

SWAZI-
LAND
1907

1884

1871   Kimberley

ORANGE
FREE STATE
1900

Bloem-
fontein

MAJUBA
HILL

BASUTO-
LAND
1871

1897

Ladysmith

Durban

DRAN

1879

1894

TO NATAL
1866

CAPE
COLONY

Graaff-
Reinet

1886

KEI R.

1879

East London

DATES ARE THOSE OF
BRITISH EXPANSION

EXPANSION
ROUTES

Capetown

FISH R.

Port Elizabeth

PRIOR TO 1860

1860-84

1885-89

1890-99

1900-1910

RAILROAD CONSTRUCTION

BUILT BEFORE 1885
"   1886-1901
"   1902-1910

BOUNDARIES IN 1899

INTERNATIONAL
INTERNAL
ZONAL

SOUTHERN
AFRICA

BRITISH EXPANSION AND
DEVELOPMENT

1867-1910

BRITISH
TERRITORIAL
EXPANSION

300 MILES
300 KMS.

TRM

19

GOLD AND EMPIRE

B Y 1886 all the territory south of Portuguese Angola and
Mozambique had been partitioned. The scramble had
started two years earlier when Bismarck annexed Southwest
Africa to the German Empire. South Africa's only unclaimed
ports, at St. Lucia Bay north of Durban, were added to the Natal
Colony later in 1884 in order to prevent either Kruger or the
Germans from seizing them. The Cape acquired all the independent Bantu chiefdoms between Albany Bay and Natal. Boer
trekkers tried to organize a "New Republic" inside Zululand,
but Britain established formal rule through the Natal government in 1887. Two years earlier, when Cecil Rhodes was acting
as the Crown representative in carrying out the London Convention, he had raised the Union Jack in the southern half of
Bechuanaland. Basically, however, the pattern for South Africa
had been determined in 1884 at the London Conference: Britain
would control all ports and the Great North Road; the Boers
would be independent but landlocked; and the Germans would
not be allowed to acquire any land that adjoined a Boer republic.

The position of the South African Republic continued to be
precarious. Her government's revenues were meager. She was essentially agrarian, withdrawn from modern religious and political
ideas, sparsely populated and lacking either railways or water

routes to transport her products. President Kruger thought that Hofmeyer's moderate Afrikanerbond, in the Cape Colony, was too willing to compromise with British politicians and Scottish churches. He also shunned the Afrikaans-language movement, fearing that it too would modify the established High Dutch tradition. Ties with the Free State, which profited from trade with Kimberley and accepted liberal immigrants, were weakening. This neighbor seemed gradually to be joining the British Cape and Bantu-inhabited Bechuanaland in reaping the benefits of economic development.

Increasingly Rhodes and his agents were becoming the dominant power in South Africa. By 1880 Rhodes was the largest diamond producer and the sponsor of railways that transported Free State produce and threatened to by-pass the Transvaal. He was also an increasingly powerful member of the Cape Parliament. A political alliance with Hofmeyer helped him to become Prime Minister at Capetown in 1890. Kruger and the Transvaal recognized and resented this combination of political and economic power. Rhodes' preëminence in Bechuanaland was established by 1885, and his "British South Africa Company" began four years later to push northward to the Zambezi. In 1890 he acquired his partner's interest in the diamond fields and bought out his greatest competitor, Barney Barnato. Rhodes' new corporation, the De Beers Consolidated Mines, Ltd., had already begun to combine all the Kimberley claims and to transform the diggings into one vast, mechanized open-pit mine. Thereafter De Beers controlled diamond production and diamond pricing throughout the world. Nothing illustrates Rhodes' strength more clearly than the fact that his personal income for 1885-86 was greater than the total revenues of the South African Republic.

In 1886 the republic's position and its problems changed radically. Gold was discovered in the hills of Witwatersrand. Johannesburg, established in September, became South Africa's second great mining camp. Prospectors immigrated. Capital followed, and big business soon developed. The "Rand" became the metropolis of a country that had never had cities. Policing, the registration of land titles, customs and immigration policies had to be devised for a nation that had neither experience nor interest in these matters. Within two years the Transvaal revenues had nearly quadrupled; by 1889 they were up 900 percent, and a decade later, 2400 percent. Kruger and the Transvaal Volksraad (Parliament), who considered the strike a mixed blessing, used its revenue and prestige for political advantage. At the same time they hoped the gold rush would be temporary. The agrarian Boers, who continued to prefer isolation and simplicity, rarely mixed with the prospectors and laborers. Kruger also hoped to regulate and dominate the industry by controlling a vital step in production, so the importation, manufacture and distribution of dynamite became a government monopoly. Miners protested the high prices, but the State made a profit.

Cecil Rhodes invested in the Transvaal mines but did not even acquire a majority interest. He envisioned an empire in South and Central Africa based upon the diamond-endowed Cape. Gold had strengthened the Transvaal's independent position, which threatened the Great North Road and opposed the Anglo-Boer coöperation that Rhodes depended upon. In 1892 —two years after he began to head the Cape government—he organized the National Union Movement in order to confirm his political alliance with Hofmeyer and the Cape Afrikaners. The interior republics, now independently wealthy, resented the industrial, political and cultural implications that such a fusion represented. The independent Boer viewpoint became increasingly different from that of the Afrikaners, who remained on British soil.

Rhodes' interest in the Great North Road had been protected first by the Convention of London, which in 1884 blocked the Transvaal's westward expansion, and then by the Crown's proclamation of a protectorate over southern Bechuanaland during the following year. The railway pressed northward from Kimberley, skirting the western border of the booming Transvaal, and simplifying communications between the Cape and the Zambezi watershed. In the latter area the Bantu-speaking people were still feeling the effects of the Zulu migrations (Ngoni and Matabele) earlier in the nineteenth century. Northeast of the Transvaal the Shona tribes had been dispersed from Zimbabwe and thrown into disorder by the Ngoni invasions of 1835. The Matabele, who had carved a homeland northwest of the Transvaal, preyed upon the Shona from time to time and contributed to their chaos.

Mzilikazi, the rebellious Zulu warrior who had created the Matabele nation, died in 1878. Occasionally he had dealt with pioneer traders and negotiated with LMS missionaries, but his rule had continued to be cunning, absolute and sometimes capricious. The gold mines at Tati, which had attracted some European prospectors in the 1860's, were almost forgotten during the rush for Kimberley. Mzilikazi exasperated the missionaries, and the LMS had virtually collapsed. New approaches by the Scottish and Paris evangelical societies were directed toward tribes farther north. The Matabele dealt largely with traders after 1870, and after 1880 they were subject to the rule of Mzilikazi's wiliest son, Lobengula.

Although he tried to avoid offending his older brother, the legal heir whom Mzilikazi had exiled, Lobengula was virtually drafted into the chieftaincy. He was as capricious and as absolute as his father had been. Missionaries had to petition his permission to transit the Matabele country, and traders were forced to pay obeisance. Entry into the Shona territory was subject to his approval, even though he did not exercise systematic sovereignty over it. The boundaries by which Lobengula defined his own area (Matabeleland) and the Shona reserve (Mashonaland) have been maintained in modern Rhodesia. Many visitors at his court in Bulawayo were impressed with his stately, if portly, carriage; others were more struck with his indiscriminate, cruel application of complete authority.

In 1887 Lobengula granted virtual autonomy to the gold diggers at Tati and recognized their right to travel at will along the Great North Road. Before year's end Rhodes was informed that Piet Grobler from the Transvaal had concluded an alliance with the Matabele chieftain. Lobengula later pleaded that he did not understand the treaty terms, and the British believed that Grobler had violated the London Convention. The treaty was therefore illegal, but it is important because it demonstrates the interest that Matabeleland was attracting and because it excited Rhodes' own ambition and possessiveness. Early in 1888 the Bechuanaland Protectorate agent, John Moffat, acceded to Rhodes' demands and negotiated another treaty with Lobengula. Britain thereby acquired not a protectorate but the right to veto all agreements that the Matabele might make with any foreign power. Lobengula was inexorably coming under European influence, carefully though he tried to maneuver his own power.

Rhodes began to lose patience with the Crown's relatively cautious attitude toward expansion. Late in 1888 he sent his agents, including an old Oxford acquaintance named Charles Dunnell Rudd, to negotiate an agreement at Bulawayo. Many European syndicates were seeking privileges at the chief's court, but Rudd's proposal was simple and sweeping. Lobengula received arms, a pension and a steamboat for the Zambezi, and he was protected from the confusion caused by numerous privilege seekers; Rhodes acquired a monopoly over all mineral resources in Matabeleland. The Rudd Concession, which the Crown approved, immediately became the basis for British domination north of the Transvaal. The expanding force, however, was a private company with political power, not a European government. Rhodes now had to keep the chieftain contented, and to charter and capitalize a company to exploit the concession. To manage and impress Lobengula, he chose his smooth-tongued physician in Kimberley, Dr. Leander Starr Jameson; to acquire the charter, he had to defeat those who advocated government-sponsored conquest and the direct, humanitarian protection of indigenous tribes. People who feared any possibility of an increase in government expense or responsibility also opposed him. Rhodes sided with the opponents of government imperialism—those who believed that "progress" was the combination of "philanthropy" and a "5 percent" dividend.

The charter of the British South Africa Company, as issued in October, 1889, included commercial and political powers. The BSA Company would control mining, trade, immigration and communication; it would also provide police and a legal system. Rhodes had appeased the Crown by offering to pay for telegraph lines within the Cape Colony that would connect with the company wires and railways running along the Great North Road, and he promised to contribute toward the expenses of the Crown representative in Bulawayo. The government also took two seats on the Board of Directors, required fair compensation for the rights of rival firms, and made the charter contingent upon Lobengula's free consent.

The last requirement was difficult to meet. The chief had repudiated the Rudd Concession. Portugal revived its sixteenth-century claims in Mashonaland, but the British Foreign Office issued an ultimatum that Lisbon respected. Only the Transvaal remained to question Rhodes' new power. Leaving Lobengula's stubbornness unassuaged for the moment, the chartered company negotiated with Kruger, who was now most concerned with his eastern frontier. Zululand had been partitioned—most of the Bantu tribesmen were now "protected" by British Natal, and the Boer "New Republic" was incorporated into the Transvaal—but the Swazi people were still independent. Kruger wanted to build a railway from the Rand goldfields across Swaziland to the Portuguese harbor at Lourenço Marques. Rhodes, concerned for the north, for the prosperity of his own railways, and, by the terms of his charter, for ancillary concessions in Swaziland, was directly involved. The Crown represented the Cape and Natal, whose ports and tariffs would be by-passed by Kruger's railway. Britain was willing to give the Transvaal limited rights in Swaziland if Kruger's railway would go to Natal. Rhodes tried to buy the Portuguese harbor and, with Britain, forced Kruger to accept a customs union. The negotiations continued intermittently until 1893. By then the railway from Cape-town had reached Johannesburg. Kruger was finally allowed to establish a protectorate over Swaziland and to build his railway to Lourenço Marques in Portuguese Mozambique. Rhodes' interest in Swaziland may well have been a feint, for it had now declined—Bechuanaland, Matabeleland and mining prospects were more immediate concerns.

The British South Africa Company had already hastened to exercise its chartered rights. Dr. Jameson humored the stubborn Lobengula, supported him when he complained about the Portuguese, and ultimately persuaded the chief that Rhodes' Company was the best alternative to choose. Early in 1890 Lobengula told Jameson that digging would be allowed "in one hole." Jameson hurried south, and six days later Rhodes announced that occupation of the entire country had been authorized. The government, believing Rhodes, assumed that Lobengula had ratified the charter. Jameson returned to Bulawayo in order to placate the chief, and the Crown granted full recognition to the Company. On June 27, 1890 two hundred carefully selected "Pioneers" entered Matabeleland in search of gold and land. Lobengula asked why two hundred men were needed to "dig in one hole." When he also wondered why there were five hundred Company police to accompany the Pioneers, Jameson pointed to the necessity for defense against the Boers, Portugal and "anyone else." Rightly interpreting this as a threat to his power, Lobengula protested to the queen, but yielded diplomatically instead of fighting. The Pioneers passed well south and east of Bulawayo, across rough terrain, in an orderly and steady march from Bechuanaland to Mashonaland. On September 12 they reached the base of Mount Hampden. Salisbury was founded, and each man received a land grant of 3,165 acres.

Company agents had also been busy farther north while the Pioneers were beating their road. In June the well-organized Barotse tribe, northwest of Victoria Falls, had signed a treaty. Boundary agreements were concluded with Germany and Portugal during July and August. The Company and the Congo

Free State raced for, and ultimately partitioned, the Katanga-Rhodesia copper belt. Harry Johnston negotiated treaties on the shores of Lake Nyasa, and the commerce in that area came temporarily under Rhodes' control. After the Pioneers had settled they found most smaller tribes willing to accept the Company's offer of protection against the Matabele and the Portuguese. By April 13, 1891 the High Commissioner at Capetown could proclaim the existence of an effective British sphere of influence wherein power was exercised by the Chartered Company. Dr. Jameson subsequently became Chief Magistrate, ruling for Rhodes but subject to the queen's "sufferance."

The Cape Colony, Bechuanaland and Rhodes' Charterland —northward to the Congo and Lake Tanganyika—were now under the diamond magnate's firm political or economic control. Nevertheless, there were questions: how to establish legal jurisdiction in the Company territory once it became known that Lobengula had not officially ceded authority? how to organize and administer territory within the structure of a profit-making corporation? how to acquire direct power and a railway grant in Bechuanaland, which was officially a protectorate guaranteeing the integrity of Bantu states? and, how to increase Company influence within the stubborn Transvaal?

The answer to the first question came during 1893. Matabele *impis* continued to raid in Mashonaland, even after Jameson had become the Company Administrator as well as the legal Chief Magistrate. European cattle were stolen. Mashona employees on the Pioneers' plantations were attacked. Company police at Fort Victoria gave sanctuary to many Mashona. Jameson ordered the *impis* back toward Bulawayo. Lobengula insisted there was no boundary separating his tribe from the Mashona. Jameson, the Pioneers, and the Company police prepared for war. Negotiations through intermediary messengers continued. On one occasion Lobengula's emissaries, imprisoned on a suspicion of espionage, apparently panicked. The Company guard slew two of the messengers, and the Matabele War ensued.

Jameson moved quickly because the rainy season was imminent. A few of the newly invented machine guns shattered the Matabele at Shangani. Bulawayo fell and Lobengula fled, but by trapping and annihilating a gallant Company reconnaissance patrol he created a major legend in the annals of white settlement. Before Christmas Lobengula was mired in the rains near Victoria Falls, and early in 1894 he succumbed to smallpox. It will never be known whether he died proud or bitter, defiant or disillusioned. Matabeleland, by virtue of conquest and royal death, was now legally a province within the Rhodes Company Charterland.

Capitalizing and executing the company charter had been hardly less spectacular than the conquest and settlement itself. The Rudd Concession of 1888 served as Rhodes' initial cornerstone, but it remained distinct from the British South Africa Company that later emerged. The Rudd privileges were consolidated with other concessions by the Central Search Association, which also sponsored the charter application. The BSA Company was to operate the Central Search concessions in return for 50 percent of the profits. The latter firm reorganized itself into the United Concessions Company and proceeded to recapitalize itself at £4,000,000. The BSA, capitalized at £1,000,-000, secretly agreed to absorb the United Concessions. Since this would have given four-fifths of the merged stock to the concessionaires, the BSA's shareholders became alarmed. Rhodes cut expenses by reducing the strength of Company police, and he borrowed from De Beers in order to finance the administration in Mashonaland. The conquest of Matabeleland in 1893 improved his bargaining position because the rebellious shareholders believed there would be gold in the ground under Bulawayo. The Company floated bonds to pay for the conquest and postponed the merger plan to 1896.

Within the Charterland Jameson proceeded to administer justice, to establish order and to assign land for settlement. Nominally his authority extended from the Transvaal border to Lake Tanganyika, but it was effective only in Matabeleland and

Mashonaland, below the Zambezi. His police grew stronger. Concessions were prospected, but the yields proved disappointing. The Bechuanaland Railway raised new capital and pushed northward. In May of 1895 the BSA Company proudly gave the name "Rhodesia" to its Charterland.

Bechuanaland remained a problem that Rhodes could never solve to his complete satisfaction. Portions of it as far north as Mafeking, 222 miles beyond Kimberley, were incorporated into the Cape Colony in 1895. The greater portion, however, remained a Protectorate under the British Crown. Two years later the Bechuanaland Railway reached Bulawayo. Rhodes dreamed of extending it northward to Lake Tanganyika—perhaps to Uganda, and even to Cairo—but the line did not even reach the Zambezi during his lifetime. The Bechuanaland section continued to be the weakest link in Rhodes' basic network because it was always a tenant-at-will upon Crown land in the protectorate. However, the government remained sympathetic throughout the period of Company rule in Rhodesia, and the Company even acquired the right to station and move its private militia along the line without serious interference.

The Transvaal continued to be the primary obstacle to Rhodes' scheme for Anglo-Boer coöperation. The Consolidated Goldfields of South Africa, Ltd., belonged to him, but it could not acquire a monopoly on the Rand. By controlling the dynamite supply, Kruger continued to hold the mining enterprises in a state of sufferance. In 1894 the long-sought outlet through Portuguese Mozambique was opened: the Nederlands Railway, linking Johannesburg with Lourenço Marques, eliminated the Transvaal's dependence upon British ports and Rhodes' railways.

Rhodes nevertheless continued to press for South African federation. Piecemeal attempts at educational, judicial, or tariff union had all failed. As the Cape Prime Minister, he attempted to induce joint policy toward the "natives" by reducing tenants' rights and increasing the property qualification for voting. Such moves pleased the Afrikaners but failed to soften the republics' defiance. The tightening of control over Bantu reserves was supposed to appeal to the Boers, but they interpreted it as a sign of an imperial greed for territory that also threatened them.

The Transvaal also became increasingly apprehensive about the numerous immigrants who flocked to the Rand. Kruger doubted their loyalty and suspected their political intentions. On the other hand, Rhodes began to think of them as potential instruments for achieving his own ends. The Boers had gradually devised legislation and enforcement suitable for the booming settlements, and had warily but sensibly negotiated many laws and provisions with the Witwatersrand (later Transvaal) Chamber of Mines, which represented the foreign investors. Immigrant miners, laborers and investors paid nearly all the taxes and earned most of the foreign exchange; and by 1895 they outnumbered the Boers two to one. However, being foreigners ("Uitlanders"), they had no franchise, no voice in the making of Transvaal policy.

Immigrants had formerly voted after one year of residence; the requirement was increased to five years in 1882, and fourteen in 1890. Certain individuals—particularly a few sympathetic Cape Afrikaners—occasionally were enfranchised more rapidly. The London Convention (1884) guaranteed civil rights to the Uitlanders but specified no terms for naturalization or ballot rights. Some British and Cape immigrants even demanded dual citizenship and franchise—in the Transvaal and at home—but Kruger jealously guarded his sovereignty. The Boers maintained the Dutch language, insisted upon the absolute jurisdiction of the Volksraad (Parliament) over the courts, and, in general, maintained the republic as the sanctuary of a chosen people.

Uitlander laborers and merchants turned to the British government, their employers and the Cape for support. Transvaal tariffs increased the cost of imports just at the point when the new railways should have made them cheaper. Cecil Rhodes, investor, politician and empire builder, realized that the Uitlanders were suitable allies. His National Union Movement took root in Johannesburg. The Volksraad in 1894 revised

the franchise law in a way that virtually precluded any Uitlander voting. An open Uitlander rebellion seemed possible,
but the Crown advised the National Unionists in Johannesburg
to remain conciliatory. The investors and mine managers began
to abandon their neutral political position and join the Uitlander agitators. Rhodes, realizing by this time that Rhodesia
might not yield much gold, revived his interest in the Rand and
began to establish active contact with the Uitlanders.

Such, then, was the balance of power in the Transvaal in
1895. Rhodes' spheres in the Cape and Bechuanaland were already established. In Rhodesia Dr. Jameson ruled for him—with
the Queen's permission, but not her control—over the political,
economic and military machinery. After 1895, events in all four
of these areas are closely related, and only in the context of all
of them do subsequent developments become intelligible.

President Kruger opened the final phase of the struggle for
domination in Southern Africa. The Nederlands Railway, which
controlled all lines in the Transvaal, levied prohibitive charges
upon traffic to and from Natal, the Cape and the Free State.
Virtual isolation, with contact and trade only through Mozambique, seemed at hand. The British railways continued to serve
the Rand by ox-wagon connection, but in November, 1895 Kruger closed the *drifts* (fords) by which the carts crossed the Vaal
River.

Rhodes asked the Bechuanaland government for a military
zone, ostensibly as a staging area for protection of the railway
from Bechuana tribesmen. He then sent his brother into Johannesburg, secretly told the High Commissioner in Capetown to
prepare for an "economic federation" with the Transvaal, and
acquired a territorial cession near Mafeking for the Company.
Dr. Jameson started south, with the Company police from Rhodesia, late in October. At the same time, arms and ammunition
were smuggled to the Uitlanders.

Joseph Chamberlain, an open advocate of expansion and
now Secretary of State for the Colonies, let it be known that
Rhodes should "allow a decent interval" between any provoca-

tion and the attack. Kruger relieved the tension by reopening the *drifts*, but Chamberlain had already begun embarking troops in England. The arrangements were therefore completed for direct intervention as soon as the Uitlanders were ready to stage an uprising.

The National Union Movement in Johannesburg exasperated Jameson, Rhodes and Chamberlain. Some Uitlanders were serious; others hoped to gain their ends simply by creating a diplomatic crisis. Many of them were reluctant to disrupt the business boom that developed during the autumn months. The uprising was postponed until the end of the racing season. National Unionists debated over the flag to be used while the Chartered Company fumed. During Christmas week Uitlander volunteers drilled openly in Johannesburg. Kruger made conciliatory gestures, and the Uitlanders agreed with Rhodes to call off the plot. The High Commissioner and Chamberlain were not surprised, for they had already been advised that Jameson might be more likely to start trouble than the Uitlanders themselves. Chamberlain cabled orders to prevent any such embarrassing developments.

But Dr. Jameson had acted. Self-confident, accustomed to freedom of action limited only by Rhodes' general instructions, he had cut the telegraph lines and led the Rhodesian Chartered Company police out of Mafeking. Rhodes' wire canceling the plans never reached him.

Late on December 30, 1895 the Uitlanders learned that Jameson had been advancing through Transvaal territory for a day and a half. A revolutionary committee was hastily assembled, Kruger's police retreated from the Rand, and General Pieter Arnoldus Cronjé assembled a Boer commando at Krugersdorp. The High Commissioner repudiated the plotters and the Uitlanders accepted an armistice. Cronjé stopped Jameson on New Year's Day and captured him near Doornkop the next morning.

Kruger released the Jameson Raiders to the British courts, but he refused Chamberlain's demand for an Uitlander compromise. The queen's government, however, found itself in a dangerous position. The United States was threatening to support Venezuela against the British in Guiana. The German Kaiser dispatched a threatening note to London, a congratulatory telegram to Kruger, and a warship to East Africa. Russia and France pleaded neutrality, so Germany withdrew its threats, but the British position in Southern Africa had changed radically.

Hofmeyer, the Afrikaners and many English merchants repudiated Rhodes. The Prime Ministry in Capetown passed immediately to Sir Gordon Sprigg. Rhodes' political career was terminated, and his direction of Rhodesia was temporarily suspended. The Crown even threatened to annul the British South Africa Company Charter. The Free State moved from neutrality to an alliance with the Transvaal. Moderate Boers began to admire the conservative Kruger. Afrikaner leaders, such as the brilliant lawyer Jan Smuts, trekked northward from the Cape and took high posts in the republics. The Bechuanaland Railway lost its military zones and came under the more direct imperial surveillance. Gone were the economic and political strands with which Rhodes had hoped to build a federation.

Chamberlain took direct control of the Company police and planned to inaugurate more thorough supervision of Rhodesian politics. Lord Grey arrived at Salisbury late in March, only to learn that rinderpest was decimating both the Bantu and the European cattle. Moreover, Jameson had taken the best policemen into the Transvaal, whence most of them had been deported to England, so law and order depended upon the support of loyal Matabele constables. Forty-eight hours after Lord Grey arrived, that tribe vented its grievances in open rebellion.

Jameson's land grant in 1894 had not compensated the Matabele for the loss of Bulawayo, which was more fertile and better watered than the new reserve. Imperial troops came from Bechuanaland and settler volunteers from Salisbury converged on the tribesmen, who retreated into the Matoppo Hills. Then, while heavy guerrilla fighting continued to occupy the white men in Matabeleland during June of 1896, the Mashona in the east launched a revolt. The English settlers who gathered in the main towns were able to endure, and by October the Mashona had scattered before the Company's hastily assembled relief columns. Final peace was not achieved until, in his life's finest moment, Rhodes went unarmed to negotiate with the rebels in the Matoppos. Thereafter, though the Company was burdened with war debts, Rhodesia was stable.

Rhodesia was subsequently divided, by orders from London, into three areas—Southern, Northeastern and Northwestern—each under a Resident Commissioner responsible to the High Commissioner in Capetown. Company rule continued, but it was subject to Crown supervision and the separation of authority into virtually autonomous sections. Rhodes complained about government interference, but the High Commissioner was determined not to let the Company make political or military policy as it had done in the Jameson era. Development and settlement schemes were allocated to independent enterprises, primarily because the Chartered Company had dissipated both its prestige and its capital. In 1899 the settlers in Southern Rhodesia were given a Legislative Council which assumed limited political, policy-making and policing powers formerly held by the Company. At the same time, a new railway financed by Rhodes reached Salisbury from Beira, Mozambique. Since this route was more economical than the Cape route, ties with South Africa began to weaken. Subsequent events in the Boer republics and the eventual discovery of copper north of the Zambezi confirmed the independence of Rhodesia. The break was symbolized when Cecil Rhodes died in 1902: he was buried not at Capetown, the base for his operations, but in the Matoppo Hills where he had brought the modern Rhodesia into being.

Events in South Africa seemed to follow an inexorable course after Jameson's Raid. On the Rand an economic recession developed. As the mines went deeper, the expense of extraction rose until, for small corporations, it exceeded the value of the gold ore. Kruger harassed the Uitlanders with petty laws and suppressed two of their newspapers. The prosperous Free State, which had coöperated with Rhodes and the Cape for a quarter-century, became noticeably nationalistic and isolationist. Early in 1897 she seized control of her British-owned railway grid.

In the British colonies tension increased. The Afrikaner-bond withdrew from Cape politics and its English opponents organized a South African League. The Natal Colony disassociated itself from the crisis-torn Cape and, having acquired self-government in 1893 and a railway to the Rand in 1895, began to compete with the old colony for Transvaal commerce.

During 1897—the year of Queen Victoria's Diamond Jubilee—Chamberlain appointed a new High Commissioner, Sir Alfred Milner. When the Transvaal entered into treaties with foreign powers, bought arms in Germany, and signed the Geneva Convention, Chamberlain warned Kruger that Britain might invoke the London Convention and disallow these acts. Early in 1898 Kruger stood for reëlection and, on the platform "Beware of Rhodes and keep your powder dry," he won handily.

Many high-ranking figures were promptly dismissed from the Transvaal Government—including many Netherlands advisers, the Chief Justice, and the State Secretary (Foreign Relations)—and a new hard-core of loyal Boers and refugee Afrikaners took their place. The new government offered to give the franchise after five years' residence, but the Uitlanders were suspicious and the British government demanded effective, permanent guarantees. Kruger interpreted Chamberlain's vague, critical note of August 28, 1899 as a rebuff, and withdrew the offer. Peace, free trade and South African federation seemed increasingly impossible without overthrowing the conservative Kruger clique in the Transvaal. Milner had already set this as his goal. An election in the Cape had put William P. Schreiner, a moderate Afrikaner, and the Liberal imperialist settlers in charge of the colonial government.

Britain had reasserted her claim to "suzerainty" over the Transvaal early in 1899. Both suzerainty and independence had been mentioned in the Pretoria Convention of 1881, but neither point arose in the London Convention of 1884. During June Kruger, Milner and President Marthinus Steyn of the Free State met in Bloemfontein to reëxamine the two Conventions. Kruger claimed that the second Convention had replaced the first; Milner insisted that it was merely an amendment. Did the London Convention therefore eliminate suzerainty, as Kruger claimed, or was Milner correct in saying that such an interpretation would also have terminated independence? Milner probably could have convinced Kruger to yield control over foreign relations, but the Boers would never have granted either an Uitlander franchise or imperial review over internal affairs. In point of fact, the juridical situation was as contradictory as the emotional atmosphere in South Africa.

The Uitlanders renewed their demands and gained the support of both the sensationalist press and *The Times* in London. Britain's foreign relations were conveniently tranquil. She had just joined Germany in making a loan to Portugal; should payments lapse, a secret agreement provided for the Anglo-German partition of the Portuguese Empire. The Czar was allied to France, and France was preoccupied with the conquest of the Niger basin. The United States was suppressing a rebellion in the Philippines, which had recently been taken from Spain. India was peaceful, and the Dominions loyal.

Milner left Bloemfontein on September 8, 1899. In the Near and Middle East, 10,000 imperial troops embarked for South Africa. Kimberley was reinforced, and the Free State Volksraad voted on the twenty-second to uphold the Transvaal alliance. President Steyn asked for American mediation, but the Crown would allow no such threat to the prerogatives of its "suzerainty." The Great North Road and Natal were mobilized while Boers gathered on the frontiers. On October 9 Kruger and Steyn cabled a joint ultimatum which the queen rejected. Three days later, in the land of Goshen, the South African War began.

20

UNIFICATION AND DIVISION

HISTORICAL factors that caused the Boer War also dominated the fighting campaigns. Republican armies outnumbered the British forces two to one. A wise strategist would have sent them into the Cape Colony in order to oust the British from their bases. The Afrikaners, coolly neutral since 1896, might then have taken an active role against the Crown; certainly the British would then have had to invade and conquer from overseas. However, the Boers turned their efforts toward targets that, notwithstanding their emotional significance, had merely tactical value. The Free State moved toward the Kimberley mines, while the Transvaal closed on Mafeking and then on Ladysmith, a junction point on the Natal Railway south of Majuba Hill.

Control of access to these points may have been desirable, but the initial advantages should have been pursued. Nevertheless, instead of heading for Durban, Capetown and Bulawayo, the Boer commandos dug in for debilitating sieges.

In the "Black Week" of mid-December, 1899 the imperial forces retired on every side, unable to stage a counterattack. Meanwhile, with the Cape's transport still secure and its agricultural resources undiminished, Britain prepared to take the offensive. Nearly all of the Indian Army, plus volunteers from Canada and Australia, poured into Capetown. Also from India came Lord Roberts—formerly Sir Frederick Roberts, hero of the Khyber Pass—as Commander-in-Chief.

By February the British reinforcements had stabilized the battle line, and on the twenty-seventh of that month the Boers were driven back. Rhodes first forced Roberts to relieve Kimberley, but Bloemfontein fell soon afterwards. The Republics sued for peace, but the British would tolerate neither their request for independence nor their pleas for foreign mediation. Disease enervated Roberts' forces, halted their advance, and gave the Boers time to regroup. Louis Botha took command for the Transvaal, and Christian De Wet directed the Free State commandos.

Roberts resumed the initiative in May, coördinating attacks from Mafeking, Bloemfontein and Ladysmith. The Free State, annexed as the Orange River Colony, lay behind when he entered the Rand early in June of 1900. Johannesburg and Pretoria fell with ease. The Republican governments retreated down the Nederlands Railway, fought their last battle at Dalmanutha, and sought Portuguese asylum during August.

Within a month Kruger exiled himself in the Netherlands. Roberts annexed the Transvaal, declared peace and returned to England in time for Christmas. The only remaining task seemed to be peacetime readjustment, for which Lord Kitchener (Sir H. H. Kitchener, the conqueror of Khartoum) was eminently qualified.

Peace did not ensue. Boer commandos emerged at the end of the year in the southern part of the Orange River Colony. Others soon appeared across the Cape, in the Transvaal and along the Drakensbergs. Martial law was proclaimed everywhere outside of Capetown, and the Cape Parliament was prorogued. Lord Kitchener hastened to protect the railway lines by stringing barbed wire and erecting blockhouses. Farms that harbored snipers were promptly destroyed. Milner and the Cape government, both realizing the reconstruction problems that would result from such a policy, tried to stop the destruction program. Kitchener discussed the terms with General Botha, but the Boers still expected independence. Fighting, with a relentless policy of farm-burning dictated by military necessity, resumed in March of 1901.

All the railways and the cities were securely British, but beyond the barbed wire that crisscrossed the veld the commandos were free. Within each enclave, between the fortified railways, the farms and pastures—which every Boer knew intimately—supported a guerrilla campaign. The British Army gave attention to one such enclave at a time, sweeping and mopping up until all the Boers had been defeated. Commando tactics hampered the operations: the guerrillas could hide, disappear, regroup and reëmerge, all with the help and support of a sympathetic rural population. To complete the clearing of each zone, Kitchener devised a scheme of total war. Men not killed were held on the Cape Peninsula, or exiled to the islands of St. Helena, Bermuda and Ceylon. Women, children and native servants were concentrated in separate guarded camps. Farmhouses, crops, herds and equipment were fired or destroyed in order to prevent a guerrilla revival. One by one, each zone was cleared and subdued in this manner.

Concentration camps had been invented by the Spanish in Cuba a few years earlier, but never had they been so widely used. Each South African colony had a different method of administering its camps, so conditions varied greatly from one installation to another. Supervision was lax, disease and food shortages ravaged the inmates, and graft reduced the operating funds. Milner and volunteer ladies pressed reforms, and experts from India taught the guards how to handle starving mobs. By the middle of 1902 nearly 250,000 Boers were dependent upon a concentration- or prison-camp ration, and since all the farms had been destroyed, the Crown was importing food at prodigious cost from North America.

Milner had rightly warned that "concentration" would not work. Quite apart from the lingering animosity that mass detention soon created, the separation had in many ways helped the Boers to hold out. Unencumbered by civilians, not responsible for their families, the commandos fought both more desperately and more agilely than before. General Jan Christian Smuts, who had risen rapidly in Kruger's service, swept deeply into the Cape late in 1901. Other Boers continued to roam the Orange River Colony and the Transvaal into the spring of 1902. British operations were hampered by Kitchener's insistence upon traditional tactics. Miners rushing back to Johannesburg and the distribution of food to the concentration camps put so heavy a load on the railways that military supplies were often delayed. Kimberley and the Rand bid against the army for Bantu manpower, but Milner resolved this problem by hiring laborers in Portuguese Mozambique.

During the period of guerrilla fighting, the Crown and the colonies had given much thought to postwar reorganization. Milner was afraid that the self-governing Cape and Natal would refuse to coöperate with the newly annexed, directly ruled Orange River and Transvaal regions. His program called for suspension of the established constitutions in order to give all of South Africa equal status at the proposed federation conference. Milner also hoped that English immigration and the distribution of Englishmen in rural areas would reduce the Boers and Afrikaners to a controllable minority in every colony. Active Suspensionist propagandization by the South African League, rabidly pro-English, alienated many of the High Commissioner's supporters. Moderate Cape settlers, British and Afrikaner, held fast to the rights of self-government. Support for their views by Canada and Australia, which were jealous of their own young constitutions, forced Milner to withdraw the Suspension plan.

Peace in the Boer War came unexpectedly amid the Suspension quarrel. Kitchener's corps were pushing Smuts, Steyn and De Wet against the barbed wire and blockhouses in the Transvaal. On April 9, 1902 the Transvaal and Free State governments were allowed to meet under flags of truce. Less than one month later Milner joined the republics' delegations for talks at Vereeniging on the Vaal River.

Smuts and Botha led a delegation for the South African

(Transvaal) Republic, which had been the immediate causus belli. After Smuts reported that the Cape could never be incited to rebellion, the Transvaalers were ready to yield. Steyn, De Wet and Hertzog headed the Free State representation; save perhaps Hertzog, they favored continuing the war. Steyn tried to say that the Free State had entered the war not for a cause but to honor an alliance; now, he complained, the Transvaal would yield and the Free State would lose its independence. Kitchener intimated that the opposition party in England might be lenient, and De Wet pressed a moderate view upon his countrymen. On May 31, 1902 the Peace of Vereeniging was concluded.

The republics became colonies of the Crown. However, Britain proposed grants and loans for reconstruction, and promised not to give any new voting rights to nonwhite people until the colonies had acquired self-government.

Within two months Kruger—by now in Switzerland—had died. The living heroes were the leaders to the end, the Boer commanders: Botha, De Wet, Hertzog, Smuts. Neutral Afrikaners had no such glamour, and the British, as the actual administrators, had to bear the brunt of criticism and the disappointment of compromise. Before long, Kitchener departed, leaving Milner in full charge of a civilian government.

Rehabilitation was a considerable task. The Boers had put 87,000 men under arms—nearly all in the field—and the Empire had mobilized about 450,000 during the war. Many of the British forces were engaged in guard or supply duty behind the lines, and others either rotated or trained. In the months after Vereeniging Milner had responsibility for about 1,300,000 people in the conquered colonies. About two-fifths of them constituted special problems: 35,000 Boer prisoners-of-war; 210,000 women, children and their Bantu servants, in concentration camps; 200,000 British troops impatient for discharge; and at least 45,000 newly arrived gold diggers. Within ten months the troops had gone, and virtually all the Boers had been released from detention and reinstated in homes, although Royal subsistence grants to distressed families continued for several years. Milner provided plows for devastated farms on the veld, but drought ruined the crops of 1903. Without animals, and unable to pay the inflated wages for Bantu labor, the returned farmers could not produce as the government hoped. Poverty-stricken white tenants, not welcome on the land when they returned from the disbanded commandos and the concentration camps, flocked to relief projects and to the booming cities. The hopes for a wave of English immigration were frustrated by prosperity in the mother country. British South Africans continued to prefer the urban economy to rural life, so the Boers— now all Afrikaners, or Dutch-speaking subjects of the Crown —continued to dominate the farms and the politics of the former republics. To many of them the prosperity of the English-speaking cities seemed to be a calculated rebuff to the newly subjugated rural population.

Preparations for federation proceeded rapidly. The Orange River and Transvaal colonies received nominated legislatures in the spring of 1903, though Milner retained executive independence. Southern Rhodesia, the four South African territories and the Bantu reserves in Basutoland and Swaziland were drawn together in a tariff union. As High Commissioner for all of them, Milner at the Bloemfontein Customs Conference also pressed for a common policy toward labor and the Bantu.

Labor supplies in the postwar years were particularly unsatisfactory. Many of the Bantu workmen, happy with wartime savings and needed for railway construction, refused to work in the underground mines. Portuguese colonial recruits on short-term contracts were expensive to train and limited in number. One Rand miner, Frederic Creswell, tried to introduce a white-labor system, but his competitors and the Crown feared that the high wage scale would force many mines into bankruptcy. English immigration and white-labor proposals having both failed, Chamberlain and Milner now hoped to transform South African society by expanding its industry and its urban population. Sir George Farrar, a former Uitlander leader, suggested that the immigration of Chinese coolies would create a labor reserve for mine and industrial development. Chamberlain and the Cape expressed opposition, but Westminster approved and 43,000 coolies arrived in 1904-05.

The mines prospered in subsequent years, but South Africa's social complexion—Afrikaner, British, Bantu, Hottentot, Colored, Malay, Chinese and Indian—became more tense. Coloreds and Indians reacted particularly against the addition, the former seeing a threat to their tenuous economic and political privileges and the latter being already pressed by restrictive legislation. Natal had tried since 1891 to return its laborers to India, first by withdrawing the land grants, then by imposing educational tests, franchise restrictions and special taxes. The Free State sealed its borders against Indians. The other colonies imposed limitations on their movement, residence and employment. Mohandas K. Gandhi, a newly arrived Indian barrister, organized nonviolent protests which preserved the peace but did not weaken the white man's restrictions.

Maneuvers toward federation proceeded in all the colonies. Dr. Leander Starr Jameson took the Cape Prime Ministry on a "vote British" ticket, but after creating a series of new pro-British urban constituencies, he soft-pedaled imperialism and restored the franchise to former Boer rebels. Hertzog continued to encourage the Free State extremists in their disdain for the Transvaal's surrender. However, the promise of self-government gave the Afrikaners an identity and a hope that overshadowed the bitterness. Milner's insistence upon English-language schooling had driven the Afrikaners to establish private Dutch instruction in the conquered colonies. National sentiment and political activity developed within the school committees and the churches, and the restless Uitlanders pressed the Crown for new liberties. Hofmeyer's Afrikanerbond transformed itself into the South African Party, in a bid for the support of moderate English and Afrikaner elements. Some of the aloof Boer military heroes slowly came together in Het Volk, a movement to demand immediate self-government. By 1906 Milner had retired, amenable Liberals had replaced the reigning Tories in the London government, and Chinese labor had become a source of strife and crime on the Witwatersrand.

Self-government the following year put Botha and Het Volk in command of the Transvaal. New legislation provided for bilingual education, the deportation of all Chinese within three years, and railway construction to aid the depressed rural areas. Hertzog and Steyn at the same time assumed control of a responsible government in the former Free State.

Aside from the post of High Commissioner, the Intercolonial Railway Committee was the only remaining institution that united the self-governing South African colonies with the Chartered Company's Rhodesias. Early in 1908, even that connection came into question. Dr. Jameson's ministry in Capetown, which included two Company directors, was defeated at the polls by the Anglo-Africaner South African Party. The central issue before the voters was Company influence in the self-governing territories. John Xavier Merriman's new Cape government was easily drawn into a political alliance with the Transvaal's Botha-Smuts regime against the Chartered Company. Railway and customs arrangements—always primary in imperial thought—were really secondary to the political basis for union which the colonies themselves had found. Furthermore, economic coöperation had now become more valuable for the depressed farms of all regions than for the select interests of commerce and industry.

Unification, even excluding the Rhodesias, was still not feasible without Natal. Settlers in that decidedly British colony had become increasingly disdainful of the polyglot Cape, and ever more proud of their own self-government. The settler population remained small and scattered, but the Zulu threat had not abated. The nineteenth-century Shepstone policy had preserved, if not strengthened, the tribal system. Continuing expansion of the European plantations, coupled with stringent labor regulations and a hated head-tax, brought the Zulu to rebellion during 1906. Dinizulu, son and heir of Cetewayo, launched once more the terrifying *impis*. Unable to defend themselves, the British colonists turned to their neighbors for help and support. Gandhi's activity among the Indians increased Natal's awareness that hope lay only in unity. By 1908 the Cape and the Transvaal had persuaded the Garden Colony to participate in federation talks.

When the National Convention met in Durban on October 12, 1908, there was no quarrel about the monarch's position, the establishment of a bicameral legislature, or the creation of a Supreme Court. The Crown was willing to grant full power save for three "entrenched" clauses which could not be altered without special procedures. However, five controversial issues were not resolved for nearly four months.

Initial debate centered on the merits of federation versus a unitary centralism. The Canadian federation of French and English seemed to be a parallel to Anglo-Afrikaner South Africa, but Sir Henry de Villiers, Cape Chief Justice and Convention President, convinced the delegates that the system was weak. Ex-President Steyn of the Orange River Colony agreed with de Villiers because he wanted South Africa to have strength in facing Britain and the European powers. Hofmeyer, the leading federalist, stayed at home in the mistaken confidence that unification would never be possible. Natal alone fought for federalism but failed to impress the other colonies upon whom she had so recently depended. Indeed, the centralists were determined to suppress Natal's tendency to create special courts of dubious legality. The South African government would therefore be supreme, with authority allotted to the provincial legislatures only in matters that did not conflict with national policy.

Franchise qualifications were more difficult to define. The Cape delegation worked to protect the rights that Colored voters had held since 1853. The High Commissioner proposed to extend this privilege by setting a civilization standard rather than a racial definition for the entire country, but Natal and the former republics were determined to protect the poor whites' superior rights as guaranteed by existing law. A compromise solution gave Cape Colored voters the protection of an "entrenched" clause, difficult to repeal, but limited the Union Parliament to white members only.

Hardly less delicate was the apportionment of seats. The Senate, all agreed, would have eight members from each province plus eight Crown nominees to guard the interests of nonwhite people. The Cape lost the right to count nonwhite voters in figuring apportionment. Reallocation of seats was to be automatic on the basis of each census of adult male Europeans, but the Judicial Commission was authorized to tolerate discrepancies of as much as 15 percent in favor of rural areas.

The choice of a capital nearly destroyed the National Convention. Proposals for creation of a new city were quickly rejected. No one city pleased a majority since each delegation campaigned for its own province. The solution was anomalous: parliament in Capetown, the Executive in Pretoria, and the Supreme Court in Bloemfontein; Natal, on the side, was given a guarantee that 30 percent of the Rand's rail traffic would pass through Durban, but all subsequent railway questions were left to "business principles" rather than politics.

Lastly, the Crown required that guarantees be given to protect the interests of five neighboring states that might conceivably join the Union. There was talk of a special commission to rule these areas—Basutoland, Swaziland, Bechuanaland and the Rhodesias—but, after brief debate, the delegates agreed to offer a customs union, recognition of tribal land titles, and a protectorate system to any future applicants. Thus, the draft of a South Africa Bill was transmitted to London for presentation in the British Parliament.

The Rhodesias never took advantage of the opportunity to join the Union of South Africa. The development of a separate railway outlet through Beira, the antipathy of South Africa toward the Chartered Company, and the ultimate development of Northern Rhodesia caused the two regions to withdraw from one another.

Crown supervision in Rhodes' Charterland had increased

markedly after the Jameson Raid, which had been executed from Company bases. There had been a tripartite division of the Chartered sphere, limitations upon the police, and the development of representative government in Southern Rhodesia. During the Boer War the Rhodesias had been loyal, but at the same time they were encouraged by strategic isolation to develop an independent economy. The personal prestige of Cecil Rhodes, which commanded devotion from both settlers and Bantu, had given unity and direction to the Rhodesias, but after his death, there was neither a personality nor a symbol capable of replacing him. Jameson, who probably would have been too vitriolic and unpredictable for the task, was committed to Cape politics and barred from Company territory.

Effective power from Jameson's Raid to the First World War rested in the hands of Sir William Milton, Administrator for the Crown. The Southern Rhodesia Legislative Council, surprising many by its independent attitude toward the Company, worked with Milton to establish effective government over the expanding frontier. Legislators elected by the settlers were equal in number to Company delegates after 1903, and a majority after 1907. Four years later the British government decreed the merger of the Northeastern and Northwestern regions into a unified Northern Rhodesia Administration. The Company thereafter assumed that its strength lay not in politics but in its title to all unclaimed land. The Legislative Council rejected the claim, and in 1914 sued to place that land under the Crown in trust for the settlers. Philanthropists pleaded for Matabele and Mashona title, and the Crown itself also filed an unconditional claim. The Privy Council subsequently determined that the Company was an agent, licensed to conquer and to administer, subject to the pleasure of the Crown. In substance, the settlers won, but the imperial government retained complete freedom of action.

Since the land was owned by the Crown, even though it had never been annexed, the British South Africa Company decided not to invest in more development. The settlers, who had supported renewal of the Charter that expired in 1914, now bore the costs themselves. After the Privy Council decision, pressure mounted to terminate the Company rule. Changes ultimately were made during the general colonial readjustment after World War I, but the position of the Company had become increasingly nominal since Rhodes' death.

The greatest potential in Rhodesia had already been found outside the Company's jurisdiction. Independent gold claims, which the Company had licensed in its search for income, began to produce in reasonable quantities during the Boer War. Company efforts to increase the settler population had led to a significant development in agriculture and cattle raising in the years after 1904, but the Company lost control of these open lands after 1918. A third resource, the copper of Northern Rhodesia, was discovered in 1902 but only intermittently exploited. The ores, which seem poor near the surface, did not compete with those of neighboring Belgian Katanga until the introduction of deep digging and massed capital during the twenties.

The increasing diversity of Rhodesian and South African interests was therefore noticeable, but not fully realized, when the South Africa Bill came before the British Parliament in 1909. Debaters in the House of Commons said little about Rhodesia; their main concern was the unitary government, the franchise definition and nonwhite rights as proposed by the Durban Conference. Federalists from the Cape were reassured that the "entrenched" clauses could never be repealed. The Liberal government in London promised never to turn Basutoland or Swaziland over to the Union without prior consultation and Parliamentary consideration. Prime Minister H. H. Asquith, when interrogated about the lack of guarantees for nonwhites, expressed confidence that example and delicacy would accomplish what specific statement might fail to do. In the end, the Act was passed and received the Royal Assent, September 20, 1909. Late the following May, on the eighth anniversary of the Peace of Vereeniging, the Union was pro-

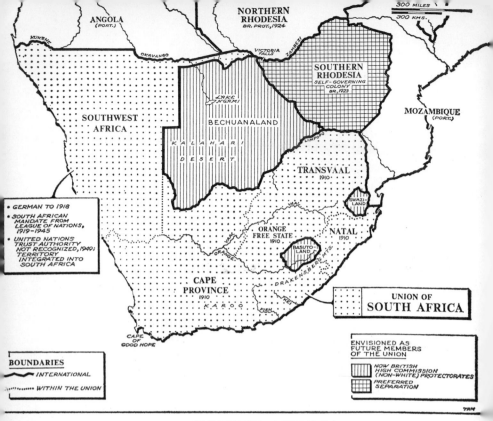

Legend and map labels:

ANGOLA (PORT.)

NORTHERN RHODESIA
BR. PROT., 1924

300 MILES
300 KMS.

KUNENE

OKAVANGO

VICTORIA FALLS

ZAMBEZI

SOUTHERN RHODESIA
SELF-GOVERNING COLONY
BR. 1923

MOZAMBIQUE (PORT.)

SOUTHWEST AFRICA

BECHUANALAND

LAKE NGAMI

KALAHARI DESERT

LIMPOPO

TRANSVAAL
1910

SWAZILAND

• GERMAN TO 1918
• SOUTH AFRICAN MANDATE FROM LEAGUE OF NATIONS, 1919–1945
• UNITED NATIONS TRUST AUTHORITY NOT RECOGNIZED, 1949; TERRITORY INTEGRATED INTO SOUTH AFRICA

VAAL

ORANGE FREE STATE
1910

NATAL
1910

ORANGE

BASUTO-LAND

DRAKENSBERG MTS.

CAPE PROVINCE
1910

KAROO

FISH

FET

UNION OF SOUTH AFRICA

CAPE OF GOOD HOPE

ENVISIONED AS FUTURE MEMBERS OF THE UNION

NOW BRITISH HIGH COMMISSION (NON-WHITE) PROTECTORATES
PREFERRED SEPARATION

BOUNDARIES
⌇⌇⌇ INTERNATIONAL
·········· WITHIN THE UNION

TRM

UNIFICATION OF SOUTH AFRICA, 1910–1952

claimed and General Botha became the first Prime Minister.

Elections immediately followed in which Natal voted Independent while the other three provinces fell into two broad, hastily constructed parties. Botha pulled together Het Volk, the Afrikanerbond's South African Party and the Labor groups into an alliance called the South African National Party. Supporting him were General Smuts, Frederic Creswell from the Rand, the moderate Cape English and a Unionist movement under Dr. Jameson, who was, as always, eager to support a unifier in South Africa. The combination was almost more than General Hertzog and Ex-President Steyn of the Orange Free State could tolerate, but they remained within Botha's bloc as a Nationalist wing.

Educational policy, reserved to the provinces by the South

Africa Act, quickly became a matter of Union concern. The Cape's system, the most advanced, was supported by a well-established local tax system, whereas the other provinces depended upon grants of the central government. English-language instruction predominated in the old colonies, but the Transvaal had a bilingual option and General Hertzog, Education Minister in the Free State, made Dutch virtually mandatory. Cape contributions to the central treasury helped to finance the Hertzog schools; Hertzog and the Afrikaners on the other hand expected the Union to enforce the teaching of Dutch in the English provinces. After much wrangling, compromises were effected under which teachers could qualify in either language and parents chose the language of instruction. Partly to save expenses, separate systems for each language were not required below Standard Five.

Other problems became intertwined with Union politics. Afrikaners began to believe that the poor-white class was a product of the Boer War. It had always been present, but the turmoil of war and the concentration camps made that fact easy to forget. At the same time, Rand mining had become more systematic and the rift between labor and management had become more obvious. Poor whites, protected from cheaper Bantu laborers by traditional color bars, held a precarious position between capital and the nonwhites. Impoverished refugees from the unrevived veld increased the tension. The Labor Party, more representative of the displaced Afrikaner newcomers than of any proletarian cause, pressed at once for stronger color barriers and the right to strike. In this atmosphere, one might note, it is not surprising that the Rhodesias looked away from the Union toward the seemingly brighter promise of their own farms and mines.

Jameson's Unionists continued to attack the Nationalist wing on matters of education and language. Hertzog opposed the imperial tariff preferences that Commonwealth status usually included, and he reacted vehemently to the dedication of a Rhodes Memorial outside Capetown. By mid-July, 1912 Her-

tzog was demanding "South Africa first," with the Empire subordinate, and he insisted that the English and the Afrikaner live
in "separate streams" until the Afrikaners were ready to dominate. Botha tried to bridge the two white cultures, but Hertzog
refused either to resign or to recant. Ultimately Hertzog was
ousted from the government, only to continue his threatening
denigrations of Anglo-South Africans. In November, 1913 he
followed General De Wet out of Botha's party, thus splitting
the Afrikaner population and creating an extreme Nationalist
opposition. Botha's bloc, dropping the word "National," now
became the South African Party. In it were included liberal
Unionists on one side and the special-interest Labor Party on
the other.

In July of 1914, when the political storms again subsided,
the Prime Minister visited Southern Rhodesia. There were to
be opportunities for exploratory negotiations on the unification question, but the Austro-Serbian crisis sent him home
posthaste. The Union promised to relieve the British forces
and to attack the German bases in Southwest Africa.

Hertzog's Nationalists condemned the government when
the Union Parliament assembled in August. Jacobus de la Rey,
a former Transvaal general who had long been plotting a Boer
rebellion, called out the commandos. Germany, rumors said,
would support an anti-imperial republic. De la Rey was acci-
dentally shot by a nervous sentry, but General De Wet assumed
the mantle. At first he merely demanded a declaration of neutrality toward the Germans. However, when a Union garrison
near the border made a compact with the Kaiser's officers,
De Wet brought the Free State into rebellion. Botha led loyal
commandos into the field, pitting one Boer veteran against another. Within eight weeks martial law was lifted and Botha sent
Smuts in an organized campaign against the German forces.

Some Unionists blamed German agents for the revolt, but
the basic cause was the extreme Nationalist belief that Botha
and Smuts had betrayed their people by coöperating with the
British Crown. Hertzog, himself surprisingly silent during the

crisis, became the idol of a strengthened opposition. Nationalist groups also appeared in new areas—in the Cape under the
Reverend Dr. Daniel François Malan, and a strong faction
within the Labor Party—but the greatest danger was the Free
State, where, in 1915, the anti-Botha Nationalists captured a
majority of votes. South Africa was rapidly breaking into not
two but three white groups: Imperialists, Botha's weakening
Anglo-Boer bloc, and the extreme Afrikaner Nationalists.

There was of course no such division among the Rhodesian
settlers. The two Company colonies were sparsely settled—
their value was one of supply, not manpower—but loyal settlers
became increasingly disdainful of the Union's problems. If anything, the First World War confirmed the Rhodesias' separation from the South. Thus, although unification was achieved
near the Cape, it was a union deeply torn within and definitely
divorced from its stepchildren astride the Zambezi.

BOOK THREE

NEW AFRICA

21

THE ROOTS OF IDENTITY

AFRICAN nations gradually acquired their identity in the interaction of alien influences with indigenous circumstances. At first, contact between Africans and the Europeans tended to obliterate or subordinate the established patterns. The occupying powers were inclined to draw colonial people into their own economic and cultural spheres. However, contact and exchange between people create in time an awareness by one group of the differences separating it from the other, and out of this consciousness there can develop a sense of distinct identity.

In the process of exploiting or developing parts of Africa, the Europeans created new factors which unintentionally made national feeling more important than tribal identity. Economic and religious programs influenced Africa in ways that the conquerors and administrators did not anticipate, and the response to these stimuli was frequently contrary to the rulers' expectations.

Frequently the Europeans' arrival caused a sudden and far-reaching change in political and economic orientation. Colonial boundaries were usually determined by the conquerors' diplomatic, military and commercial situation, which in many cases arbitrarily contradicted the traditional tribal allegiances and established trade routes. Kenya was annexed simply as an access corridor for Uganda, and, though later transformed into a white colony, its European-designed boundaries and land titles totally disregarded the existing social and political structures. The homogeneous Hausa confederation, for centuries an integrated commercial power dependent upon established markets and caravan routes to the north, was partitioned in a race among competing European powers; the greater portion of Hausaland, joined without precedent to the coastal rain forest, had to develop entirely new outlets and a substantially different economy. Routes running inland from the Gold Coast continued to be important, but the introduction of new crops substantially altered the nature of the trade that was conducted. New routes in the Congo, French West Africa, the Zambezi basin and elsewhere served to reorient the economic and political life of all indigenous people. Each colony strove to become a viable economic unit, as self-contained as possible, intentionally isolated from its neighbors, and dependent upon the products and markets of the mother country. Since European boundaries and commerce dictated the means of livelihood as well as the lines of communication, daily life depended upon the peace and prosperity of a whole colony. Administrators expected the Africans to identify themselves with the new economic and political units rather than the traditional associations, and assumed that they would become loyal to the ruling power.

As ocean transportation replaced the traditional overland routes, port towns and a longshoreman class became important. Efforts to develop self-sufficiency and new forms of commerce within each colony led inevitably to the growth of light industry. The resulting cities were a new phenomenon in African society. People from diverse tribes intermingled freely in the new environment, which had been created by European economic and political innovation. Instead of diverse tribal laws and traditional chiefs, there were standard Metropolitan Police and a city government to rule the newly urbanized Africans. Industrial working conditions and labor unions replaced the farm and the clan in daily life. The European language was the only means of communication among people who arrived speaking many African tongues. Crowded slums, barracks or planned developments superseded the village huts. Barter and agriculture gave way to a new economy in which food, clothing and the gadgets associated with urban living had to be bought with money earned in the European manner. Africans in cities were separated from their traditions in countless ways, but their contact with Europeans was relatively superficial. Big business, the large labor union, the metropolitan bureaucracy were usually impersonal. European law was frequently misunderstood and therefore often evaded. Colonial governments were reluctant to spend money for education, and missions usually lacked both the personnel and the money for extensive programs in the densely populated cities. Tribal religion frequently became a social ritual, devoid of contact with established priests and sometimes meaningless because the worshiper was separated from the clan and the ancestral home. Tribal rivalries lost their justification and meaning in the new environment but were perpetuated in social clubs and political movements. Sometimes such movements, lacking control either by a responsible chief or by tribal law, degenerated into public disturbances. Underlying factors were usually economic competition, personal grudges or imagined grievances. Without the check of traditional law, such outbreaks could become more vicious than tribal fighting had ever been. African cities therefore contained many people who were said to be "detribalized"—separated from their own meaningful traditions and authorities, but not exposed to or influenced by any but the impersonal and materialistic aspects of European life.

Generalizations cannot be applied to all detribalized Africans, but large numbers of such people are found in every city south of the Sahara: Johannesburg, Durban, Nairobi, Léopoldville, Ibadan, Dakar, and others. Detribalization also became a phenomenon observed among Africans who became tenants

on European lands in Kenya or the Rhodesias, among the
Congo tribes whose chiefs were replaced by Belgian civil service administrators, and among the laboring classes in the Union
of South Africa. In every case, whether urban or not, the detribalized people have lost one culture without acquiring
another. Therefore, instead of replacing tribalism with loyalty
to the mother country, the European influence has created a
powerful class whose identity is defined by the economy and
commerce of a colonial territory, but whose chief grievance is
the European ruler and trader.

Although the detribalized Africans and the tribesmen have
separate identities, they do share a common resentment of the
occupying power. The diverse groups in colonial Nigeria—
Hausa and Fulani, small Delta clans and the larger Yoruba
tribe, and the urban dwellers of Lagos and Ibadan—had no political or economic tradition to hold them together. After making their economies interdependent, and ruling them all, Britain
allowed the United Africa Company to control 40 percent of
the overseas trade. Nigerians may have had many identities, but
they came to agree that Britain was the common enemy who
blocked progress by supporting economic subjugation. Similar
feelings united divergent groups on the Gold Coast in dislike
for the (British) West African Merchants Association which
dominated two-thirds of all commerce. Union in opposition
therefore developed before the emergence of a common sense
of identity. Such views, which resembled those of the seventeenth-century Boers toward the Dutch East India Company,
were also present to a lesser extent in East Africa. However,
much of the resentment in Kenya, for example, was directed
toward Indians and Arabs who respectively controlled the small
shops and the coastal plantations.

Rural and remote areas of the African continent contributed individuals to the developing cities but were not themselves greatly affected by detribalization. Christian missions, on
the other hand, usually had much more impact upon the back
country than upon the cities. Britain and France both barred

European churches from the predominantly Moslem regions, so Islamic possessions tended to remain aloof from the Christian influences. However, throughout the rain forests, and rural areas farther south, missionaries were for many years the main link between Europe and the tribes.

Christian missionaries usually expect their converts to renounce the tribes' traditional social and cultural patterns. Initiation ceremonies, polygamy, dancing and ancestor veneration were particularly subject to condemnation. Until recent years churchmen rarely understood that these practices were only partly religious. The ceremonies also symbolized the unity, authority and loyalty of tribal organization through a period of history. By attacking them, the missionary contributed to the weakening of tribal continuity and the increasing of social dislocation. Other mission influences are much clearer in retrospect than they were at the time. For every African converted by a missionary, there were many who saw only his strange dress or his material possessions. Missionaries tried to be simple and to emphasize the gospel, but Africans who did not hear or understand them were impressed only by their automobiles, their houses, or their equipment. Some were converted, but many learned only to desire gadgets and machines. People who misunderstood or lost interest in the Christian message were also likely to draw incomplete or inverted ideas from the missionaries' presence.

Education always was important in the missionary program. Government schools were scarce or unknown in most areas, but mission schools were long required to follow a European curriculum. In Nigeria English law and history, as well as the English language, were mandatory. French officials laid down similar rules for their language, as did the Germans. Belgium required French instruction, and the Portuguese insisted that all schools—even those run by American Protestants—must use the mother country's tongue. Such policies necessarily increased the missions' tendency to equate Christianity with European culture. An educated African therefore learned rela-

tively little that would help him live in or improve his own society. A school diploma was valuable only in applying for a government post or for commercial employment. Literate graduates
therefore looked toward the cities for careers, and about half
of the educated Africans became clerks for a colonial government. Furthermore, Christian charity generally could not afford
to train more than 2 or 3 percent of the total population. Consequently, the population in many places increased more rapidly than did the number of students. Schools were therefore
much less influential in remolding rural areas than the missionaries had hoped.

Education often attracted the lowest or poorest groups in
a traditional society because it presented an opportunity for
advancement. After becoming the Europeans' right hand, these
groups found that only the lower clerkships were open to them.
The educated African therefore tended to become separate
from his own society rather than to leaven it, and he ultimately
became an instigator of anti-European feeling. Educational efforts thus added to the detribalized group that courted European favors in urban centers. These selected, literate and experienced people soon identified themselves with the national
rather than the tribal interest.

Before the end of the nineteenth century rural and urban
Africans began to express resentment of the missionaries. Christianity was criticized as a religion that spread by disrupting and
destroying established culture. Even the church leaders who
realized the difference between culture and religion insisted
that converts reject customs that contradicted the new faith.
The critics retaliated by forming "Ethiopian" (i.e., African)
sects that tried to reconcile indigenous and Christian customs.

The splinter churches were not merely tribal reassertions.
Since they stood for an amalgam of some indigenous traditions
with a selection of European ideas, they were a factor in the
breakdown rather than the preservation of African patterns.
Organizers and believers had to conform to the colonial boundaries as Europeans had defined them, so the movement in each

colony tended to be separate from that of any other colony. At the same time, colonial postal and road service facilitated contact with all dissident factions within a given possession. Ethiopianism therefore became a focus for both antitribal and anti-European feeling within a colony, and a factor in the development of a national identity.

By the end of World War I the leading mission societies realized the dangers which resulted from a confusion of religion with European culture. A Christian universality, which could give meaning to many cultures, was stressed. However, the awakening came late in mission history and only slowly influenced missionaries in the field who had long been accustomed to the older attitude. Consequently, the European Christian often continued to confuse or to weaken the old pattern rather than to strengthen any new one.

Ethiopian Christians usually justified African practices by drawing analogies from the Old Testament. Polygamy, tribal ritual and occasionally slavery could be supported by the interpretation of select passages. The Ethiopian definition of African culture therefore tended to become an isolationist, rigidifying force which established and preserved a nontribal, non-European cultural concept. As such, it resembled and frequently influenced the detribalized people, but Ethiopianism usually continued to be a distinct and more withdrawn factor in African society. Separatist churches were greatly concerned with the difference between theology and daily practice, and some considered themselves a purification movement within Christianity. One Nigerian newspaper epitomized this sentiment in observing: "Europeans came to Africa with Christ and the gospel. On their way back they left both here."

Missionaries also continued to encounter the handicap of their white skins and European citizenship. Their language, behavior and culture resembled those of the colonial rulers. In rural areas they were often more numerous than the political authorities. Even if the officials and missionaries came from different countries, Africans in some areas either suspected a conspiracy between the two or tried to ingratiate themselves with both. Christian churches as well as European rulers tended to become something against which to unite.

The auxiliary effects of mission work contrasted markedly with the original intentions. A European education undermined the traditional identity, but it inevitably implanted new political and patriotic concepts. Admiration for European institutions led to an African class that, having learned how to organize and to operate a colonial possession, considered itself an elite equipped to lead a new nation. Missions and governments both operated within the new colonial boundaries and economies, thus contributing to a new national consciousness. By weakening established institutions, they opened the door for disruption and cultural changes which rarely were wholly European in character. Upon such incomplete transitions, distinct national identities could readily be built.

Cultural problems in each colony contributed to the rise of dissatisfaction, but the direct movements toward African awareness had somewhat different origins. Separatist "Ethiopian" churches had found sympathy and support among the schismatic white and Negro sects that emerged in the United States after the American Civil War. All three groups, feeling a bond uniting them against the established denominations, worked together in financial, theological and personnel problems. Rarely was the contact continuous or systematic, but it afforded the African leaders their first opportunities to visit North America, to witness "Jim Crow" in the American South, and to observe the Negro position in the independent New World. Most of the early influences passed from Negroes in the United States and the British West Indies through the independent settlements in Liberia and Sierra Leone.

The initial impetus for African identity came from Edward Wilmot Blyden. Born of British West Indian Negro parents in the Danish Virgin Islands, barred by his color from an American university, he migrated to Liberia in 1850. Twelve years later he published the first of a series of books advocating

Negro progress by assertion of a unique "African personality," rather than by imitating or accepting alien ideas. His primary contact, both in travel and in writing, was with the American Negroes, but before his death in 1912 he had also become an idol in the British West African cities. His key slogans, "the right to be different" and "Africa for the African," were widely quoted. John Payne Jackson, a Liberian who edited Nigeria's *Lagos Weekly Record* from 1891 to 1918, developed the racial consciousness inherent in Blyden's concepts and thereby made his paper the most influential mouthpiece for detribalized Africans. Small, polemical presses quickly appeared in urban areas, each seeking to outdo the other in popular appeal.

Blyden's work was relatively moderate and secular, but the religious movements—which he also encouraged—had a more immediate impact. Nigeria's first Ethiopian churches were organized on his recommendation in 1891, and the splinter movement was well developed throughout West Africa by World War I. In South Africa a similar trend after 1896, particularly among the Zulus in Natal, was sponsored by Bishop H. M. Turner, head of the African Methodist Episcopal Church in America. A number of converted Bantu "Ethiopians" studied or visited in the United States before 1924, but the South African government prevented any subsequent contacts. Another liaison between American and African splinter sects culminated in a violent uprising against the British in Nyasaland during 1915. Fear of analogous disturbances had led the Belgians in the Congo to detain American Negro missionaries in 1908, and the British to impose restrictions on the Gold Coast in 1914. The Ethiopianist sects were also condemned by an international mission conference in 1926.

Negroes around the world first came together to protest against white colonialism in 1908. A Pan-African Conference was organized jointly by Henry Sylvester-Williams, a West Indian barrister who had represented many African chiefs in Great Britain, and Alexander Walters, Bishop of the African Methodist Episcopal Zionists in North America. The expansion of Cecil Rhodes' Chartered Company, the Boer War, and African rights everywhere received particular attention. The movement collapsed with the death of its founders, but the Conference memorial, prepared by the American Negro, William Edward Burghardt Du Bois, contained the claim that "The problem of the Twentieth Century is the color line."

Du Bois was a well-born Massachusetts mulatto, trained at Harvard and Berlin, whose scholarly and editorial work gave new intellectual depth to African and American Negro opinions. As a sociologist, he attacked the racist theories of Social Darwinism and the early anthropologists. Du Bois' research also documented forgotten aspects of Negro history. His legal arguments for implementation of the Fourteenth and Fifteenth Amendments of the United States Constitution were the first serious challenge to the "separate but equal" segregation which Dr. Booker T. Washington had accepted. Washington's statement, the so-called "Atlanta Compromise," had been interpreted by many whites as abdication of the claim to full equality. Tuskegee Institute, founded by Dr. Washington, became the model and inspiration for education both in Negro America and in Africa, but Du Bois' claims set the dominant tone in political matters.

With William Monroe Taylor, a Negro journalist, Du Bois convened a conference of the American Negro intelligentsia at Niagara Falls in 1905. Du Bois' program for voting rights, freedom of association, abolition of the color bar, and advanced education was given organized and continuing support. When the Niagara Movement met again the following year, it directed its protests toward segregation on railway trains, a practice which had become widespread only in the preceding two decades.

The antiforeign, white-supremacist Ku Klux Klan increased its activity in the North and the South, but in 1910 the Niagara Movement joined with Northern liberals to form the National Association for the Advancement of Colored People. Negro rights were to be acquired by systematic appeal to constitutional law, and Dr. Du Bois became editor of *The Crisis*, a propaganda paper that was soon read by influential Negroes overseas.

The expanding distribution of *The Crisis* was matched by the extension of Du Bois' own interests to colonial Africa. During the First World War his editorials also included attacks upon Negro segregation in the American Expeditionary Force in France. By coming into contact with British and French colonial forces, these troops had further increased the connections between the NAACP and African dissatisfaction. Shortly after the armistice Du Bois—supported by Negroes in colonial Africa and the United States—summoned a Pan-African Congress. American Negroes were denied passports and, distracted by racial violence and isolationism at home, were unable to give the movement full support. Nevertheless, Du Bois—already abroad on a research project—coöperated with Blaise Diagne, an assimilated African who represented Senegal in the French Chamber of Deputies. Under their leadership, delegates from Africa and the West Indies met in Paris. The Congress petitioned the Versailles Powers to adopt an international code guaranteeing native rights in tropical Africa and establishing a plan for progressive self-government. An NAACP plan for the internationalization of all colonial territories failed to gain approval.

The proposals made no impression except in the redistribution of German colonies. For these, the Powers adopted a "Mandate" system. Britain, France, Belgium and South Africa each took portions of the Kaiser's empire, which therefore disappeared from Africa. Each mandated territory was supposed to be governed in the interests of its inhabitants, but no provision was made either for foreign inspection or for African representation.

American opposition to internationalism also deprived Du Bois of white liberal support in the NAACP and cast a pall over the Second Pan-African Congress in 1921. The opening sessions, meeting in London, were addressed by Fabian Socialists from the Colonial Office. The second sessions, at Brussels, asked the League of Nations to study Negro problems and to condemn all color bars. Belgian politicians, concerned both for the Congo profits and the emotions of European voters, accused the Congress of preaching disorder and taking Soviet Russian pay. However, no Congress speaker had even mentioned Marx, Lenin or dialectic materialism. Indeed, both Moscow and the Communist International were specifically attacking the Negroes for their "bourgeois nationalism" and for "destroying proletarian unity." Meanwhile, the Second Congress held its anticlimactic third sessions in Paris, where the League was asked to put a Negro on the Mandate Commission.

Du Bois' Third Congress (Lisbon, 1923), although poorly attended, demanded elections, trial by jury, free education, and a labor code for Africa. Britain subsequently granted voting rights to a few middle-class West African townspeople, but none of the other requests were granted. In New York in 1927 the Fourth Pan-African Congress—composed largely of American Negro churchwomen—devoted most of its efforts to social and religious welfare. Plans for a Fifth Congress, aimed largely at proselytizing Africa through an international Negro mission program, were thwarted by the depression of 1929, which severely reduced the American donations upon which Du Bois depended.

Movements for the establishment of African identity had by this time developed many facets. Booker T. Washington's influence had culminated in 1927 in the founding of Achimota College on the Gold Coast. The Vice-Principal, Dr. James E. Kwegir Aggrey, advocated racial coöperation for African development. Aggrey's simple philosophy—exemplified by his statement that beautiful piano music must be played on both black and white keys—had more influence on public education than on politics. However, the Negro world of the 1920's was dominated by a less moderate concept, expressed by Marcus Aurelius Garvey.

Preaching "Africa for the Africans, at home and abroad," Garvey created an emotional, mass-supported racist cult that appealed to Negroes first in America, then in Africa. His position in Jamaica, where he was born a pure Negro and considered inferior both to whites and mulattoes, greatly embittered his subsequent attitudes. He was also influenced by Egyptian nationalists, the biography of Napoleon Bonaparte, and religious fervor. After proclaiming himself the Negro Moses, he sailed to New York in 1916 to preach the salvation of Negritude. Proposing that pure Negroes were the chosen race, he insisted that whites were base inferiors and the mulattoes merely defiled hybrids. American Negro leaders, who had long advocated disregard for racial definitions, denounced Garvey's racism. On the other hand, the Ku Klux Klan gave Garvey open support in his crusade against the so-called mulatto-led NAACP.

On August 1, 1920, after decreeing himself Provisional President of Africa, Marcus Garvey convened his first "Parliament" in uptown New York. The Universal Negro Improvement and African Communities League was created to acquire territory. The Provisional President became His Highness, the Potentate of Africa, and aristocratic titles were awarded—Baron Zambesi, Overlord of Uganda, and the Order of Mozambique, among others. In order to liberate Africa, the Universal Black Cross Nurses, the Black Eagle Flying Corps and a Black Star (steamship) Line were also organized. New York's Harlem had never seen an inaugural procession such as that which followed. Kilt-clad youth corps, trainees for "the imperialism of independent African states," marched behind His Grace Archbishop Alexander McGuire, Patriarch of Garvey's new African Orthodox Church.

The Negro World carried Garvey's clarion throughout Africa in three languages, surpassing *The Crisis* both in circulation and in influence for at least five years, even though the paper was banned by most colonial governments. American followers were estimated to number nearly three million, and preparations were made to establish a base in southern Liberia. Garvey was delighted when white politicians in Mississippi suggested that the United States take the European colonies, cancel the mother countries' World War I debts, and turn the land over to Negroes who would be deported en masse from the American South. The Liberian government promised land grants for a more reasonable settlement, but canceled the concession when it became known that Garvey was planning to subvert the traditional True Whig Party in the republic. Universal Negro Improvement Association property was confiscated and sold in order to ease Liberia's own financial crisis.

In 1925 Garvey's career closed abruptly. The United States courts convicted him of using the mail to defraud and sentenced him to prison. Two years later he was deported to his native Jamaica. The U.N.I.A., *The Negro World* and the empire scheme quickly collapsed, much to the relief of moderate Negro leaders and the NAACP. Until his death in 1940 Garvey spent his later years orating in London at Hyde Park Corner. On one such occasion he admitted that "we were the first Fascists. . . . Mussolini copied fascism from me, but the Negro reactionaries sabotaged it [my plan]." The danger had been not his greed but his egoism and megalomania. Africa reacted less to his specific plans than to the stimulus of his vision and to his defiance of white paternalism. He therefore emerged as a major force in the definition and coalescence of African nationalism, and, through his writings, inspired confidence among later nationalists, even though their specific actions were much less grandiose.

Garvey had a greater impact upon Africa than Du Bois. He and his African Orthodox Church, rather than Pan-Africanism, excited the African cities and worried the colonial governments. "Pan-Africanism," Du Bois later wrote, was in the twenties primarily "American rather than African."

After Garveyism collapsed and the depression began, five major sources of African nationalism remained. The first two—Ethiopian Christianity, and the secular colonial leadership exemplified by Joseph Casely Hayford—can best be treated in subsequent discussions of various regions. Communism and Pan-Africanism, the third and fourth factors, coincide with a fifth strand represented by the Africans who studied abroad after the First World War. Ultimately, as these students returned to their colonial homes, nationalism in Africa acquired sophisticated leadership and coherent direction.

Marxist theories did not particularly apply to Africa when they were conceived in 1848. Karl Marx claimed that historical forces, beyond human control, would soon cause an inevitable revolution in which capitalism would fall. The economy would then be subject to a "dictatorship of the proletariat," if the "workers of the world" were united. The theory applied to Western Europe, which was at that time the dominant power and the only industrial region in the world.

The expected revolution did not occur. Instead, by the end of the nineteenth century, working conditions had improved and capitalism had continued to grow. Three Marxists eventually tried to explain the failure of the theory.

In 1898 Eduard Bernstein "revised" the theory, claiming that in a democracy, capitalism and industrial monopoly could be transformed simply by popular vote. Revolution, a "dictatorship" and a rigid theory of history were therefore unnecessary. Upon these "revisions," Western European moderates built the modern Social Democratic, Christian Democratic and Labor parties.

A fanatical minority rejected this democratic revisionist socialism and called themselves "Communist-Socialists." The French extremists or "Syndicalists" created a General Confederation of Labor, which would cause a revolution by calling a massive general strike. The other extremist, V. I. Lenin, made an addition rather than a revision for Marx's original theories.

Lenin claimed that capitalism had unexpectedly invented "imperialism," thus forestalling the revolution and overriding the laws of history. Monopolistic exploitation of foreign countries, he said, had revived capitalism and made it possible to placate the European workers. Direct action was therefore necessary to crush capitalism and to restore history so that Marx's predictions could be fulfilled. The best allies against "imperialism" would be its Asian and African victims. As soon as Lenin's Communists had seized Russia (1917-1921), a meeting of the

Communist International (Comintern) decided to direct its campaign toward the American Negroes, because "the United States is the true center of world-wide Negro culture." The Comintern dismissed the NAACP as "opportunistic and insufficiently emancipated from bourgeois prejudice," and instructed the American Communist Party to recruit Negro comrades.

Garveyism, the NAACP and economic prosperity helped to frustrate the Party plans. By 1924 North Africa and the Near East had joined America on the list of primary objectives. Although a secret Colonial Committee began to propagandize, sub-Saharan Africa still remained peripheral.

In 1924-1925, Lenin's emerging successor, Joseph Stalin, ordered the Communist parties of Africa and Asia to infiltrate the "bourgeois nationalist" movements and to redirect them along class lines. An attempt to do this in China, directed by the Communist general Chiang Kai-shek, backfired: Chiang joined the nationalists and captured the Party (Kuomintang). Stalin was nearly discredited but he managed to consolidate his power within Russia. His chief critic, Leon Trotsky, who advocated action through peasants in Asia and tribal organization in Africa, was exiled in 1927.

The Comintern meeting of 1928 was therefore completely Stalinist. Notwithstanding the experience in China, Communists in the colonies were told to continue the infiltration of nationalist movements. Other orders established a Pan-Negro movement, which Stalin hoped would be as popular as Garveyism had been. Independent Negro republics were to be established in the southern United States and in South Africa. Communism therefore stood for two contradictory ideas regarding Africa: racial separation and working-class struggle.

Neither of Stalin's plans took root. First of all, the racial sentiment was misjudged. Garveyism had been popular not for its racism, but for its expression of hope and self-confidence. Negroes wanted equality and integration, not racial separation. In America they therefore turned to the NAACP, not to Moscow. In South Africa communism appealed primarily to the ultra-racist, segregationist white laborers. The second policy, calling for worker infiltration of nationalist movements, also failed. Labor organizations in tropical Africa were still too weak, too scarce, or too short-lived; and powerful or mass nationalist movements had not yet emerged. Communism therefore reached the colonial areas only through isolated aliens and relatively insignificant propaganda.

After 1935 Stalin tried to coöperate with the democracies against Hitler, so he curtailed programs that might displease them. The Comintern therefore had relatively little to say when Italy invaded Ethiopia. Russia's pact with Nazi Germany severely weakened the overseas Party in 1939. During the following war, in which Russia finally allied with the colonial powers, subversion inside Africa was rare.

In the interwar years the danger from Comintern agents and propaganda was relatively small. The Soviet Union failed to understand conditions inside Africa, and the ruling powers from time to time imposed restrictions on Russian contacts. However, the contact between Africa and Communists in the mother countries was harder to control. Nevertheless, none of the European parties, save that of France, was large enough or strong enough to sustain a significant campaign. The French Communists operated through the General Confederation of Labor, which had become more peaceful if no less Marxist than its founders intended. Yet there was no significant labor movement with which the GCL could work in French Africa until the forties.

Moscow's most significant contacts before World War II were with African students in Europe and America. Neither Lenin nor Stalin anticipated this, except of course for their own very different Afro-Asian cadre program at Kutvu University. American and British Communist Party meetings were frequently attended by Africans, who listened, and often learned, but had already acquired enough education to reserve their own judgments.

West Africans had studied abroad in slowly increasing

numbers since the 1890's. The earliest of them stayed only
briefly at preparatory schools and the training centers of small
Protestant denominations. Of the few who did advanced work
before World War I, most remained in England. West Indians
had usually preceded them, so the Africans tended to associate
with and to join their moderate social organizations. A small
number, intending to return home from studies in London,
eschewed the exiles and in 1917 formed the pioneer Union for
Students of African Descent.

Not until the twenties did students go abroad in significant numbers. Small clubs for men from each colony did not
last. However, the West African Students Union (WASU),
founded in 1925 by law students, quickly became the permanent center for African life in greater London. Originally intended as a residence free of color-prejudice, WASU developed
social and political functions. Interracial good-will, African research and information, "self-help, unity and coöperation," and
"a spirit of national consciousness and racial pride" were declared objectives. A monthly journal, WASU, became an outlet
for literary and nationalist expression. Most of the nationalist
leaders of British Africa have at some time been associated with
this independent coöperative hostel. The "nation" to which the
students would be loyal was not always clear, but it was usually
either a Pan-African Federation or a unified British West African Republic. However, when they returned to their homelands,
individual students found that economic and political realities,
reinforced by the regional loyalty that detribalized urban masses
were developing, had created a more fertile field for separate
nationalisms in each colony. Pan-Africanism therefore remained
primarily an ideal for students abroad rather than a practical
goal for nationalist movements within Africa.

Outside of London, organizations of British African students were rare. Cambridge and Oxford boarded all students, so
an African association and African nationalism never developed.
In other universities, there were not enough Africans to justify
any permanent arrangements.

French colonial subjects were less likely to study in the mother country than the British Africans. Those who did go usually found accommodation either with Moslems or with racially tolerant Parisians. Most visitors from the colonies, however, were either laborers under GCL auspices or military conscripts on active duty. Belgium never brought Africans to Brussels, save occasionally on special business. Portuguese colonial people could not travel unless they belonged to the small "assimilated" group, in which case there was virtually no legal or social bar.

British West Africans therefore constituted the greatest proportion of overseas students. Although more went to London than to any other university, a considerable number also studied in the United States. Many came under mission sponsorship. A smaller proportion won college and university scholarships, and a few came to earn their own way. Most of them during the twenties and thirties enrolled in Negro colleges in the American South, but Lincoln University in Pennsylvania graduated the largest number. Some took postgraduate degrees, usually at Columbia or the University of Pennsylvania, and all were markedly influenced by their American sojourns.

The southern states left a particularly sharp impression on the West Africans. Unaccustomed to complete social restriction at home, every one of the prewar students had a brush with Jim Crow and segregation in America. Some were terrified by KKK raids in the twenties. Others, dependent upon extra jobs during the depression years, became familiar with the American Negroes' economic insecurity and chafed against unequal pay for work identical to that of white labor. Many found solace or acceptance only in New York's Harlem, which some likened to a ghetto. Alert and impressionable, they were swept up first in Du Bois' Pan-Africanism, then Garvey's "Black Nationalism." More than one witnessed a race riot, fled from a lynch mob, or was barred from a segregationist church.

Communist Party meetings were exciting phenomena, but the students always suspected its white leadership—Russian,

French, British or American—of ulterior motives. The main attraction of Marxist activity was its quasi-illegal character, which appealed to the defiant streak in brilliant students, and the ingenuity of Communist organization, which some of them tried to copy. The Party ideology and international discipline were much less influential because the Negro wanted identity, independence and interclass racial unity rather than the Communists' alien-dominated class-conscious abstraction.

African students also drew heavily, if not uniformly, upon the host country's environment. The impatience, dynamism and forthrightness of the American people left indelible marks upon the policies, journalistic writings and behavior of those who studied in the New World. WASU scholars absorbed much more the British emphasis on national unity, strong Parliamentary party discipline, and evolutionary reformism. Furthermore, virtually every future nationalist absorbed more than one of the many influences from abroad. Garveyism, Pan-Africanism, American Negro and British West Indian influences interacted with impressions of the American people and the southern United States, British institutions and Communist Party techniques. Numerous varieties of these then combined with the Ethiopianism, mission impact and detribalization of Africa itself. The product was a leadership that was at once diverse and complex, which in turn contributed to the differentiation of Africa's many emerging nationalisms.

Interwoven with the student influence and the Communist approach was the later history of W.E.B. Du Bois' Pan-Africanist movement. The four Pan-African congresses between 1919 and 1927 had been increasingly dominated by the American Negroes. As already mentioned, plans for a fifth meeting were disrupted by the 1929 depression. The organized movement collapsed in the diplomatic and economic disappointments of the thirties. Du Bois, largely disregarded and disillusioned by the NAACP's concentration on American domestic problems, escaped from his isolation by accepting Moscow's promises. Stalin's subsequent turns of mind and the death of the Comintern dashed Du Bois' hopes. After breaking with Moscow during the war, he called the long-delayed Fifth Pan-African Congress. At its meetings in 1945, in London, WASU members such as Kwame Nkrumah of the Gold Coast and Jomo Kenyatta from Kenya listened with interest and sympathy. Trade union movements, which had grown and stabilized during the wartime prosperity, were strongly represented alongside students and politicians. The Congress drew on Negro colonial populations, a cross section rather than a special class of African people. The driving forces were British, African and West Indian rather than American; anticolonialism, not ideology, was stressed, and the resolutions opposed both Russian and Western domination. The delegates called for political independence, economic control by indigenous people, and social improvement. Civil rights, equality with white settlers and the separation of Christianity from colonial politics and economics were demanded. The Congress' ambitions were systematic and extensive, but the ruling powers reacted warily and the general Pan-Africanist analyses were not always suited to the specific needs of individual colonies.

After 1945 the nationalist movements within Africa tended to become increasingly distinct from one another. Pan-Africanism continued as an ideal but not as a working institution. The shell of Pan-African organization therefore became quite separate from the effective nationalist movements. Before Communists infiltrated the Congress organization in 1948, the Pan-Africanist ideal had already been transferred to the independent local movements scattered across Africa. The Communist front therefore represented an organization that no longer had any real influence. Postwar agitation for self-government in Africa varied from one colony to another. Communism remained essentially external, still working from outside while the basic work took place inside Africa. The achievement of independence in Africa, albeit a result of contact with European ideas, has occurred entirely within the individual emerging nations.

22

COMMONWEALTH IN WEST AFRICA

SECULAR political activity in West Africa had a rudimentary but significant beginning in the late nineteenth
century. In Lagos, whose urban population was already partially detribalized, Africans in 1896 protested that most of their
taxes seemed to be going toward the improvement of European
residential areas. On the Gold Coast a year later the governor
recognized an Aborigines' Rights Protection Society which Fanti
chiefs and lawyers were then organizing.

A law regulating the "public land" of the Gold Coast
alarmed the Africans. Previously the Crown had claimed ownership of no land save the old factory sites. The Aborigines' Society failed to halt this Lands Bill in the colonial Legislative
Council, which officials controlled, but London heeded the protests and disallowed the measure. Subsequently the Society
served as a self-appointed African voice which, though separate
from the Legislative Council, advised the governor on a variety
of local matters. An enlargement of the Council in 1916 was intended to eliminate this anomaly, but official appointees still
dominated the proceedings and the Aborigines' Protection Society continued to function separately.

Cautious progress failed to satisfy many West Africans,
who had been told that World War I would "make the world

safe for democracy." In 1920 a National Congress of British West Africa proposed a federal dominion that would exercise "self-determination" and eliminate "taxation without representation." The founder, Joseph E. Casely Hayford, had been a Fanti barrister, an editor and, for four years, one of the nominated members of the Legislative Council. The Congress drew heavily on the Congress movement and Gandhi in India. Hayford's ideas stimulated the Nigerian cities, but, because of poor communications, they had little impact upon Sierra Leone and Gambia. The West African National Congress asked Britain for a partially elected "Assembly," fiscal and judicial control, and a university. However, the Aborigines' Society chiefs repudiated the plan, which would have threatened their traditional position. With the chiefs thus contradicting the educated Africans, the government felt that it could safely reject the application. The Congress movement nevertheless continued its activities until Casely Hayford died in 1930.

Dissatisfaction in Nigeria then manifested itself in a wave of Garveyism, imported from New York, while the Aborigines' Society retained its power on the Gold Coast until the constitutional reform of 1925. The governor who wrote the new law, Sir Gordon Guggisberg, an exceptionally sensitive and popular official, greatly changed both the economy and politics of the Gold Coast, Ashanti and the Northern Territories. Cocoa production, which had spread gradually since its introduction from Fernando Po in 1879, began to be the leading industry. At Takoradi the government built an artificial harbor which offered the only sheltered anchorage and the first wharves on the Guinea Gulf Coast. Guggisberg also increased his prestige in the Ashanti Colony by judiciously handling two fortuitous developments. The long-sought Golden Stool turned up during 1920 in the course of a highway excavation project, but the governor promptly renounced Britain's claims and helped the Ashanti to prosecute two thieves who had desecrated the precious symbol. Four years later he also allowed the ashantihene to return from exile and recover his Stool.

Guggisberg's political changes, although influenced by Casely Hayford's ideas, were much more controversial. Ashanti and the Northern Territories came under indirect rule, whereby established chiefs, advised by British officials, reported directly to the governor. In the Gold Coast Colony, which already had direct rule and a Legislative Council, the number of legislative seats was increased from twenty-one to twenty-nine. Officials retained a one-vote majority. Of the fourteen unofficial members, five represented European merchants, miners and other interests. The nine remaining seats—just under one third of the total—were reserved for representatives of the African population: six from the provincial councils and one to be elected from each of the three main cities. Property requirements restricted the electorate to about 6 percent of the urban population, or one out of every two hundred people in the whole colony.

Observers abroad—including the Pan-African Congress—hailed the reform, but the Aborigines' Rights Protection Society did not. Its newspapers labeled the African members "dummies" whom Britain would use "to gag the people." Chiefs were told to boycott the provincial councils, and educated Africans were forbidden to contest the municipal seats. Casely Hayford, many chiefs and some merchants disobeyed, but in the city of Cape Coast, the seat of Aborigines' activity, there was no election. Guggisberg, as expected, ceased to consult the Society, which gradually became a center for intransigent local discontent rather than a movement toward national identity. The Society's situation in 1925 demonstrated that educated Africans could not work for democracy and nationhood within an institution dominated by the aristocratic interests of traditional local chiefs.

Sierra Leone had its first elections in 1924, in which three Africans were elected from the coastal colony. In addition, two others were appointed by the British, and paramount chiefs from the interior protectorate were admitted to the Council, which advised the Governor on all matters. The government machinery was therefore identical for both the colony and the protectorate, although, in the latter, traditional chiefs retained greater control over local affairs.

Southern Nigeria and the Lagos Colony had actually preceded the Gold Coast and Sierra Leone by having elections in 1923. The West African National Congress may have been less of an impetus toward this reform than the continued demands of detribalized Lagos Africans. Their movement, directed since 1908 by a volatile politician, Herbert Macauley, was sometimes powerful within the city but never popular elsewhere. Macauley appealed both to the laborers and to the powerful market women with his personal dynamism, but insisted upon so direct a control over his political machine that it could never establish effective branches outside Lagos. Sometimes known as "the father of Nigerian nationalism," he was a vital force both in the 1923 reforms and in subsequent elections. Essentially Macauley remained a city politician rather than an effective national leader.

Political developments in each British West African colony subsequently diverged markedly. The electoral innovations of 1923-25, along with the early groundwork of the Aborigines' Society, Casely Hayford and Macauley, gave each area a superficially similar political beginning. However, later evolution was strongly influenced by the unique problems within each territory. Nevertheless, there was a period in every case when emerging nationalists and their foreign supporters looked to nearby Liberia—free since 1847—for examples and precedents. They rarely found any, save perhaps the desire to succeed where Liberia had failed. The factors in Liberia that caused this reaction should therefore be understood before considering the national development of the Gold Coast, Nigeria and Sierra Leone.

For the first years of the twentieth century the government of Liberia—controlled by the 12,000 descendants of liberated slaves—was sustained by foreign loans. The customs houses came under joint control by Britain, France, Germany and the United States, but the outbreak of war in 1914 caused disagree-

ment among these four receivers. Trade dwindled, customs collections declined and the interior tribes (especially the Kru)
began to revolt. Liberian police and munitions were transported
by the American Navy. The United States pressed for fiscal and
social reforms but could not enforce its wishes upon Liberia,
which had joined the allied cause. American Army officers organized the frontier forces, thus helping to restore peace. The
United States then offered to grant $5,000,000 but demanded
in return the right to control the treasury. Liberia's Congress
denied the request. Then, in 1922, President Warren G. Har-
ding proposed an American Protectorate, but the Senate in
Washington rejected the idea.

Two years later the four-power receivers sold their loans,
which had long been in default, to the Firestone Tire and Rubber Company. From the Liberian government Harvey S. Firestone also acquired a ninety-nine-year lease on one million acres
of tropical land, although such an arrangement seemed to contradict the constitutional ban on "alien landholding." In addition to the concession, which served as collateral for the loan,
Liberia promised to pay a substantial rate of interest. In the
depression year of 1931 the annual charge amounted to one-half
the government's total revenue. Liberia refused to pay the debt,
and the League of Nations proceeded to investigate.

The League commission was less concerned with the Firestone debt than with the rumors of active slave trading. The investigators reported that government soldiers were periodically
attacking the tribes, kidnaping children and selling them to the
Vice-President. Some then worked on the coastal plantations,
but others were exported to the estates of Portuguese São Thomé
and Spanish Fernando Po. The League Assembly approved a
scheme for international administration of the country, but
Liberia was able to veto the plan. Slaving gradually disappeared
and the League in 1934 rescinded its proposals. One year later
Liberia again came to terms with Firestone. The company received new mineral rights and, in lieu of overdue interest, an
exemption from taxation. Slow economic improvement then

permitted Liberia to meet the interest payments, but there was almost no money for education, welfare or diversified economic development.

During the Second World War, under pressure from the American government, Firestone surrendered 800,000 acres—80 percent of the concession—which had never been used. Furthermore, a new agreement between Liberia and the company eliminated the monopoly guarantees and provided for a revision in the interest payment system. A priority formula in the Liberian budget balanced public education and welfare requirements against the Firestone loan in a way that guaranteed the maintenance of essential services in bad years, but provided for high amortization payments in the good years. The United States also licensed Pan-American Airways to build and maintain Roberts Field. During the war this air base became a major strategic link, and after 1945, together with an American harbor-improvement program, it became the cornerstone of economic development. Iron exploitation since 1956 has given the country its first railway and raised Liberia's hopes for a competitive, diversified economy. Well-planned missionary programs, supported by the government, have begun to educate the interior tribes and to prepare them for participation in politics. By 1960 the first few had begun to qualify for the ballot and to participate in the new economy. Government revenue has increased, and the Firestone debt should be discharged before 1966.

The improvement, however, has come only since World War II, due largely to prolonged international prosperity. Until recent years the country appeared to keep its precarious freedom only by fortuitous circumstance and a delicate balance of foreign interests. This unhappy era, a period in which the elite coastal minority either disregarded or dominated the tribal majority, was the one that impressed both Europeans and the rest of Africa. The colonial powers interpreted it as a warning against independence, but the African nationalists saw in Liberia a regressive elite on one hand and an economic colonialism on the other. Indeed, it still is uncertain whether the Europeanized coastal settlers and their one-party oligarchy will accept the indigenous majority who, aside from a superficial racial similarity, constitute a very different cultural and social force. For these reasons, the rest of Africa still considers Liberia simply the germ of an idea rather than either a model or a full ally.

In the Gold Coast Colony, Guggisberg's political innovations were not entirely successful. Withdrawal of recognition from the Aborigines' Rights Protection Society had eliminated the consultative system by which British governors kept in touch with African sentiment. Under the 1925 Constitution the traditional chiefs operating through the provincial and legislative councils had a stronger voice than the educated detribalized Africans. The urban intelligentsia felt increasingly that power had passed to a coalition of chiefs and colonial officials, both of whom would have to be abolished in order to obtain freedom and democracy.

Economic depression during the 1930's strengthened the popular movement against traditionalism and the Empire. The cocoa industry, which had captured half the world market, created a new class of individual farmers who farmed intensively and efficiently on individually owned plots of land. Having neither tribal or urban connections, these yeomen sold their cocoa through a series of African brokers to a number of competitive European wholesalers. By 1929 export sales had passed into the hands of the United Africa Company, a virtual monopoly built upon the merger of Lever Brothers, the old Royal Niger Company, and a number of smaller firms. A few months later the depression caused cocoa prices to plummet. The small cocoa farmers immediately felt the loss and, in 1930-31, they tried unsuccessfully to break the monopoly price by staging a boycott. In 1937 the major wholesalers formed a "pool" in order to restrict competition and to control the price. Cocoa prices fell 50 percent within a few weeks. The Governor at first protested but soon retreated to a neutral position. The farmers tried another boycott, during which many mortgaged themselves heavily to their brokers.

Early in 1938 the Colonial Office dispatched a commission, led by William Nowell, to investigate. After discovering both manipulation and hardship within the cocoa industry, the Nowell Commission recommended the establishment of a farmers' association that would collect and market the entire cocoa crop. World War II began before such a cocoa coöperative could be established, but the British war cabinet ordered the Food Ministry to buy all crops directly from the growers. The wholesalers' pool, including the United Africa Company, was thereby eliminated. When emergency agencies ceased operation in 1947, the government replaced a wartime system with a permanent Gold Coast Marketing Board, which would purchase, grade and export all cocoa, while guarding the prosperity of the producers.

The Marketing Board system, which destroyed the European export monopoly, tried particularly to prevent a recurrence of the severe price and demand fluctuations that characterized the twenties and thirties. It paid the small farmers a fairly standard price for each crop, banking the excess in a good year and expecting to draw upon it in a bad year. However, prices rose steadily during and after the Second World War, so the surplus—a so-called "Equalization Fund"—grew steadily. Management of the fund, and of the entire marketing system, rested with the African producers.

Most of the fund was saved, but some went into capital development, scholarships and educational improvement, especially for the cocoa growers' families. At the same time, other Africans were becoming increasingly concerned with the lack of educational opportunities. Poor tax revenues during the depression had thwarted earlier hopes for a schooling program, and the British taxpayer had been unable or unwilling to subsidize such a system for the entire colonial population. Even in the late forties most schools continued to rely upon mission support. Not more than 15 percent of the people were literate,

and most of those who were lived in the urban centers along the
southern coast.

The 1946 constitution, which Governor Sir Alan Burns introduced, was not well received. Ashanti and the Northern Territories were given their first seats on the Legislative Council,
but chiefs and tribal councils chose the representatives because
the literacy rate among the interior population was so low. These
indirectly elected northern chiefs, combined with directly elected
representatives of the coastal towns and farms, composed a majority of the council seats. Nevertheless, the chiefs tended to
ally with the officially nominated minority in controlling the
legislature. Cocoa growers, the urbanized and the educated—
together a substantial majority of the population—began to
consider the constitution a device for perpetuating foreign domination. The new British Labor Government had considered
it "enlightened," even though the Governor still was not responsible to the Legislative Council, so the negative reaction
dismayed the Crown.

Shortly after the constitution was promulgated, the Gold
Coast government began to encounter an increasing amount of
economic criticism. A "swollen shoot" disease began to disrupt
the vital cocoa industry in 1947. In order to halt it, all trees in
an infected district—even the uninjured ones—had to be destroyed. Money was appropriated for such a program, but farmers
suspected that the government was plotting either to favor another colony or to weaken the economy so that the Gold Coast
could not develop a working government. At the same time,
postwar inflation and the shortage of consumer goods caused
inflation, which the Africans blamed on the European import
firms. Farmers complained the Marketing Board paid too little
for cocoa, and put too much money into the "Equalization
Fund."

By 1947 an opposition movement had become evident.
Africans who had fought abroad in World War II, especially in
India and Burma, demanded for their country the same inde-
pendence that India had just achieved. Under the leadership

of Dr. J. B. Danquah, an urban lawyer, the dissatisfied masses —veterans, educated youths, urbanized and detribalized Africans, and many cocoa growers—formed the United Gold Coast Convention. The UGCC advocated mass pressure, immediate self-government and a new constitution. Danquah called upon Kwame Nkrumah to direct the party organization.

Nkrumah had been abroad since 1935, first an undergraduate at Lincoln University in the United States, then a graduate student at the University of Pennsylvania. At the end of the war, he went to London for Du Bois' Fifth Pan-African Congress, and remained in Britain as an active leader in the West African Students Union. His personal charm, indefatigable energy and organizing ability were well known to educated, urbanized Gold Coast Africans. Nkrumah therefore seemed to be the logical man to direct a popular movement against aristocratic chiefs and colonial rule.

As its organization strengthened, the UGCC pressed its demands. In 1948 the party led a boycott of European goods. On February 28 the boycotting masses marched on the Governor's palace. The police responded with gunfire. Rioting broke out in Accra, the capital, and spread quickly to several other cities. Danquah cabled to the Colonial Secretary, claiming that the civil government had broken down and asking for authority to form a ministry that could restore order. However, determined to disprove the cabled statements, the Government detained Danquah, Nkrumah and four other UGCC leaders. A commission under Aiken Watson flew out to investigate.

The Watson report stressed the economic complaints, but added that these had led to political frustration. Faster progress, more public information, and less support for the chiefs were advocated. British economic power and the cocoa marketing system needed reform. More Africans in the higher civil service posts, additional educational facilities and new agricultural services were recommended. The commission pointed out that the government had to convince farmers to cut down cocoa trees, to pay higher prices for imports, and to sell their crops below the market price. Disturbances should not have been a surprise, concluded the report, but the grievances should have been recognized before they had become so bitter. In other words, political self-government probably would have prevented the crisis.

The Governor promptly appointed J. H. Coussey, Chairman, and thirty-five other Africans to a constitutional committee which deliberated through most of 1949. The resulting report attempted to strike a balance between African self-government and the gradualism that Britain desired, yet to satisfy both urban people and the rural chiefs. The Coussey Committee proposed a legislature, with nearly all members chosen by election, which would have the power to dismiss an executive, though the Governor could continue to legislate if necessary without such check.

Britain accepted the Coussey Report, though her officials doubted that a responsible government without political parties would be feasible. African legislators had always criticized policies, but none had either executed them or formulated alternatives. There was only one party, the UGCC, which contained all advocates of self-government; on secondary matters, Africans disagreed along personal or regional lines that were devoid of either party or policy. The Colonial Office therefore decided to retain a separate Executive Council, responsible to London rather than to the legislature. However, individual members of the Executive Council would be dismissed if the legislators so requested, and a responsible cabinet would be allowed as soon as opposition parties emerged.

Gold Coast voters did not respect the British argument. Opinion turned against Dr. Danquah, who was trying to negotiate with the Coussey Committee. Kwame Nkrumah, the organization manager of Danquah's United Gold Coast Convention, demanded "Self-Government Now," rejected all compromise, and formed a new Convention People's Party. The CPP took over the final word of the UGCC's name and then most of its mass support. Nkrumah called a boycott and general strike early in 1950. Although the CPP wanted to emulate Gandhian nonviolent techniques to discredit the government, disorders erupted in the tense atmosphere. Nkrumah was promptly sent to jail.

The trial backfired. CPP supporters firmly believed that British justice was merely an arm of the political authorities. The colonial government did not make it clear that the sentence was solely a punishment for violence. Instead, the masses believed that Nkrumah was simply a political prisoner. He therefore became a popular hero whom colonial injustice seemed to have martyred.

Fortunately the Crown did not delay the promised new constitution. A unicameral Assembly was created with eighty-four members: thirty-eight elected by popular vote, thirty-seven by chiefs' councils, and nine appointed by the Governor. Africans would manage the executive departments, and would be responsible to the Assembly, but the chief executive would still be a British governor, nonpartisan, accountable only to London, and holding in reserve the power of decree.

In addition to the change in executive machinery, the 1951 Constitution also gave half the legislative seats to the chiefs instead of only one-third, as the Coussey Committee had recommended. The CPP immediately protested against these revisions. The Constitution could have been thwarted by fresh unrest, but the party agreed to coöperate with the Governor in the new system. The first elections were scheduled for February, 1951, and civil servants worked with the British authorities to instruct the masses in voting procedure. Of the thirty-eight seats filled by popular election, the CPP captured thirty-four. Danquah's UGCC took only three, and an independent held one. Traditional chiefs chose several small factions to fill their thirty-seven seats, and the Governor appointed nine European official and commercial representatives. Nkrumah carried a district in the capital, although he was in prison throughout the electoral campaign. Since the CPP controlled the largest bloc of seats, its coöperation was essential for effective operation of the Constitution. Governor Sir Charles Arden-Clarke therefore pardoned Nkrumah, consulted with him immediately, and accepted him as the (Parliamentary) Leader of Government Business.

Nkrumah relied heavily upon his organizing ability in order to restrain the impatient wing of his party. Primary attention was given to the extension of education and to the replacement of Englishmen in the civil service. Agricultural development, road building, modernization of the railways, harbors, public water supply, and health services all were pressed. Foreign and British capital was far from adequate, so the Nkrumah government relied upon tax revenues for its programs. At the same time, the Cocoa Marketing Board assumed a larger role in economic development by providing loans and auxiliary improvements among its own members. Danquah accused the Board of favoring CPP members, but when the charges were sustained by a legislative investigation (Jibowu Commission), the CPP government tightened the regulations and asked the Assembly to maintain stricter supervision.

Governor Arden-Clarke realized that the CPP had become an effective Parliamentary party, and that its voting strength gave it the power to sustain or disrupt the executive any time it wished. Nkrumah therefore became Prime Minister in March, 1952, and his ministers became a cabinet. The chiefs' representatives in the Assembly had already been made responsible to local councils that were closer to the people in tribal areas, but the chiefs themselves still continued to exercise more influence over these councils than the democratically minded CPP wished to permit. Nkrumah's cabinet now realized the need for time and for legal clarity in the final steps toward independence. In 1954 the Assembly passed a new constitution which, after receiving British approval, provided that all legislative seats would be filled by direct election and that all Europeans would be eliminated from the cabinet. However, the Governor was allowed to retain his special powers during the transitional period. The CPP then submitted to a general election, from which it emerged with 71 of the 104 seats. The opposition represented special aristocratic, religious or ethnic interests—chiefs, privileged intelligentsia, Moslems, tribalists—rather than any national or parliamentary parties. The strongest of these groups, the Northern People's Party (NPP), became the official opposition, although Nkrumah was afraid that its emphasis upon regional interests, especially those of the Northern Territories, would disrupt the progress toward national independence.

Subsequent to the election of 1954, the government increased the duty on cocoa exports. The new revenue, essentially an indirect levy upon the cocoa farmers, was intended to control inflation and to finance more economic development. Many farmers understood, but some in Ashanti interpreted the move as an attack upon their prosperity. The objectors soon began to demand financial autonomy for Ashanti, and talked about "the creeping dictatorship" of the South, where a majority of the population lived. A National Liberation Movement (NLM) emerged in Ashanti, which the ashantihene supported, and the Crown was asked to investigate the possibility of creating a federal constitution. The Colonial Secretary pointed out that this would be foreign interference in a problem that potentially independent countries should settle by themselves.

Conferences between the NLM and the CPP broke down because the latter felt that it had a direct electoral mandate in favor of the 1954 Constitution. An English constitutional expert, whom the government then appointed to arbitrate the issue, advised against the division of so small a country. He did recommend the creation of strong local governments, and the protection of chiefs' prerogatives, but the CPP rejected this. The NLM and the Ashanti Council thereupon asked Britain to postpone the grant of independence, but the Colonial Secretary recommended instead a general Gold Coast election to resolve the dispute.

A similar contest between regionalism and nationalism was moving toward resolution on the eastern boundary of the Gold

Coast. The former German colony of Togo had been partitioned into two League of Nations mandates, one French and one British. The Ewe tribe was therefore split into two groups. Some of the Ewe advocated tribal reunification, but others favored the CPP's Gold Coast nationalism. Britain notified the United Nations, which was heir to the League mandates, that the trusteeship would have to be transferred either to the Gold Coast or to another power (presumably, France or a reunited Togo). On May 9, 1956 the voters of British Togo chose the Gold Coast by a reasonable majority, a transfer which the UN General Assembly subsequently approved.

Nkrumah called a general election for July, 1956. The CPP stood for a unitary government, popularly elected. The NLM and NPP lacked cohesiveness until the Ashanti Council gave them a platform in which political parties and majority voting were condemned. The essential issue was national unity and democracy versus regional interest and the chiefs' traditional prerogatives.

All seats in the southern colony went to the CPP, as did a majority of those in Togoland. Ashanti went six to four for its local NLM, and the north gave a moderate edge to the NPP. The CPP, which held a clear majority of the total popular vote, was the only party to win seats in all four regions, and it increased its Parliamentary strength to 72 out of 104. Nkrumah cited the returns as proof that his party alone supported the Constitution, and the British government accepted the election as a mandate for the CPP.

The Legislative Assembly thereupon met to write a constitution for sovereign self-government, and to ask Britain for formal independence. The opposition parties demanded a special Constitutional Convention. In denying this request, Nkrumah pointed out that constitutions according to British law are always made by the regular legislature. The opposition thereupon walked out of the Assembly, leaving the chamber to the CPP, which constituted both a quorum and a majority. The

Independence Petition was therefore debated and passed by a vote of 72-0.

The British Parliament passed the Independence Act and, at the request of both Danquah and Nkrumah, the country was named Ghana. The ancient kingdom of that name was at least 400 miles farther northwest, but the CPP, supported by some scholars, claimed that its followers were the heirs of the old empire who had migrated to the coast. Many students doubt that there was anything more than a transmission of ideas from the earlier culture. Nevertheless, the adoption of the Ghanaian name linked a proud historical tradition with the first independent state in twentieth-century tropical Africa.

The influence of both colonial and precolonial history has been noticeable in Ghana since Independence Day. The date itself—March 6, 1957—coincided with the anniversary of the Anglo-Fanti Bond of 1844. The African government, having assumed the responsibilities formerly held by Great Britain, has maintained the Cocoa Marketing Board as a government-sponsored commercial coöperative, which now has to strike a balance among national welfare, foreign markets and the farmers' interests. The effort to stimulate development on a national scale has given political as well as economic importance to new railways, harbors, hydroelectric projects and bauxite mines. Some capital has come from abroad—particularly British and Canadian funds—but such resources, which have always been insufficient in tropical Africa, are now being augmented by public appropriations. This tendency toward government financing is enhanced by the recollection of long periods during which relatively small foreign investment was usually associated with much direct control over the country. Educational facilities have been expanded; literacy has increased from 20 percent, the rate prevailing when Nkrumah's first Education Act was passed in 1952, to something over 80 percent in 1959.

The constitutional controversy has continued. The federalist-minded minority, NLM and NPP, represented tribal, privileged or regional interests. The governing CPP claimed that they were pressure groups, not parties, which constituted a virtually seditious secessionist threat against the national constitution. As long as identity had not been secured, the centralists said, there could be no basic policy disagreement on the national level.

The CPP government has dealt severely with critics of either national unity or the Constitution. Britain apparently did not successfully impart the concept of a judiciary separate from the executive. Therefore, law enforcement in major political disputes tends to depend upon the legislature rather than the courts. This resembles the English situation about 300 years ago, when political prisoners were sentenced by "Bills of Attainder," debated and passed in the British Parliament. Since 1957 the Ghanaian Parliament has for similar reasons passed comparable measures restricting, exiling or unseating the more vociferous opposition critics. It remains to be seen whether, over a long period of time, some system of justice less subject to political influence can be developed for the preservation of constitutionalism and national unity.

Complex historical factors are equally noticeable in the personality and policies of Prime Minister Nkrumah. The internal structure of his Convention People's Party resembles a British parliamentary party in its insistence upon firm discipline and upon national interest rather than regional representation. The centralized organizational command is similar to that of most successful pressure groups throughout the world—nationalist, Communist, Falangist, trade-unionist, or the Gandhian Congress movement in India. However, the party's function and actual operation is influenced more by American political machines and English mutual-benefit societies than by abstract or dogmatic ideology. Some of the Garveyite sense of racial unity is evident, as is much of the Pan-Africanist thinking with which Nkrumah was familiar as a student.

A United Party emerged in the fall of 1957 out of the opposition factions in Ghana, but the new organization still represented the interior regions and supported traditional authorities. Firmly convinced that the opposition constituted a threat to domestic unity and Pan-Africanism, the government continued to restrict or to silence the United Party leadership. Nkrumah also became increasingly concerned with the position of the British monarch in Ghana's constitution. Though the queen's function was purely symbolic, it might have barred any federation with African countries that did not belong to the Commonwealth. He also feared that the Army might capitalize on political dissension in order to increase its own power. The CPP therefore proposed a republic, similar to that of India, still within the Commonwealth, but with a president whose power more closely resembled that of the chief executive in America and the new French Fifth Republic. The United Party demanded instead a series of elective provincial monarchies, with paramount chiefs of all the regions rotating automatically as the federal chief executive. In April, 1960 the people voted seven to one in favor of the new constitution, chose Nkrumah as president, and gave him authority to curb political activity within the Army. Ghana therefore became a republic on July 1, 1960. The queen was simply Head of the Commonwealth, and Nkrumah her representative in Ghana in lieu of a governor-general, but all other Commonwealth ties remained unchanged. The president will hold office for five years, but if he loses Assembly support, there must be a general election. Provision was also made for the modification or extension of the constitution should the country federate with another African nation.

Ghana served both as a pioneer and as a model in the achievement of African independence by essentially peaceful means. However, the example was by no means entirely suited to other colonies whose problems, characteristics and attitudes were very different. Nigeria, which was the second British colony to acquire freedom, clearly illustrates these contrasts, even though she was so near to Ghana and subject to the same colonial ruler. The colonies and protectorates of Nigeria were more than four times the size of Ghana, and contained about seven times as many people. Both countries were composed of three regions plus a small strip under United Nations trusteeship, but the differences otherwise were pronounced. Ghana was dominated by the Gold Coast Colony, the richest, most Westernized section, which contained a majority of the population. However, the Nigerian regions were more evenly populated and somewhat more equal economically. Furthermore, all of Nigeria—except for the enclave of Lagos—came under British rule in the course of only sixteen years, whereas European control had expanded slowly in Ghana in the course of more than 400 years.

There had never been any unity in Nigeria until the various colonial possessions were federated under Lord Lugard in 1914. Even then, the unification was largely for European administrative and economic convenience. Each region was intentionally allowed to retain its distinctive characteristics. As late as 1920 a British governor—Sir Hugh Clifford—ridiculed the idea

> "that this collection of self-contained and mutually independent Native States separated from one another . . . by . . . distances . . . history and tradition . . . political, social and religious barriers, were indeed capable of being welded into a single homogeneous nation. . . ." [1]

However, the West African National Congress under Casely Hayford was exerting pressure for unification. This movement failed to take roots in Nigeria, but it did stimulate demands by Herbert Macauley and in the coastal cities for representation in the government. Yielding to the pressure in 1922, Governor Clifford created a Legislative Council for Nigeria, and allowed the election of three African representatives—two from Lagos, one from Calabar. The Legislative Council was actually dominated by the governor's appointees. Therefore, by giving new

---

[1] Quoted in Kalu Ezera, *Constitutional Developments in Nigeria*, Cambridge, 1960, p. 26.

power to his officials, he weakened Lugard's older system of indirect rule, which relied upon the established chiefs.

From indirect rule, with federation limited to the European administration, to the emergence of a national state, took only thirty-eight years. For most of this time, nationalist activity was autonomous in each region, and the advocates of self-government appealed primarily to the needs and desires of their local areas. Developments were therefore parallel rather than closely interrelated: in the West, Britain exerted an extensive, direct influence over the fairly well organized Yoruba; in the East, about 700 autonomous villages (mostly Ibo) were indirectly controlled; and in the North, the Hausa and Fulani emirs were allowed to retain their traditional functions. Nigeria could not be called a nation until each region had become aware first of its own identity, then of its interdependence with the other regions.

Nnamdi Azikiwe, a detribalized Ibo from the East, was the first Nigerian to study in the United States and the first African to take a degree from an accredited American university. He entered a small college in 1925, completed his B.A. at Lincoln, and his M.A. at the University of Pennsylvania. Segregation in the American South, the last phases of Garveyism in New York, and the NAACP's goals left deep impressions. Determined upon his return in 1934 to liberate the Negro, he started a newspaper chain and the Nigerian Youth Movement (NYM). His journalism, which resembled the American tabloid style rather than the English sensationalist press, became both influential and profitable. The NYM quickly acquired a following among the multitribal, urban Africans in Lagos—particularly the younger generation, those whose parents had supported the Macauley machine. Azikiwe's fellow Ibos did not dominate the NYM, but their influence was strong. Observers have not been able to agree whether the Ibos who pioneered in these early nationalist years were seeking an identity that their disunited tribe had lacked, or simply competing with the more Europeanized and wealthier Yoruba of the Western region.

By 1941 the Yoruba had reasserted themselves. Under the leadership of Obafemi Awolowo, an indefatigable entrepreneur in local transport, they acquired control of the National Youth Movement. Azikiwe's multitribalism disappeared, so he resigned in order to concentrate upon journalistic development and agitation. After returning in 1944 to Iboland, in the Eastern region, he formed a new movement, the National Council of Nigeria and the Cameroons (NCNC). Azikiwe wanted an intertribal organization, but the actual following was more restricted. Herbert Macauley brought his detribalized, anti-Yoruba Lagos movement into the NCNC, which could therefore claim members whose origins lay in more than a hundred tribes. However, Azikiwe's fellow Ibos were the only group with active tribal connections. The NCNC demanded independence within the Commonwealth by 1958, while the older NYM concentrated on economic issues, local-government representation and the preservation of Yoruba preëminence.

The British Labor Party accepted the principle of colonial self-government when it came to power in 1945. However, there was less agreement about the method of putting the ideal into practice. The tendency, at least in the early years of Labor's tenure, was to accept the advice of experienced officials in the field. The initiative in Nigeria therefore rested with the incumbent governors, whose chief concern was the disparity and contrast among the country's various regions.

Under the 1922 Constitution the North had no representation of any kind in the Legislative Council except for Englishmen appointed by the governor, and the northern emirs did not seem to wish any change. In 1942 Governor Sir Bernard Bourdillon persuaded them to participate, although he found them most reluctant to break their isolationism. The next wartime governor, Sir Arthur Richards (later Lord Milverton), attempted to assuage their fears by guaranteeing their distinctive regional autocracy within a federal Nigerian structure. However, in view of the difficulties he had just had with nationalists in Jamaica, Richards' transfer to Africa in 1944 may have been unfortunate. A year later, without any warning, consultation or test of public opinion, Richards published a new constitution. The officials controlling the Legislative Council quickly gave their approval, and both parties in the British Parliament ratified it after a few minutes of debate. Promulgated in 1946, the so-called Richards Constitution provided for a federal Legislative Council, 91 percent of whose members were appointed either by the governor or by the traditional Native Authorities. In addition, each region had its own legislature. However, the function of the latter councils was purely advisory and none of the seats in them were to be filled by election. In the North the system was bicameral: a House of Chiefs, in which all principal rulers and selected lesser ranks had seats; and a House of Assembly, with membership selected by the Native Authorities or the governor. The East and West each had a unicameral House of Assembly, with about 60 percent of the members nominated by the government and 40 percent chosen by the tribal councils.

The Constitution clearly reflects two problems that had begun to concern the British planners. Believing primarily that tribes and emirs were the "natural" government, but wishing also to build a new nation, they decided to create artificial provinces. In the initial preparatory stage the new provinces would absorb the traditional authorities, change the orientation from tribes to a comprehensible territorial government, and give training in political techniques. Through this device, national unity would gradually acquire meaning. The official planners wisely avoided the election of representatives to assemblies that would have no legislative power, but they did this by making sure that British nominees outnumbered both the chiefs and the nationalists on all levels. The result was less than satisfactory.

The educated and nationalistic leaders in the eastern and western regions were disappointed. Many of them felt that the Colonial Office was deliberately frustrating self-government. In fact, Richards had intended to "democratize" the Native Authorities so that they would, in time, merge politically with the urbanized and detribalized movements. The NCNC and the NYM both wanted to start managing the government—not just "discussion," one spokesman said, but "participation." Awolowo complained that the structure of the regional Assemblies was determined "by a consideration of the number of Official members available in each Region, and not by the desire to give wider and [more] adequate representation to the people." Others believed the chiefs would ally with Britain against the masses, and some claimed that the chiefs who entered popular politics would lose prestige. There was particular bitterness because elective representation had not been increased. Awolowo agreed to work with the constitution, though his NYM followers later balked. The NCNC, which protested vehemently from the beginning, soon began to produce an extremist wing.

Two months after publishing his constitution Richards accused Azikiwe's newspapers of misrepresenting facts. The governor then suspended the papers, but nationalist agitation continued to appear in other journals. Azikiwe then went into hiding, notified influential people that his life was threatened, and petitioned the Colonial Office for protection. Richards dismissed "a certain journalist" for his "silly invention," but the newspaper-reading public, less familiar with sensationalist journalism, became alarmed. By seeming to be the victim of a colonialist plot, "Zik" made himself a popular idol. Some of the press—particularly the NYM organs—condemned his "colossal falsehood." Feelings sharpened. The faithful formed a Zikist Movement, which defined itself as "African irredentism," "a creative impulse," and, ultimately, an instrument for the immortalization of Zik as the "Prophet" of the National Church of Nigeria. Tribal support for this Ethiopianist movement was considerable. Zik did not encourage the traditionalist element, which threatened to blur his nationalist cause. He denied being a "New Messiah," and apparently did not direct the extremist fringe. However, he did attend National Church services, in which, as in his papers, he was openly "compared" to Christ. Actually, Azikiwe was more concerned with the NCNC's 1946 lecture tour through the North. His eulogy at Macauley's funeral, which unexpectedly became the climax of the Northern tour, attracted 100,000 mourners.

Zikism declined rapidly after Sir John Macpherson succeeded Richards in 1948. Moderation, tact and positive reforms —designed in large part by the British Labor Party's Fabian Colonial Bureau—restored balance and compromise to the Nigerian political scene. Azikiwe abandoned his boycott of the Legislative Council. Macpherson promised a new constitution, the Africanization of high positions, the democratization of tribes, and a national university. Labor unrest in the eastern region contributed to a brief revival of Zikist extremism late in 1949, but Azikiwe himself, the NCNC and the NYM, continuing the trend toward Anglo-Nigerian coöperation, let the governor outlaw the movement, which had now become noticeably seditious.

Macpherson inaugurated the University College at Ibadan within the first year, thus giving British West Africa its first fully accredited institution of higher education. Lower levels of education, financed by local taxes, were for the first time provided for every region. Then "if it is the wish of the country," the governor announced, "constitutional changes should be made. . . ." Attention was paid to the Watson and Coussey Reports, which came out of the Gold Coast within the next year. Nigerian opinion was meanwhile sampled with great care, and consultations among all interested factions consumed two more years. The new governor and the imperial cabinet, under Clement Attlee, wanted at all costs to counteract the autocratic impression that Richards had created in promulgating the previous constitution.

During the lengthy constitutional negotiations, the nationalist factions throughout Nigeria regrouped and ultimately emerged as functioning political parties. Only at this penultimate stage did nationalism take root in the Northern region. Earlier NCNC and NYM penetration into that area had found some audience in the cities, but was strongly resented by the

Fulani emirs, who had become grateful for British government support. Northern nationalism did not become effective until it developed distinct roots of its own, particularly among Hausa students, the first of whom did not go abroad until 1945. One of these, Alhaji Abubakar Tafawa Balewa, built a Northern Peoples Congress in alliance with the reigning emirs. This NPC, deliberately aimed to counteract the spread of southern nationalism, was a conservative response rather than reformist aspiration. Nevertheless, it in turn generated an oppositon of its own. A Northern Elements Progressive Union, seeking support largely from the anti-Fulani minorities, such as the Nupe, developed its appeal by calling the emirs opponents of reform and obstructors of democracy. NEPU found a ready ally in the NCNC, which tried to use tribal sentiment as a stepping stone to political power in federal politics.

The NCNC itself was put into an uncomfortable position by the new constitutional and political developments. Azikiwe came to the conclusion that the NPC and the Awolowo bloc were advocating federalism as a front for the dismemberment of Nigeria. Therefore, the NCNC proposed a unitary state consisting of ten ethnic or linguistic departments. Yet, at the same time, Azikiwe fought—albeit unsuccessfully—to preserve the artificial distinction between Lagos and the western region. By using this issue, he hoped to gain support from minorities in these areas so that the NCNC could become an interregional, nationwide party.

Awolowo effectively opposed this, primarily by organizing a new "Action Group" to replace the old NYM. This new party's sophisticated organization, thorough program and elaborate campaigning captured the Yoruba and gave "Awo" full control of the west. Clearly believing that success in one region was the most direct path to national political power, Awolowo made more realistic and influential use of the party system than any of his opponents. From its firm position in the western region, the Action Group could afford to issue stronger demands for self-government than any other party. Awolowo's success was a major impetus toward the federalist thinking that ultimately predominated in Nigeria. Meanwhile, the NCNC's main demand—revision of the constitution—was already being directed by Governor Macpherson. The resulting revisions, determined by careful polling, were so overwhelmingly federalist as to be a sharp check to the NCNC platform. Azikiwe was more nationalist, but Awolowo, as the more regionalist politician, was the more realistic.

The short-lived Macpherson Constitution, promulgated on June 29, 1951, committed Nigeria to a stronger federation than Richards' plan. In trying at once to protect the regions and to prevent secessionism, the authors had followed the Canadian precedent of a central government that held all residual powers. The device proved ill suited to a system of regional parties. The attempt to represent all shades of opinion had led to the inclusion of several unworkable anomalies. Hope turned first into exasperation, then into dogmatic quarreling and bitter frustration. Southern attempts to demand independence by 1956 were met by British wariness. The NPC feared that the North would be overrun by hasty extremists. Competitive political rallies in the northern cities culminated in a frenzied riot at Kano. The new constitution was manifestly unworkable, an addition rather than a solution to Nigeria's problems.

This time, the British government followed a very different line of constitutional negotiation. Party leaders were called to London in 1953, then reassembled in Lagos early the next year. After a series of delicate negotiations among the experienced politicians, another constitution came into force. Thereby, residual powers reverted to the regional governments on October 1, 1954. The federal elections were separated from the regional contests. Public services and economic responsibilities reverted to the regions, and Lagos became a Federal (capital) District separate from any region. Regional self-government was scheduled for 1956, at which time future developments were to be reconsidered.

The new compromises, notably similar to those in the

United States Constitution, worked peacefully. The timetable was followed in principle, though postponed one year with Nigerian consent. The federal legislature gradually assumed control over policy, and relations with Britain improved rapidly. The royal tour of 1956 elicited support from all parties, both for the queen and for the Commonwealth ideal. The final conferences on independence and the constitution then took place in London during 1957.

Most serious was the weakness of the federal executive. The Macpherson Constitution had not provided for such a post, partly because the British Governor was in charge, partly because no region would accept another region's candidate. The 1954 revisions were based on the assumption that one faction would gain a majority, but with three nearly equal regional parties, this did not happen. The final conference therefore arranged for a federal prime minister who nominated his cabinet. Effective government by coalition and plurality of strength was henceforth possible, and it was agreed that Alhaji Abubakar Tafawa Balewa immediately should become the first incumbent.

The new government set April 2, 1960 as the target date for independence. Britain did not immediately reply, primarily because hesitation and lack of education in the North continued to be a problem. By 1959 the signs of progress and a spirit of realistic federal coöperation were more promising, so all parties agreed to make the transition on October 1, 1960. The final period preceding independence was preëminently devoted to the development of an effective machinery of parliamentary compromise, preparation for educational expansion and economic viability, and the organization of laws and precedents. The greatest danger continued to be federal-state relations, many observers and politicians fearing a secessionist sentiment which the American-style constitution did not entirely preclude. However, by working consciously to avoid such an event, the politicians as well as the voters became accustomed to parliamentary subtleties and compromise coalitions. Both before independence and after, the cabinet represented an alliance of the NPC and the NCNC-NEPU bloc, bound together largely by personal contacts, a recognition of the need for national unity, and a mutual desire to restrain Awolowo's well-disciplined, Yoruba-dominated Action Group. All parties favored active Commonwealth ties, if only because they contributed to the sense of common loyalty. There was common consent to the goals of nationwide democracy based upon expanded educational opportunity, although the northern emirs wished to realize this less rapidly than the others. At the same time, the influential Sardauna of Sokoto, proud of the realism and astuteness of his political judgment, discouraged any dogmatic or rebellious notions among the other aristocrats.

Nigeria's foreign policy represents a sense of realism comparable to that so evident in internal politics. All parties seem to be aware that the country's large size and considerable diversity are unique, so Nigeria tends to be less interested than Ghana in the Pan-African ideal. Such association, many feel, would pose federal problems even greater than those that Nigeria already has. The government inclines toward the belief that its policy should rest upon diplomatic imagination, the example of internal balance, and the prestige of being Africa's most populous country. In opposition, the Action Group advocates more active entry into power politics.

With the largest population, most diverse society and one of the most complex constitutions in the tropical Commonwealth, Nigeria contrasts markedly with Sierra Leone, which is the smallest and newest member. About 120,000 "Creoles"—half descended from ex-slaves, half absorbed from neighboring tribes—have led a Europeanized, commercially oriented life in the coastal colony. Fifteen times as many people, in indigenous tribes under traditional chiefs, occupied the loosely controlled interior protectorate. After 1924 certain paramount chiefs sat in the colony's Legislative Council, but law, administration and development continued to be different in each area. Nationalism was relatively slow to develop, partly because the

British government did not offer enough resistance to encourage its coalescence, but largely because Creoles concentrated on maintaining their privileged commercial and political position relative to the protectorate.

Freetown harbor, the best in West Africa, developed suddenly during the Second World War. To operate the port, laborers were recruited from the protectorate. Their contact with the Creoles sharpened competition between the colony and the interior. African membership in the Legislative Council was increased in 1943, but the government's proposal to strengthen protectorate participation caused a stalemate that prevented further evolution. By order in Council, Britain imposed a new constitution in 1951. The executive remained British, but the legislature was reconstituted: seven British officials and two British merchants, all appointed; seven members from the colony, elected by property owners; and fourteen—a majority being chiefs—elected by local councils in the protectorate.

Ghanaian progress toward independence intensified nationalist feeling, which manifested itself first in Creole riots against the chiefs in 1955, then in protectorate disturbances a year later. In 1957 the constitution was amended to provide for more elected members in the legislature and to allow a responsible, self-governing cabinet. Of the fifty-one representatives, fourteen came from the colony and twenty-five from the protectorate, by general election; the remaining twelve were chiefs, selected indirectly through the protectorate's councils. Official representation dropped to four, and executive control passed to Sir Milton Margai, a native of the protectorate who had retired from a career as a physician in the colonial Government Medical Service. His Sierra Leone People's Party won a majority on a relatively conservative platform that included independence by 1962. As a result of an unusual move to hasten this step, Sierra Leone received freedom and Commonwealth membership a year earlier, on April 27, 1961.

Stable, prosperous development depends upon the fulfillment of two pressing demands. Recent economic advance

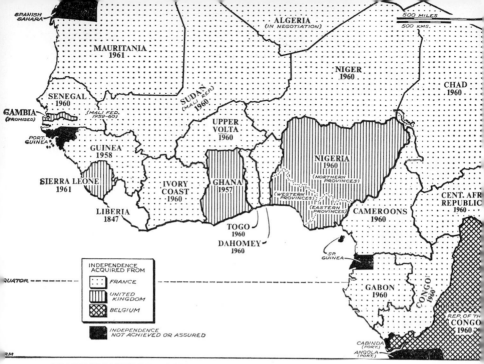

NATIONALISM AND INDEPENDENCE IN WEST AFRICA

has resulted, in some degree, from individual prospecting in alluvial diamond deposits. The law requires resale at controlled prices to the De Beers company, but illicit marketing—from which no tax revenue accrues—prevails. Many Sierra Leonians hope to replace smuggling and profiteering middlemen with a coöperative or nationalized marketing outlet. The other challenge is the pressure to hasten the extension of education, legal uniformity and democratic administration to the former protectorate.

Except for Gambia, a small enclave whose future has not been decided, the British West African Empire has been transformed into three sovereign Commonwealth members, two of them monarchies and one a republic. Because she is so small, Sierra Leone has the greatest degree of economic dependency upon the Commonwealth. Loyalty and respect are vital elements of Nigeria's participation, but Ghana, as the pioneer who fought most bitterly for her position, remains less intimately involved in the international community. However, for all three, the Commonwealth system serves as a source of capital, an aid to marketing through its preferential-tariff arrangements, and a symbol of certain common institutions in history, law and politics.

23

TOWARD THE COMMUNITY

THE First World War put the French colonial system to a severe test. Since 1905 the West African territories from Senegal to Lake Chad had been subject to a highly centralized, bureaucratic system. After 1907 a similar but less effective central control was artificially imposed upon the possessions between Lake Chad and the north bank of the Congo. The private concessions that had dominated the latter area were less powerful, less long-lived and less profitable than their counterparts in the Belgian Congo, but their abuses were widely publicized and roundly condemned by French public opinion, which had begun to think of centralized government rule as the panacea for colonial scandals.

Theoretically the African colonial people would be gallicized and assimilated into the Republic in the perhaps distant future. Meanwhile, the French West African government—completely controlled by an independent bureaucracy and supported by powerful Moslem authorities—did not have to face the practical problems that would have been posed by any real assimilation or representative government. Such a dichotomy between vague theory and actual practice also prevailed in French Equatorial Africa, except that the latter's population, more thinly scattered and rarely subject to the influence of strong Moslem authority, was less effectively or systematically governed.

Each of the two French colonial federations was dominated until 1940 by its own monomania. West Africa continued to serve as a reserve source of manpower for the economy of metropolitan France, and the Army depended increasingly upon African recruits to fill its ranks. Equatorial Africa, incapable of making a comparable contribution from its sparse population, remained primarily a battleground between concessionaires and humanitarians.

Manpower was therefore the basic problem in both federations—as a resource in the West, and as something lacking on the equator. The common solution, throughout French Africa between the World Wars, was the corvée of forced labor. Usually the conscripts were engaged in public works—especially transportation projects—but private use, such as that required by the equatorial concessionaires and private enterprises, was not unknown. Though not necessarily efficient or enlightened, the system seemed to work moderately well in West Africa. However, when it applied to the oft-forgotten Equatorial federation, corvée remained abusive and confused: there were not enough conscripts for both public and private needs; the Congo-Ocean Railway, which eventually reduced the demand for large numbers of porters, was not completed until 1935, and the concessions were hampered by the intermittent incursions of public works and half-hearted reforms. A number of travelers —particularly René Maran in 1921, and André Gide in 1925-26 —called attention to the contradictions in Equatorial policy, but the resulting indignation was never organized into an effective movement for solving them.

France decided in 1919 to apply military conscription in the colonies. Severe losses in the European war had weakened the military potential of the mother country, whose rate of population growth had long been lower than that of Germany and Britain. The main burden of the new legislation fell on West Africa, especially Senegal. African males reported for service at the age of nineteen, but spent three years on active duty instead of the eighteen months required of full-fledged Frenchmen. The results were less satisfactory than Paris had hoped: nine-tenths of the eligible men were rejected for medical reasons, and those accepted often proved ill-suited for military life in other climates. One in eight died while on duty in France, Indo-China or Syria; one in twelve contracted tuberculosis. Those who survived were Europeanized—at least, adjusted to barracks life—and usually remained in France as unskilled or semiskilled laborers. Some who returned home found themselves either restless and impatient or suspected and resented in African society. The result was a sharp break between the conscripts and their homes, and the creation of a class dependent upon the European economy and society but not fully assimilated.

This semi-Europeanized group also contained a very limited number of educated Africans. Theoretically the government school system "diffused spoken French among the mass of the population," but in practice it produced only a few candidates for the civil service examinations. Most of these met the French-language requirement for appointment as a chief. The remainder entered the central bureaucracy or associated with the semi-Europeanized veterans.

The earlier imperial dreams of commerce and prosperity had failed to materialize. Frenchmen were unwilling to invest in risky or long-range projects for the Sudan. However, after the army had occupied the West African rain forests, an interest developed in plantations. In addition to the older groundnut (peanut) estates in Senegal, there now appeared cocoa, coffee and bananas on the Ivory Coast, palm oil in Dahomey and bananas in Guinea. Africans soon emulated the planters, so agricultural production increased rapidly. As trade developed, the government acquired enough revenue to finance ports and railways. Tracks from Guinea, Senegal, Dahomey and the Ivory Coast had each reached four to five hundred miles into the interior by the 1930's. Although the newly opened Sudan was producing little that France wanted, new labor supplies could be tapped and more extensive inland development became possible.

At the end of World War I the League of Nations had given France mandates over two of the former German territories: most of the Cameroons and slightly more than half of Togoland. A narrow strip along the western boundary of each colony was integrated with the adjacent British territory—the Cameroonian enclave with Nigeria, and West Togo with the Gold Coast—but the French zones continued to be separate entities. In the latter, the methods and policies of administration paralleled those of the West and Equatorial territories, the League's only requirement being a ban on monopolies. Neither mandate joined the French federal colonies, but decrees from Paris usually applied without distinction to both types of possessions.

No significant constitutional changes took place in French Africa between the wars. The central bureaucracies in Dakar and Brazzaville continued to make all decisions. The railways had been improved, coastal agriculture had developed, and the concessions in the Congo basin had been weakened—more by depression than by reform—but corvée, military conscription and the separation of a small class of educated "évolués" had not been modified. The Equatorial area was still underfinanced, ill-staffed and weakly governed; West Africa remained authoritarian, preoccupied with economic and manpower problems. Within this context World War II at first caused simply a rapid rise in exports to France and a concentrated effort to strengthen the colonial forces. Conscription and corvée were greatly intensified.

When the metropolitan government capitulated to Germany, most of the bureaucracy remained loyal to the collaborationist regime in Vichy. Although West Africa withdrew from the Allied camp, German forces were never allowed in Dakar, the strategically located capital of French West Africa, and the borders with British colonies came under an unofficial truce.

However, the bureaucrats of Equatorial Africa turned from Vichy to the "Free French" exile leader, General Charles De Gaulle. Perhaps the often-forgotten officials at Brazzaville, many of whom were less senior or less favored than those at Dakar, were more willing to risk their chances for promotions and pensions. The action of one—Félix Eboué, born in French Guiana, the highest-ranking Negro in the French service and governor of the Chad territory—provided De Gaulle with his first concrete support and a crucial strategic position. Equatorial Africans volunteered for the Allied cause, accepted another increase in corvée, and converted their homeland from a colonial stepchild to the headquarters of French resistance. Quick joint action from Chad, the Congo and Nigeria saved the Cameroons and the Gabon territory from Vichyite control. Roads hastily built from Brazzaville, the Cameroons and Nigeria facilitated the concentration of forces in the Chad. With a remarkable dash into Libya, across nearly 500 miles of unexplored desert, late in 1941, Colonel Leclerc threw French troops —84 percent African—back into battle against the Axis powers.

De Gaulle elevated Eboué to the Governor-Generalship at Brazzaville and radically reorganized the Equatorial federation. Mining, rubber and cotton exploitation, and the banking system, were thoroughly mobilized. The concessions were canceled and traditional chieftains restored to power. Eboué planned to destroy the bureaucratic elite and to replace it with popular leadership. African judges, modified customary law, a broadly based school system, and indigenous control of industry were established. European planters were transformed into a special corps in order to educate a peasant yeomanry. Migrants—both corvée and free—were encouraged to bring their families with them. The effect was profound: African morale rose and the traditional French colonial administrative system was broken. Under the stress of wartime effort individual living standards actually declined, but the wherewithal and enthusiasm for subsequent improvement had been strongly implanted by 1945. The territorial governments and local authorities, strengthened and released from the former system of rigid central control, proved to be more adaptable to regional variations and more sensitive to the needs of a scattered population.

The new colonial approach was codified at a conference of Free French administrators and politicians in Brazzaville during January of 1944. Africans were not represented. The political proposals were cautious: gradual representation and decentralization of the colonies, without any rights of either autonomy or secession. However, the economic and social revisions were relatively radical: coördinated planning for the development of resources, industry and living standards; and the broadening of educational and medical services. The influence of Eboué's ideas and the example of wartime Equatorial Africa were clearly represented in the Brazzaville Plan.

Eboué died in 1944. De Gaulle assumed power in France after the liberation but was turned out of office when the Fourth Republic came into existence in 1946. There had not been time for the Brazzaville scheme to take full effect, and the postwar government strove first of all to restore order and organization in the empire. The French Constituent Assembly of 1945-46 adopted much of the Brazzaville Plan. Forced labor was abolished, certain civil rights and legal citizenship were granted, and African colonial delegates participated in the central legislature for the first time. However, the trend toward Franco-colonial federation was abruptly checked when the metropolitan voters rejected the completed constitution. France had become conservative. The colonies reacted with a radical turn of opinion.

The second constitution in October, 1946 restored the traditional centralization policy and revived the ideal of assimilation in the distant future. The rights and representative institutions of "overseas citizens" remained undefined, although elective assemblies were established by decree as soon as the constitution was ratified. For the next twelve years colonial politics and French policy were in large measure dominated by the struggle between the realities of the 1946 constitution and the intermittent resurrection of federalist sentiment. The Africans indeed were not of one mind on the practicability of either system.

The structure of government after 1946 was fairly complex, albeit unitary and carefully weighted to assure the predominance of European power. Each of the territories (eight in West Africa, four in Equatorial Africa) had a bicameral legislature, the General Council or Territorial Assembly. European residents elected the upper house, and Africans the lower. (In Senegal, the Territorial Assembly was unicameral, and, in this case, no distinction was made between European and African voters.) Each house then selected its own delegates to the Council of the Republic (so-called Senate) in Paris. (Upper Houses in the four Equatorial African territories acted in two pairs, and Senegal's delegates were chosen by the single chamber.) Deputies for the National Assembly were elected in a joint session of the two houses in each territory, but 96 percent of the seats in Paris were reserved for metropolitan France. Furthermore, each Territorial Assembly—both houses again sitting jointly—chose delegates to the appropriate Grand Council, which, sitting at Dakar and Brazzaville, advised the respective governors-general of the West and Central African federations. Lastly, each Territorial Assembly, still in joint session, selected delegates to the French Union Assembly, where France's own representation—about 50 percent—was proportional to the actual size of her population.

Some Africans hoped the Union Assembly would evolve into a federal parliament, but it remained purely advisory while the National Assembly continued to exercise complete legislative supremacy through the governors-general in Dakar and Brazzaville. These central authorities continued to prepare the budgets and set the basic tax rates for their respective federations. The General Councils and Territorial Assemblies could add to either, but could not block or reduce the governor-generals' appropriations. Legality was given to the entire arrangement by the Lamine-Gueye Law of 1946, which provided for two classes of citizens; those of the Republic and those of the Union. The National Assembly, representing the unitary Republic, exercised effective power. The Union Assembly embodied the potentially federalist long-range ideal.

Three political parties emerged within the 1946 system, each embodying one of the alternatives in interpreting the complex constitutional arrangements. Lamine-Gueye, representing Senegal, headed an African section of the French Socialist Party. This movement was too closely allied with and centered upon European politics for the Senegalese voter, who soon preferred a program that appealed to his local and territorial interests. The European Socialists soon declined, and Lamine-Gueye himself was eventually rebuffed at the polls. The other two political movements took deeper root in French Africa.

Félix Houphouët-Boigny from the Ivory Coast inaugurated the Rassemblement Démocratique Africain in Bamako, Sudan, in 1946. In creating subordinate parties within each territory, the RDA followed the Pan-Africanist example. However, in ideology, Houphouët-Boigny envisioned the achievement of African economic and political power within the structure of the unitary Fourth French Republic. Each territorial party communicated directly with the others—Guinea, Ivory Coast, Sudan, Dahomey, Chad, Middle Congo, etc.—so Houphouët-Boigny, as the popular head of the Ivory Coast "section," kept more effective control over politics than the central RDA directorate. At the same time, this form of organization made possible a considerable scope of opinion within the RDA federation, ranging from moderate right in one section to radical left in another territory.

The second enduring party, the Indépendants d'Outre-Mer (IOM), directed by Léopold S. Senghor of Senegal, advocated a federal system such as that which had been proposed at Brazzaville, but the movement was less widely spread and less effectively organized than the RDA.

In Equatorial Africa, local sections of the French Gaullist party (Rassemblement du Peuple Français) enjoyed considerable popularity after 1945, but by 1953 Africans changed from it to the RDA much as they did from the Socialist movement in West Africa.

French Communists attempted to operate throughout the colonies, usually by establishing African branches of Georges Sorel's old syndicalist union, the Confédération Générale du Travail (CGT). Between 1947 and 1951, when Equatorial Africa reacted angrily to the CGT's attacks upon De Gaulle, the Communist Party changed its policy toward the whole Empire. The Marxists then concentrated on infiltration of the RDA in both West and Equatorial Africa. Particular efforts in the latter federation again failed because repeated visits by leading French Communists were interpreted as European interference contrary to local interests. Communist penetration again became the kiss of death: the RDA's early promise steadily gave way to the opposition, which represented a variety of personality groupings and territorial nationalists. Gabon leaned toward Jean Aubame and Léon Mba, rival and relatively isolationist local politicians who remained independent but sympathized with the Senegalese IOM. Oubangui-Chari became the province of Barthélemy Boganda, the magnetic and imaginative founder of the Mouvement d'Evolution Sociale en Afrique Noire (MESAN). The Middle Congo leaned toward a disfrocked priest, Fulbert Youlou, who, like Gabriel Lisette, the Martinique-born leader of Chad, maintained some connections with the Houphouët-Boigny wing of the RDA.

The West African political scene was much more amenable to leftist tutelage. Bitterness remained from the war, in which corvée and racial segregation had both increased markedly, and the Communist bureaucrats in the French regime took advantage of it. Although Houphouët-Boigny's personal appeal soon superseded that of the Marxist abstraction, the Communists persistently tried to turn the RDA from its goal of Franco-African unity toward the fomenting of class struggle and anti-imperialist agitation. By 1950 Houphouët-Boigny realized that communism was threatening rather than helping the African politicians. The RDA then revealed an acrimonious correspondence that had been exchanged with the Marxists, and made a complete break with the French and Soviet parties. The French government had already begun to squeeze Communists out of the colonies, and it so strongly manipulated the colonial elections in 1951 that the RDA seemed about to follow its former supporters into oblivion.

Thereafter RDA survival depended largely upon Houphouët-Boigny's magnetism and the ability of territorial sections to develop their own local policies and grass-roots organization. The initiative in Middle Congo passed to Youlou. In Guinea, power rested with Sekou Touré, a third-generation descendant by the female line of Samory, one of France's most stubborn opponents in the nineteenth century. An agile and turbulent organizer, Touré had built a labor union that entered politics under the broad RDA label. Houphouët-Boigny himself, having made a spectacular comeback at the polls of his native Ivory Coast, retained titular command of the RDA federation. His influence now tended to be a check on extremism, on infiltration from abroad, and on decentralizing tendencies. By 1955 every territory save Senegal and Gabon stood under the banner of the RDA, but the local sections advocated increasingly divergent sets of ideas.

Fully as crucial as the political excitement was a program of economic development throughout French Africa. At Brazzaville in 1944, broad outlines were drawn for educational, medical and technological expansion. Both of France's Constituent Assemblies in 1946 took steps toward long-range implementation of these schemes, but colonial Africa continued to suffer from serious inflation and chronic shortages. Private capital, scarce enough in postwar Europe, was more reluctant than ever to take the necessary risks. Indeed, as French industry regained strength, it tried to prevent African industrialization and tariff reform. The experts that the Brazzaville planners wanted to consult were barred from office because of their associations with Vichy, but the need was too great to permit delay. Africa, therefore, came haphazardly under the overseas sections of the

Monnet Plan for Modernization and Equipment, which was inaugurated in 1946. Money from France and the territories was channeled into the Fonds d'Investissement pour le Développement Economique et Social (FIDES), which covered research, public services, increased production and social improvement. FIDES took some time to accumulate capital, to acquire equipment and to correct serious initial planning errors. Africans resented the dominance of Paris planners and criticized many early projects. Most of the money went into transportation and loans to speculative private or public corporations. Education, rural areas and productive capacity were virtually neglected.

The errors were revealed in 1949 and 1950—precisely the period when communism was at its height in French Africa. FIDES now undertook to increase production "in the light of the long-term evolution of French economy," but the social development of Africa was still neglected. France's successive obligations in Korea, Indo-China, Algeria, the North Atlantic Treaty Organization and the Suez War diverted funds from the plan after 1951. Territorial governments found that FIDES projects—roads, schools, railways—cost more to maintain than the local taxpayers could possibly afford. The World Bank subsequently lent money for repairs so that territorial resources could be devoted to other development projects. In time such improvements should create a broader, more balanced economy that can support the new facilities. Furthermore, the French National Assembly finally required FIDES to devote at least 20 percent of its funds to projects that would improve local productivity and taxable income.

France contributed approximately 400,000,000,000 francs ($1,000,000,000) in fourteen years, but the effects were often unsatisfactory. African towns, roads and ports were transformed, but production and social conditions improved only slowly. Africans with any sense of responsibility had to remain under French influence in order to maintain and to redeem the seriously unbalanced economic situation. Criticism and disillusionment were increasingly noticeable in France and in Africa as the problems remained unsolved in the mid-1950's.

An unusually dramatic effort was then attempted to rearrange the political relations and economic interconnections in the French Empire. The *loi cadre* (enabling act) of June 23, 1956 granted sweeping reform powers to the Overseas Ministry. Houphouët-Boigny, having just taken a ministry without portfolio in the Guy Mollet cabinet, wrote most of the law, which authorized political reorganization by official decree. The new arrangements were intended to strike a balance between French power and African political aspirations, thus creating an atmosphere wherein political or economic grievances could be less autocratically redressed. Twelve specific decrees then put the *loi cadre* into effect. Executive powers in each territory were transferred to cabinets chosen by the elected Assemblies, which were also given full internal legislative jurisdiction. The Governors-General lost all powers except those of economic coördination. Territorial governors became figurehead advisers. The difference between Citizens of the Republic and those of the Union was abolished for territorial or local elections. Territorial Assemblies were authorized to levy fines upon bureaucrats who disobeyed the cabinets or the laws. And, finally, the territories acquired exclusive rights to the collection and disposition of taxes. France retained the right to collect import duties, and she could still control their disposition and the distribution of grants from the Métropole.

Although the central government retained control over defense and foreign affairs, the internal administration was virtually federal in character. The Overseas Ministry's decree power was efficient and systematic, but unfortunately it was not used in consultation with African politicians. Some of the difficulties in implementing the reforms were later attributed to this fact, and the tempo of nationalism—spurred by the example of Ghana, which acquired complete independence in 1957—made the *loi cadre* soon seem outdated. Notwithstanding these reservations, there was a strong current of feeling in Africa favoring the attempt to make the system work.

Application of the *loi cadre* decrees fell largely to RDA men throughout French Africa. Both the Socialists and the IOM had lost in Senegal. Gabon remained under Independent control, and Oubangui-Chari supported the MESAN, but in the other ten territories Houphouët-Boigny and the RDA set the dominant tone. In large part, the *loi cadre* decrees and the territorial voters supported the RDA's concept of separate African states, each in direct association with the French Métropole.

Despite the defeat of his IOM, Léopold Senghor launched an offensive against the *loi cadre* decrees. Houphouët-Boigny was accused of disrupting unity by Balkanizing Africa. Senghor then transformed the IOM into a more broadly based inter-territorial party, the Convention Africaine, which tried to attract the opponents of Houphouët-Boigny's increasing conservatism. The party campaigned for a form of the Brazzaville Plan to replace the *loi cadre*. However, the Convention never became a force outside Senghor's own territory of Senegal. Instead, radicals first turned to Lamine-Gueye, whose revival of Socialist organization was widespread but brief, and then settled in the rebellious labor wing of the RDA.

By September, 1957 disillusionment with the *loi cadre*, now fourteen months old, had begun to set in. In a conference at Bamako, Sudan, the RDA decided to demand a federal empire in which all territories would be equal partners with the French Republic. On this platform the party agreed with and soon absorbed the Convention Africaine. However, Houphouët-Boigny remained on the periphery, still advocating a direct link between each territory and the central power in Paris. On the other hand, Sekou Touré went to the other extreme in demanding an independent, federated West African republic that would be equal in power and position with France, with whom there would be only limited economic links. Equatorial Africa followed its own path, deciding at this time to discard its regional federation entirely. Youlou in Middle Congo and Boganda of Oubangui-Chari dreamed of a new "Latin Africa," stretching from the Sahara to Angola, but Gabon and Chad were strongly opposed.

Subsequent developments seemed to be divisive and half-hearted. There arose sincere doubts whether any structure, either of the whole French empire or any group of states therein, could find a workable basis for political and economic association. The decline in hopes was suddenly checked on the thirteenth of May, 1958.

Rightist paratroops of the French Army seized Algeria, then Corsica. The Fourth Republic reacted feebly, then turned to Charles de Gaulle, long retired but ready for the call. The new constitution, unprecedented for France, installed the General as a strong President and provided for a radical reorganization of the Empire. The Brazzaville Plan, modified and considerably modernized, was put to the voters in France and Overseas in the month of September.

Provisionally De Gaulle designated each of the twelve territories as an electoral unit. Each one could become an autonomous nation within the "Community," although the new Fifth Republic would retain control over foreign and defense affairs. Alternatively a nation could secede—either immediately or at any future date—or France herself could oust a nation from the Community. Furthermore, the Africans would have the right to merge, to subdivide or to readjust their own boundaries at any time. Each republic—France, Senegal, Dahomey, etc.— would have its own Assembly and Prime Minister; all the latter would form an Executive Council of the Community. A federal Senate in Paris would have representatives from every member nation in proportion to its population. Supreme over all, De Gaulle—or his successor—would be chosen, by a complex federal electoral system, to exercise broad executive and emergency powers.

The plebescite in September, 1958 sampled opinion by

universal suffrage on parts of four continents and several South Pacific islands. France and its overseas departments (Algeria, the West Indies, and Réunion Island) approved the constitution. The small Pacific possessions and French Somaliland agreed to remain as dependent territories. Eleven of the twelve African territories, plus Madagascar, accepted by wide margins the status of autonomous national republics within the Community. In one case, Niger, the French army may have influenced the results. Guinea alone, following the lead of Sekou Touré, opted for prompt secession.

Within hours France withdrew completely from the Guinea Republic. Officials, schoolteachers and technicians left immediately. Military and police units abandoned their posts without hesitation. Guinea was independent, but totally devoid of any banking system, any experienced administrators or any technical personnel. Furthermore, Touré was now divorced from the RDA and completely independent of Houphouët-Boigny. Anarchy, save for the personality of Sekou Touré and the none-too-certain discipline of his union organization, was indeed at hand.

Guinea was alone for less than a day. Planeloads of advisers and engineers soon arrived from Czechoslovakia and Russia, and materiel for war, for industry and for agriculture followed promptly. The republic had really exchanged one foreign organizer for another, but the difference was that the newly arrived Communists had neither legal title nor reliable native organizations to rely upon. Touré appealed to the Western powers but received no assurances: the United States took three months to reply, longer to send even a consul, and twelve to arrange aid; West Germany organized more quickly, but not in quantity. Britain hesitated to offend France. Ghana provided help, albeit minor since she lacked resources at home, but in conferences with Nkrumah, Touré tried to devise ways to protect his national independence. The future of Guinea in this context remained in doubt. By virtue of his personality and effective nationalist appeals, Touré maintained order and loyalty within the country. Dependence upon him and his party was, after

1958, essential for the nation's survival. By 1961 there was still hope but not assurance that his domestic leadership and his ingenious international diplomacy would preserve some measure of economic as well as political independence.

Both Togo and the Cameroons had become United Nations Trust Territories in 1945, but their development continued to parallel that of France's colonies. Territorial Assemblies appeared under the 1946 constitution, and the *loi cadre* a decade later also applied. A UN plebescite then determined that British Togo should join Ghana, notwithstanding vehement protests from the Ewe tribe, whose partition in 1918 was thereby made permanent. French Togo became an autonomous republic of the French Union and acquired complete independence on April 27, 1960. Its truncated shape and arbitrary origin have given Togo economic problems which Sylvanus Olympio, the moderate and personable President, is committed to solving without bowing either to the French Community or to Ghana.

An autonomous republic also emerged in the French Cameroons at the end of 1956. Exceptional use was made of the United Nations Trusteeship Council as a forum for internal politics. The primary issue, the inability to create real nationalism, resulted largely from the diversity of forest and savanna people, which was complicated by the country's artificial boundaries and repeated partitions. An extremist movement, the Union des Populations du Cameroun (UPC), centered on tribal dissidence but, willing to accept Communist support and instruction, conducted a campaign of propaganda and terror. The 1956 government of Ahmadou Ahidjo, a moderate who relied heavily upon French support, was severely criticized in the United Nations for not holding subsequent elections. However, independence was scheduled for January 1, 1960. Ghana, Guinea and the U.S.S.R., claiming that Ahidjo's government was a front for colonialism, demanded that it first be tested at the polls. When the problem became associated with power diplomacy, the merits of the case took second place. The Soviet bloc supported the call for elections but was defeated by the

Western opposition. In the same voting, Ghana and Guinea both thought of their own histories, rather than either the issue or the power struggle. The Cameroonian Republic came to independence as planned, without elections, but the event was marred by UPC terrorism, the continued presence of French troops, and a chilly attitude by Sekou Touré and Kwame Nkrumah. Four months later Ahidjo won a tenuous electoral victory, mainly by carrying the Moslem regions of the northern interior. The UPC's power, like its terrorism, began to yield ground to more legitimate opposition movements. However, the government's position became less secure when, during 1961, the southern part of the British Cameroons chose to join the republic. Though small and relatively stable, the new area tended to support the moderate anti-Ahidjo opposition, which had not yet acquired cohesion or experience.

The eleven nations that accepted the Community faced considerably different problems. Political orientations shifted rapidly, but the peacefulness and adaptability of the new institutions surprised many observers. Relations between Africa and France became both smoother and more distant, while those within Africa entered a period of readjustment and flux. President de Gaulle, in playing the role of an arbiter, tried to demonstrate that the Community was much more subtle and flexible than the new constitution implied.

Coastal republics competed with one another for trade and prestige in the interior. Through a revived Convention Africaine, Senegal pressed for a "Federation of Mali" which would make her ports the outlet for the Sudan, Upper Volta and Niger. As the leader of the orthodox RDA, Houphouët-Boigny opposed such formal regrouping, believing instead that his Ivory Coast was in a position to predominate if the interior retained separate autonomy. The third republic with seaports, Dahomey, weaker and less advantageously located, was for some time uncertain which of the two proposals best suited her interests. The Mali scheme was widely discussed, but when Niger and Upper Volta chose Houphouët-Boigny's system, all others except the

Sudan withdrew. In reality, Upper Volta was tied to the Ivory Coast by rail, Niger to Dahomey by river and rail, and Sudan to Senegal by the oldest railway of all. The latter pair formed Mali, and the other four entered into a loosely structured economic "Entente."

In Equatorial Africa the four territories had agreed in 1957 to dissolve the colonial federation. The new constitution simply hastened this step. Chad became completely landlocked, totally dependent upon long road or air routes to the outside world, but its Moslem population welcomed separation from the forest states. Gabon's isolationism, already a marked tendency, was enhanced by the discovery of iron reserves which were being profitably leased to European and American developers. Oubangui-Chari and the Congo Republic (formerly Middle-Congo) continued to seek a new federation, but their interest —defined largely by their Congo River transport connections— attracted the others only to the point of a customs union.

By the beginning of 1960 there were therefore ten republics in the Community—nine unitary states, and one federation of two former territories. All of them were keenly aware of the problems that secessionist Guinea had encountered, yet they also wished to assert their national sovereignty apart from Paris. Leadership in resolving these demands came from Mali, especially from Léopold Senghor's Parti de la Fédération Africaine (PFA), successor to the Convention Africaine, which had been advocating sovereign equality within the Community. In consultation with De Gaulle, a constitutional adjustment was arranged. Mali accordingly became a sovereign, federal republic, regulating its own foreign and defense affairs, on June 20, 1960. Madagascar followed suit six days later, its name now becoming Malagache.

The leaders of the four Entente republics initially opposed any change in relations with France, but popular opinion quickly forced them to revise their views. In order to recapture nationalist support, they demanded a break not only with France, but with the Community as well, until independence had been granted. By agreement, Dahomey therefore became a sovereign, unitary republic on August first, Niger on the third, Upper Volta on the fifth, and the Ivory Coast on the seventh. Equatorial Africa immediately followed: Chad, August 11; the Central African Republic (formerly Oubangui-Chari), August 13; the Congo, August 15; and (despite its reluctance) Gabon on August 17. Mauritania hesitated for several weeks, unsure first of Morocco's or Mali's attitudes, and anxious to guarantee capital for iron mining which would finance the state, but full freedom arrived on November 28. The French empire in Africa had changed into ten contiguous nations in just over five months—fourteen nations, if the two mandates, Madagascar and the older state of Guinea are counted.

Only eight weeks after it had set the precedent for independence, the Mali Federation disintegrated. The rupture's immediate cause seemed to be a political deadlock over the apportionment of high federal posts between the two members, but underlying factors included the Sudan's feeling that the Mali Federation now offered no more independence than the other republics had. On August 19 Senegal and the Sudan became separate, independent republics. Sudan proclaimed itself the unitary state of Mali, denounced all connections with the Community, closed the railway to Senegal, and started channeling its meager commerce through Guinea and the Ivory Coast. Not wishing to repeat its abrupt behavior in Guinea, France did not acknowledge the withdrawal from the Community. Czechoslovakia once again served as a funnel for Communist contributions, but the Soviet effort appeared to be about as inconclusive as it had been in Guinea. Sudan's two great problems—commercial access and severe trade imbalance—could only be solved in coöperation with her immediate neighbors, Senegal, Guinea and the Entente states.

In the four allied republics of the Entente, Houphouët-Boigny's Ivory Coast controlled both the purse and the key to prosperity. Here alone was there any remnant of the old RDA, whose power within three of the states was now precarious. Dahomey was torn between the urban-centered RDA and a rural pro-federalist movement. In Niger the RDA faced opposition of the Guinean variety, and in Upper Volta, political sentiment was amorphous, centered on regional personalities. Ivory Coast alone was united in loyalty to the RDA, although even there a tribal opposition was incipient. In order to alleviate the danger of factionalism, all four Entente republics have decided that the party receiving the most votes shall have all Assembly seats—a procedure which, though democratic, is certainly not conducive to constituency representation.

In relations with France the Community has become increasingly loose in character. The republics hold complete sovereignty. France aids all of them, except Guinea, though Sudan (Mali) and the four Entente states also do not recognize the Community arrangement. The Senate of the Community was dissolved in March of 1961.

Sometimes less friendly with one another than with France, the African republics—save for Sudan (Mali) and Guinea— have tended toward increasingly conservative policies. The entrenched elite leadership in each country clearly aims to perpetuate its own power and independence. Therefore, it firmly opposes outside influences such as communism, European economic or political domination, and—with equal strength—any Pan-African or Pan-Community federalism. The economic and diplomatic connections necessary for survival will not be settled for some time.

24

TRIBES AND SETTLERS
IN TRANSITION

EAST AFRICA felt the impact of World War I more keenly than any other part of the continent. Europeans had been ruling the area for less than twenty-five years, so the fighting came at a crucial point in the readjustment and development of the indigenous people. Furthermore, the Kaiser's forces, under General Paul von Lettow-Vorbeck, kept German East Africa and its neighbors in constant warfare for four years. General J. C. Smuts chased them with a combined British Imperial Army, drawn from South Africa, the Rhodesias, Uganda and British East Africa (Kenya); Belgium attacked from the Congo basin; and Portugal made a contribution. The other German colonies fell by 1916, but von Lettow-Vorbeck was still in the field—inside Northern Rhodesia—three days after the armistice came in November, 1918. The Versailles powers then agreed to partition the East African colony into two mandates, the greater portion going to Britain as Tanganyika, and Ruanda-Urundi becoming Belgian. Portugal also received a minor slice, which was integrated with Mozambique.

Social dislocation and the problem of discharged veterans plagued the British in Kenya and Uganda after the wartime emer-

gency had ended. Although the immediate impact on both possessions was similar, the background and future developments
in each were markedly different. Uganda's strong Bantu-speaking
kingdoms and African-controlled cotton economy contrasted significantly with the Kikuyu, the dominant tribe of Kenya, many
of whom were tenants upon the European settlers' coffee estates.

For three years following the war a shortage of labor amid
an insatiable world-wide demand caused a boom in Uganda's cotton production. European estates had been bought or rented
from the Baganda chiefs, but peasant producers preferred increasingly to work their own lands. Indian entrepreneurs—some
from Kenya, others directly from Bombay—acquired strong footholds in ginning, marketing and general retailing. However, as
the slump of 1921 developed into a prolonged recession, markets disappeared and unemployment resulted. In an effort to
protect indigenous society and alleviate dissatisfaction, the protectorate government persuaded the native authorities, including
the Baganda Lukiiko (council), to put a ban on alien land-
ownership.

The presence of comparable difficulties elsewhere in East
Africa led the British government to investigate the possibilities
of a unified, interterritorial policy, but the federation schemes
—which will be discussed later—were thwarted by regional resentment and English hesitation. Within Buganda, however,
land and economic problems came to a head in the Bataka Movement of 1922. Having been the heads of clans that ruled Buganda
before the Lukiiko or the post of kabaka had developed, the
Bataka traditionally held special privileges on the clan burial
grounds. These rights, overlooked in the 1900 Agreement, were
disregarded by the Lukiiko chiefs when they apportioned the new
mailo freeholds among themselves. Peasants continued to respect
Bataka, but the Kabaka, the Lukiiko and the protectorate government did not, so the Bataka elders were reduced to the status of
common tenants. The Kabaka agreed during the 1922 recession
to apply a British proposal for compensation, but the Lukiiko—

clearly exercising its power as a ruling oligarchy—barred reform. The Bataka appealed to the British authorities. Four years later the Colonial Secretary ruled against them because the restitution of their privileges would disrupt agricultural development and create chaos in the *mailo* system, which had already prevailed for twenty-five years.

By that time prosperity had returned to the protectorate economy. Cotton production increased. Sugar crops and small mining industries began to appear. Local railways and a road network developed rapidly. By 1931 a branch of the Kenya-Uganda Railway opened for service and, because of its vantage point on Lake Victoria, Buganda became the East African headquarters for intercontinental flying-boats. A pioneer technical school at Makerere, opened in 1922, became the cornerstone of an educational program that within four years included tropical Africa's first widespread system of government-sponsored primary schools. Educational experts expected to use Swahili, the lingua franca of East Africa, instead of the local Bantu tongues, but plans were changed after the British Parliament—in a rare display of interest in colonial details—found in 1931 that most Africans would prefer instruction in English. During the enlightened, humanitarian administration of Governor Sir Philip Mitchell in 1938, Makerere became a Higher College for East Africa, licensed to prepare students for the University of London. Except for Fourah Bay in Sierra Leone, it was the first such institution in tropical Africa. Degree-granting powers were eventually added in 1950.

The years following 1930 were inevitably affected by the world-wide depression. Public revenues as well as the indigenous economy suffered seriously. The tax system was modernized and made more efficient in 1932. Further, three years later, African-owned marketing societies, which had been developing steadily since the 1921 recession, came together in a Uganda Growers' Coöperative Union. Governor Mitchell's efforts in public health increased not only life expectancy but the peasants' capacity to develop their own potential. During the Second World

War Mitchell continued to encourage indigenous initiative, which permitted Uganda to sustain itself and to contribute sterling income as well as able-bodied men to the British cause.

The first Legislative Council convened in 1920, primarily in order to advise the Governor on the labor and land problems that followed World War I. Only the Europeans, whose immigration was not yet being discouraged, held unofficial seats. Indians were invited to join but, in an attempt to increase the size of their representation, they boycotted the Council until 1926. Baganda authorities were inclined to feel that participation would compromise their semi-independent position under the 1900 Agreement, but some of the official members were supposed to guard African interests. Indian representation increased during the 1930's, but the substantive function and character of the Legislative Council did not change until 1945.

Subtle constitutional changes were nevertheless evident during the twenties in the native provincial governments, due to an increase in both British intervention and Lukiiko stubbornness. Closer supervision of finance became necessary when the *mailo* chiefs began to misuse their rent- and tax-collection privileges. In order to eliminate the corruptible system whereby chiefs took a 10 percent commission on tax collections, the British authorities instituted regular salaries. The kabaka supported and enforced this reform upon the Lukiiko. However, the attempt to restrict abusive landlords met determined opposition. The increased prosperity of the mid-twenties encouraged the *mailo* chiefs to levy a fee, payable in crops or cash, upon products grown by tenants. The Lukiiko tried to legalize the custom, but the protectorate government disallowed the measure. An investigating commission in 1926 estimated that landowners commandeered up to one-third of the peasants' crops, and the Lukiiko again authorized the practice, the rates being fixed at 10 to 35 percent, depending upon the crop involved. The British had believed that the recognition of private property was a virtue of the 1900 Agreement, but were not now willing to allow the exploitation of peasant tenants that had subsequently developed. Again the act was vetoed, thus bringing British power into direct conflict with the Lukiiko in Buganda's internal affairs. A compromise was finally reached in 1927, providing for a more moderate levy, but another issue had already led to even more positive intervention.

In a minor issue—excessive beer-drinking in an urban area —the local British Commissioner accused the kabaka's Chief Minister of uncoöperative behavior, and threatened to suspend the 1900 Agreement. Both the kabaka and the governor were drawn into the controversy, which had raised the constitutional question of Buganda's status. Kabaka Daudi Chwa put the matter on record in a pamphlet. The Minister's resignation in 1926 clearly indicated that final authority over Baganda appointees had passed to the protectorate government. Thereafter, Buganda was essentially a province under British authority, the political agreement of 1900 notwithstanding.

The Lukiiko's position began to change considerably. On one hand, the *mailo* chiefs had acquired, unprecedentedly, absolute control over both land and wealth. For a time these leaders exercised a new degree of legislative independence—as seen in the *mailo* distributions and in the levies upon tenants' crops—yet the change also had adverse consequences. Before 1926 the chiefs' primary allegiance was to Britain, which had created their new power, instead of the kabaka; after that date, the Lukiiko chiefs were subordinate to British policy. By the 1930's Baganda peasants and urban dwellers had begun to feel that the Lukiiko was an increasingly entrenched oligarchy, less concerned with Buganda than with its own special privilege. An increased and more secure income permitted the chiefs to live apart from the people. The spread of Christianity and of education had destroyed the traditional religious ties. The Lukiiko had become a secular institution, the object of democratic criticism and economic discontent.

Prosperity and emergency restrictions preserved stability during World War II. Political development also awaited the maturity of the new kabaka, Frederick Mutesa II, who inherited the throne in 1939 at the age of fifteen.

By 1945 Baganda patience was exhausted. Personal quarrels among chiefs dominated the Lukiiko. The prestige of tradition reached a new low. Obedience to the 1900 Agreement would have isolated Buganda from the protectorate's development. On the other hand, disregard for the treaty would have encouraged disrespect for constitutional law and stimulated separatist Baganda nationalism. During January, strikes for wage increases developed into political demonstrations, demands for representative elections and, ultimately, purposeless rioting. Politicians fled, civil servants were tested for loyalty, and the Chief Minister was assassinated as he entered a cathedral. His successor, determined and inflexible, restored a semblance of order.

The Lukiiko opened thirty-one of its eighty-nine seats to representatives who were chosen by a complex system of indirect election. Although nearly two-thirds of the council was still composed of hereditary chiefs, the 1946 reform was an initial step toward democratic government in Buganda Province. At the same time, the protectorate government also created the first African seats on the Legislative Council: one for Buganda, one for the Western Province, and one for the East. Fearing a compromise of its sovereignty, Buganda hesitated to participate, though the Lukiiko finally sent a delegate. The other provinces were, on the contrary, far from reluctant.

British efforts to create provinces as strong as Buganda had not been wholly successful. Chiefs had been elevated to the positions of constitutional monarchs, all quite artificially. Imitations of the Lukiiko had been encouraged. Nevertheless, the newly created authorities were slow to take charge, and when they did, the new institutions were noticeably different from those of Buganda. In no case did the new provincial chiefs acquire land or financial independence. There was no *mailo*, no oligarchy. Provincial councils tended to become democratic forums—or, at least, councils representative of several small tribes that were being arbitrarily fused. In time, Buganda had become, both to the other provinces and to Britain, a rather uncertain model for achievement. Instead of regions as distinct as Buganda, the new governments began to think of themselves as local units under a centralized state—that is, as districts of Uganda. Indeed, it may not be too much to say that they found in unity a balance to Buganda power. Britain's problems in Uganda were not only the constitutional differences between Buganda and the other provinces, but as well the increasingly serious divergence of Baganda separatism and broader Ugandan nationalism.

Kenya meanwhile had become concerned with contradictory land claims and political balances. Both the land and the government were controlled by Europeans—the former since settlement in 1902, the latter after a Legislative Council was created in 1907. Technically Kenya was the "British East African Protectorate" until 1920, at which time the Arab sugar plantations along the coast became the Kenya Protectorate and the interior became a Crown Colony. In practice, however, the Kenya Colony and Protectorate, like its predecessor, was administered as one unit.

The government had preceded the settlers and preëmpted the resources, so that there were numerous economic and political disputes that had to be resolved in the first Legislative Council. For this reason two European settlers were appointed to sit with the official advisers. One of these was Hugh Cholmondeley, Lord Delamere, age thirty-seven, a wealthy young baron who had arrived in 1903 after twelve years of dissolute living, reckless adventure and purposeless extravagance. Strong-willed, ill-tempered, bombastic but brilliant, Lord Delamere was suspended from the 1907 legislature for unruly behavior. Nevertheless, his reckless pioneer endeavors were a major element in early Kenya development. His outspokenness and stubbornness also made him the hero of those who hated bureaucracy, and the enemy of those who valued social amenities. Lord Delamere delighted in wrestling, and in an evening of shooting street lights or smashing windowpanes. He tried to turn 100,000 acres of empty land into sheep pastures, but soil deficiencies starved the flock. Cattle succumbed to tropical ticks. After plowing and fencing the virgin land, Delamere raised wheat, only to see it hit by rust. Not yet defeated, he mortgaged his English manor in order to finance rust research. After eight years, expending two fortunes and prodigious effort, he produced a hybrid wheat ("Equator," named for his ranch), defeated the cattle ticks, remineralized the sheep-grazing soil, and started to invest in other new industries: flour milling, timber cutting, hotel building, big-game hunting (he also invented the "photographing-safari"), ostrich raising, and tobacco curing. Coffee, cotton, pigs, sugar and wattles (twig-like reeds for matting and basket weaving) were all introduced or adapted by Lord Delamere. Between 1914 and 1918 he organized and financed a corps of Masai tribesmen for intelligence work in German East Africa. In the twenties Delamere introduced not only dairying but the coöperative creameries and breeding facilities upon which a major industry rapidly grew. Yet, throughout his career, the indefatigable baron represented the settler community in demanding an effective system for encouraging the Africans to work on the developing European estates. Out of his efforts, political and agricultural, the foundations of modern Kenya had clearly emerged before his death in 1931.

World War I left deep marks upon Kenya: 65 percent of the European population—most of whom were young men—was under arms, and a hundred thousand Africans served as porters. Field losses were heavy, agriculture was neglected, and animals died for want of veterinarians. The war ended with drought, famine, repercussions of the world-wide influenza epidemic, and a crumbling transportation system. In 1919 several thousand "soldier settlers" were drawn to the colony, where they were given land commandeered from an African reserve. Reconstruction and development once again raised the issue of forced labor, but the Colonial Office forbade this device except in cases of special emergency.

When the European Highlands became a Colony in 1920, the Legislative Council was expanded to include twenty-two members, half of them elected by the British settlers. A year later the Indians, who outnumbered the Europeans two to one, were invited to fill two seats. However, considering such small representation to be an insult, they boycotted the elections. The government instead nominated their representatives. The Wood-Winterton Commission, which investigated the dispute, recommended a common roll, regardless of race, but the British settlers protested vehemently and the government wavered. In 1923 the problem was reconsidered in the Devonshire White Paper, which granted the Indians five legislative seats but retained the separate roll. In addition, Indian immigration was restricted by a quota, and non-Europeans were forbidden to buy land in the highlands. Not until four years later, when a new constitution went into effect, did the Indians yield, but even then, the problem had not been permanently resolved. The 1927 Constitution furthermore provided for eleven European representatives, one Arab, and one European acting for the African masses, in addition to the five Indians and the usual majority of government officials. The first African was not admitted until 1944, and he by appointment rather than by election.

As European settlement spread after World War I, African interest in the highlands also increased. The immigrants' estates had presumably been created on unoccupied land in 1902 and again in 1919, but in some cases, Kikuyu spokesmen who had protested were given a nominal payment. Europeans held 999-year leases from the government, which, they believed, owned this land, but the tribesmen usually failed to understand this. In traditional law, land could not be sold to "alien tribes." Furthermore, the required religious ceremonies and consent of the whole clan had not been secured. At best, therefore, the European estates were on land that Africans believed they had lent or leased to the Crown, subject to the pleasure of the tribal owner. Nevertheless, the issue did not become serious until the twenties, when the Kikuyu began to recover from their earlier disasters. Movements for reacquisition of highland properties were then encouraged by Kikuyu war veterans. Having participated in the campaign against von Lettow-Vorbeck, they expected equal treatment and political advances as a reward for patriotic service.

Agitation coalesced in the Kikuyu Central Association of

1922, which stressed political rights, tribal solidarity and—to a lesser degree—educational advances. The KCA also demanded the return of lands that it claimed had been "stolen." However, the main strength of the organization lay less in the traditional tribes than in the urbanized, tenant and semi-Europeanized Kikuyu who became increasingly distinct from their clan affiliations. European education and mission affiliation were cause for automatic dismissal from tribal life. The Kikuyu population seemed to explode, largely because health services reduced the death rate. Birth rates also rose as people lost contact with the traditional society whose mores had included a system of birth control. The KCA pressed the government for "tidley-dee" (title-deeds), but the Crown Lands Ordinance of 1926 ruled that the Africans were only "tenants-at-will of the Crown." The British had no real understanding of the traditional land laws until the Kikuyu Land Inquiry Commission wrote its report in 1929. By that time European occupation was well established, and, as the Commission's report pointed out, the Africans' position was thoroughly confused because wealthy, detribalized Kikuyu had either bought or falsified traditional claims, often in violation of the tribe's own laws.

The presence of confusion did not, of course, assuage the rising hunger for land. However, in 1932, the Carter Land Commission devised a compromise solution that the government hoped would be permanent. KCA claims were disregarded as extravagant and insolubly contradictory, but the Native Reserves were considerably increased and the European Highlands definitely restricted. As an answer to the immediate needs of traditional tribes, the award was fairly satisfactory, but there had been no real amelioration of conditions among the three most dissatisfied African groups—the urbanized, the tenants and the detribalized. Each of these posed problems that rapidly became more severe during the depression years and the Second World War.

As increasing numbers of Africans took employment in the cities, especially Nairobi, an urban housing and policing problem developed. Removed from traditional society, dependent upon industrial and clerical income, they became a class partly Europeanized in both social and political attitudes. Yet settler insistence and government reluctance prevented legal recognition of their status. On the theory that they would return to the tribe when not needed, they were denied either unemployment insurance or retirement pensions. Towns were therefore temporary, almost transient in character. Crime increased alarmingly. Many of the urbanized Africans usually tried to acquire rural land as a hedge against depression and old age. However, since the tribes frowned on migrants who had been under European influence, the land had to be outside of the Native Reserves. Such areas were of course reserved for European estates. For these reasons urban dwellers were tense, restless, intermittently lawless and sympathetic to extreme land-reform movements.

Kikuyu tenants on the European estates at first seemed to fare better than tribesmen in the reserves. Better land, European agricultural techniques and a wage economy gave them a considerable advantage. However, both the European and the tenant population grew. The Europeans utilized and developed more of their land. Africans were frequently evicted or the size of their holdings was reduced. They became more dependent upon employment. Wages declined because labor supplies exceeded demands, a situation that was aggravated by the depression. Unable to return to tribal reserves, which by the late thirties were themselves becoming overcrowded, the rootless Africans became a serious social problem. Wartime conditions during the early forties alleviated the pressure somewhat, but the problem of the "landless tenants" reappeared with new urgency after 1945. The highland African was economically dependent, largely detribalized, often unemployed, and frequently bitter about his condition.

As a result of the urbanization and land-title complications, detribalization was a more acute problem in Kenya than in many other parts of Africa. Inevitably missionary efforts and educational developments also became involved with the problem. Schools were first introduced for the children of European settlers. A second, separate system was then created in response to the demands of Indian merchants and farmers. African education remained entirely in the hands of missionaries, who did not begin extensive work until the end of World War I. The segregation policy in government schools was reaffirmed in 1926, although the authorities still did not plan to finance the education of any but European and Asian children. For Africans development was therefore restricted by the missions' limited resources and usually connected with religious instruction.

In the main, the Kenya missions were among the more modern and moderate in Africa. However, the Kikuyu ritual of female circumcision (clitoridectomy) was one practice that the humanitarians considered intolerable. Persistent efforts to stamp it out were less than successful. Missionaries made no progress within the Kikuyu Reserve; the traditional tribes promptly ostracized all neophytes and converts, who perforce were detribalized. Among the urban, tenant and exiled Kikuyu—the detribalized—the churches made considerable progress. However, one of the characteristics of detribalization is incomplete or partial culture-change. In Kenya there was a persistent tendency to retain clitoridectomy as a social rite, even though it had lost its original function as a religious ritual. A number of Kikuyu were converted to the Christian position, but many of the detribalized people participated in a reaction against the missionaries. Separatist "Ethiopian" churches gave a Biblical aura to indigenous customs, but they also provided a system of "mission schools" for the education that many Africans wanted. The core of separatist education was the Kenya Teacher's College, headed by Jomo Kenyatta and supported by the active Kikuyu Central Association. In the years following World War II, the nucleus formed by Kenyatta, the KCA and the separatist schools became associated with the violent Mau Mau emergency, which will be considered in a later context.

South of Kenya the territory of Tanganyika was the most war-devastated area of Africa when Great Britain initiated mandate government in 1918. Disease, famine, scuttled railways and factories, and a reduced population were found. Influenza in 1919 exacted a heavy toll from the indigenous population.

The task of reorganization and reconstruction fell to Sir Horace Byatt, the first British governor. All German settlers were deported, and their freeholds were redistributed to Africans and new immigrants on ninety-nine-year leases. Germans were readmitted on these terms in 1925, but ousted permanently during World War II, when they openly espoused Nazi expansionist ideas. Under the mandate agriculture revived rapidly, making Tanganyika financially self-sufficient by 1923 and, two years later, twice as productive as it had ever been. Byatt's efficiency and decisiveness made him the architect of a foundation upon which Sir Donald Cameron, his successor in 1925, built a unique reputation.

Cameron's genius lay in his capacity for realistic assessment and conscientious executive supervision. His reports to the League of Nations' Mandate Commission were models of their kind, seldom if ever matched elsewhere. Certainly not a radical, either in thought or in action, he nevertheless was one of the first administrators to take concrete steps to prepare Africans for self-government at an early date. He induced honesty in his subordinates and remained exceptionally attentive to complaints and criticism. Taking advantage of Byatt's reorganizational work, Cameron concentrated on the task of locating the rightful chiefs whom tribesmen respected. Then he trained them, restored their power and turned over local justice as well as tax collection to their exclusive jurisdiction. Observers called this a system of "indirect rule," but the governor—precise, as always—preferred to call it simply "native administration."

The Legislative Council that Cameron introduced in 1926— nominated, with an official majority—remained unaltered for nineteen years. The railway system was thoroughly rebuilt and, in 1928, a branch reached Lake Victoria. Tanganyika's main crop, sisal fiber for the making of twine and rope, predominated in markets around the world. Most of it was grown by Indians and

Europeans, but the indigenous Africans—concentrating on food and coffee—benefited directly from the consequent stimulus to internal commerce. Racial problems were much less pressing than those of Kenya, largely because the Europeans were less numerous, widely scattered, and representative of several different nationalities. The more serious questions were Asian domination of retailing, irrigation for agriculture, and control of the tsetse fly that infected the cattle.

All three of these problems were attacked at the end of World War II. The Legislative Council of 1945 was formed with "balanced representation"—that is, equal representation for each race (Asian, African, European)—an experiment that for the moment seemed to satisfy all parties. The needs for economic and medical development were to be met by a British government project, the Overseas Food Corporation.

Popularly known as the Great Groundnut Scheme, the plan envisioned the production of peanuts, which would meet Britain's need for oleomargarine, cattle feed and edible oils. Confident that the inclusiveness and extravagance of wartime undertakings would make the greatest impact, the Overseas Food Corporation took over five hundred square miles in southeastern Tanganyika, invested roughly £35,000,000, built an artificial port and 150 miles of railway, and stockpiled a prodigious amount of construction machinery. Within five years production was supposed to reach 600,000 tons, twice as much as the yield in Nigeria, where peanuts are a major crop. Machines could not, however, conquer forests, plant disease and confusion. Indeed, in no country—not even the United States—could peanuts be grown on vast, mechanized plantations. The labor supply was insufficient. When the wooden railway ties (sleepers) rotted, expensive steel ones were laid. The plan expired in 1951 after yielding only 9,000 tons of nuts, about 1½ percent of the expectations.

Important lessons were nevertheless learned from the Groundnut Scheme. No agricultural project so large or so hastily conceived was ever again attempted, nor was another idea issued by European planning boards put into practice without prior

tests in the field. Furthermore, the Scheme was eventually transformed into a very different project, which benefited Tanganyika
considerably and eventually became the model for future developments throughout Africa. Much of the groundnut-scheme machinery was useless, but some of it and much of the material was
salvageable. An African Tenant Scheme experimented with mechanized tropical agriculture and studied ways of improving peasant
methods. Other projects contributed to stock raising, road construction and, perhaps most important, to the building of rural
schools. The concept of the "pilot project," as distinguished from
the "master scheme," eventually emerged. In the end Tanganyika received a variety of minor, scattered improvements which
may well have been a more important stimulus for overall development than the original concentrated scheme could possibly
have been. Nevertheless, the lessons were learned in an expensive
way.

British expectations for East Africa—Uganda, Kenya and
Tanganyika—had begun to center by 1948 upon the idea of a
federation. There have been times in colonial history when such
dreams have borne fruit, with countries such as Nigeria, Canada,
and Australia. Others have had less impressive records—South
Africa, the British West Indies, India and Pakistan, the Rhodesias—but few were as firmly thwarted as was the East African
Federation. Initial proposals appeared in the early 1920's but,
aside from a standardization of East African currency, the only
result was a semiannual Governors' Conference. Strategic considerations during World War II demonstrated the economic
value of coöperation. By 1948 the Colonial Office therefore
decided to press for a permanent link among the three possessions.

An East African High Commission, composed of the three
governors, was created. Each territory also sent four representatives to sit in the Central Legislative Assembly, which took charge
of railways, harbors, postal and telegraph-telephone services, customs, research and the income tax. However, efforts to create
further powers or to plan any self-government for the High Com-

mission federation encountered stubborn opposition. Except for Tanganyika, which for economic reasons expressed a guarded interest, the proposals seemed only to stimulate separatism and to awaken nationalism. Most firmly rejecting the idea, Buganda aimed to preserve her monarchical institutions and her predominance within Uganda. Kenya's white settlers would accept federation only if their preëminence were permanently guaranteed, which no other territory would ever permit. On the other hand, Kenya's nonwhites were uncertain: would unification weaken the whites or entrench them? Indian merchants outside Kenya favored the prospective economic advantages, but were less confident of the possibilities for protecting their distinction in a large state that would be dominated by either whites or Africans. In economic terms, which seemed to be uppermost in British thinking, there can be little doubt that all territories would have derived some advantage. As a political maneuver, however, the proposals were poorly timed. The subsequent developments in each territory have indicated that serious difficulties might have ensued if the plan had been put into action. A Royal Commission in 1953-55 stressed once again the economic considerations, but was able only to recommend an African control which many East African residents, either for racial or regionalistic reasons, would not accept.

Although Zanzibar Island, despite her long associations with East Africa, was not included in the federation proposals, she deserves brief mention. The sultan continued to rule the main island, along with neighboring Pemba, but British advisers penetrated deeply into routine administration. There had been a Legislative Council, largely composed of officials, since 1926. The clove monopoly continued to assure financial stability, and, as corruption was reduced, the traditional revenue system was able to support new, modernized government services. British authorities, paid by the sultan, operated the courts and dominated the bureaucracy. Political feelings tended to coalesce along linguistic lines —Arab, Indian, Bantu and the Swahili mixture—rather than in multiracial groupings. Within each language group there were further divisions between those who supported and those who criticized the established economic and political hierarchy. Agitation for self-government increased during the 1950's, but the Colonial Office postponed any promises until "the appropriate time." Presumably this will be when responsible, durable national parties and programs have been more acceptably defined. Delay may also be necessary until decisions have been made regarding the protectorate strip in Kenya, about which Britain promises to consult the Zanzibari Sultan.

The excitement created by the federation scheme seemed to mark a turning point in East African history. Uganda's apparent tranquility and systematic economic development took second place to a series of constitutional crises which were associated with the prospects of self-government. Political tension among Kenya's racial groups increased in the face of acute, often violent economic and social unrest. Tanganyika suddenly began a rapid transition toward independence.

The change in tempo for Uganda became apparent in a resurgence of Bataka agitation during 1948. Although the movement purported to originate with the traditional clan heads (Bataka), their disabilities were only an excuse for opportunists who played upon Baganda antifederalist sentiments. In the following year the so-called Bataka Movement asked the kabaka to dismiss the oligarchical chiefs, to make the Lukiiko an elective assembly, and to give Africans control over retailing and marketing, which were largely Indian enterprises. The kabaka agreed to consider the economic complaints but, in denying the political demands, he set the stage for riots throughout Buganda. The rest of Uganda watched these developments with calm disdain.

The protectorate government, inquiring into the disturbances in 1950, found the cause to be a desire by self-interested politicians to disrupt the legal Baganda regime. The only legitimate complaints were those related to limited malfunctions within the agricultural price-stabilization fund. However, the British forestalled any further unrest by introducing a system of popular elections for Provincial Councils, including the Lukiiko.

Buganda accepted this step but based its representation upon the *ssazas* (chiefs' districts)—some of which were 100 times as populous as others—instead of creating equitable electoral constituencies. Provincial Councils elsewhere in Uganda were now beginning to function effectively, so each of them was asked to send two delegates to the Protectorate Legislative Council. The Lukiiko refused to do so, claiming that the 1900 Agreement made the kabaka the sole link between Buganda and the central government. For a while direct conflict was avoided by allowing the kabaka to appoint the Baganda representatives, but this practice did not please those who anticipated progressive democratization.

The British authorities had meanwhile been making efforts to improve and to industralize the protectorate's economy. After an investigation in 1948 had pointed out the inefficiency, corruption and wastefulness of cotton gins and markets owned by Indians and Europeans, the government instituted a supervisory Marketing Board. When the unrest in Kenya increased, particularly in the face of Mau Mau, capital investors became wary of all East Africa. The Uganda government, therefore, started purchasing the established gins and investing in new ones. In 1952 the Conservative administration in London sold these nationalized holdings to African coöperatives on long-term mortgages. As a result, the indigenous farmers and townspeople gained possession of the gins and markets—a pioneer example of nationwide, African-owned capital industry. Nevertheless, there persisted a fear that industrialization would lead to a rigid color bar, but this was allayed by the categorical promises of the new governor, Sir Andrew Cohen, upon his arrival in 1952.

Although Cohen's experience in Africa was slight, he had exerted a major influence, as head of the Africa Division in the Colonial Office, in making the policy that led to West Africa's rapid postwar political advancement. Sensitive, pensive and faithful to policies once they were determined, he represented the British expectation of early self-government for Uganda. In March of 1953 the promises were confirmed by two major developments:

the reconstitution of local government and a substantial modification of the Legislative Council.

Believing that educational, medical and agricultural services in a unitary state should be controlled by the lowest level of government, the protectorate proceeded to turn these powers over to the District Councils rather than the provinces. However, in view of the special circumstances of the 1900 Agreement, it seemed wise in the case of Buganda to deal with the provincial authorities. In return for Britain's surrender of these powers, the kabaka promised to increase the proportion of elective seats on the Lukiiko from 34 to 67 percent, thus weakening the traditional chiefs, increasing democracy, and substituting local control for British domination. At the same time, the Legislative Council members were to be chosen by the representative District Councils rather than the more artificial provincial bodies, but an exception was again granted to the Lukiiko, which would select the delegates for Buganda. Furthermore, Governor Cohen made it clear that the kabaka could appoint representatives if the Lukiiko refused to do so. However, when the council met in 1954, the kabaka also withdrew all support from the developing central government, so the British had the awkward task of filling Buganda's seats by official appointment.

Unexpected crosscurrents then began to create tension. A Uganda National Congress, mostly Baganda but sympathetic to a unitary government, had been formed in 1952. The young kabaka, poised, Cambridge-educated, and more sensitive to popular opinion than his predecessors, took insult at the Coronation of Queen Elizabeth II in June, 1953 when he was ranked below the Sultan of Zanzibar and the Queen of Tonga. It was later quite clear that, having decided to depend on popular support rather than traditional prerogatives, the kabaka simultaneously approved democratic reforms and opposed the customary alliance of powerful chiefs with the British authorities. Regionalist feelings came to the surface in response to a speech by the Colonial Secretary that implied a federation scheme including the Rhodesias as well as East Africa. On August 6 the kabaka demanded that Buganda be transferred to the Foreign Office and given a plan for complete independence.

Sir Andrew Cohen pointed out that this request violated the 1900 Agreement, which required the kabaka to coöperate with the Colonial Office, but the demand was not withdrawn. The Governor therefore invoked Article Six of the treaty, withdrew recognition of the kabaka, and on November 30, 1953, deported Frederick Mutesa to Great Britain.

An impressive upsurge of Baganda loyalty quickly ensued. In a bid for popularity, the Uganda National Congress turned from its unification policy to support for the kabaka. The Lukiiko refused to approve either a regency or a new kabaka, which according to law was its prerogative; on the other hand, without a kabaka's formal assent, the Lukiiko members elected under the new reforms could not take their seats. Popular support in Buganda rallied behind the chiefs, despite their earlier unpopularity, and the British found themselves constitutionally stymied.

The Colonial Office appointed Sir Keith Hancock, Director of Commonwealth Studies in the University of London, to negotiate with a committee chosen by the Lukiiko. The talks nearly collapsed when Cohen vetoed the chiefs' appointment of a "non-Baganda," Dr. Ralph Bunche, the American Negro who mediated in Palestine for the United Nations Truce Commission. Feelings rose, but an alternate was finally chosen. Meanwhile the Congress in protest called a boycott of European goods. The governor refused to negotiate under such pressure, but Hancock proceeded toward a compromise in a series of informal conversations with the Lukiiko committee. The concluding agreement contained much vague language, which when published caused confusion and tension, but subsequent clarification of the terms quieted Buganda's fears. One of the noticeable characteristics of the entire crisis, it should be noted, was the peaceful behavior of all concerned parties, African and British.

According to the compromise, the kabaka could return if the Lukiiko so requested, provided the 1900 Agreement were altered to make him a constitutional figurehead. Buganda would therefore be a monarchical county within a unitary democratic Uganda nation. The Lukiiko also agreed to send delegates to the Legislative Council, which would be granted limited cabinet representation, but Britain promised not to incorporate Uganda into a federation without first getting popular approval. Kabaka Frederick Mutesa II therefore returned to his throne in October, 1954, and accepted a revision of the 1900 Agreement.

The 1955 Agreement embodied the Lukiiko and Legislative Council reforms. The kabaka was placed under constitutional limits, his reign being subject to continued interest in and support by the Baganda people. However, the new arrangement provided no means of enforcement; bilateral Anglo-Baganda consent was required either for deposing the kabaka or for abrogating the treaty. Notwithstanding the clauses affirming the unitary nature of Uganda authority, the constitutional prerogatives accorded to Buganda are clearly those of a state within a federation. Furthermore, the xenophobic propensities in Buganda had been increased, the Protectorate could not contravene the democratized Lukiiko as readily as it had earlier done, and the kabaka, as a constitutional monarch, was a less valuable channel for outside influence than the formerly autocratic ruler.

After the kabaka had been restored, nationalist movements seemed to have no concrete programs to hold them together. Their vaguely defined aspirations for self-government seemed to be developing under British aegis, the main threat being Baganda intransigence rather than government opposition. The Uganda National Congress' close association with the Baganda crisis had not pleased many of its supporters in the other provinces. Its place in protectorate politics was gradually taken by two offshoots, both favoring a unitary national republic but distinguished by the religious division so long dormant in Uganda. The Democratic Party, formed in 1956, tended to represent Roman Catholics. Then, a number of splinter groups, none more than three years old, united in 1960 to form the Uganda People's Congress, which appeared to be primarily a Protestant voice. In the interim the development of Ghana, where the central government had steadily destroyed traditional authorities, began to alarm the Kabaka and the Lukiiko. Buganda therefore boycotted the Legislative Council after 1958. Under the 1955 Agreement, there seemed to be no way in which Britain could constitutionally force coöperation.

A routine statement from the protectorate government guaranteeing the rights of the Indian minority provoked unexpectedly great alarm during the following year. Baganda resentment of the Indian merchants rose rapidly, despite British counterassurances, culminating in a mass boycott of all Indian retail establishments. The economy suffered considerably, probably unnecessarily in view of the relatively small number of Indians actually living in Uganda, but by forcing many merchants to bankruptcy and emigration, the Africans felt that their own position had been enhanced. The British then summoned an investigating commission, mostly African in composition, to make recommendations for alleviating the tension. The resulting Wild Report suggested that a Legislative Council be chosen by popular election, with all voters on a common roll.

General elections to fill eighty-two seats in the Uganda National Assembly therefore took place in March, 1961. The Uganda People's Congress won a clear majority of the popular votes. However, the kabaka's continued boycott kept all but a few Roman Catholic dissidents away from the polls in Buganda. Therefore, by capturing all Baganda seats on a very light vote, the minority Democratic Party acquired an absolute majority in the National Assembly. A national Uganda government, with an African cabinet, is therefore ready to assume self-government if and when Buganda's position is satisfactorily defined. The Lukiiko continued to demand constitutional guarantees to protect its semidemocratized traditional system against the corrosion of popular, unitary republicanism.

At constitutional talks in London during December, 1961, Uganda was promised independence by October, 1962. Representatives of Britain, Buganda and the smaller states agreed readily to create a "semifederal" national government, with the balance of local and central powers substantially unchanged. Buganda thus retained her traditional institutions, but abandoned all claims to separate independence. The Lukiiko received the right to choose Buganda's twenty-one-member delegation to the central Parliament in which popularly elected legislators from the other states would fill sixty-two seats.

Instead of the tension among divergent regions, as in Uganda, the Colony and Protectorate of Kenya since 1948 has experienced deep divisions among contrasting races, cultures and economies. Constitutional development at first appeared to be resolving some of the difficulties. The 1948 Legislative Council introduced an unofficial majority chosen by four separate voter rolls: eleven elected Europeans, three elected non-Moslem Indians, two elected Moslem Indians, and one elected Arab. In addition, four Africans and one Arab were nominated by the government. Apparently quite satisfied with their parliamentary position, the European settlers seemed to become less intransigent. Many of them hoped for self-government, perhaps even based on a broadened electorate. However, deep-seated, unreconciled African grievances erupted unexpectedly, and peaceful development was thwarted for the next seven years.

The Mau Mau was beginning to emerge. Neither settlers nor the authorities had any inkling of its formation, although extremists among them had frequently been panicky, and there was no one who understood the movement when it did erupt. The history of Mau Mau has many unclear facets, but subsequent anthropological and sociological analyses have brought the outlines into focus.

No beginning date is known for the Mau Mau, whose name probably was intentionally meaningless and mysterious. Undoubtedly the movement was several months—perhaps years—in creation; the first dated Mau Mau "oath" was in 1949. Mau Mau's greatest strength lay not among the tribes but among disgruntled tenants on the European estates. Basically it was a secretive, coercive, antiwhite, anti-Christian movement, standing firmly on profoundly warped interpretations of the Kikuyu tribal traditions.

Apparently the movement began as a negative, secret revolt against all manner of change, probably among an isolated group of detribalized Africans. Violence was not to occur until the very distant future. The idea spread by word of mouth, but some who heard the secret apparently were not guarding it carefully. The Mau Mau organization therefore adapted the traditional Kikuyu oath in order to enforce loyalty.

The Kikuyu oath was highly complex, very specific in purpose and used only on the rarest occasions. It was intimately connected with tribal religion, and constituted the basic device for maintaining order among the autonomous Kikuyu *rugongos* ("ridges," or sovereign local governments). Indeed, the oath functioned in an ingenious manner: internal disputes could almost always be resolved by the council of elders, and disputes between two different *rugongos* could usually be compromised by palaver or a joint hearing of the two councils having jurisdiction. However, if truth could not be determined, or a solution found, the parties to the dispute would be told that the oath would be administered if the answer were not found within a certain length of time. This tactic nearly always revealed the guilty party or the liar. If not, the oath was administered—and, it should be noted, only as a last resort to determine the truth— to both disputants. Each of them then swore that his statement was true, and religiously proclaimed that if it were false, "may I be killed by this oath." The effectiveness of this oath is self-explanatory: it was so deeply respected and literally believed that no one in the wrong would dare to take it. To do so under such conditions was simply unthinkable in the strongly disciplined religious context of tribal society. As a result, the oath was so rarely tested that its validity and power never came into question.

Far different, then, was the Mau Mau oath. A terrorized victim was forced to take the oath, which in the Mau Mau perversion had no connection with the separation of truth from false-hood. Furthermore, the oath taker was required to promise never to tell the true secret—another reversal of the tradition. Also, by administering an oath that bound the taker for unlimited time, Mau Mau twisted the original idea. In short, the Mau Mau oath was itself a direct travesty of the Kikuyu tradition. In administer-ing it, the organization was playing upon two basic facts: the de-tribalized victim did not know the difference between a real tradition and a false tradition; yet the victim still was overawed by the vague terror of a traditional oath, which he almost cer-tainly had never seen in actual use.

The Mau Mau ceremony required that "if I do anything to give away the organization to the enemy, may I be killed by this oath." It is quite obvious that such an experience, regardless how awesome or grisly, would not silence every lip among thousands. The organization thus found that it had at once to force an ever-expanding number of people to take the oath, and it also had to eradicate untrustworthy people who had heard—or might have heard—the Mau Mau secret. By 1952 the secret had gotten out of hand. Africans were being sworn, forcibly and rapidly. Some, in panic, joined the secret campaign. Others who might talk were themselves wiped out. The authorities became alarmed at an in-creasing amount of arson, murder and inexplicable coercion, first among the highland tenants, then among the urbanized Africans. Inevitably the members of so frenzied a movement began to ap-ply the secret itself. Only at this final stage, between 1952 and 1955, were European lives and property at stake. Nevertheless, the government had only the barest idea of the Mau Mau secret. Believing for some time that the terrorism was totally untrace-able, the authorities labeled it a revolt and declared a state of emergency.

The Mau Mau was not broken by military action, although that obviously reduced the immediate effects of unbridled ter-rorism. The answer instead came from the Kikuyu themselves, and in large part from a counterdevice that they explained to the government. Mau Mau attempts to infiltrate the firmly converted

Kikuyu Christians were the beginning of the organization's undoing. Having no fear of the secret oath, even if they had been forced to take it, these Africans promptly sought police protection and gave the British the first extensive explanations. The Movement also started to penetrate the tribal reserves, where the tribal traditions still were maintained. Tribesmen promptly discounted the false oath, so they too reported to the authorities and explained what had happened. The tribe also had the answer to Mau Mau's advance: a traditional counteroath, or cleansing ceremony, which the British administered en masse throughout Kenya during 1954-55. Hard-core elements continued to be a threat for some time, and there always remains the danger of some resurgence or a new perversion. Nevertheless, a full-scale revival of the original Mau Mau is extremely unlikely, because the government is now keenly aware of the problems created by changing or misunderstood traditions, and steps have been taken to reduce some of the most pressing detribalized grievances out of which extremism might grow.

In the process of mopping up the Mau Mau, the British forces became suspicious of the long-established Kikuyu Central Association (renamed Kenya African Union), the "Ethiopian" church schools and the Kenya Teacher's College. Their virulent opposition to Christian missions, persistent defense of the clitoridectomy tradition, and obvious anti-European propaganda were a circumstantial link with the Mau Mau. Accordingly the principal of the Teacher's College, Jomo Kenyatta, was taken into custody and brought to trial. A specially constituted court heard the case, the publicity of which helped to sustain tension among the detribalized Africans. Kenyatta was convicted of lending active support, perhaps leadership to the Mau Mau, and sentenced to detention in northern Kenya.

Kenyatta was born to a family of witch doctors and spiritual counselors in Kikuyuland, about 1893. When Britain proclaimed the protectorate, Kenyatta was about two years old. Shortly thereafter he abandoned his tribal upbringing in order to attend a Scottish mission school. He then became a houseboy for a European settler who, in turn, found him a government job. Between 1929 and 1946 Kenyatta lived all but one year in England, where he worked on farms, attended a Quaker school, studied anthropology, and wrote an unusually important analysis of the Kikuyu tradition. In 1945 he was active with Du Bois and Nkrumah in the English branch of the Pan-Africanist movement. Soon back in Kenya after his long absence, he pressed constitutional reforms. His precise role in the subsequent Mau Mau terrorism has never been fully clarified. The court that tried him has been criticized for submitting to pressure, either from colonial officials or from politicians in England who were forced to find a scapegoat. Many questions remained unanswered. Was Kenyatta the organizer of the Mau Mau, or merely a politician who underestimated the bitterness of his constituents? Was he basically a tribalist, a Europeanized "modernist," or essentially detribalized? Critics saw irrationally barbarous quirks in him; sympathizers found pacifism, sensitivity and cultivation. Acquaintances have described him as quiet, quixotic, sometimes lonely, perhaps charismatic; some have said that he is often ill at ease among indigenous Africans but comfortable among the educated and the whites. He once visited Moscow but left with observations to the effect that communism was too restrictive and charged too high a price. Imprisonment after 1953 removed him from active politics, but his image remained vivid in all Kenya minds—an image of horror to white settlers, of unity to most African politicians and voters. Some British authorities began to wonder whether Kenyatta, as a result of his detention, might become a nationalist martyr. Many officials also felt that an early release would undermine respect for the law, whereas holding him too long might encourage irresponsible extremists.

In addition to the mistrust and suspicion engendered in the Mau Mau period, there were two Emergency regulations that had considerable effect upon Kenya's subsequent history. As a safety measure, 90,000 Kikuyu were dismissed from their jobs and expelled from metropolitan Nairobi. Luo tribesmen who filled their places were resented, and unemployment became chronic in

Kikuyuland. Also, a ban on large organizations and public meetings severely restricted the growth of African nationalist parties. The liveliest movement under the regulations was that of Tom Mboya, a self-educated Luo union leader. Long restricted to Nairobi itself, his People's Convention Party—a name clearly borrowed from the nationalists in Ghana—became the foundation for the Kenya Independence Movement when the restrictions were withdrawn.

Constitutional reforms, introduced in 1954 by Colonial Secretary Oliver Lyttelton, marked the first step toward the restoration of normalcy. Africans were granted the right to vote—on a separate roll—and given one of the six cabinet ministries. Nationalists rejected the concessions as insufficient, but Europeans were equally disturbed at the thought of a nonwhite cabinet. The first elections in 1956-1957 served only to increase dissension, primarily because of the peculiar Coutts system of voting, which granted extra ballots to "responsible" Africans but made no such distinction on the European or Indian rolls. The African legislators continued to reject both the Lyttelton Constitution and any cabinet post. The Electoral Union, which had represented all Europeans since 1920, began to disintegrate into competing factions—some favoring the constitution, others holding it too liberal, still others criticizing its conservatism. The collapse of a European front frightened those who saw the white man as Kenya's saving master, but heartened the advocates of interracial national consciousness.

It is not therefore surprising that a new constitution, taking advantage of recent politics, was promulgated in 1957. The racially elected representation was frozen at fourteen Africans, fourteen Europeans and eight Asians. This destroyed the European settlers' "parity," a concept by which Europeans would outnumber the representatives of the other two races. The new Colonial Secretary, Alan Lennox-Boyd, then incorporated a novel device into the constitution: twelve Legislative Council seats, four from each race, to be chosen by the Council itself. These so-called "Specially Elected Members" promised to be a nonracial element in the government but the purpose was thwarted. Some of the special seats went to prowhite elements because the African elected members, who were still boycotting the Council, did not participate in the voting. European and Asian members therefore chose the special members, including several Africans who thereby became very unpopular among the African voters. The fourteen popularly elected Africans later quit the Council completely, returning only in January, 1960, when the British government convened another Constitutional Conference.

Political alliances were very tenuous under the Lennox-Boyd Constitution and at the 1960 conferences. Nationwide African parties had been forbidden until the end of the Emergency in 1955, and most of those that later emerged trace their origins to Mboya's Kenya Independence Movement. The KIM advocated a single roll for all voters, African settlement in the Highlands, universal compulsory education and the release of Jomo Kenyatta. Being at once popular and stubborn, Mboya had personal qualities that were a source of strength but which also made it difficult for him to adjust to the compromises of practical politics. To a considerable extent, Mboya's ascendancy originated among the Luo, who gained control of urban Nairobi during the Emergency. When restrictions were lifted, the more numerous Kikuyu began to reassert their political strength. They continued to respect Mboya's leadership, though men such as Ronald Ngala—representing smaller, less powerful tribes—became more acceptable to many African voters.

Liberal European opinion coalesced around Michael Blundell, a planter who favored the common roll, free education and a compromise on the land question. His New Kenya Party gained some African support, though no African representatives in the legislature, but the early promise of moderate interracial policy failed to develop into a positive, active force. Instead, a revival of the older Kenya Party—long quite dormant—attracted the strongest multiracial support. Its policy, as put forth by Sir Ernest Vasey, drew upon the statements of the Capricorn Society which, in 1956, had argued the advantages of interfactional coöperation for the development of East and Central Africa. The KP appeal was lower keyed and less flamboyant than those of other parties, but it had the valuable qualities of endurance and of policies that it not only accepted but sincerely desired. Other groups—an extreme settler faction, a moderate African movement, and the Asian parties—were relatively weak, and either ephemeral or silent.

The context of the 1960 constitutional talks was also influenced by two major British decisions which may have contributed to the reduction of intractable factional rigidity. The first of these was a wholesale resettlement and reorganization of the Kikuyu tribe. About 1,500,000 people were given new houses in planned villages, with a radical social and economic reorientation. The government hoped that, along with markets, public utilities and school facilities (built, but not maintained, by the government), the new system would alleviate the tribal divisions and detribalized unrest that led to Mau Mau. There is hope—presumably well-calculated in this case—that such wholesale changes will create contentment instead of new detribalization or culture-change crises. A second step, taken in 1959, established an appointed, interracial Central Advisory Board to supervise ". . . the basis of tenure and management of agricultural land." Buyers of any piece of land must not already be owners of large tracts and they must indicate that they plan to work the soil efficiently. The Board must also ensure that the rules for purchasing or owning land "will be the same throughout Kenya, regardless of race or tribe." There was, however, no restriction on land prices, which were already very high, especially in the Highlands. The KIM continued to agitate on this point, which may have prevented much African purchase in the foreseeable future, but the multiracial principle in the land question had nevertheless been established.

Guided by Iain Macleod, successor to Lennox-Boyd in the Colonial Office, the Constitutional Conference of 1960 was attended by representatives of every faction in the Legislative Council. Mboya, Ngala, Blundell and Captain Briggs—leader of a conservative European movement to partition Kenya—were present. Each party was also allowed to bring one adviser. The African counsel was Thurgood Marshall, an officer of the American NAACP. When the Africans elected Ngala to lead them at the conference, the displaced Mboya made a startling move to revive his prestige. He demanded as a second adviser one of Jomo Kenyatta's close friends. The conference nearly collapsed on this technicality, but Macleod arranged a compromise that permitted the talks to resume. Blundell and Ngala together held the extremists of all races in check, especially in the delicate question of voting qualifications.

The resulting Macleod Constitution contained several noteworthy provisions: a common voter roll, regardless of race, with moderate educational and property-owning qualifications for the franchise; an African-dominated Legislative Council (up to thirty-three out of fifty-three elective seats) and cabinet; a guaranteed representation for minority groups (the electorate must fill ten European, eight Asian and two Arab seats, by choosing among candidates who have won the support of their respective groups in primary elections); and twelve nonracial appointments, to be voted by the elected legislators. Macleod also promised to add a bill of rights containing guarantees desired by Europeans against the expropriation of property.

Ngala and Blundell were warmly welcomed by Africans when they returned to Kenya. Briggs' United Party, representing the European right, rejected the settlement and appealed for support, but found that the majority of whites were not willing to block the constitution. Mboya's dependence upon the Kikuyus, who outnumber his own Luo people, forced him to step up the appealing demand for Kenyatta's freedom. Many Kenyans, including influential white settlers, began to feel that Kenyatta would be a practical, national leader if he were restored to active politics.

Against this background Kenya went to the polls in February, 1961. Personalities predominated over party organization, but despite some European dissatisfaction the minorities' primaries and common voting roll both functioned smoothly. Mboya emerged with unexpected strength, nominally leading the victorious Kenya African National Union (successor to the KIM). Kikuyu attempts to exercise tribal strength, either by dividing Mboya's KANU or by supporting the opposition KADU (Kenya African Democratic Union), seemed to fail. Mboya's appeal was national rather than tribal, but, by relying on the image of Kenyatta, he put himself in a position where he might have to take second place if Kenyatta were ever allowed to re-enter politics. KADU could have formed a weak government by allying with the European and Asian minority representatives. However, realizing the political suicide of such a step, KADU instead supported KANU's demand for the release of Kenyatta. As the plurality party that alone could rule effectively, KANU therefore refused to form any government without Kenyatta. The British governor, Sir Phillip Renison, on the other hand, refused to pardon the leader until a government had been formed. Blundell's New Kenya Party, the third largest group (though small when compared with the African factions), expressed willingness to work with Kenyatta. This leader's release awaited only the development of a technical formula that would give him political freedom without either embarrassing the British government or infuriating too many white settlers. Such an arrangement, announced late in the summer of 1961, permits Kenyatta to assume leadership as the colony progresses toward self-government.

Certain facets of the constitution—notably the prime ministry and the bill of rights—remained uncertain. Nevertheless, the prospect of a workable polity, multiracial but not totally controlled by one race, seemed to be a possibility. Peace and development still depend upon the successful achievement and maintenance of national loyalty over economic and racial interest. A framework for the protection of individual rights, without restricting the function of universal suffrage, would appear to be a crucial factor in any workable resolution.

The contrast between Kenya and Tanganyika has been marked, despite the presence of many comparable racial and economic problems. British administration under United Nations trusteeship has been dedicated to nationwide development of the entire population, devoid of much of the equivocation and hesitation that characterized earlier Kenya policy. White settlers were less firmly established and less vociferous in their own defense. Land was not so scarce. Capital for national development came less from European individuals, more from the trust administrators. From fresh beginnings after the Germans left in 1918, the patterns set by Byatt and Cameron in the twenties did much to prepare for a peaceful, unspectacular achievement of independence.

Pilot projects growing out of the Groundnut Scheme were of major importance in strengthening the rural economy and educational system of Tanganyika. The simultaneous expansion of sisal production, though carried out largely by Asians and Europeans, was an important contribution to increased prosperity and racial interdependence in the economy. Africans were not admitted to the nominated Legislative Council until 1945, but within three years that body included equal (so-called "balanced") representation by all three races.

A new constitution in 1955 continued the principle of a "balanced," nominated legislature, but the Council's size and jurisdiction were expanded. Local government reforms pointed the way toward the first elections, which took place in 1958. The franchise was broad, with low qualifications, but each voter was given three votes—one for a European candidate, one for an Asian, and one for an African. Each race therefore retained "balanced" representation, but the candidates all had to appeal to a broad, interracial electorate. The government thus hoped to orient political thinking toward the nation instead of any one interest group. British approval of a white-directed interracial United Tanganyika Party was that movement's kiss of death, so an overwhelming victory went to the Tanganyika African

National Union (TANU). Its multiracial slate put the party's African leader, Julius Nyerere, into the predominant position, although there also emerged an equally moderate but strong opposition, the Tanganyika Elected Members' Organization (TEMO). An extremist African National Congress appeared to be very weak, though a serious failure of the TANU policy could enhance its appeal.

Nyerere was a slightly built, soft-spoken, intensely serious Roman Catholic history teacher, who gained prominence by spreading the TANU organization into rural areas. A graduate of Makerere and the University of Edinburgh, he formed TANU in 1954, the year in which a United Nations commission forecast at least twenty more years of European trusteeship. Nyerere's sophisticated speeches directed TANU toward a policy of constitutional moderation, but made it clear that there would be no compromise with the goal of independence by 1965. Nationalist sentiment took root with astonishing rapidity and remarkably little friction for such a large, lightly populated country. Many observers were also inclined to feel that the Tanganyikan experience had a salutary effect upon the negotiations that led to the Macleod Constitution in Kenya.

The second general elections in August, 1960 gave TANU control of all but one of the legislative seats. The franchise was broader, with less emphasis on racial balance but more on national unity, so racial feeling played at most a negligible role. Cabinet government, allowed immediately after the election, was increased to internal self-government on May 1, 1961. With that step Nyerere formally received the title of Prime Minister. The British government had by then announced that Tanganyika would receive independence on December 9, 1961. At that time the country was formally admitted to membership in the Commonwealth of Nations.

The Nyerere government has taken steps to develop the transportation and communication systems, which are indispensable bases for economic and social development in such a large country. New railways and trunk highways are under construction, but particular attention is being given to a network of simple secondary roads in agricultural regions.

The example of Tanganyika's multiracial coöperation and development will be noticed in neighboring countries having comparable problems, but observers are not sure whether it will be a helpful lesson or merely a stimulus to increased tension.

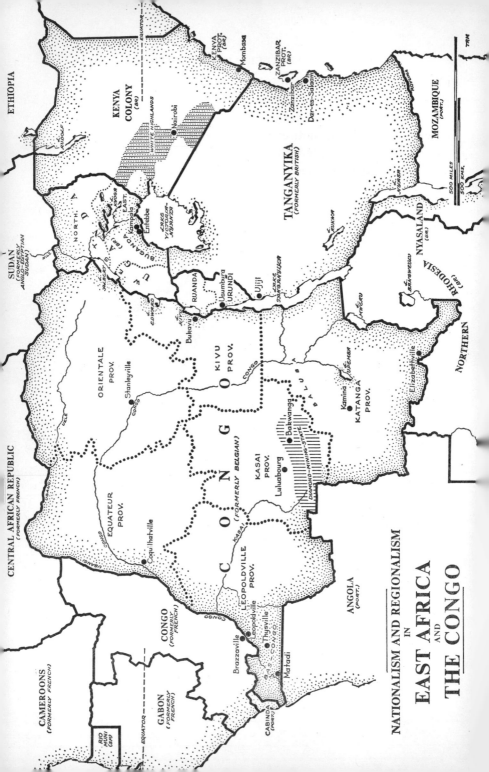

NATIONALISM AND REGIONALISM
IN
EAST AFRICA
AND
THE CONGO

25

THE CONGO

"It is the Whites who have killed Christ," the blacks used
to say. "We have nothing to do with it. Whites who kill a
White?—old tribal quarrel. Leave us alone in our village."

Charles-André Gilis, *Kimbangu*

IN asserting sovereignty over the Congo, the Belgian Parliament in 1908 aimed simply to thwart the corruption and
personal aggrandizement that had characterized the earlier
Congo Free State under King Leopold. The reforms established
bureaucracies and incorruptible councils to accomplish this purpose, but the powerful economic concessions, the source of all
capital, were left untouched. The colonial government itself became a depersonalized mechanical corporate entity whose functions were the maintenance of order and the development of
basic communications. By World War I the changeover had
largely been completed, although many minor services, some remote areas and most of the abstract official humanitarianism
had yet to be organized. The Belgian colonial system was not in
full operation until the 1920's.

Undoubtedly Belgium's responsibility was enormous.
Seventy-eight times the size of the mother country, the Congo
was as large as the United States east of the Mississippi. How-

ever, the estimated population was small—only slightly larger
than Belgium's, and less than that of New York State. In Africa,
Nigeria alone had three times as many people, British East
Africa almost twice as many. It is not therefore surprising that
communications and the labor supply became the two greatest
Belgian problems.

Even as late as 1951, Belgian officials could find no definition of their colonial policies—political or social—although they
spoke confidently of "first realizations" (i.e., pioneer accomplish-
ments) and the "rightness of their intentions." In practice, the
independent bureaucracy and the monopoly concessions were
separate, nearly equal powers. The Christian religion acquired
similar status in 1925, so there was subsequently a trinity of independent colonial authorities. For twenty years the Roman
Catholic church represented religion, controlled all education,
and received state aid, but Protestant missions played an auxiliary, sometimes moderating, role. After 1946 the latter also received tax support. The overall three-headed structure was not
modified until 1959.

Government, business and the church retained control of
all initiative and determined all policies. The African was
neither consulted nor tested, though experts pondered his condition at great length. As late as 1958 the Belgians openly and
proudly described their system as "paternalistic." None of the
three authorities ever doubted that the colony existed for economic gain and for humanitarianism, and that the second would
automatically follow from the first. Economic motives therefore
explained and justified all policies, including even the social and
religious programs. Such an interpretation of cause and effect
in human history is usually characteristic of Marxist theory,
though in the Congo it was actually preached by a conservative
bureaucracy closely supported by large private businesses. The
theory was remarkably successful insofar as such a long tenure
without major change cannot be matched in any other phase
of modern colonial history. Indeed, the Congo's history for fifty
years was made largely according to an authoritarian plan. How-

ever, the end of the regime in 1960 was caused not by economic factors, but by the social and political questions that the authorities had overlooked for so long. Ironically the ensuing chaos invited Russian Communist propaganda couched in the purely economic terms that Congolese Africans had been trained to accept.

Each of the three colonial authorities held broad, virtually autonomous power over its respective sphere of life in the Congo. The government concentrated on basic communications, transportation, the regulation of labor supplies, and the maintenance of order. The concessionaires directed economic development and industrial production. Educational services that coördinated with these programs were placed under the church.

Railways and water transport formed the core of the government's development program. The established lines, which usually by-passed rapids in the river, were modernized and their termini made more efficient. New branches facilitated access to mines and waterways that the Free State had not exploited. River steamers were centralized under new concessions and linked more closely with the rail system. By 1918 reliable, economical rail-steamer routes reached both Lake Tanganyika and the Katanga, but it took three to five weeks, with six transfers, for either products or goods to make such journeys. A more direct railway into Katanga, opened in 1928, halved the time and the number of transhipments. Nevertheless, the transportation network did little to unify the Congo colony, because it was designed simply to provide the cheapest possible outlet for the exportation of raw materials. River services stimulated some local commerce, but were too slow for perishable foods and too expensive, too intermittent for much human contact. Railway lines merely augmented this system, moving mined ores, agricultural produce and Europeans, but doing relatively little to develop the interprovincial movement of African people. When roads were built in later years, their function was similar to that of the railways. Airplanes eventually provided the speed and convenience that would have contributed to Congolese interdependence and unification, but they were too costly for the movement of bulk cargo or masses of people. Africans were rarely permitted to travel, except as contract labor, so regional isolation continued to be characteristic of indigenous life.

To maintain order and efficiency, the government created a strong colonial army, the Force Publique. Appropriations and recruitment were centrally controlled, but the preservation of tight discipline and fighting preparedness was entrusted to a small, independent corps of volunteer white officers, most of whom were Flemish. African recruits were required to break completely with their tribes and to give unswerving loyalty to the Force. The officers inspired devotion by valiant example, by instilling fear, and by exercising unquestioned authority over the recruits' personal lives. In return, the Force Publique was well paid, given a high standard of living, and accorded much prestige. Its primary tasks were to protect trade, to quell unrest, and to prevent any political or social movements that threatened the colonial system.

After its creation in 1908, the administration expected to revive the traditional chieftains in tribal areas. However, most of the Congolese tribes had been seriously disarranged by Free State exploitation, so there were few legitimate chiefs to be found. Most of the chiefs whom Belgium recognized between 1910 and 1920 were therefore artificially strengthened, untraditional authorities.

Two factors then served to disrupt the tribal system again. The first was a thorough reorganization of tribes and chiefs, instigated by Louis Franck, Minister of Colonies, in 1920. For the next thirty-five years the colonial administrators proceeded systematically to replace tribes and chieftains with a system of uniform, arbitrary "sectors"—each ruled by a newly selected, appointed, and salaried African "chief." In this manner, some 6,100 traditional tribes—or the remnants thereof—were compressed into about 550 "sectors." Membership in the sector councils and courts was determined not by tradition or chiefly status, but by the Belgian District Commissioner who was guided by the government's unilaterally revised codes of African law. Unlike comparable consolidations in other colonies, the Congo "sector" system was rigid, unrealistically systematic and without regard for popular sentiment. Chiefs were paid in proportion to their efficiency rating, but in practice the government simply tended to disregard or to by-pass those who seemed for any reason to be unsatisfactory.

Rapid urbanization, the second element in hastening tribal disintegration, became significant after World War I. The depression retarded industrialization, but urban concentration increased markedly after 1940. As late as 1938 eleven out of every twelve Africans lived in a "traditional" sector or tribal remnant. Ten of the twelve were still there in 1946, nine in 1953 and only seven—about 60 percent—in 1960. The other 40 percent had taken employment in the booming cities. To rule the mixed urban populations, the government created "extra-customary [untraditional] centers," which were the counterparts of rural sectors. The colonial District Commissioners chose "Chiefs of the Centers" among the African residents, or, if none of them seemed suitable, he appointed Belgian officials to rule the centers. In addition, a Belgian Territorial Agent exercised strong— perhaps controlling—influence. Every center was then supervised by a "Protector Committee," composed of Europeans and appointed by the Governor-General.

In 1945 the creation of centers was discontinued. Subsequent urban developments became *cités indigènes* (indigenous cities) or *villes* (towns), under the direct rule of the provincial governor and a special committee of Belgian advisers. Subordinate to each of them was a European "city chief" and a group of appointed African "neighborhood chiefs." There was no system of election or representation, and the African settlements were always some distance from the European communities.

Urbanization was not necessarily well received in rural areas of the Congo. There was plenty of land, although tenure and tribal cohesiveness were often uncertain. Wholesale recruiting, such as the Free State had permitted, was forbidden by the

1908 reforms, but coercion continued to be common. Since the government owned substantial proportions of the concession companies, officials were not discouraged from using pressure to help recruiters. Chiefs were frequently bribed, despite humanitarian protests, and the legal quotas were regularly exceeded. Open connivance was effectively repressed after 1933, and wartime pay increases stimulated the volume of voluntary contracts, but most labor continued to be channeled through the draft system. By law no more than one-fourth of the population could be contracted, but drafts after 1940 usually took more than 30 percent of the rural males.

Africans came into contact with the concessions in the matter of land tenure as well as the labor draft. Free State decrees, which permitted African tribes or clans to occupy land but not to own it, remained in force after 1908. Small families or individuals had no such rights. The claims frequently conflicted with those of concessionaires or other tribes. There being no shortage of land in most areas, the government felt little need for definitive action. After 1908, concessions already chartered by the Free State were allowed to keep freehold title to about 42,000,000 acres. By 1940, when the policy was changed, Belgian authorities had granted leases or freeholds for another 9,000,000 acres. In cases where these grants have been used for agriculture, the benefits have been considerable, particularly in developing alternatives to the African system of shifting cultivation. However, most speculators found—as the indigenous farmers knew—that the forest soil was too shallow and too weak for sustained planting. Unless these ventures had capital, technology and patience, they either failed or adopted the indigenous tradition of moving to fresh land every year.

Industrial and mining concessions have been more important than the agricultural schemes. Logging developed primarily to supply fuel for industry, but exotic hardwoods have often been exported. Hydroelectric power, though only superficially exploited (the Congo has one-quarter of the world's potential), made industrial development economically feasible. The resulting complex of capital in Katanga and Kasai concessions quickly became the core of the colony's prosperity.

Katanga's copper reserves had been worked lightly since prehistoric times, but European development did not begin until 1911. Diamonds were first produced in Kasai two years later, largely for commercial use. Both exploitations were cornerstones of the interlocking structure of Belgian colonial capital, the pattern for which descended from the Free State concession system. King Leopold II, who established the parent system, controlled 50 percent of the stock of all Congo companies. In 1908 these rights passed by law to the Belgian government, which matched them with money from private investors to form a new holding company, the Société Générale de Belgique. The government thus owned half the Société, which in turn held half the stock of each concession. The Forminière concession (Kasai diamonds), all transportation, and most other Congo investments were controlled by this system.

In Katanga, however, a special situation had already arisen. Instead of a limited concession, the Katanga Company had arranged with the Congo Free State for joint administration and exploitation of the entire province by a Special Committee of the Katanga. After 1908 two-thirds of the Special Committee belonged to the Société Générale, and one-third to the Katanga Company (reorganized as Union Minière du Haut Katanga). The Committee, conversely, owned one-fourth of the Union Minière, which thenceforth controlled the mines of Southern Katanga, but no longer all property. The Special Committee, rather than the government, continued to regulate all mining, to supervise land sales, railway construction and urban resettlement. It also directed African affairs in Katanga province. By the end of World War II the Committee's domain produced more than half the colony's exports and the government's tax revenues. Profits regularly ran about 30 percent of the value of production; indeed, the profits of all concession companies, if combined, would have been one-seventh of the Congo's annual gross national product. African agriculture rated poorly in monetary terms, in part for want of transportation for perishables, but African industrial wages were better than half the colony's national income.

Undoubtedly the Congolese African standard of living was higher than that of any neighboring territory, perhaps higher than that of any nonwhite population in Africa. In this respect Belgium's policy succeeded remarkably, far surpassing the achievements of any other African colonial administration. However, in attaining their goal, the authorities subordinated or postponed all noneconomic considerations.

Although no humanitarian organizations were legally barred, official preference and state support before 1946 went only to Belgian Catholic institutions. Foreign and Protestant missions were subsequently given grants-in-aid, and, in 1948, all discrepancies were eliminated. At that time, unsupported Protestant schools were educating slightly more than half the total number of students. From the government's point of view the church served two purposes: maintaining peace by controlling social institutions, and providing a broad base of elementary education. From time to time, separatist or "Ethiopianist" dissention threatened political tranquility and economic efficiency, but the church, the Force Publique and the government in close coöperation tried to suppress such tendencies promptly.

Belgian educational philosophy envisioned not Europeanization but orientation of Africans to their own social and economic needs. Rudimentary general background plus technological training were emphasized, on the theory that social development depended upon the Congolese ability to develop local resources. Missions therefore offered a four-year primary program, in which by the 1950's were enrolled about half the 500,000 children who reached school age during each year. However, more advanced schools were forbidden until 1948. Thereafter there was a "post-primary" system, severely restricted both in student enrollment and in subject matter, that annually accepted about 3,000 Africans: half for an eight-year secondary course, and half for a four-year technological-vocational program. Concession companies had operated small employee-training schools since the First World War, but the curricula were oriented exclusively toward specific industrial skills. In addition, the monopolies supported a broad primary-school system for the families of urbanized Africans, and, in conjunction with the state, they offered fundamental training courses for midwives, carpenters and hospital attendants. Literary, philosophical and cultural education was profoundly distrusted and never offered, except in the special schools that were established for European children in the Congo. Primary education was always conducted in the African languages; French instruction was given only as a necessary adjunct to advanced technical training. There was no system of higher education until 1955, and no Africans were permitted to study either in Belgium itself or elsewhere abroad. The government confidently believed that, by this broad but limited system, it would create a rudimentarily trained mass of people who would have no dissatisfied, elite or incongruously advanced leadership. As late as 1953 the authorities expected to postpone the creation of such a class for at least thirty more years. Meanwhile, all efforts were directed toward the creation of a prosperous, industrially oriented, technologically trained African middle class upon which, in the distant future, political and social institutions could be grafted.

There was an implicit assumption that economic development would satisfy a changing society, a confidence that political and social expression could be subordinated according to a preconceived plan. However, increasingly frequent indications of human unpredictability had already begun to emerge. The Congolese search for and expression of noneconomic ambitions was evident as early as the 1920's, but it did not become a persistent clamor until the years following World War II. To most officials, such movements—which were quickly suppressed—seemed quite minor when compared with the impressive economic achievements.

Religious agitation was the first sign of African restlessness. Within a year after "sectors" had begun to replace tribal remnants, the first cohesive Messianic sect appeared. The prophet was Simon Kimbangu, about twenty-five, originally baptized by Protestant missionaries, who began to preach and to heal among the Bakongo in the spring of 1921. Reports of his miracles spread quickly, attracting pilgrimages of the lame and discouraged. Protestant attempts to conciliate him failed; Catholics, merchants and the government became alarmed. Disciples in his name spread African xenophobia and cataclysmic fears, but Kimbangu himself seems to have been peaceful, stressing the Bible over tribal beliefs, the next world over this. To him, Christianity was a scriptural truth that satisfied traditional African emotional yearnings. As the Prophet of the Bantu, he carried a message and, in order to convince traditional skeptics, he performed impressive physical miracles. Nevertheless, he denied being either a Christ or a liberator: "Follow God alone, and not me," said Kimbangu, whose message was transcendental rather than temporal.

Within six months the Territorial Administrator decided to arrest him for disrupting order and weakening the state church. Kimbangu hid until the Force Publique used violence to flush him out. Tried, admitting his prophetic mission, and sentenced to death, Kimbangu was later reprieved, then exiled to Katanga, where he died after thirty years in prison. However, he left behind a church, the Kimbanguistes, rich with modifications of Christian liturgy, slightly less xenophobic than the original disciples, but quick to elevate their prophet to Christlike stature. From his prison cell Kimbangu had the experience— almost unique in religious history—of watching his own deification, contrary to his original intentions and without his encouragement. The Kimbanguiste church remained strong in the lower Congo, spread eventually to Katanga, and exerted considerable influence in Portuguese Angola. Some of its operations were secretive, though the organization was not systematically repressed; it stimulated resentment against European rule, but did not condone either violence or threats against individual whites. Not itself nationalistic, the new church nevertheless encouraged African dissatisfaction, sheltered separatist thought, and stimulated the growth of other movements that were more direct. Kimbanguism became, in time, less systematic and more eclectic in doctrine, not only a religious vehicle but a social and political outlet for African aspirations. Finally, by the late 1950's, this church began to take an active role in Congolese politics, particularly among the Bakongo people near Léopold-ville. At least nominally, the Kimbanguistes follow the leadership of the prophet's three sons, who reign in council.

Although Kimbanguism itself was not a nationalist movement, later prophets and competitors, operating independently, gave separatist religions an increasingly political tone. Some new preachers, especially in the growing cities, suggested anarchism. Another movement, led by Simon Mpadi, a cold-blooded, imaginative prophet with a penchant for bizarre peccadillos, secretly asked Nazi agents in 1939 for Hitler's help in liberating the Negroes. In a Katanga prison twenty years later, Mpadi proudly confessed his acts, claimed to be a Christian healer, not a prophet, and a follower of Kimbangu, a prophet who, Mpadi said, "Later . . . made errors." Mpadi in 1959 demanded political power in the lower Congo, but neither Belgium nor the nationalists would recognize him.

Kimbanguiste doctrine was not far removed from apocalyptic vision. The impetus for such interpretations originated with the Watchtower movement of the Jehovah's Witnesses in the United States. The Belgian authorities expelled their missionaries, but could not stamp out the ferment they had caused near Stanleyville. The indigenous Witnesses, called Kitawala, combined Kimbanguiste prophecy and Watchtower millennial thought, but some of their ideas differed considerably from those of the forerunners. There was a god with three sons, an Asiatic Jew, a European and a Negro. The first two then committed atrocities on the third that mocked him and made him inferior. According to Kitawala, an imminent apocalypse would rectify this degradation—not by ennobling the Negro, but by giving him a white skin. At this point, of course, the existing government would be replaced by theocratic rule. Furthermore, convinced that faithful Negroes, duly whitened, would alone survive the cataclysm, Kitawala demanded total renunciation of all present governments and contacts with white men. Xenophobia, political disobedience and apocalyptic martyrdom were therefore encouraged. On the eve of World War II the Kitawala doctrine was the most virulent and disruptive form of anti-Belgian feeling in the eastern Congo. Persistent repression actually fed the faith, which subsequently exerted a considerable influence upon nationalist politics.

In large measure, religious ferment—especially in its radical forms—seems to have been a reaction against foreign rule. Without tribes, firm land titles, or political institutions—even advisory or intermediary—the demand for social and cultural identity found expression only in amorphous or dramatic cults. The political implications became increasingly noticeable during the depression years. Legal outlets were forbidden and older traditions abolished, so there was no check upon extremist frenzy in the new religions.

Wartime exigencies, after 1939, exerted a profound influence upon Congolese life. After the fall of Belgium, the colonial government was virtually autonomous. Languishing industries, such as rubber, underwent a speculative boom. More important, the Katanga mines provided vital war material, especially copper. Uranium production, hitherto a small industry, developed rapidly in utmost secrecy; by 1945, when atomic research was first revealed, Congo mines were producing more than half the world's supply of fissionable materials. Urbanization, the volume of production and European settlement had all nearly doubled during the course of the war. An overwhelming majority of the Congolese population—at least those who knew much about the conflict—were loyal, sometimes active in the Allied cause, and the wartime Governor-General, Pierre Ryckmans, acquired considerable renown as an organizer—stern and efficient, but benevolent.

There were isolated strikes, sometimes with violence, during the war. One Force Publique garrison mutinied in 1944. Nevertheless, the postwar government, pleased with the Congo's overall wartime contribution, gave the colony its first native-welfare program, the *Fonds du bien-être indigène*. Ninety-five percent of the $50,000,000 grant was actually a lottery privilege and compensation for emergency Congolese war expenses. The bulk of it went into the government's first program of rural medical services, and about one-sixth to public utilities and education. A smaller project also began to establish "indigenous peasants" on small, defined plots of land, but the administrators failed to obtain clear land titles and too often disregarded peculiar soil conditions. In point of fact, the government recognized native "registration" of land, but never granted proprietary titles to any non Europeans.

The Congolese colonial system began to weaken about 1947. For several years the change was subtle and slow. Long-standing paternalistic policies were rarely reëxamined, certainly not revised.

The economy boomed. African living conditions were unprecedentedly good. Nevertheless, African discontent was coalescing. Big business and the church—two of the three ruling authorities—began to reassess their positions. "Man becomes a kind of vegetable," wrote a Belgian anthropologist, but, he added, man soon finds "freedom in misery more attractive than slavery in comfort. We must immediately start deproletarianizing the native. . . . Man can receive his real happiness only from his own hands." [1]

Most of the dissatisfaction seemed to center in the cities, around the industries and among the wage-earning Africans. Belgian colonial policy anticipated the development of a sympathetic, loyal *évolué* group—a middle class within the European system—but the authorities expected the process to be slower than it was. The original plan encouraged the lower-school graduates to form "Former Students' Clubs" (ADAPES), which gradually became social and study groups.

[1] G. Malengreau, *La Revue Nouvelle*, vol. 2, February 1947, p. 101.

The ranks of such *évolués*, proud of their French, European manners and urban prestige, increased rapidly during and after World War II. Along with several small associations that imitated it, ADAPES expanded rapidly among detribalized Africans in mining centers, lower levels of the bureaucracy, indigenous cities and even the headquarters of many rural "sector" administrations. In 1946 African clerks and government employees formed an "Indigenous Personnel Association" (APIC), and churches launched their own social and discussion groups, notably the "Social Interests Union" (UNISCO).

Club activities took a turn that the planners had not foreseen. As membership rolls expanded, recreation, social service projects and abstract discussions gave way to practical questions—working conditions or job opportunities, racial problems, regional pride, political feelings and ideological complaints. New voices put club sentiments into coherent demands. There was Joseph Kasavubu, a clerk in the colonial government, advocating "equal pay for equal work," racial equality and the recognition of regional autonomy, particularly for the Bakongo "sector" from which he came. Kasavubu's strongest opposition, composed of migrants from the upper Congo and Uele basins who predominated in urban Léopoldville, lacked cohesion and leadership. Eventually these groups gave enthusiastic support to Patrice Lumumba, the spokesman for clubs in Stanleyville who adamantly opposed all forms of regionalism. Elsewhere in the Belgian Congo, leadership was more fragmented. *Evolué* associations within the rural "sectors," which had replaced the tribes, competed with one another and with silver-tongued orators in urban "centers," each presenting his own case for regional exclusiveness and special privilege. Representative of such smaller groups were Moise Tshombe and Jason Sendwe of Katanga, Albert Kalonji of Kasai, and Antoine Gizenga in Orientale Province. The Belgian policy of "domination for service" had regrouped traditional tribes, but it also preserved many characteristics of dividing in order to rule. There was no effective traditional leadership. The social and study associations had got out of hand. Finally demagogues had begun to acquire considerable prestige, without either elections or administrative responsibility to test their potential.

The government attempted to give the new sentiments an outlet by granting the right of *immatriculation*. In theory, Africans had this privilege as early as 1892, but none had exercised it because the authorities had never established a procedure for or a definition of immatriculation. The Minister for Colonies issued the enabling decree in 1952, after three years of study. He clearly hoped that, by gradually admitting a limited number of Africans to the status of Belgian citizens, the dissatisfied *évolués* would be mollified. Anyone who demonstrated "a state of civilization implying the aptitude for enjoying laws and fulfilling duties" would then be entitled to European justice, civil rights and racial equality on all public transportation. However, few Africans were either satisfied by this or willing to disassociate themselves from their brethren as the decree required. But even more serious was the refusal of most European colonials to accept Africans who did immatriculate.

Big business, high officials and the churches were largely sympathetic to the immatriculation decree, but the majority of foreigners—especially those who had come to the Congo after the war—were small businessmen, individual entrepreneurs and some agricultural settlers. This group of Belgian *colons*, themselves resenting the governing bodies as strongly as the Africans did, feared and distrusted the *immatriculés*. The governor-general forbade discrimination and segregation, but could not prevail against the *colons* who effectively defied him. Then, determined to protect themselves from official domination, the *colons* demanded voting rights and representative institutions.

White demands for self-government were promptly denied, but the issue shook the Belgian system severely. The united front of colonial power had begun to split. Africans could not but notice the example, which immediately encouraged them to think in terms of their own self-interest and self-government. Protestant churches had joined the Catholics in receiving state support after 1946, and both concurrently began to be impatient with the government's cautious policies. Education became unsystematic, with missions opening secondary schools, the government hesitating or at best making only piecemeal adjustments in its long-range plans. The concession companies also hastened to assuage their African employees by improving working conditions, living standards and educational facilities. Ultimately, in 1954-55, a new government came to power in Brussels and policies were extensively overhauled. Nevertheless, reform ensued only after bitter public quarrels between the Colonial Ministry in Belgium and the steadfast bureaucracy in the Congo. The apparent unanimity, implacability and rigidity of white rule had suddenly given way to deep divisions: big business versus the *colons;* Brussels authorities versus Belgian officials in the Congo; Protestants, liberal Catholics and the Minister of Colonies versus the long-preferred state-supported Catholic-school policy.

First of all, secular government schools were set up. There had been a few, for European children, since 1946, but the system was now extended to all races. Subsidies for church schools were reduced. The churches—particularly the Catholics, whom the new government strongly criticized—threatened to strike against the innovations, thus crippling education during the transition period. Two factions emerged, not only in Belgium but also in Africa, and the Congolese for the first time realized that politics in the Belgian motherland could be turned to African advantage. The reform party eventually carried its point against the Catholic traditionalists by citing the "irresistible pressure" of Congolese opinion.

Following the introduction of secular schools in 1954, events moved with increasing rapidity. A new university, Louvanium, soon opened its doors in Léopoldville, and a university college was planned for Elisabethville. The Jesuit order established new liberal schools that were designed to foster Congolese Catholic nationalism. Professor A. A. J. Van Bilsen,[2] a dynamic liberal scholar at the University of Antwerp, put forward a thirty-year plan for African independence, an idea that created no little sensation in both Belgium and the Congo. *Colon* sentiment hardened. Africans published their first journals and organized their first political parties. Their demands became increasingly vehement, although consistently more regional than national in emphasis.

The first and strongest African movement, Joseph Kasavubu's Association des Bakongo (Abako), dominated the lower Congo. With a longer detailed history, stronger tribal organization and larger numbers than any other Congolese tribal "sector," the Bakongo had survived colonial rule with exceptional cohesion and sense of identity. Kasavubu capitalized on these characteristics, and the idea of a reconstituted Bakongo nation enhanced his appeal. One of Africa's older nationalists, having been born in 1909, Kasavubu accepted support both from the Kimbanguiste church and Professor Van Bilsen. One of the few Congolese politicians to be immatriculated, stubborn and wilful, long a student of Thomistic Catholic theology, he nevertheless distrusted Belgium. Colonial officials alternately praised and attacked him, they being never quite certain whether to respect his apparent sophistication or to suspect his regionalist separatism.

The only other widespread movement, perhaps the sole advocate of strong national unity, was the Mouvement National Congolais (MNC), which coalesced behind Patrice Lumumba. By disregarding regional loyalties, which no other Congolese politician did, Lumumba became the object of both widespread nationalist respect and unparalleled regionalistic detestation. Prestige and precariousness both suited his mercurial temperament, which was dominated by three characteristics: unswerving belief in national unity, profound fear of paternalism, and a noticeable lack of decisiveness on all other matters. Since the

[2] "Un plan de trente ans pour l'émancipation politique de l'Afrique belge," *Les dossiers de l'Action Sociale Catholique*, Brussels, February, 1956.

first two attitudes were uppermost in many Congolese minds, Lumumba gained widespread support which he did not dissipate by committing himself on any other debatable subjects. His enemies were ideas, never personalities—regionalism, but not Kasavubu; paternalism, but not all Belgian individuals. Foreigners described him as a monomaniac, unsophisticated, confused, even ineffectual, but his followers—and many people throughout Africa—admired him because of his consistency on the only two points that really seemed to matter.

Born in 1925 to devout Catholic parents among the small Batetala tribe of northeastern Kasai, Patrice Lumumba received the limited primary education then customary in the Congo. Once of age, he joined the urbanized *évolué* community in Stanleyville and became a postal clerk. He frequently wrote articles for local newspapers, then for some of the widely distributed African journals that emerged after 1954. Unlike most such writers, who stressed their traditional heritage, Lumumba campaigned for nonracial, nationwide equality. In 1956 he was arrested for embezzling 126,000 francs ($2,520) from the post office—some say he was "framed" to cover others' crimes—and sentenced to two years' imprisonment. *Evolué* friends covered the missing funds, so, after being freed in 1957, he became the sales manager of a brewery in Léopoldville.

Lumumba was in no way prepared or organized for the local elections that Belgium allowed in 1957. Abako alone was able to present a slate of candidates, though this party stood only in the lower Congo. Essentially these initial elections were a pilot, a cautious test, applied only in selected wards of a few "indigenous cities." The most significant outcome was Kasavubu's victory in the Dendale district of Léopoldville where, as mayor, he acquired an official position from which to lead both the Abako and the urban *évolués*.

Time and events beyond Belgian control had already begun to feed nationalist sentiment. Ghana's independence earlier in 1957 inspired nationalists throughout the Congo. Excitement increased when General de Gaulle, President of the French

Community, visited Brazzaville, only four miles from Léopold-ville, in 1958. The Middle Congo, in former French Equatorial Africa, had become an autonomous republic; the many Bakongo within its borders were now free, and independent Africans began to frequent the streets and markets of nearby Léopold-ville.

Throughout 1958 the colonial government attempted to put its best foot forward at the Brussels World's Fair. A typical African village, complete even to a miniature school with authentic students, was installed in the Congo Exposition Building. In order to work at the fair, leading *évolués* made their first trips to Brussels where—also for the first time—they met and talked with one another. Hundreds saw Belgian life, with its impressive prosperity, and they contrasted whites in Europe with those who ruled them in Africa. At the same time the Congolese exhibit became controversial. Some tourists reportedly threw food to the "natives" on display. The *évolués* were indignant, other tourists complained, and the exhibit had to be withdrawn. The government provided all African personnel with board and accommodations at a special Center where discussions of the fair soon expanded to include Belgium, the Congo, and, inevitably, independence. When they returned home at the end of their unprecedented summer, nationalists had both new life and new direction.

Meanwhile Lumumba had remained in Léopoldville, where he became active in three *évolué* clubs. In one of them, the Social Research Study Center, he met Joseph Ileo and Joseph Ngalula, each of whom had edited well-known nationalist journals for more than a year. Ileo's *Conscience Africaine*, which in 1956 had published an independence manifesto based upon Professor Van Bilsen's thirty-year plan, was primarily the organ of the urbanized Bangala people who predominated in Léopold-ville. Ngalula's *Presence Congolaise*, a Christian-supported paper, was also connected with the Mouvement National Congo-lais (MNC), which was then a small, moderate nationalist group that supported Ileo's manifesto calling for independence in 1986. Lumumba was active in all of these movements, political and editorial. He became chairman of the MNC Central Committee in October, 1958, pulled all the groups together into one front, and proclaimed a "national movement [for] . . . national liberation."

The Bangala of Léopoldville followed Ileo into the MNC, which thereby acquired a strong foothold in traditional Bakongo territory. Kasavubu's Abako, weakened and greatly alarmed by this incursion into its bailiwick, changed its policy quite radically. Separatism was still latent among the Bakongo, but their party now sought either an alliance with other regionalists or a guarantee that all other parties would refrain from activity in the lower Congo. At this point Kasavubu fell out of favor with the Belgian authorities, who openly preferred Lumumba's nationwide MNC.

The government then decided to let Congolese delegates attend the All-African People's Conference, a meeting of independent and aspiring nationalists, in Accra, Ghana. The authorities could neither deny nor control the influence of other African nationalists, so exit permits were granted to four leaders —Lumumba, Ngalula, Kasavubu, and Gaston Diomi, the mayor of another "indigenous city" in Léopoldville. Kasavubu was then prevented from leaving the Congo, presumably because his medical papers were not in order, so Lumumba became undisputed leader of the Congo contingent. Of all major figures in later developments, he alone had met Nkrumah; he alone had presented the Congo's case, the case for national independence and against regionalism or paternalism. Other African nationalists—particularly those of Ghana and Guinea—were therefore convinced that Lumumba was the only true Congolese nationalist. This impression was of considerable significance in the 1960 crisis. At Accra Lumumba and the MNC were themselves converted to the idea that independence must come, not by 1986, but by 1961. The Congo atmosphere was therefore heavily charged when the eventful year 1958 came to a close.

On January 4, 1959, one week after Lumumba returned from Accra, Congolese sentiment exploded. Lumumba and the MNC had no role in the riots that occurred in Léopoldville. Abako was responsible, but it would not heed even Kasavubu's call for moderation. The government had already promised to issue a new policy statement in mid-January. Rumors interpreted this to mean independence within a fortnight. Unemployment had been growing steadily since 1956, due primarily to the low price of copper and to excessive urbanization. The government took an optimistic long-term view of the economy, but the restless Abako membership reacted to the immediate poverty. A mass of economic and social resentments, fed by the new political impatience, came to the surface. Abako meetings were banned, protest marches ensued, and quick repression by the Force Publique fanned the flames. Many Europeans were hidden by African friends, but others, misled by calming propaganda from the government radio, were caught in the rioting. The uprising was sharp but short-lived—forty-nine Europeans, forty-nine Africans officially reported killed—yet its roots were obviously deep.

Divisions of Belgian opinion, noticeable since 1954, became greater. The Brussels government was inclined to hasten its liberalization policy, but the colonial authorities still inclined toward repressive enforcement of detailed regulations. This official dichotomy probably explained the last-minute ban on Kasavubu's trip to Accra as well as the manner in which the riots had been stopped. European *colons* meanwhile formed a third white party, at once considering "committees of public safety" and criticizing both the home and colonial authorities. Abako was banned, and Kasavubu temporarily deported, but the governor-generalship passed to a tough, progressive reformer, Maurice Van Hemelrijck.

King Baudouin's address and the government declaration on January 13 came as no little surprise to Africans and Belgians alike. The King's adulatory reference to his grandfather, Leopold II, was not as well received as the body of the message, which instituted a barrage of sudden changes. Many of these had been hastily developed in Brussels during the preceding week. The declaration was therefore substantially more sweeping than the government had anticipated a fortnight earlier. Independence, heretofore never mentioned by the government, would follow, neither too slowly nor too quickly, the monarch promised. All local offices were to be filled by universal suffrage before the end of 1959 and a rudimentary Congolese parliament, indirectly chosen, would convene in 1960. Racial integration, higher minimum wages, educational expansion and African promotion to upper government posts were guaranteed by sweeping fiat. By thus seizing the initiative, the Brussels regime increased its prestige markedly. However, unexplained delay in implementing the social goals began to weaken the government's advantage. Many *colons* and some of the established bureaucracy fought or undermined the new policies. Kasavubu returned from exile within three months, but Governor-General Van Hemelrijck came under fire from both the *colons* and the political right in Belgium. The great concessionaires, accustomed to time in which to think, failed to make a decision either for or against his administration. Van Hemelrijck felt that prompt reform was necessary in order to prevent the rise of Congolese extremism, but the right demanded slower change, a blockade on contacts with the rest of Africa, and the preservation of Belgian privileges. Intrigues connected with this quarrel spread to the Congo. *Colon* petitions and demonstrations began to alarm the Africans. Brussels hesitated. Van Hemelrijck, now left without support, resigned in September, 1959. His successor, Auguste DeSchrijver, instituted a compromise program of slower, less thorough reform. Africans interpreted his appointment as a retreat from the January promises. In fact, DeSchrijver was well qualified and sensitive to many Congolese problems. Earlier in the year he had directed an unprecedented Parliamentary investigation that revealed many improprieties and propagandistic devices by which the old order had maintained its position.

Van Hemelrijck's departure marked the point at which Belgian control and African nationalism became openly incompatible, although there had already been much evidence that the educational, political and social reforms in January, 1959, if not those of 1954-55, were too late. Under DeSchrijver, discontent again rose. The Force Publique once more enforced official desires with repressive measures, and the *colons* boasted of their victory.

Two African parties predominated: Kasavubu's Abako, regionalist with a tendency toward federalism, still strongly opposed by the Belgian authorities; and the MNC, under Lumumba, the one pan-Congolese movement, with particular strength in Léopoldville and Stanleyville. Other movements that coalesced during 1959 represented smaller interests, essentially regional in orientation, but related in complex ways to the two main political opponents. In every case, some traditional background plus the pronounced effects of former Belgian policies were noticeable.

The minority parties organized themselves by regions and "sectors," not by traditional tribes. In some cases, interests within the colonial administrative provinces corresponded roughly with common ethnic backgrounds, but traditional chiefs and customary organization had much less significance than the *évolués* who rose to power in the "sector" system of local government. Good examples of such movements were the Bangala people of Equateur Province, who, with their kinfolk in urban Léopoldville, were represented by Ileo and Ngalula. Their Bangala organization, fighting primarily against Bakongo influence in Léopoldville, increased its strength in 1958 by joining Lumumba's MNC. Other MNC allies included the spokesman of Baluba diamond miners, in southern Kasai, a quiet, earnest former teacher named Albert Kalonji. Numerous other groups, even smaller, supported the MNC, not because they necessarily wanted centralization, but because they feared the exclusivist pressure-group approach often employed by the larger regional factions. The MNC was still the only national party, but much of its support was actually the product of common dislikes rather than positive belief. This became evident in the summer of 1959 when Kalonji's Baluba in Kasai, as well as the Bangala of Equateur and Léopoldville, seceded from the MNC. In both cases, the breakaways, who preferred federalism to complete unity, realized that opposition to Abako or other powerful regionalists was not necessarily the same as support for Lumumba's centralist MNC. However, the latter recouped part of the loss by making new allies in Kasai. These were the Lulua, former Baluba overlords, who still lived in rural "sectors." Lumumba then accused the Baluba of "tribalism." This was clever propaganda, but not realistic in view of the fact that Kalonji's supporters were more *évolué*, urbanized and detribalized than Lumumba's new Lulua allies. After this arbitrary realignment in 1959, bitterness and violence were endemic in Kasai.

The particularly delicate situation in Katanga demonstrates both the nontraditional and the opportunistic character of Congolese politics on the eve of independence. Katanga Province was by no means an ethnic unit. Luvale tribesmen were the traditional occupants of the copper-mining region, but the new urbanized population of Elisabethville and Jadotville, drawn from many tribes, outnumbered them after World War II. Some of the Baluba, whose brethren in Kasai supported Kalonji, predominated in the northern part of Katanga. Nationalist political alliances in the province cut boldly across these traditional lines. The Katanga Baluba, the rural Luvale and several minor groups supported the federated Balubakat (Balubas du Katanga), which was led by Jason Sendwe, a conscientious former medical student whom the old educational system had barred from becoming a doctor. The government and most missions supported Balubakat, which allied with Lumumba, and continued to do so even after Lumumba supported the Lulua faction against the Baluba in Kasai. Opposing Balubakat was the Confédération des Associations Tribaux du Katanga (Conakat), led by Moise Tshombe. As its name implies, this party was also intertribal—or, properly, nontribal—representing the *évolués* and polyglot urbanized populations of Katanga. Con cerned primarily for practical politics, Tshombe also accepted the active support of Belgian *colons,* who were just numerous enough to give Conakat a slim majority in Katanga's provincial legislature. Since Tshombe's power depended upon this tenuous support, the colonial government considered him simply an unimportant, transient figure in African politics.

The final phase of Belgian rule began in October, 1959. Governor-General DeSchrijver called local elections for December and scheduled a series of indirect elections throughout 1960 that would eventually culminate in an experimental parliament. Lumumba demanded a faster timetable; Kalonji and Kasavubu, who accepted the elections, nevertheless irritated the government by pressing for federalist guarantees; Tshombe, who maintained a discreet silence, was disregarded. The authorities were then frightened by a marked increase in Kasai violence and in Lumumba's demands for haste. DeSchrijver again toughened: Lumumba was arrested, and the Force Publique marched into Kasai. Yet, at the same time, nationwide elections for local offices went ahead as scheduled.

Abako's boycott of the polls played into the hands of the Lumumbists, who added Léopoldville victories to their impregnable position in Stanleyville. Nevertheless, the Abako action demonstrated that party's strength, even though it meant the temporary loss of political power. Tshombe, Kalonji and Ileo all retained control of their own regions. The colorless, leaderless Parti National du Progrès (PNP), which won most rural contests and emerged as the largest faction, was in fact scandalously discredited, because it soon became known that the colonial government had financed its campaign and selected its candidates.

The Belgian government began to feel that order and control could no longer be maintained. A round-table conference with the Congolese was therefore called for January, 1960, in Brussels. Invitations were planned in such a way that extremists would be in the minority—out of eighty-one delegates, nineteen represented traditional tribal "sectors," twenty-two the officially sponsored PNP, and the forty others were popular politicians. By placing all its hopes on the PNP, the government threw away its last bridge of contact with the other political leaders. Brussels newspapers ridiculed Kasavubu, who strove to build his prestige but seemed weak because his party had lost all its posts in Léopoldville. Tshombe, who tried to create an air of *évolué* elegance, was again overlooked, and Lumumba, who displayed wounds allegedly acquired from prison torture, overtaxed the Belgian patience.

The Round Table quickly discarded the agenda. Unexpectedly presented with a nearly unanimous resolution, the government agreed to grant independence by June 30. DeSchrijver asked for that much delay so that a temporary Basic Law, Parliamentary enabling acts and preparatory elections could be arranged. Thenceforth events moved at a chaotic pace, although the Belgian government continued to give the impression that all developments could be controlled according to plan. Officials favored Lumumba for a couple of months, during which the Basic Law was written. The Congolese state thereby became highly centralized, as it had been under Belgium and as Lumumba wanted it to remain. But on other details, Lumumba and the colonial government began to disagree: Belgium would retain ultimate control over the Central Congolese Bank; and all aid programs would be administered—Soviet-satellite style— by a special department of the Belgian Embassy, not subject to Congolese control or review.

By February it was obvious that the Congo would not give Belgium any special concessions until independence had been granted. In March Kalonji and Lumumba reunited their forces, the Kasai returned to peace, and Kasavubu began to revive the strength of Abako. In Brussels, Parliament passed the enabling acts. Political campaigning started in April and elections followed in mid-May. During the last week of June, Parliament convened, the cabinet was formed and, on the thirtieth, the Congo became an independent republic.

In one respect the Congo was better prepared for independence than any other tropical African country. The economy was strong and the standard of living high. Although agriculture in the northeast was not greatly developed, Katangan mining and commerce in the lower Congo more than compensated for it. Industry was not well diversified, but the presence of many essential products guaranteed a good income from foreign markets.

Social development was less solid, though hasty strides in recent years encouraged some observers. Educational facilities had expanded considerably, but only fifteen Congolese had yet taken any university level work. Some Protestant churches had begun to pass from the missionaries to indigenous control. Medical facilities were fairly widespread, though they still depended exclusively upon European physicians and surgeons. For all social services, the new government had to rely heavily upon foreign employees.

The political picture was the least encouraging. Lumumba's program of national independence, both from colonial and from paternal control, seemed momentarily to have gained the upper hand. The May elections had confirmed the patterns that emerged in 1959: the MNC predominated with thirty-three Parliamentary seats out of 137, including some victories in every province and total control over Orientale. Abako and its allies won twenty-five—all but one of those allotted to Léopoldville and the lower Congo—and Tshombe's Conakat, a coalition of *colons* and urbanized Africans, retained a slight edge over its Balubakat opponents in the Katanga delegation. The Belgian-sponsored PNP was virtually wiped out. Lumumba built his cabinet upon the tenuous coöperation of Sendwe's Balubakat, the Bangala under Ileo and several minor groups. By reaching a remarkable agreement with Kasavubu, who became the figure-head president, he also added Abako to his coalition. Fragile at

best, the new government rested largely upon the distribution
of twenty-three cabinet posts among twelve different parties.
Only one minister was a university graduate, and none had ever
administered anything larger than a township. Tshombe's party
resented having been given only one ministry; Kalonji—rated
as a minor ally—received none. Bangala delegates, bitter because
the presidency had not been given to them, weakened in their
allegiance to Lumumba.

Subsequent events are too recent to permit the formation
of a historical judgment. A brief outline of certain trends, understood in the light of their earlier history, would alone be possible.

In the chaotic months following Congolese independence,
world opinion and many foreign governments depended heavily
upon journalists, the shortcomings of whose reports were exceptionally serious. Frequently not familiar with peculiar Congolese
institutions and movements, they were faced in many cases
with conflicting or unconfirmed rumors from distant areas, and
repeatedly required to explain quickly or dramatically many
complex or subtly defined problems. A barrage of contradictory
propaganda—Russian, Belgian, *colon*, Ghanaian, Lumumbist,
regionalist or religious—influenced many who, because of terror,
confusion or lack of linguistic and historical background, did
not travel widely in the country or delve deeply into the situation. There was a persistent tendency to confuse true tribalism
(which was rarely the problem) with the "sector" system and
the pressure groups in African urban "centers."

The political factions were numerous. Lumumba remained
the standard-bearer of centralization, modeled upon the Belgian
colonial precedent, but he was determined to overthrow every-
thing else reminiscent of economic or social paternalism, white-
settler privilege and European political influence. Kasavubu's
Abako, encouraged by its role in the struggling coalition government, turned from secessionism to alternative confederal or federalist ideas. Tshombe and Kalonji remained secessionist, the
former still very dependent upon *colon* support in Katanga.

Groups such as the Bangala of Equateur, who gradually shifted toward Kasavubu, and the Baluba of Katanga, accepted temporary alliances that seemed to meet their requirements at any given moment. Last but not least, there were the Force Publique, still Belgian-officered and impatient—as always—with all politicians and local interests, and unstable fanatics of Kitawala inclination, ready to take unpredictable advantage of any weakness in white strength, African political authority or popular feeling.

Six days after independence the Force Publique mutinied against its officers, against Lumumba's concessions to Kasavubu, and in favor of higher pay and promotions. Lumumba dismissed the Belgians and promoted all the enlisted men. Whites panicked and technicians fled the country, which without communications seemed to be more chaotic than it really was. The Force Publique, carried away by its newly found sense of power and despising local politics, attacked white and Negro civilians in two towns. On July 11 Belgian paratroopers seized the three main cities. On the advice of Nkrumah, Lumumba the next day asked for United Nations aid, and, within the week, Tshombe proclaimed the independence of Katanga, under unofficial but extensive Belgian *colon* and military influence.

The UN became a pawn for international diplomacy and the bête noire of internal politics. Security Council resolutions, which forbade the use of force, were designed primarily to halt Belgian intervention. Lumumba wanted the international police, drawn from smaller nations on five continents, to crush the Katangan secessionists. The Soviet Union attempted to use the UN to further its own purposes in the crisis. Kalonji turned against Lumumba, proclaimed the sovereign Diamond Mining State (of which he later became king), and Lulua-Baluba fighting recommenced. UN Secretary-General Dag Hammarskjöld, assisted by Dr. Ralph Bunche, his American Negro undersecretary, tried to counteract Belgian and Russian influence while neutralizing Lumumba, Kasavubu, Kalonji, Tshombe, the Balubakat and the Lulua.

Now afraid that the UN might perpetuate regionalism and revive paternalism, Lumumba began to accept Russian aid and to tolerate Soviet infiltration in Orientale Province, where his strongest support was concentrated. In completely disregarding the diplomatic struggle between the Communist and Western powers, he received strong sympathy from several other African countries who continued to believe that national independence and unity was still the main issue.

Kasavubu took advantage of the internal dissension and Western anti-Communist feelings to depose Lumumba and appoint Ileo to the prime ministry. The legal power to do this was uncertain, the temporary Basic Law that Belgium had provided being unclear, and Lumumba retaliated by dismissing the president. On September 14 the Force Publique once more rose, arrested Kasavubu, Lumumba and Ileo, and put Colonel Joseph Mobutu into power. Parliament was prorogued. The rule of martial law, ostensibly intended to neutralize politics, was supported by an advisory "College of High Commissioners," composed of all of the Congo's fifteen university graduates. Communist diplomats, who publicly admitted that Lumumba had exasperated them, were soon deported from the country.

Mobutu was unable to organize the logistics necessary for the subjugation of eastern and southern regions from his Léopoldville base. Tshombe, still allied with the white *colons* of Katanga, remained independent. Orientale turned to Antoine Gizenga, a quiet but efficient Lumumbist aide who claimed to be the true heir of MNC centralism, and, in defiance of his authority, fanatical anti-European violence of the Kitawala type began to increase in the east. Communist influence declined in the winter of 1960-61 as regionalists gained strength, but Ghana and Guinea continued to help Gizenga in the belief that he alone had the answer to the problem of economic and political disintegration. In February 1961 Lumumba tried to escape from Mobutu's control. He was caught and killed while crossing parts of rural Katanga that were loyal to Tshombe, who promptly transferred the blame to "disgruntled tribesmen." Meanwhile

Kasavubu—now unchallenged in the lower Congo—began, with UN help, to resume control over the Force Publique.

During the spring of 1961 the UN made agreements with Kasavubu which effectively separated international obligations from local politics. The UN undertook to retrain the Force Publique so that it could become a responsible national army under African civilian control. Kasavubu, Tshombe and Kalonji developed a federation scheme in a meeting at Tananarive in the Malagasy Republic (Madagascar), though a second session at Coquilhatville in Equateur Province was disrupted first by Gizenga's continued boycott, then by the Force Publique, which arrested Tshombe in violation of safe-conduct guarantees. However, the Coquilhatville Plan for a federated United States of the Congo slowly gained ground. Katanga agreed to participate in a reunited Parliament if Tshombe were released, and Gizenga's supporters planned to attend under UN assurances of safe conduct. Once freed, Tshombe repudiated his government's promises, but Parliament nevertheless met in order to seek a modus vivendi among all the other groups.

A new cabinet was promptly formed with Cyrille Adoula, a Kasavubu supporter, as Premier and Gizenga as Deputy Premier. Lacking Katanga's coöperation, the central government now had no counterweight to the increasing pressure from Gizenga's Communist-influenced supporters. A UN attempt to conquer Katanga, thus reuniting the non-Communist Congo, failed in September. Secretary-General Hammarskjöld, en route to negotiations with Tshombe, died in a mysterious air crash in Northern Rhodesia, and the fighting ended in a truce that left Katanga independent.

The UN was immobilized by a prolonged debate among the Great Powers which delayed the selection of a new Secretary-General until November. Tshombe meanwhile interned over 100,000 of the anti-Communist but pro-centralist Balubakat opposition and ousted its elected representatives from his legislature. Gizenga used his position as Deputy Premier not to participate in Adoula's government but to spread leftist influence; he considered himself the "President-General" of the country and labeled his movement the Party of African Solidarity. His erstwhile supporters among the old Force Publique began to join hands with antiwhite terrorists who ranged out of control in Orientale and Kivu provinces.

In December, after U Thant of Burma had been installed as Acting Secretary-General, the UN resumed military action—this time with more success—against Tshombe's secessionists. The UN command and the central Congolese government seemed to believe that internal lawlessness, regional defiance and outright secession would weaken the Congo's ability to resist either European or Communist influences. The re-incorporation of Katanga, which could effectively counterbalance the growing threat to the central authority from Eastern intrigue or disorder, was apparently considered an urgent and indispensable first step. By January, 1962, even though Katanga's promise to federate was still theoretical, the Adoula government—with significant UN assistance—had arrested Gizenga, deposed him from the deputy premiership, and begun to send loyal forces into the disaffected regions.

The persistent difficulties in the independent Congo had created much confusion in international affairs, but the balances of forces inside the country were quite well defined and virtually all the violence was confined to four specific areas: the brief initial Force Publique mutiny in July, 1960 near Léopoldville; the sporadic quarrel between the Lulua and Baluba "sectors" around Luluabourg; the terrorism against whites, missions, the central government and the UN in the two provinces under Gizenga's intermittent influence; and the fighting in Katanga, first between Tshombe and his Balubakat opposition in the northern part of the province, then between his supporters and the UN. Tax collection was disrupted—it virtually ceased in the East, fell to one-third in areas under the central government, and dropped to about two-thirds of normal in Katanga—but business and economic development has not suffered appreciably. The productive plant and physical assets remain intact, and almost every industry and service has maintained—in many cases exceeded—its best pre-independence levels. For example, certain agricultural and processing industries in areas under the central government have set all-time production records. Consumer industries, textiles and mining in all regions except the East have done almost as well. Large firms such as the Société Générale de Belgique throughout the Congo and the Union Minière in Katanga—notwithstanding the claims of both right- and left-wing propaganda abroad—have largely eschewed doctrinaire politics, maintained neutrality toward all secessionists and hoped primarily for peace and sound fiscal policies.

The economic potential initially so encouraging for the Congo's future thus remains. Yet to be achieved are the realistic, flexible political and social attitudes that form the basis for a workable nation.

26

DIVIDED DEPENDENCIES

T HE last major territories under European control, seven
African regions below the Equator, all contained populations that were seriously disunited. Two of them, Ruanda and
Urundi, were United Nations Trust Territories under Belgian
administration; Britain controlled three, the two Rhodesias and
Nyasaland, and the Portuguese remained, as they had been for
nearly five centuries, in Angola and Mozambique. Independence was officially anticipated for all but the Lusitanian territories, but, in every case, deep-seated racial and cultural conflicts had yet to be resolved.

German rule had scarcely touched the elaborately structured, densely populated traditional kingdoms in Ruanda and
Urundi. When transferred to Belgian mandate by the League
of Nations, these two states were still dominated by a small
class of aristocratic Batutsi, who descended from the pre-European Nilotic conquerors. These traditional rulers monopolized
the cattle, which were symbols of great prestige, and maintained
a dependent group of Pygmies, the Batwa, as servants and shep-
herds. The Bahutu, a Bantu-speaking people who constituted
the bulk of the population, were agricultural peasants, formerly
bound in serfdom to the Batutsi overlords. The latter continued to exercise exclusive political authority.

Situated in high, healthy, fertile country, Ruanda-Urundi is populated four times more densely than any other part of Africa—about as crowded as France, Pennsylvania or rural India, and fifteen times the figure for the nearby Congo. The pressure of numbers constitutes a major problem that steady migration into Uganda does not begin to solve. Except for Belgium's new, small administrative seats, there are no urban centers and no resources that would support any. Ruanda and Rundi (Urundi) government, though tightly organized, traditionally functioned from movable sites.

The League of Nations and the UN permitted Belgium to administer these countries as part of the Congo colony. However, unique local conditions and certain special policies continued to give Ruanda and Urundi a distinct history. The judiciary and finance remained separate, and the Vice-Governor-General, sitting in Usumbura, held special powers of decree. The two traditional rulers (Bami, plural; Mwami, singular) were subject to European "Residents"—one for each of them— such as the Germans had required. Belgium, again following the German example, treated both Bami in identical fashion, even though the Mwami of Ruanda had originally held more centralized power than the Mwami of Urundi. The preservation of both Bami, whose powers were limited only when the Residents issued countermanding orders, substantially modified the impact of Belgian native policy. The Batutsi tradition of hierarchical administration lent itself readily to the organization of colonial districts. Government revenue continued to be collected in the traditional tribute form, though monetary payment was allowed after 1931 and required by 1952.

Social services were extensions of the Congo programs, technically administered through the government of Katanga Province, but their application differed slightly. Education received less emphasis, partly because the presence of traditional governments seemed to make it less important, but medical and agricultural work—in view of the peculiar population problems—were more intense. Except for mission stations and two large national parks, virtually all land was reserved for African use. European settlement would not have been prohibited, but immigrants fortunately did not choose to enter the already crowded country. The parks were scenically spectacular. However, they were intended primarily to conserve the forests and soils from damage caused by excessive grazing and overpopulation. After World War II, Belgian agronomists augmented them with a widespread system of ditches and hedges. Later programs proceeded to deinfest the low-lying, underpopulated river valleys, which thereby became suitable for planned grazing and intensified, more diversified agriculture. All of these undertakings received enthusiastic popular support.

After 1945 the Belgian government initiated "planned and deliberate" political reforms. Although the program was gradual, its avowed goal—ultimate independence—contrasted sharply with the vague Congo policies. Five "indigenous cities" and immatriculation procedures were developed on the Congo model, but Ruanda-Urundi had only small urban centers in which to apply them. Educational standards were added to the traditional hereditary qualifications for high office, and some Bahutu gained admission to the ruling aristocracy. Elections on the local level—by interview rather than by ballot—were introduced in 1952. These District Councils then nominated the Bami's advisers. Corvée duties, traditionally required by each Mwami, were restricted to public works, and the term of service was reduced. Similar levies could also be used in order to teach modern farming techniques. Finally traditional chiefs and immatriculated commoners came together to form joint educational planning boards.

UN investigating teams submitted favorable reports to the Trusteeship Council in 1951 and again in 1954, although neither commission could find any organizations to express African opinion. The 1954 report recommended that steps be taken to prepare for full independence within twenty years.

Belgian policy appears to have undergone a radical change about 1956. Events in the Congo at that time probably influenced this decision, which remained secret for some time. The new plan aimed at the rapid creation of egalitarian populism. The government therefore began to ally itself with the Bahutu peasant masses, who in 1957 issued a republican manifesto. Reforms within the existing system, which was now marked for destruction, came to a halt.

In July, 1959 Mwami Charles Mutara Rudahigwa of Ruanda died suddenly at the age of forty-seven. According to rumor, he had been poisoned. In an attempt to maintain their position, the Batutsi Council of Ritual Chiefs immediately installed a successor, Mwami Kigeri V. Reinforced colonial police preserved order, and the Bahutu people were drawn together in an Association pour la Promotion des Masses (Aprosoma). Four months later, under the impression that the Mwami would crush them before Belgium could come to their aid, the Aprosoma Bahutu revolted against their traditional government. Several hundred on both sides were dead by the middle of November. The Belgian government called it "tribal warfare." The fighting was in fact a civil war—no more "tribal" than the War of the Roses in fifteenth-century England. Finally, on November 11, the Colonial Ministry revealed its real aim: figurehead constitutional monarchies and popular elections inside six months.

In a European context, these would have been desirable goals. However, there is grave doubt whether stable democracy or respect for law can be attained by a colonial government that engineers a sudden, violent revolution against its own standing policies. The Belgians had learned the dangers of excessive rigidity earlier in the year at Léopoldville; in Ruanda, they now seemed to foster the other extreme.

By December protests began to come from several sources. Julius Nyerere, the moderate African leader in neighboring Tanganyika, accused Belgium of "fabricating" the entire incident. He asked the UN to assume direct control of the trust territories. Meanwhile the Church Missionary Society, the main British Protestant organization, provided further details. When the fighting started early in November, said the Society's journal, the Force Publique was called in from the Congo. Instead of restoring order, these forces were ordered to join the attacking Bahutu peasants. In much of Ruanda, Batutsi property and cattle were looted or destroyed.

The old order had been effectively broken. Bahutu populism emerged supreme, but its newly organized voice, the Aprosoma Party, still relied upon Belgian guidance.

A UN mission recommended during the following spring that a round-table conference, free elections and complete independence from Belgium be achieved as soon as possible, preferably by 1961. Belgium, however, followed her earlier plan, which included elections in July of 1960. As expected, the Bahutu parties—Aprosoma and the new Parti d'Emancipation des Bahutu (Parmehutu)—won 84 percent of the votes.

Then, in January, 1961, Belgium and the Ruanda parties agreed to hold elections in March. However, once again acting suddenly, the Belgians allowed Ruanda to declare itself an independent, sovereign republic on January 30. This posed a delicate problem for the United Nations—no trust territory had ever taken such a unilateral step—but no one officially recognized the situation. Openly supported by Belgium, Ruanda proceeded to establish the machinery of self-government. The provisional Legislative Assembly, representing the District Councils that had been elected the previous July, became a Parliament. Mwami Kigeri V was formally deposed. The presidency went to Dominque Mbonyemutwa, the head of Parmehutu, and Gregoire Kayibanda, a popular newspaper editor, became the Premier. The Batutsi boycotted the entire proceeding.

Both trust territories remained subject to Belgian administration. Ruanda's republicanism did not take root in Urundi, where the Mwami's traditional power may have aroused less popular resentment because it is less centralized than that of the former Ruanda overlords. The diverging forms of government, under which both regimes expect to receive independence late in 1962, may therefore become an interesting subject for future comparative historical examination.

Few areas of the world have been so little known as Portuguese Africa. There is a long history, undoubtedly involving many social phenomena, but the portions of it that have been authoritatively revealed are largely those relating to administrative theory. Foreign travelers have not been allowed to observe extensively, and the Portuguese reports are deeply tinged with chauvinism. Unresolved controversy and contridictory rumor, therefore, characterize most detailed accounts of the actual practices.

Because Portugal has long held both claims and some actual authority in Mozambique and Angola, there has been a tendency to assume that neither policy nor practice has ever changed. The direct character of Portuguese rule and the lack of economic development have been persistent, but noticeable variations have occurred in attitude and in the effectiveness of local rule. The ambitions of other colonial powers have at times been dominating influences, and in the twentieth century, Portuguese policy has often tried to anticipate or to answer foreign criticism. This reaction often appears to be more legalistic than practical but, in the absence of any contradictory proof, it protects the Portuguese position. Agile diplomats have also taken advantage of the conflicts of interest among the major powers.

Interest and activity in Portuguese Africa had centered largely on the American slave trade, which declined rapidly during the 1880's. The colonial economy languished, and occupation was confined essentially to a few coastal points and some widely scattered half-castes' plantations. Other powers began to intrude upon Portugal's claims. By 1890 Germany, Britain, France and the Congo Free State had all established firm footholds in territory that had formerly been under Portuguese influence. Britain and Germany even considered a partition of the remainder, so, to preserve its position, the Lisbon government attempted to resume the "effective occupation" of forgotten regions, both in East Africa and south of the Congo basin. Lacking capital and finding few resources, the Portuguese concentrated largely on the revival of their national prestige. Only in the nineties did Portugal find it necessary to develop such a conscious policy and rationale for its modern empire.

Critics accused Portugal of abusively exploiting African labor. However, the colonial authorities claimed that the national civilizing mission must begin by teaching the moral and material value of work. Labor, even if coerced, was therefore essential to African development. The long terms of corvée service and the great distances that conscripts were transported, so serious as to be labeled "A Modern Slavery," were modified or suppressed in answer to foreign criticism on the eve of World War I.

Extensive reform did not follow from the official changes in policy. A republican government that overthrew the monarchy in 1910 promised to liberalize the colonies, but internal dissension and the war delayed action. Loosened colonial ties served largely to increase the independence of established administrators who maintained the previous system in defiance of the new theories. With two-thirds of the homeland still illiterate, democratic public opinion in Portugal was unable to exert an effective influence. Improvements and modifications in Angola and Mozambique occurred as the result of luck or default rather than by direct effort. Labor continued to be the main resource for each colony, though the procedure for its exploitation seemed to be less overtly obnoxious and less centrally directed than it had been.

Colonial manpower has been an important source of revenue for the government. Portugal itself, rural and underpopulated, had little capital, and that could be attracted to the colonies only by granting very broad monopoly powers over the labor supply. Foreign investors were never allowed to participate in colonial development because of a near-xenophobic sense that they would destroy the unique character of Portuguese national civilization in the overseas territories. British interests were permitted to build railways and ports to serve Katanga and the Rhodesias but, aside from a prosperous veneer near three harbors, these contributed little to Mozambique or Angola as a whole. Indeed, Portugal seriously questioned whether development was desirable. She cited her own colonial history, which was longer than that of any other power, as proof that under-development was the wisest policy. According to this theory, dissatisfaction is caused solely by alien meddling and the impatience of inexperience. Colonial rule probably can be perpetuated by tolerating ignorance, fostering stagnation and discouraging rapid social change, but the moral premises of this position are open to serious question.

In Portugal's policy, which has always envisioned a vague process of hundreds or thousands of years, Africa constituted a complete social and cultural vacuum that must follow three patient steps: first, to learn to work, work being the basis of all social and cultural achievement; secondly, to absorb the Portuguese interpretation of Christian civilization; and, finally, to become loyal citizens, fully integrated into the long Portuguese historical tradition. In short, there would be a very lengthy process of transforming Africa into an extension of the Portuguese nation, which would then be a powerful world-wide state dominated by Africans.

Such concepts clearly dominated the thinking of the New State, an "anti-progressive" benevolent dictatorship, which Dr. Oliveira Salazar established in 1932. A former student of theology and of law, now professor of political economy in the University of Coimbra, the new premier was retiring, studious and unusually immune to personal interest. Convinced that there could be no political disagreement among any true Portuguese, Salazar stressed the unity, preservation and indestructibility of all national institutions. Colonial policy changed—that is, its earlier nationalistic and isolationist forms were revived, and the former republic's progressive promises forgotten—and the idea of absorbing Africa into the nation was proclaimed an immutable goal.

The New State consistently refused to sign the international agreements limiting forced labor, the argument being that no restrictions should be placed on the essential task of teaching the value of work. Much emphasis was placed on the theory of "assimilating" advanced Africans, though in fact the number of people in this class (37,000 out of 8,000,000 Negroes) increased very little if at all. More than 100,000 Portuguese peasants have been resettled in Angola since 1932, but their tendency to settle in groups has materially weakened the integrationist pattern of which colonial theorists were long so proud.

There has never been any legal recognition of African law, custom, chiefs or tribes. Africans, for whom indeed the Portuguese do not even have a legal name, are considered untutored, unorganized, unmotivated masses. Actual practice, however, varies widely: magistrates in some districts take cognizance of custom, others do not, and there is no overall system whatsoever. There are chiefs—some survivors of tradition, others created or bolstered by local administrators—yet in many districts all vestiges of tradition have been disregarded. Labor recruitment has remained, partly because theory approves it, partly because it is practical or profitable. Legal authority to force labor had been withdrawn by the republic in 1928 and was not revived, but there are no general rules, except for abstract ideals, to prevent the survival of many similar practices. The law now does not authorize any corvée except for punishment or in lieu of taxes, but it does require all able-bodied men to hold acceptable, gainful employment for at least six months out of every year. Such men are supposed to volunteer for work. However, if their identity cards show no employment—employers are said to charge fees for making such entries on the cards—the government retains the right to assign them on contract to any public project or "essential" private enterprise that needs laborers. In this manner about 100,000 workers from Mozambique—some 10 percent of the eligible force in that colony—are contracted each year to the Witwatersrand Native Labour Association for work in the South African goldfields. The Portuguese Government collects their pay, which, after tax deductions, is doled out to the men when they return to Mozambique. Similar contracts, which run from six to eighteen months, are issued to unemployed Angolans, most of whom serve the government, plantations, fisheries or Diamang (Diamonds of Angola Company, a Portuguese monopoly concession that sells to De Beers). There seems to be little doubt that much recent recruitment, the law notwithstanding, has involved arbitrary quotas, official bribes and connivance with petty chiefs. Practices apparently continue to vary greatly, there being some districts, with either conscientious officials or frequent foreign visitors, where the irregularities are not tolerated. Nevertheless, there are enough Portuguese undertakings to demonstrate, in spite of falsified statistics, that a minimum of capital investment is being augmented with a remarkable amount of mass labor.

The New State is firmly convinced that a consistent, antiprogressive policy could not generate any African reaction different from the listless acceptance that has characterized most of the last four centuries. Local Portuguese administrators, who themselves sometimes live much like their subjects, believe that Africans cannot imagine any alternative to the Portuguese colonial system. The government has therefore been confident that African nationalism would never develop in the colonies.

Nevertheless, boundaries within Africa are sometimes quite arbitrary and African feelings cannot be directed by simple decrees. The Bakongo people of the lower Congo were divided among French, Belgian and Portuguese rulers, but they retained a common language, social contacts and a sense of their own past traditions. Congolese religious movements, such as Kimbanguism, spread into Angola during the twenties and thirties. Kasavubu's political movement, Abako, and the development of French Congo influenced and inspired all segments of the once-united Bakongo. Other Angolans smuggled themselves into the prosperous mining areas of Katanga and Northern Rhodesia. Out of 100,000 men who went each year from Mozambique to South Africa, some unavoidably absorbed ideas and found common cause among the East and South African Negro laborers with whom they associated. The rigidly segregated atmosphere of the Transvaal mines encouraged the growth of an African sense of identity. That Portugal realized this is also certain from the way in which her police watched all who had returned from South Africa.

When unrest did increase in the Portuguese colonies, the New State drew seemingly logical conclusions: the nationalist ideas, being unprecedented, must have come from outside the presumably stable Portuguese colonial tradition; as something new to the colonies, they were necessarily the results of alien progressivism, which Salazar had already defined as a Communist-type evil; and, being anti-Portuguese, they were ipso facto anti-Christian.

Although the government insisted that it was merely following a centuries-old plan, it actually seems to have made two adjustments to the modern African situation. The first of these, in 1956, disbanded the colonial system and integrated all the overseas territories into the mother country. In practice, this posed few real problems. Only white settlers, a few half-castes and the small "assimilated" population were recognized as legal citizens. There were also no effective elections by which the new overseas provinces could either protest their integration or unseat the Portuguese authorities, who, in effect, continued to rule as before. The New State maintained—perhaps ingeniously—that its consistent policy had merely prepared Africa for admission to the Portuguese historical tradition, wherein opinion is always unanimous. Furthermore, by being able to point to its political uniformity, the government felt better prepared to argue that all foreign criticism constituted interference in the internal affairs of a sovereign country. The second decision, apparently reached over a long period of time, was based on the assumption that discontent and African nationalism could only occur among the unassimilated. The government in effect stopped admitting Africans to the loyal assimilated ranks, hoping thereby to demonstrate that African nationalism was an alien idea that appealed only to uncivilized, immature people who were not ready for absorption and citizenship.

There has been no effective way of circumventing Portuguese restrictions in order to determine the nature or extent of dissatisfaction inside Mozambique and Angola. It is known that Africans, in numbers varying from seven to a hundred thousand a year for forty years, have taken refuge in British territories. In all, the exodus seems to have been equal to at least 10, perhaps 15 percent, of the Portuguese African population. Angolan refugee organizations are scattered throughout West and Central Africa, some of them taking a considerable interest in politics.

Similar movements also exist for Mozambique. There has been little unity among them; some, feeling desperate, have taken support wherever it was available—especially from the Soviet Union—but most have been too small or too divided to be of much direct value to factions within their home territories.

An increase in unrest within Angola became apparent during 1959, and persistent violence in the north, predominantly a Bakongo region, erupted late in the following year. The Portuguese reaction was direct and thorough. Whenever possible, agitators were shot or jailed without charges. Torture, forced labor and indiscriminate military round-ups were reportedly common. Ghana in particular, but even other colonial powers, were charged with fomenting the disturbances. The New State labeled all events "Communist," but Salazar so brands anyone who questions his authority. There is undoubtedly dissent within Portugal itself, as exemplified by those of his domestic opponents who—like Henrique Galvão—flee the country in order to organize resistance to the New State. Galvão is himself an interesting case. A high colonial official, an aide to the Inspector-General of Angola, and a well-known historian, he was jailed in 1951 for submitting a report criticizing "neo-slavery" in the colony. Galvão later escaped, joined an exile faction in Brazil, and, early in 1961, seized a Portuguese ship in the Caribbean. His plan apparently included an assault on Angola, but it was thwarted by Portugal's NATO allies, largely because piracy on the high seas is illegal regardless of political circumstances. Galvão had become recklessly desperate, and there were increasing signs that Angola at that time was similarly frantic.

Casualties and brutalities on both sides in the 1961 fighting far exceeded those of any disturbances elsewhere in modern Africa, including Kenya's Mau Mau, the Congo or Ruanda-Urundi. The rebellious factions seemed to be more desperate than systematic. Some Africans, whether loyal, frightened or wary, sought Portuguese protection. Tight censorship, strong measures and the expulsion of foreign visitors prevented any objective assessment of the nature, extent or prospects of either the rebellion or the Portuguese military reaction. There seemed to be no cohesive nationalist leadership, yet the Portuguese apparently could not repress the movement with any of their traditional methods or policies. The conflict unquestionably had deep roots. Neither side showed any disposition toward compromise, and there has been much reason to believe that discontent—without much order, purpose, or sense of national identity—would spread despite unalterably firm Portuguese repression.

Between Mozambique and Angola, on the undulating veld and dry forest of the Central African interior, the three British territories—Northern and Southern Rhodesia, and Nyasaland—have also acquired multiracial problems which, though not at all secret, are even more complex. Each British possession had distinct origins, and a noticeably different status, prior to the federal unification of 1953. Bantu-dominated Nyasaland had been a protectorate under Crown control since 1891. In Southern Rhodesia, which was a self-governing colony of white settlers after 1923, the British government had annexed the sovereign lands formerly held by the pioneer British South Africa Company. However, the Protectorate of Northern Rhodesia, proclaimed in 1924, was solely an administrative system whereunder the Company retained exclusive, independent title to all native treaties and territory.

Each of the three possessions contains about 2,500,000 Africans, which is approximately a three-fold increase since the end of World War I. In the same period of time, European settlement in all the territories increased from 40,000 to 300,000,

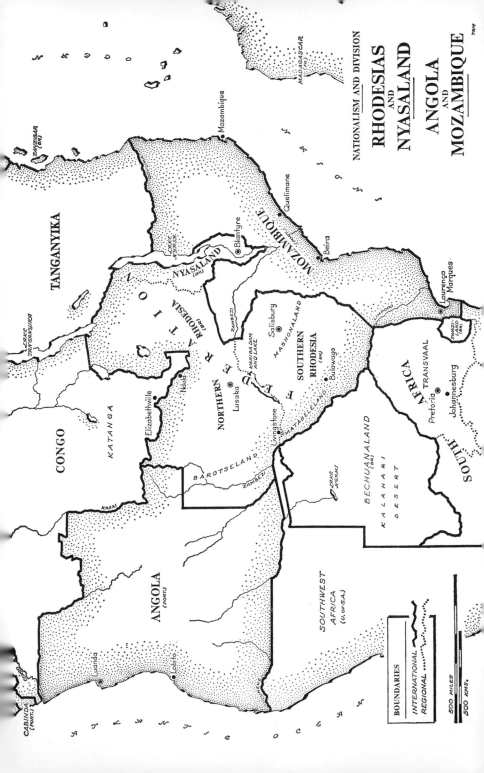

NATIONALISM AND DIVISION

RHODESIAS
AND
NYASALAND

ANGOLA
AND
MOZAMBIQUE

TANGANYIKA

ZANZIBAR
(BR.)

MADAGASCAR
(FR.)

Mozambique

MOZAMBIQUE

Quelimane

Blantyre

NYASALAND
(BR.)

Beira

FEDERATION

NORTHERN
RHODESIA
(BR.)

ZAMBEZI

KARIBA DAM
AND LAKE

Salisbury

MASHONALAND

SOUTHERN
RHODESIA
(BR.)

Lourenço
Marques

SWAZI-
LAND
(BR.)

CONGO

KATANGA

Elizabethville

Ndola

Lusaka

Livingstone

MATABELELAND

Bulawayo

LIMPOPO

SOUTH

AFRICA

TRANSVAAL

Pretoria

Johannesburg

LAKE
TANGANYIKA

LAKE
MWERU

BAROTSELAND

ZAMBEZI

LAKE
NGAMI

BECHUANALAND
(BR.)

KALAHARI

DESERT

KASAI

ANGOLA
(PORT.)

Luanda

Lobito

SOUTHWEST
AFRICA
(U. OF S.A.)

CABINDA
(PORT.)

ATLANTIC

OCEAN

BOUNDARIES

INTERNATIONAL
REGIONAL

500 MILES
500 KMS.

due largely to immigration following World War II. Southern Rhodesia, which had 90 percent of the white population in 1921, still has fully three-quarters of it. Nevertheless, indigenous Africans continue to outnumber the settlers ten to one in that territory. Whites in Northern Rhodesia, attracted by the opening of copper mines in the late twenties, have increased in number from 3600 to 60,000, but there are twenty times that many Africans. Agricultural Nyasaland, where a European planter population declined from 400 to 300, acquired a larger administrative class, but remained unquestionably (99.7 percent) an African territory. Already six times more crowded than either of the Rhodesias, the country has an overpopulation problem that has been aggravated by an influx of several hundred thousand refugees from Portuguese East Africa.

Early European settlers in the Shiré Highlands, south of Lake Nyasa, introduced the cultivation of coffee. After 1910 tobacco proved to be more profitable. Africans became increasingly accustomed to tending this crop, which they could raise more cheaply than the Europeans, and some of them abandoned their traditional seminomadic shifting-field procedures in favor of fixed plots. Many settlers withdrew, subdividing their estates among the rising African peasantry, but most of them turned to tea, which after 1933 became the predominant European plantation crop. Africans did not have the capital, technical facilities or marketing organization that would have been necessary for successful competition. The immigrants' plantations, occupying about 5 percent of the arable land, have encouraged the spread of modern agricultural methods. However, early hopes that plantation labor would form the nucleus of a wage-earning economy have been disappointed because large work crews were required only during the short harvesting season.

When H. H. Johnston granted the original settler freeholds in the Shiré Highlands, few Africans lived in that area. Plantation employment attracted about 50,000 from the lake shore farther north, but some 150,000 others—the Nguru (Alomwe) people, refugees from Portuguese Mozambique—comprise the great bulk of those who became tenants. By 1930 the Highlands had been transformed from an underpopulated area into the most crowded rural area of Africa between Ruanda-Urundi and Natal. Nyasaland between the World Wars developed a notable phenomenon: most of the older tribal areas around the lake, subject primarily to the long-standing missionary influences, continued to be relatively stable and traditional; the newly occupied south, its population complicated by tenant, refugee and developing wage-labor problems, quickly became a densely populated homeland for heterogeneous, newly detribalized populations.

As early as 1903 Nyasa laborers began to go abroad on regular contracts. Employment in the Shiré Highlands was too temporary and did not yield enough to pay taxes that were now imposed. Nyasaland itself was too crowded for all to farm, and too isolated from most markets. The wages of a foreign job were therefore especially attractive. By 1913 Southern Rhodesian settlers, the South African goldfields and the Katanga mines were hiring 10,000 men each year. South Africa withdrew from the system between 1914 and 1932, under the mistaken impression that tropical Negroes were particularly susceptible to disease. A British investigating commission in 1937 estimated that one-fifth of all adult males were working in other countries. After World War II, contract recruitment doubled—20,000 annually —and another 100,000 went abroad voluntarily. Reasonable estimates classified Nyasaland's postwar labor supply as about one-third dependent upon foreign mining contracts and one-third engaged in agriculture at home. The remainder were Highland tenants or urbanized. Customarily people moved from one category to another, and the contract workers provided nearly half the country's total income. Rural areas suffered badly, with serious losses in both manpower and production. Moreover, traditional tribes and missionaries' achievements were noticeably eroded.

Social change at home, plus association with urban laborers

throughout Central and South Africa, made Nyasaland a particularly suitable focus of African nationalist thinking. Men returning from the Rand, from Katanga and from the Rhodesias compared impressions and news. Internal economic and population problems attracted their interest, and a political movement, built on the Indian Congress model, began to emerge following World War II. Yet the roots of Nyasa nationalism reached back to much earlier years of the twentieth century.

Migrant laborers, in their first jobs abroad, received two influential impressions, both of which continued to have a strong impact on successive waves of contract workers. Wherever they went, Africans and Europeans alike referred to them not by tribe but as the "Nyasa boys." As such, they were treated similarly, housed together, and, consequently, they reacted as one group, regardless of their differences at home. Furthermore, they encountered everywhere—the Rand, Katanga, the Rhodesian plantations—a similar pattern of discriminatory restrictions. Police methods, the pass laws, color bars and general native policy all contrasted markedly with the benevolent, protective missions and government of their own country. This awareness gave Nyasaland a national identity, the object—however distant it may have been—of their pride and loyalty. The migrants' sense of identity found expression in two early forms: Nyasa labor unions in the foreign mine fields, and Native Associations in the mission districts at home.

The North Nyasa Native Association, organized in 1912, soon fathered similar groups in the west and central regions, and the movement reached southern Nyasaland at the end of World War I. The associations provided manpower for the allied campaigns against German East Africa—up to 60,000 men at one time—and pressed particularly for educational improvements.

Encouragement and continuing support came from Dr. Robert Laws, head of the venerated Livingstonia Mission, and humanitarian heir to the antislavery mantle of Livingstone and Johnston. He advised the government to be sympathetic, and in 1920, suggested that preparations be made for elected representation. Constitutional means were uppermost in Association thinking, and the organizations received active support from traditional chiefs.

Not all agitation was so sophisticated. The Association movement did not reach the composite, detribalized tenant populations in the Shiré Highlands until the 1920's. Earlier movements in this southern region lacked direction: social upheaval was becoming increasingly severe, missions were small and noticeably competitive, and individual, unsponsored missionaries had gained a foothold. Among these last was an Australian, Joseph Booth, Seventh-Day Adventist and pacifist, who arrived alone in the Shiré country during 1892. He advocated an independent, semitheocratic African Christian Union, preached to the Ethiopianists of Zululand, and revived Edward Blyden's earlier slogan, "Africa for the Africans." Between 1898 and 1900, his favorite Nyasa convert, John Chilembwe, attended a Negro evangelists' training center in Lynchburg, Virginia, U.S.A., where civil-rights agitation was strong and racial conflict frequently occurred. Chilembwe gained the support of a fundamentalist Negro Baptist Church in Germantown, a suburb of Philadelphia. He then broke with Booth, who accepted sponsorship first from white Seventh-Day Adventists, then from the Watchtower. Although Booth originally inspired him, Chilembwe now rejected all white guidance. "Africa's sons," he preached, "only need the quickening and enlightening influence of the Gospel of Christ to lift them from . . . degradation, and make them suitable members of the great human family."

Chilembwe was typical of several nativist and American Negro missions that dismayed the government and the established churches in Nyasaland. Nevertheless, Chilembwe's mission was built by hard work and aided by an aura of legend that grew around him. He chafed at tax increases in 1911, and resented the European planters who encouraged Africans to become tenants in order to earn tax money.

In 1914 Nyasaland's strategic communications were mobilized for the campaign against the German colonies. "We understand that this," wrote Chilembwe the prophet, "is a war of free nations against a devilish system. . . ." A plotter and deliverer as well, he then launched an anticolonial uprising in 1915. His full object was not clear, but agitation was widespread, and two European planters died. British troops quickly chased, ambushed and shot Chilembwe, but the uprising had three noticeable sequels: a brief expectation that the leader, having escaped to America as a bird, would soon return as an emancipator; stricter government control over minor missions; and a new government concern with land titles, tenants' rights, and, ultimately, education.

Still convinced that European settlement—at least temporarily—would stimulate African progress and economic development, the government in 1917 instituted a system of leaseholds for immigrant planters. However, tenants received no protection—a 1920 commission erroneously assumed that there was no shortage of African land—and, when guarantees were instituted after 1928, the leases were seriously undermined by a sharp increase in taxation. By the 1950's some attempts were being made to resettle tenants on Crown lands with titles of their own, but an ever-increasing population continued to be dependent upon insecure "residential rights" on the European estates. A major cause for Chilembwe's uprising therefore remained to stimulate unrest in 1933, 1943, 1945 and again in 1953. Nevertheless, some land eventually began to pass from the planters to the peasants, and most of Nyasaland continued to be primarily an unrestricted, desegregated homeland for Africans.

Education remained primarily a mission responsibility until the end of World War II. Government grants, minimal when first offered in the twenties, covered about one-fourth of Nyasaland's school expenses during the late thirties. Since the remainder came from the limited resources of charity, literacy was limited to 37 percent of the population in 1937. Experiments in low-cost rural-adjustment education, though cheap and wide-

spread, failed to satisfy the popular demand for technical progress and political training—in other words, academic standards
were not as high as the students expected them to be.

Moderate African sentiment was organized in the crowded
south during 1924. A Blantyre Native Association, led by
Levi Z. Mumba from the North Nyasa Association, became the
leading advocate of popular grievances in the Protectorate. By
1930 Mumba was chairman of a Representative Committee of
the northern Association, which both the south and the government recognized as spokesmen for the entire country. The Committee worked primarily to preserve Nyasa rights from the restrictions that migrants experienced in other countries, and
pressed consistently for educational facilities. It remained un-
questioningly loyal to Great Britain in World War II. After 1944
the Representative Committee became the nucleus of a nationalistic movement, the Nyasaland African National Congress.
At heart, the Associations, the Committee and the Congress
were less anti-British than simply antipaternalistic.

The racial patterns of Southern Rhodesia were already
shaped when the Crown received title to the self-governing colony from the BSA Company. The Colonial Office merely recognized sovereign powers that the settlers had exercised through
an elected Legislative Assembly for a quarter-century. As a practical convenience, Negroes had been assigned to "reserves" in
1902, though thousands of them were encouraged to become
tenants on the European estates. The separate reserves—just
under one-fourth of the colony—were permanently confirmed
by a 1920 Order in Council, but many settlers protested when
they realized that Africans were not forbidden to purchase land
elsewhere. Two years later the white voters chose self-government under the Colonial Office in preference to unification
with segregationist, Afrikaner South Africa, but most of them
fully expected to pursue a similar policy of separate development. In 1925 Sir Morris Carter headed a commission that investigated the assignment of vacant land among the races. Virtually all settlers favored firm segregation—some demanded a

ban on any African ownership—usually on the grounds that nonwhite farmers would lower the value of neighboring estates or that African groups could never improve themselves. Unquestionably an underlying Social Darwinist fear of miscegenation dictated the nature of most economic and political arguments. Dr. Godfrey Huggins, a surgeon serving in the Legislative Assembly, attracted public attention by drawing an analogy between the settlers and the white position in the American South.

Segregation became law as well as practice in the Land Apportionment Act of 1930, which drew heavily on the Carter Commission recommendations. Europeans, 50,000 in number and already owning 32 percent of the land, were allowed to acquire another 19 percent. The 1,000,000 Africans could add about 8 percent to the 23 percent already reserved for them. The remaining 18 percent, infested, arid, or reserved for parks and game, was assigned forever to the Crown. By this enactment the social geography of Southern Rhodesia was firmly determined. All subsequent history revolves around the separation dilemma.

The dilemma was intentional. By restricting the native lands, yet at the same time forbidding tenantry—seemingly a liberal clause—the Act deliberately hoped to force Africans into wage employment. This, in turn, was supposed to eliminate the labor shortage which the legislature believed was retarding the development of European estates, mines and the economy in general. Not by coincidence, the European "reserves" included the best farmlands, all the minerals, and the transportation system. The dilemma was obvious: if Africans improved their productivity by adopting European ways, they would be developing not in parallel but in equal competition with the settlers and therefore should tap comparable resources; yet, if segregated and left to be different, they would soon find their "reserves" insufficient. Without resources, the African could not develop; with them, he would not have to accept white employment. The government later tried to enforce agricultural improvements, but Africans resisted any apparent dictation on lands that were legally assigned to their exclusive control.

Industrial jobs offered greater inducement and higher status than agricultural work. However, this attraction was reduced in 1934 by the Industrial Conciliation ("Color Bar") Act, which reserved preferential pay and seniority for white union labor but denied any bargaining power for Africans. Industrial segregation was serious for its social consequences, but it also disregarded Southern Rhodesia's greatest long-range potential. In passing the Color Bar Act, the government overrode its advisers who pointed out that an African, integrated into the economy, constituted in time a new producer and consumer as valuable as any European immigrant. The number of Africans always increased more rapidly than the European population, so, in the final analysis, policy determinations were based more upon social fears of this fact than upon long-range economic assessment of it.

All political parties supported land and labor separation in the interwar period. The names and membership of organized groups changed frequently, but there was a remarkable continuity in all the parties that won elections. Strict wage and property qualifications kept the franchise 99.8 percent white, so the political arena was small. Factions were, in practice, defined by personalities and friendship rather than by platform or performance. The first parties, formed in preparation for the 1922 referendum on the constitution, were the Rhodesia Union Association (favoring annexation to South Africa) and the Responsible Government Association. The latter, under Sir Charles Coghlan, prevailed and governed the country for ten years. The fluid opposition—Independent, Progressive and, finally, the Reform parties—coalesced behind Dr. Huggins who, by personal appeal, carried the election of 1933.

Huggins immediately merged the two groups into a United Party, which offered cabinet posts and lesser offices to members of both former parties. There was consequently no opposition, except for a small Rhodesian Labor Party, which pleaded for white workers' privileges. This class disappeared in the wave of prosperity following World War II, and the party's leaders split into several groups on questions of socialist theory, African membership and personalities. In its place, after 1946, there emerged a stronger Liberal Party, which was Huggins' first serious opposition in thirteen years. The new group offered an ambiguous economic program—"the economic resources of the State are best employed to foster private enterprise"—and a forthright segregation policy, under which Africans would be taught "the habits of industry, discipline and work." As an opposition, the Liberals failed, in part because they allowed themselves to become associated with Afrikaner immigrants from South Africa, one of whose leaders had been openly pro-German in World War II. Power in Southern Rhodesia continued to rest securely with Huggins' United Party, which was the only effective party in the country.

It is not therefore surprising that, despite the outwardly democratic and thoroughly Parliamentary constitutional machinery, actual administration was a simple and direct matter. Europeans constituted less than 10 percent of the total population, but they held all the professional and skilled jobs. The lowest third of an industrial society—unskilled and semiskilled occupations—did not exist in white Rhodesia. Government bureaus and commissions were composed of people sympathetic to industrial management, large farms and the most skilled artisans. Social and, sometimes, family contacts were frequent and close within the relatively small white population, so unanimity and coöperation were easily arranged. Essentially, though the government represented all the whites, most of the Europeans were themselves an unusually selective group. Political parties, election issues, government policy and white social attitudes consequently developed within a limited framework.

Africans in Southern Rhodesia were represented by a small Rhodesian Native Association, similar to that of Nyasaland, as early as 1915, but its members—all of whom were "more advanced natives"—limited their activities to mild defenses of long-recognized rights. Clements Kadalie, a Nyasa migrant la-borer, exerted some influence through the short-lived Industrial and Commercial Workers' Union after 1919. Four years later the Rhodesia Bantu Voters' Association was organized. Its membership was less than fifty, for only that many Africans could meet the ingenious wage and property qualifications for the white man's ballot. Depression unemployment and the Color Bar Act weakened both the Voters' and the Native Associations, which finally merged during 1938 into the Bantu Congress of Southern Rhodesia. A Conference of Christian Natives was also active during the thirties, particularly in requesting education and relief from the pass laws, but, like the Congress, it did not attempt to challenge any of the separation and segregation policies.

Only the Congress survived the Second World War, after which it became the Southern Rhodesia African National Congress. After taking many small African coöperative insurance societies under its wing, it pressed for the right to organize labor unions. One of these, the Rhodesia Railways African Employees' Association, had remarkable success in getting recognition by staging a well-disciplined strike late in 1945. Seven years later the Association members elected a young railwayman, Joshua Nkomo, to represent them. He was the only African labor leader to gain recognition, but the advance was only temporary because the government, under the Color Bar Act, had no obligation to bargain again.

Huggins' government had meanwhile approved a new policy whereby Africans could live in segregated townships, totally and permanently removed from their home reserves. Urbanization eased many European labor problems, but it created new problems for Africans. Their wages, which were sometimes only one-sixth those of Europeans who did identical work, scarcely provided for subsistence. Traditional rights, economic and political, guaranteed by the constitution to all Africans on the reserves, did not apply to these new urbanites. In 1948 the Africans of Bulawayo rallied behind Benjamin Burombo, a former mission bookseller and the agent of several coöperative insurance societies, to stage a mass strike. The government then set a minimum wage, which was unprecedented, but the rate was so low that the grievances were not relieved. Two years later the legislature passed a broad Subversive Activities Act that gave the Justice Minister power to ban any organization. Africans reacted with a noticeable shift from concern with local grievances to a broader racial militancy. The Congress movement began to develop new links with nationalist groups in Northern Rhodesia and Nyasaland.

The protectorate of Northern Rhodesia, mostly barren and sparsely populated, attracted few Europeans until the mid-1920's. Copper was known to exist, but it was much less accessible than Katanga's reserves. New technological methods, first tried in 1923, brought the first mines into commercial production two years later. The capital was largely British, with some American, most of it administered by the Rhodesian Selection Trust, a subsidiary of the British South Africa Company which had long held title to the copper-belt lands. Labor came first from Nyasaland—400 miles, often on foot—but was later augmented from tribes closer at hand. Rhodes' Cape-to-Cairo Railway, completed into Katanga in 1909, passed near by, and the new Angola Railway soon provided an additional outlet for Rhodesian ores. Far from being depressed during the 1930's, the copper belt boomed phenomenally.

The number of Europeans grew apace: 3600 in 1924; 14,000 in 1931; 60,000 by 1953. Africans outnumbered them 300 to one at first, 40 to one in the last year, but the settlers were if anything even more confident of their unbounded superiority than the Southern Rhodesians. The Memorandum of Native Policy, issued by Lord Passfield in 1930, came as a profound shock. Unlike its neighbor, Northern Rhodesia was to be a trusteeship wherein race, color or religion would be disregarded. Africans would be free to work for pay or for themselves, as they wished, and their development took precedence over all other considerations. The settlers' Legislative Council formally protested in December, 1930, accusing the Crown of preference for "barbarous races," but was promptly rebuffed. Thenceforth Northern Rhodesian whites tended to look for sympathy and support to their more numerous southern counterparts. The British government in the main adhered to Lord Passfield's policy, even to the point of instituting indirect rule on the Northern Nigerian model for the large, traditional Barotse tribe in 1937. Nevertheless, though the Crown respected the broad principles of the Memorandum, in fact it gave much more active support to the industrial sector than to the traditional elements.

Regular labor supplies for the copper belt continued either to be recruited in Nyasaland or to be drawn from Northern Rhodesian volunteers. Many of these Africans intended to remain permanently in the mining towns. The Selection Trust companies usually provided adequate urban housing and amenities. Native Welfare Associations, largely concerned in the early thirties with African security and mutual aid, gradually assumed many local administrative functions, either from tribal elders or from the Protectorate government. In 1946 the Welfare Associations federated and in 1948 they united as the Northern Rhodesia Congress (later, Northern Rhodesia African National Congress). Organized mass activity and a leader, Harry Nkumbula, did not emerge until 1951, at which time the Crown introduced radical proposals for future political development.

The White Paper of July, 1951 proposed that Northern Rhodesia, Southern Rhodesia and Nyasaland be drawn together in a Central African Federation. The idea was not new, it having been advanced several times since World War I, but the prospect of full official support for such a scheme materially altered the delicate balance of social and political forces in all three territories.

Both Rhodesias had nominally been administered as one during the early years of BSA Company rule, 1890-96, and, through the subsidiary African Lakes Company, Nyasaland's economy was also related to the original arrangements. Unification was not in those years a dream, but a real prospect. However, each area subsequently developed marked distinctions—

Nyasaland as a protectorate, under "trusteeship," after 1891; Southern Rhodesia, self-governing under the Company in 1898, then with a "racial separation" policy under the Crown after 1923; and Northern Rhodesia as a protectorate, transferred to Crown trusteeship, in 1923-24. Dr. Leander Starr Jameson openly voiced unification ideas for the Company in 1915, but the settlers, wishing primarily to escape from private rule, opposed such plans at that time. Another commission, headed by Sir Hilton Young in 1929, considered the possibility of uniting Northern Rhodesia and Nyasaland with East Africa, but found that communications were too poor to justify the scheme. The alternative of federation with Southern Rhodesia seemed to the commission equally unwise in view of that colony's racial policies.

The settlers of Northern and Southern Rhodesia revived the latter plan in 1936 by requesting joint white self-government. Two years later Viscount Bledisloe led a commission that investigated this possibility more fully. After hearing overwhelming evidence that Africans feared subordination to Southern Rhodesian racial policies, the Bledisloe Report recommended solely intergovernmental coöperation on practical questions. Nevertheless, the commission accepted a series of singular assumptions: that economic coöperation would eventually lead to political union, that white Rhodesian policies would become more liberal in the face of increased African progress, and that federation would ultimately attract white capital to nonwhite areas, even those that lacked resource potential. In essence, Bledisloe's commission advocated amalgamation in principle, but not in practice, on the grounds that such a step would in a relatively short time reduce the differences among the various territories. Presumably trusteeship and separation—two contradictory concepts then in practice—would be replaced by some undefined but inevitable philosophy which all African and European factions could accept.

Implementation of the Bledisloe recommendations awaited the end of World War II, but coördinated banking and research programs soon got under way. The railways of all three territories, plus those of Bechuanaland, passed from the BSA Company to unified, intercolonial government control at the end of the war. The question of closer union came up again in the postwar years, particularly in 1947 when the Northern Rhodesia whites demanded self-government. Their spokesman, Roy Welensky, a white labor leader who sat on the protectorate's Legislative Council, found the British Labor Government adamantly opposed to both white rule and amalgamation. Welensky nevertheless believed there was hope for a limited federation scheme which would unite the whites but leave the Africans under British protection. In 1949 he convinced Huggins to join him in talks with the Colonial Office on this basis. However, the Crown's ministers clearly gave the impression that unification without Africans and African approval would not be tolerated.

A skillful legal compromise between Britain's trusteeship responsibilities and the white settlers' desires emerged in the 1951 White Paper. Instead of Britain or Southern Rhodesia surrendering one to the other, they would both yield power to a new federal government which would have particularly extensive jurisdiction over economic affairs.

The Conservative Government that ruled Britain after October, 1951 was particularly optimistic about the economic potential of a federation. Northern Rhodesia contained resources, Nyasaland the labor, and Southern Rhodesia had both capital and technical knowledge. Prosperity and security would therefore be enhanced by closer connection among the three. African nationalists and white extremists, each fearing subjugation to the other, would surely weaken in the face of the development and progress that should follow from federation. In practice, however, the nature and policy of a federal government —a matter not given fullest consideration—would depend upon the extent of that authority's future sovereignty and the method of its election. Serious misgivings subsequently arose regarding both these questions, in part because the ideal concept had to

be adjusted by negotiation in order to make a workable constitution. The Colonial Office, as the protectorate authority, nevertheless took the view that a prosperous federation was more in
the long-range African interest than poverty-stricken national
independence. The scheme also appeared to be a means of
breaking down Southern Rhodesia's relatively rigid segregation
policies without directly overriding the rights of self-government.
The federation was supposed to institute "partnership" of the
races in lieu of either paternalistic "trusteeship" or legal
"separation."

The practical misgivings arose over specific points in the
Federal constitution that went into effect in 1953. African affairs in the two protectorates remained under British control,
but those of Southern Rhodesia passed to the new central government. Africans might have been persuaded to accept this—
those of Southern Rhodesia found it particularly attractive—if
the constitution had not said that a revision, perhaps independence, would be considered within ten years. It was always possible (if not probable) that the Federal government, once
independent, would then revoke the new system, revive "separation," and extend it to Africans in all regions. The danger
seemed particularly real in view of the federation's election system, which, by virtue of a rigid franchise qualification, gave
European voters control over the central government. According
to the 1953 Constitution, the voting system could not be changed
without the consent of Britain, the protectorate Legislative
Councils, and the new white-dominated Federal Parliament.

On paper, the franchise qualifications seemed to be an effective device for assuring experienced government, led by the
Europeans, until Africans had acquired sufficient education,
property and income to enter into civilized "partnership." All
people so qualified, regardless of race, were allowed to vote on a
common roll. The new system therefore offered a good chance
for evolution toward multiracial political coöperation. However,
practice again contradicted the theory, as Africans immediately
realized. Nyasas in particular, long familiar with Southern Rho-

desian working conditions, doubted that any government dominated by white caretakers would ever improve education or relax the color-bar discrepancies to the point where Africans could actually constitute a voting majority. They suspected that under partnership, they would be forever relegated to a subordinate role in all territories. Nationalists therefore found no assurance within the federation scheme, and, no longer certain that Britain would retain uncompromising trusteeship, they began to demand full and separate independence for each territory. Instead of allaying or forestalling African nationalism, the federation was its greatest stimulus and its bête noire.

Seats in the unicameral Federal Assembly were assigned on the basis of voter registration rather than population. These representatives, twenty-six in number, were elected by all English-speaking people who met one of five alternative combinations of income, property and literacy qualifications. This roll was 95 percent European in each territory, so the white population of Southern Rhodesia in effect controlled fourteen seats, the Northern Rhodesia settlers eight and the Nyasaland planters four. In addition, each territory was allowed two "special" African representatives. These were chosen by various methods: by a "special" roll of voters, 92 percent nonwhite, in Southern Rhodesia; and by indirect election, through appointed representative councils, all nonwhite, in the two protectorates. In 1957 the proportions were slightly altered by constitutional amendment: forty-four elected (twenty-four Southern Rhodesia, fourteen Northern Rhodesia, six Nyasaland) by the white-controlled rolls, and twelve "special" Africans. Nyasaland and Northern Rhodesia now chose their special representatives by general election for the first time. In both the 1953 and 1957 systems, Europeans (less than 5 percent of the population) controlled nearly three-fourths of the seats.

Political parties within the federal system were direct products of factions previously existing in each of the three territories. Dr. Huggins, now Sir Godfrey, reorganized the old United Party of Southern Rhodesia into two complementary units: a

Federal (later United Federal) movement, which acquired control of the Federal Assembly and made him the federal Prime Minister; and the party of the Southern territory, the United Rhodesians, which supported Garfield Todd as territorial Prime Minister.

The white opposition, weakly represented in the territory by the right-wing Liberals, also emerged as the federal opposition under the name of the Confederate Party. Africans from each territory continued to carry the label of their respective African National Congresses; outstanding among these were Nkumbula of Northern Rhodesia, and H. B. Chipembere and M. W. K. Chiume from Nyasaland, all outspokenly opposed to the federation scheme.

The Liberal-Confederate alliance, opposing Huggins' United Federalists and Todd's United Rhodesians, quickly disintegrated. There was then no opposition white party until the Dominion Party emerged in 1956, led by Winston Field, who advocated permanent white rule and the expulsion from the federation of non-European areas that had no resources. In 1957 Todd—a missionary from New Zealand with a liberal conscience and some flair for politics—was expelled from both his office and the United Rhodesia Party because he had advocated gradual integration and franchise extension. In the resulting election the Dominionists nearly unseated his successor, Sir Edgar Whitehead, but the Huggins machine retained a slight edge in Southern Rhodesia and firm control on the federal level. Two years earlier Huggins had become Lord Malvern, thus leaving the management of federal politics in the hands of his scrapping lieutenant, Roy Welensky, who had earlier unionized the white railwaymen of Northern Rhodesia.

Welensky, soon Sir Roy, exemplified the Rhodesian immigrants' prosperity. Still close to labor and his union backgrounds, he nevertheless spoke and acted as the representative of an unquestioned and impatient economic elite. Like all white settlers, he cherished the belief that Britain favored its emigrants. He was determined that white Rhodesia should lead its African charges, paternally and in partnership, but reserving political control for trained Europeans at least for some time. Welensky's statements, again like those of his supporters, have not always seemed consistent. He has had to please two masters—his constituents and followers, and the British government, which still usually considers itself the Africans' trustee.

No such ambivalence clouds African sentiments and aspirations. Nyasas and Northern Rhodesians have repeatedly and vehemently denounced the federation. This issue, amid political awakening, coincided with the persistent land agitation in Nyasaland. In 1953, and again in 1959, nationalist sentiment erupted into violent demonstrations. The latter incidents were aggravated by the recent arrival of Dr. Hastings Banda, nearly legendary leader of the local Congress, who had spent most of his life practicing medicine in Britain and America. Dr. Banda's return to Nyasaland eclipsed Chiume and Chipembere and gave the country a clearly nontribal, widely experienced national politician. His party, known as the Malawi Congress, was in effect a caretaker for the National Congress which Welensky had banned after the 1959 riots. By periodically detaining him and restraining his party, the federal government has tended to martyr the nationalist cause. Quite apart from the justice of either side, about which no Europeans and Africans seem to agree, Banda has become an indestructible symbol of African anti-federalism.

The constitutional review of the federation, which had been promised for 1960, was deferred by the Crown. Instead, a commission under Lord Monckton was asked to reconsider the federal future. After exhaustive consideration, the Monckton Report suggested a looser federation, gradual economic integration and a planned extension of the franchise. Africans would eventually gain control, "partnership" would become effective, and, if still dissatisfied, individual territories could later secede. However, the recommendations were badly received. The United Federal Party would accept neither secession nor the implicit threat to Southern Rhodesia's long-established white privileges. Equally opposed, but for opposite reasons, were Dr. Banda's Malawi Congress and Kenneth Kaunda, whose United National Independence Party had filled the gap left by a ban on Nkumbula and the Congress in Northern Rhodesia.

In serious respects the federation plan had run into seemingly insoluble dilemmas. Multiracial partnership had been compromised in order to avoid the trammeling of self-government previously granted to the Southern Rhodesian whites. Such modifications awakened latent African fears and stimulated strong local nationalism. Furthermore, the faith that economic interdependence would overcome social, political and racial differences had been disappointing for two reasons: the economic connection was not based upon mutual coöperation but upon an enormous labor pool, valuable only so long as it remained subordinate and cheap; and capital and technical leadership on the copper belt came not from Southern Rhodesia, but from sources overseas. Subsequent attempts to reassess the federation depend for their success upon their ability first to substitute realistic fact for wishful thinking, and then to achieve enough progress to prevent African discontent, yet caution enough to maintain the European settlers' sense of security.

The order is large. Britain faces complex choices, perhaps her last major African decisions in view of the fact that the main direction of all other territories has been determined. Unless one or more of the federation's factions yields voluntarily, the Colonial Office will apparently have to revoke at least one of its legally irrevocable commitments: self-government for Southern Rhodesia, indissoluble federation, or African trusteeship. It is to be hoped that independence will not be granted with a vague confidence in peaceful progress instead of concrete, enforceable guarantees that all interests can accept.

27

HOLISM AND APARTHEID

HIGH hopes and optimism accompanied the unification of
South Africa in 1910. Britons and Afrikaners, long in competition with one another, now seemed to be coöperating. Confident that a liberal example would best further the new trend,
England granted the Union independence within the Commonwealth.

Evidence at that time—both within the white communities and among the races—did not justify such assumptions,
but faith in progress was characteristic of the age. The errone-
ous nature of the early confidence was demonstrated by subsequent events. Meanwhile, feeling herself relieved of a pressing
problem, Britain turned to the urgent questions of European
diplomacy, the increasing German naval menace, and, ultimately, World War I.

Anglo-Afrikaner coöperation, upon which most hopes were
based, seemed to be realized in the South African National
Party, which governed the Union from 1910 to 1924. Led by
General Louis Botha of the Transvaal, the party included his
aide, General Jan Christian Smuts, the Afrikaner nationalist
faction under General James Barry Munnik Hertzog, and most
of the English-speaking population. Botha had apparently devised a formula encompassing the Commonwealth kingship,

Afrikaner nationalism, a modicum of liberalism and the advantages of economic unification. There were cracks in the coöperative structure, but they did not seem to weaken the governing bloc. In 1912 the South African National Party lost Hertzog—he established a Nationalist Party, leaving Botha's group with the name South African Party—but the pro-British Unionists, who began to coöperate with the SAP two years later, compensated for the division. Extremists within the Nationalist faction attempted to turn South Africa against Britain in the first days of World War I, but Hertzog himself demanded only neutrality. The SAP triumphed handily over the protests and contributed actively to the Allied cause. South Africans, both English and Dutch, helped to conquer the German colonies. Smuts became a leading figure in the Commonwealth's imperial war cabinet, where his trained legal and military mind affected diplomacy as well as strategy. His tactful suggestions influenced the structure of the postwar League of Nations, and the mandate system was largely the fruit of his inventiveness. When Botha died in 1919, General Smuts inherited the Prime Ministry and the mantle of Anglo-Afrikaner coöperation. In view of his service to the Commonwealth and to the world, he seemed to be fulfilling Britain's earlier hopes for South Africa.

Smuts' life had been marked by a series of changes, each of them intimately connected with his sense of moral idealism. Originally an Afrikaner lawyer at the Cape, he had emigrated to the Transvaal in protest against Rhodes' imperialism and the Jameson Raid of 1896. First an aide to President Paul Kruger, then a Boer general, he had key roles in both the peace talks at Vereeniging in 1902 and the subsequent rebirth of Afrikaner political activity. The idealism of World War I and the League stimulated his imagination. British Liberal ideas seemed to have found a strong advocate in South Africa, among not the English settlers but their arch Dutch rivals. Smuts' philosophy envisioned his nation as an autonomous amalgam of white cultures that would provide benevolent, civilized leadership in Africa and participate in the new international community.

Afrikanerdom and British culture merged into white South African civilization, which was its own master, the trustee for other races, a member of the Commonwealth, and a founder of the League. Each culture, each race retained its distinctive characteristics, but acquired full meaning only in terms of its unique, sanctified relationships to the whole. "Holism," as Smuts called his philosophy, applied to Afrikaners, English-speaking South Africans, nonwhite races and international relations. The holistic concept, produced in much the same atmosphere as the 1910 Constitution, was compatible with both the benevolent African guardianship and the optimistic League diplomacy that typified European hopes in the years following the Treaty of Versailles.

Outside South Africa Smuts often seemed to be the personification of his country's ideas. However, a number of his supporters voted not for Holism but for the prestige of his personality, which epitomized the acceptance of Afrikanerdom within the empire. Dissatisfaction with this status became increasingly noticeable. Before World War I the Nationalists had denounced white unity. Britons and Afrikaners may be equal, Hertzog said, but they must remain "two separate streams," and both cultural groups must be loyal first to South Africa, then to the empire. After some time the Afrikaner stream might absorb the new British element, so the nation should prepare for such an event by requiring all school children to learn both languages. English-speaking South Africans were greatly alarmed by "Hertzogism," but the SAP tactfully condemned compulsory bilingualism. On this specific issue Hertzog broke with Botha and Smuts in 1912.

Initially Hertzogism seemed to be primarily a revival of the Orange Free State's resentment of the more moderate Transvaal Afrikaners. By-elections during 1915 in the Free State strengthened the Nationalists, who soon became popular in the Dutch-speaking West Transvaal. White politics had already begun to divide on the cultural and language issues, though Smuts' name retained enough bicultural appeal to obscure this trend. After 1920, when the SAP absorbed the English-speaking

Unionists completely, Afrikaners continued to be split between Smuts and Hertzog. Then, following the 1924 elections, Hertzog formed a coalition government that replaced the Anglo-Afrikaner SAP. However, because his new power depended upon Labor support, Hertzog was unable to press the main Nationalist aims. Cultural differences still were not the primary basis for political divisions.

The Labor Party in South Africa occupied a unique position. Originally founded by English-speaking workers, following the Fabian Socialist model, the movement had rapidly become the spokesman for an increasing force of landless Afrikaners who flocked to the mines during World War I. This Dutch-speaking proletariat, noticeably nationalistic in feeling, feared especially the Bantu laborers who threatened their status and security. The Afrikaner trade unions therefore pressed for a stiffening of the color bar and tried to prevent Negroes from entering the skilled-labor market. The Smuts government—which allowed whites but not Negroes to strike—provided some guarantee for the poor-whites, but not enough to assuage their fears.

Negroes in the Union of South Africa were not permitted to participate in politics. Legislation and long-standing custom divided them into two broad categories: the urban and tenant Africans, regulated by a variety of residence, travel and vagrancy rules; and those who remained in tribal locations, as controlled by the Natives Land Act of 1913. Each of these two Bantu-speaking classes presented distinct problems to the white-dominated governments.

Prior to 1913 very few nonwhites ever received formal title to the land. Once a territory had been annexed, either by the British government or by one of the Boer republics, whites were allowed to stake claims anywhere. Large blocks of land—usually those most suitable for modern agriculture or commerce—were thus Europeanized before the Negroes had arrived or settled. However, much the greater part of South Africa became white man's property without regard for the claims of nonwhites who already grazed, farmed or lived on that land. The 1913 Act reserved 6 percent of the country for the "natives," who were nearly three-fourths of the population, and the government added another 7 percent (mostly in small, unconnected pieces) during the subsequent decade. Reserves were administered quite differently in each province, those of the Cape and Natal having elective councils, with considerable discretionary power, while those under the Transvaal and Free State government were ruled quite directly. The small Bantu reserves, frequently sub-marginal or inefficiently worked, could not sustain all the tribes. Many Africans therefore had to take employment on European farms or in the mines, and, as the reserve populations increased, the number of tenants and urban dwellers also rose. The move-ment away from tribal lands had been noticeable since the 1860's, but it reached marked proportions during the boom years of World War I.

In every province but the Cape, Bantu who left their re-serves were required to carry passes and, after 1923, to live only in specially supervised "locations." Curfews applied outside these "locations." If a Bantu were unemployed, he had to for-feit his urban pass and return to a reserve. Work protests and strikes were cause for criminal action under the Masters and Servants Act, but union organization did develop during the First World War. Clements Kadalie's Industrial and Commer-cial Workers' Union took root during 1917 in the Cape Prov-ince, where Colored (mixed-blood) skilled workers had already imitated the older white labor organizations. About the same time, a radical-socialist branch of the white-dominated Labor Party set up the Industrial Workers of Africa in Johannesburg. The first Negro strikes, in 1918, were broken by police arrests. Early the next year an African National Union emerged, sup-ported by masses who defiantly burned their passes and sang egali-tarian anthems. A widespread strike of unorganized nonwhites on the Rand, in 1920, was broken by the use of temporary white labor and police assaults upon barricaded "locations." During 1921 the agitation and some violence spread to the reserves. Independent Christian "Ethiopianists," usually preaching self-determination and white extermination, mistakenly believed themselves immune to police bullets.

Europeans reacted in many ways. The universities inaugurated work in African languages and anthropology. Smuts' government established an advisory Native Affairs Commission, and the mine recruiters began to propagandize Africans "on the right lines." Finally the Rand mining companies proposed to modify the color bar, to open more jobs to dissatisfied Bantu and to reduce the numbers of highly paid whites. This issue aroused great alarm within the Afrikaner-dominated Labor Party.

Already concerned with an economic recession that had followed the end of World War I, the Labor movement had become the protector of poor-white laborers who were protected from native competition only by tradition and the color bar. The mining companies' proposals were therefore particularly disquieting. In 1922 Communists penetrated the Labor Party and directed a massive strike. A Red Republic of white workers seized the Rand. The Afrikaner strikers probably did not realize that they were being used for ulterior purposes. The Smuts government crushed the incipient revolution and allowed the mining companies to dictate the strike settlement. Henceforth Labor and the Afrikaner Nationalists, under Hertzog, stood together in opposition to Smuts, to Holism and to the capitalists. The rural-based Nationalist Party and the white Laborites, linked in part by Dutch-language sentiment, united actively in their common hatred of all that Smuts represented. The Afrikaner nationalist spirit was not yet strong enough to sustain, by itself, a thorough program that could bridge the gulf between strong urban and rural interests. Hertzog's Nationalist-Labor "Pact" government, in power after 1924, therefore succeeded only in stalling Smuts' program of pan-white coöperation.

The new regime attempted to secure some reward for each of the two parties to the coalition. It took more than a decade to achieve the white-supremacy guarantees that both groups desired. By quicker but less dramatic changes, Hertzog also sought firm evidence of South Africa's sovereign independence, and concrete demonstrations of full Afrikaner equality with the English-speaking whites. World-wide prosperity fortuitously enhanced Hertzog's prestige for the first six years. During the next nine, however, depression problems disrupted his programs and ultimately changed the character of the coalition.

Determined to resolve the long-standing "native" question, the Pact government first of all assumed that all Bantu were alien intruders, in the country solely by the white man's leave. Hertzog put "segregation" on a broad, legal footing, but, sincerely desiring to be just within the framework of his assumptions, he completed the establishment of reserves under the 1913 Act. The Native Trust and Land Act of 1936 also tried to reduce the number of African tenants by increasing the efficiency of some and sending the rest back to the reserves. Attempts to enforce the act failed, so the enabling provisions were soon withdrawn, but the principle remained law. Additional legislation, passed early in the Hertzog era, effectively guaranteed preference for "civilized" workers in nonskilled jobs, thus introducing a color bar into types of work that had previously been predominantly African.

By introducing these measures almost simultaneously, the government generated a complex opposition—white labor, Africans, liberal Europeans, provincial-rights advocates, and even those who felt that Hertzog was too liberal—so much of the racial legislation was held up until 1936. Other laws also removed all Bantu from the Cape common roll, but electoral discrimination had already become fact six years earlier when whites were exempted from all educational qualifications. Thus, the basic arrangements, which had made the Cape voters' roll such a hopefully liberal device, had begun to erode.

One source of confusion was Moscow, which in 1928 ordered its South African cadres to oppose Negro integration. Nevertheless, the government proceeded to detain integrationists on the grounds that they were "Communists." In the process, all existing Bantu nationalist and nonwhite trade-union organizations were destroyed or driven underground. Meanwhile the real Communist Party, which obediently supported the Pact government in accordance with Comintern instructions, was actually scuttling itself by cutting itself off from Negro integrationist movements and by constantly purging its confused membership. The leaders who obeyed Moscow quietly emigrated, unhindered, in 1933; those in prison, albeit radicals by South African legal standards, were actually those who, in their struggle for radical or labor rights, had disregarded or defied the Communist International.

The coalition's segregation policy was by no means as systematic as the apartheid idea twenty-five years later. Hertzog's views more closely resembled the pragmatic historical approach of earlier Boer farmers and Rand industrialists. The Colored (mixed) people were not treated with any uniformity. Those in the Cape held positions politically and economically equal to whites. The few who lived in other provinces had the legal status of whites in economic matters, but separate political representation. Social relationships were consistently held to be outside the area of official concern.

On the other hand, the central government had specific responsibility for "Asiatics" (i.e., Indians in South Africa). Mohandas K. Gandhi, on the eve of World War I, had presented the Indian case to the Union authorities. He protested laws which specifically limited the immigration of "Indians and other Asiatics," and argued that, since the country was unified, there should be no more ban on the movement of Indians from Natal to other provinces. The government removed the racial clauses from the immigration laws, but retained the power to administer elastic educational tests and refused to disallow a Free State anti-Indian law. In 1914 Smuts and Gandhi reached a formal agreement on the question. Indians still could not go from Natal to other provinces, but they were relieved of a special head tax on nonindentured labor that had been carried over from the 1860's. Indians soon found means of evading the Transvaal bans on immigration, trade and property ownership, but the Union Parliament plugged the loopholes in 1919. Smuts subsequently refused to grant Indians the status of citizens, even if born and raised within South Africa.

On the Indian question, the Pact ministry made considerable progress. Not committed to rigid segregation for all non-European minorities, and not dependent upon white votes in Natal (where most Indians lived), Hertzog negotiated a reasonable settlement with the government of British India. Each side recognized the validity of the other's problems in 1927. Smuts' bills for commercial and residential segregation were shelved, and the government offered reasonable compensation to any Indians who would emigrate. The legal status of Indians did not change, but Indo-South African relations and consultative arrangements improved considerably.

The movement for Afrikaner equality with the English-speaking whites followed a course that was still distinct from the nonwhite problem. Hertzog's first act, in 1925, gave the colloquial "Taal" or dialect full equality with both Dutch and English. Gradually the newly legalized language—renamed Afrikaans—took the place of High Dutch in South Africa. Work began on an official Afrikaans dictionary, and, in 1933, there appeared an Afrikaans *Bibel*. Historically a successful translation of Scripture into the vernacular is the hallmark of success in establishing a new language, and so it was with Afrikaans. Since the 1870's there had been a considerable literary development in Afrikaans, which contains certain expressions and nuances, unique to the South African environment, that no other European tongue has. A sense of inferiority, which the dialect speakers had earlier felt, now gave way to Afrikaner pride and a stronger national self-confidence. Some English speakers resented the new trend, which they considered divisive and isolationist, but the preëminence of English in commerce and society was not immediately threatened.

Commonwealth relations had always chagrined the Afrikaner Nationalists, but Hertzog had promised his Labor allies that the issue would not be forced. Indeed, he seems to have

found in the Imperial Conference of 1926 every assurance of
South African independence. The resulting Balfour Declaration
defined the Dominions as "equal in status, in no way subordinate one to another . . . ," a concept that was embodied in the
Statute of Westminster in 1931. Great Britain no longer held—
even theoretically—any power of legislation, veto or control.
Judicial appeals could still be carried to the Privy Council in
London, but foreign relations and constitutional sovereignty
were purely South African.

Racial concerns were never far from the political surface.
Smuts' reference to northward expansion was used by the Nationalist Party as an issue in the party's election of 1929. The
"Black Manifesto," which foresaw white South Africa drowned
in a flood of equatorial Bantu and liberal Rhodesians, assured
Hertzog a simple majority in Parliament. Labor disappeared;
the SAP would not have them, and their supporters now preferred to vote directly for the Nationalists. Afrikaners were
finally in unfettered command.

There was no change in policy. Indeed, there soon was little policy of any kind except the effort of economic survival.
After 1931 South African mines and farms suffered seriously.
As the world's chief gold source, and an independent nation,
South Africa tried not to follow Britain off the gold standard.
Hertzog staked all his power and prestige on the issue, but when
gold finally had to be abandoned in 1932, he did not carry out
his resignation threat. Instead, Smuts buried the political
hatchet and brought his South African Party into Hertzog's government. All racial and cultural issues disappeared before the
question of national survival. The SAP and the Nationalists
merged into the United South African National Party, and
formed an emergency National Fusion (coalition) ministry.
The great bulk of English and Afrikaans-speaking voters then
reunited in one enormous, ponderous middle-of-the-road party
of intercultural coöperation.

The United Party seemed to hoe the safe middle because,
on either extreme, there emerged two small, dissident parties.

Confirmed Imperial subjects organized a relatively short-lived Dominion Party that defended big business and advocated a revival of direct ties with Great Britain. On the other hand, the "Purified" Nationalists, organized by the Reverend Dr. Daniel François Malan, believed that the Hertzog group, from which they seceded, had capitulated to imperialistic and capitalistic interests. A predikant of the small Dopper sect in the rural Graaff-Reinet district of the Cape, Malan had been directing theocratic political factions and editing Nationalist newspapers since 1911. He repudiated Smuts' Holism, the moderate Cape-Afrikaner tradition and the Hertzogite two-stream concept, advocating instead the resurrection of a nation governed by Afrikaner *Volkswil* (will of the Afrikaner people) as expressed in their clergy. Malan was a firm teetotaler, known for his lack of humor and tight collars that sometimes caused him to faint. Although he inspired fanatical devotion among a slowly increasing number of followers, his "purified" party did not seem to threaten the position of Hertzog's orthodox Nationalists in the coalition government.

The Fusion survived and functioned for three clear reasons: its primary goal, economic survival, appealed broadly; Hertzog's Afrikaner Nationalism involved equality with the British, not injustice or domination; and depression conditions made most politicians willing to accept the basic segregation and white-protection legislation that Hertzog had so long wanted. In short, the Fusion appeared to accomplish, by intercultural coöperation, under economic pressure, precisely those programs that the Nationalists by themselves in prosperous times had been unable to fulfill.

Not all Afrikaners were willing to accept a government based on such pragmatic action. The Purified Nationalists insisted upon the principle of Afrikaner supremacy over the "alien" British, whom they—unlike Hertzog—did not expect to absorb into the white nation. South Africa should ultimately become a pure Afrikaner republic, separate from the Commonwealth and divorced from the culture of "imperialistic, liberalistic," Britain. Nevertheless, under Dr. Malan, the party was willing to use parliamentary means to achieve its goals. Other Afrikaner-nationalist elements, which now proliferated, were eventually to be less patient.

The oldest such action group, the Broederbond, had been preaching anti-British republicanism, Afrikaans culture, and Calvinistic theocracy since 1918. Essentially a tightly controlled nationalist elite that had become steadily more strict and secretive, the Broederbond was directed by a council of "Twelve Apostles," many of whom—including Malan—were clergymen. The dictatorial power of the Twelve alarmed Hertzog much more than the political programs of the Purified Nationalist Party. Afrikaans-speaking university students formed a proto-Fascist white-supremacist Studentebond. By 1936 the ultra-nationalists had made significant inroads into white trade unions—all non-Nationalist or nonwhite unions were dismissed as Communistic, imperialistic, liberalistic or capitalistic—and the point was enforced by Nationalist Gray Shirts, then Black Shirts (Stormjaers, or storm troopers), who received financial aid from Nazi Germany. Then, to uphold all these small minority fronts, there emerged the Federasie van Afrikaanse Kultur Verenigings (Federation of Afrikaner Culture Unions, or FAK). Two years later Afrikaner Nationalism developed its first general, mass organization, the Ossewabrandwag (Ox-Waggon Sentinel, or OB).

Initially intended to preserve the Afrikaner pioneer spirit, which had been aroused by the 100th anniversary of the Great Trek in 1938, the OB quickly developed National Socialist (Nazi) overtones. Members were organized in commandoes, bound by secret oath of unquestioning obedience to a Commandant-General, and dedicated to totalitarian ethnic sovereignty under his leadership. Non-Afrikaner labor leaders were either assassinated or called Communists, which most of them were not. Nationalist newspapers launched virulent anti-British, anti-Semitic, anti-Communist campaigns, in which the Reformed Church, Transvaal sect (NHK), played an active part. The OB had totalitarian ambitions, but in practice it divided the Nationalist movement for the time being.

Boer pioneer history began to assume the proportions of a national myth. The problems and purposes of the Great Trek were overshadowed by new ideas that gave more appealing depth to the old tradition. Tales of British colonial persecutions and diabolical humanitarian plots became part of a rising folk legend. The uniqueness of Afrikaner civilization was being established, albeit more in the new propaganda than in the actual happenings a century or more before, and its exclusive isolation became the basis for claims of superiority. Alone in a corrupted, "sentimental, liberal" world stood Afrikanerdom, guarding the last hope for true religion, Christian civilization and divinely ordained separation from inherently different beings. Membership in the *Volk* nation came by blood alone. Afrikaner nationality, according to the party's more orthodox statements, could not be acquired by "aliens," who, even if they learned the language, would remain contaminated. The *Volk*—the people with cultural unity who form the Afrikaner nation—were being given an identity, a raison d'être, that alien conquerors and "liberal ideas" had allegedly repressed. In fact, the Afrikaner cause had itself become an amalgam, even if the Nationalists did not choose to admit it. Formerly agrarian and anti-industrial, the Afrikaners began to be consciously and deliberately capitalistic. A Reddingsdaadbond (RDB)—like the OB, a product of the 1938 Centenary—worked to strengthen Afrikaner business and industry. The RDB lent capital, planned development and pressed Afrikaners to buy only within their own culture group.

Afrikaner nationalism was finding more strength and making a more direct appeal than at any time since 1902, but the United Party government, under Hertzog, remained secure. In the 1938 elections, it captured 73 percent (111 out of 150) of the Parliamentary seats, which was the largest plurality in Union history. The popular vote was smaller—only 54 percent—but there were three minor parties in addition to the badly fragmented Purified Nationalists. Malan's party, which won twenty-seven seats or 30 percent of the total vote, had by no means become the vehicle for all Afrikaner politics. Many political observers believed that South Africa was still destined for coöperative Anglo-Afrikaner politics in the Holistic (or, at least, moderate Hertzogist) tradition.

One of the tests of national unity is the unanimity of response, regardless of domestic politics, to foreign dangers. In this respect, the Union's response to European fascism before and during World War II reveals significant divisions in the white society. Though never asked, nonwhites appeared to favor —sometimes quite strongly—the anti-Nazi, anti-Fascist cause. Germany was the Union's best customer in the thirties, and the Royal South African Air Force bought a number of German warplanes. When Hitler asked for African colonies in 1935, Prime Minister Hertzog seemed willing to discuss the question. Malan demanded a general redistribution of all colonies, so long as the Union kept Southwest Africa, where British and Afrikaner white immigrants predominated. At first, Foreign Minister Oswald Pirow publicly favored a Nazi mandate in the Southwest territory, but he and Hertzog later said they would insist that such a colony be elsewhere. Malan, who gave the impression that the Nationalists would neither surrender nor defend the mandate, then called for an amicable agreement to give Hitler alternative possessions. In 1938, however, Hitler overplayed his hand by demanding Southwest Africa. This threat, which coincided with the invasion of Austria, came just before the South African elections and undoubtedly contributed to the United Party victory. Hertzog approved of Neville Chamberlain's compromises at Munich, but pointed out that South Africa was bound to the League rather than the Commonwealth in both war and diplomacy. A full-fledged Nazi movement and a well-trained "fifth column" among the German minority in Southwest Africa alarmed the government in 1939. Malan asked for a declaration of South African neutrality, which Hertzog pointedly refused to issue. As an independent country that had not ratified Britain's European alliances, the Union had no military commitments, but, the Prime Minister said, South Africa's closest friend was the United Kingdom. Yet, when war came, the country—and the government itself—had by no means made up their minds to fight.

Germany's invasion of Poland, which plunged England into war, revealed the divisions in South Africa. Hertzog did not feel that the crisis affected the country, but Smuts believed that world order was at stake. The issue went before Parliament, which split eighty to sixty-seven in favor of the Allies. Hertzog and Pirow resigned to make way for the war party under Smuts, and the neutralist faction seceded from the United Party. Malan, Pirow and Hertzog promised to prevent internal violence, such as had occurred in 1914, but refused to join the active anti-Fascist campaign. Smuts' strength lay in the support of English-speaking South Africans, plus about two-fifths of the Afrikaner population.

The government relied heavily on the National Defense Force, a light army that was originally created to maintain internal order and, if necessary, to help white settlers in East or Central Africa. Most of its members were Afrikaners, supported behind the lines by a battery of nonwhite volunteers. As the war progressed, the relentless Nazi advance forced the government to back down on its original promises that no forces would go "overseas." Anglo-Afrikaner troops began to take an active part in the Ethiopian and North African campaigns. Smuts participated once more in the Allied war councils and began to talk of an international organization to replace the League in the postwar world.

Afrikaner nationalists continued to criticize the Allied cause, though deep divisions and frequent convulsions prevented them from disrupting the war effort entirely. Many Dutch Reformed clergymen dismissed the Afrikaner soldiers as "liberal stooges" or "Red lice," and some veterans were actually evicted from the Calvinist churches. Loyal police tried to smash the Ossewabrandwag, which actively plotted pro-Nazi subversion. Hertzog and Malan came together briefly in a Reunited Nationalist Party, demanding secession from the Commonwealth and a separate peace with Hitler. At a meeting of Nationalists in the Cape, Malan called for a Christian National Republic, with a constitution banning any party that threatened the Afrikaner dictatorship. At meetings in the Transvaal, Johannes Gerhardus Strijdom and Hendrik Frensch Verwoerd succeeded in expelling all Jews from the party. The Afrikaner-Republican resolutions of Nationalists in the Free State, sponsored by Charles Swart, drove the moderate Hertzogites out of the party. Hertzog then formed an Afrikaner Party, but soon retired in favor of his protégé, Nicolaas Christian Havenga, who tried to fight both "holistic imperialism" and Afrikaner totalitarianism. In subsequent by-elections, the Malan-Swart-Strijdom-Verwoerd bloc gradually gained control of most Hertzog-Havenga seats in Parliament. The Nationalists now claimed that the wartime evacuation of English school children to South Africa was a plot to drown Afrikaner blood, then criticized the Allied cause as a scheme born of Jewish rapacity. Oswald Pirow, Hertzog's former Foreign Minister, organized a New Order movement for Afrikaner National Socialism, which again divided the Nationalist front. Malan retaliated with an Afrikaner Unity Committee which would give him broad "folk-leader" powers. Pirow then established a splinter party and the OB issued "military orders" which, though soon withdrawn, threatened Malan's leadership. The Malanites therefore joined with Smuts in 1942 to crush these "subversive" movements. Later in the war Hertzog moved closer to the Nazi-modeled OB, which tried to stage a *putsch* in Natal. Nevertheless, in the 1943 elections, Smuts' pro-British United Party retained a bare edge in the popular vote and 60 percent of the legislative seats, so South Africa pursued the war against Germany and Japan to its conclusion two years later.

Peace brought no relief to the Union's troubles. The newly formed United Nations supported India's efforts on behalf of the Indians in Natal. Soviet Russia and many egalitarian Western countries also pressed for an investigation of Southwest Africa, for which Smuts—strongly encouraged by Malan—refused to accept the authority of the United Nations Trusteeship Council. However, the Prime Minister subsequently decided to submit trusteeship reports and to encourage liberal treatment of Indians, at least until the UN matured. Meanwhile racial problems became more complex as African urbanization, Colored uncertainty and Indian impatience increased. When unorganized Bantu laborers struck in the mines to gain recognition, the government replied with police action. Smuts then appointed experts to study the problem and to create jobs for outstanding Bantu, but paternalistically preserved both the color bar and the ban on nonwhite trade unionism. Yet, notwithstanding Smuts' efforts to balance factions and unite the country, the opportunity for Anglo-Afrikaner coöperation was destined to fade.

South Africans trekked once more to the polls in 1948. Standing with some pride on Smuts' record in foreign relations, the United Party continued to advocate equality and coöperation between the two white cultures. In opposition, there was a temporary alliance of the Nationalists (including Malan, Swart, Strijdom and Verwoerd), and remnants of the Afrikaner Party under Havenga. The government, whose reëlection seemed certain, promised to maintain segregation, as currently practiced, but not to disrupt the Holistic concept of multiracial interdependence which underlay the nation's economic life. Opposition candidates directly attacked the United Party program. They accused Smuts of neglecting problems in his own country in order to practice international diplomacy. Instead of segregation under Holism, the Nationalist-Afrikaner coalition would offer a new plan of apartheid, a comprehensive "apartness" of native races and the white "Christian nation."

Apartheid was original only in that it applied deeply rooted Boer beliefs and modern Afrikaner attitudes in a broad, systematic fashion. The concept therefore rested upon a series of assumptions that, according to apartheid advocates, had been demonstrated in South African history. Reformed Church communicants of Dutch origin, in the first assumption, had God's law—presumably stated in His Scriptures—placing them above and separate from all nonwhite, non-Calvinist, alien or secular-liberal contaminators. Second, the Afrikaans-speaking Afrikaner —alone among all whites in Africa—had no European mother country to support him. Finally, a series of historical interpretations was assumed to be indubitable fact: 1) The Dutch reached South Africa before the nonwhites, who then were charitably permitted to remain under white Christian trusteeship; 2) Negroes in their "natural" state were happy and contented under Boer Christians who understood and did not try to Westernize them; and 3) The root of racial trouble was misguided liberal humanitarian sentimentality (missions, Western education, equal rights, foreign capitalism, trade unionism, communism, urbanization) which personified either the alien or the secular anti-Christ.

Upon these premises a systematic apartheid theory was developed at Stellenbosch University in 1947 by several Nationalist professors, including Dr. Theophilus Dönges and Dr. Ernest Jansens. Their Suid-Afrikaanse Buro vir Rasse Aangeleenthede (Race Relations Bureau, or SABRA), a reaction against the older, more liberal Institute of Race Relations, aimed to protect and benefit all races by compulsorily separating them from the evils of contact with one another. White men would both set the pattern and obey it. Some SABRA professors wanted to deport all nonwhites—three-fourths of the population—but the majority favored the creation of "independent" nonwhite nations under Afrikaner tutelage. Thus deprived of servants and unskilled labor, the white nation would have to attract acceptable immigrants and do its own work.

For the campaign of 1948 the Nationalist Party simplified and broadened the apartheid concept. The word sometimes meant simply traditional segregation, at other times only a certain aspect of the fuller doctrine. Dr. Malan discontinued his open attacks on Britons and Jews, stressing instead only apart-

heid, which he would apply to Indians and the Coloreds as well
as the Negro people. The voter must choose, he said, either
white rule, racial purity and Christian civilization, or gradual
immersion "in the black sea." Malan seemed to face an impossible task: to win, he had to increase his Parliamentary strength
by 74 percent.

This he did. Astonishingly enough, a shift in 6 percent of
the popular vote made the difference. The Nationalist-Afrikaner
coalition, under Malan and Havenga, won seventy-nine seats to
seventy-one for the United Party-Labor bloc. Malan's willingness to work within Parliament, so often criticized by other
Nationalists, had paid off handsomely. He could scarcely claim
a mandate—the popular vote was 53 percent UP-Labor and 40
percent Nationalist-Afrikaner—but the legislative road to Afrikaner nationalism and apartheid lay open before him.

The election returns should not have surprised astute observers. The elements of Nationalist victory had been in the
making since 1910, for they were part and parcel of the unfore-
seen developments that made independent South Africa so different from Britain's original expectations.

First of all, the South African whites had gradually polar-
ized into increasingly antagonistic English and Afrikaans-
speaking camps. Afrikaners were a majority in every electoral
district that the Nationalists won in 1948, and the United Party
(or a splinter) won nearly all predominantly English-speaking
districts; only two constituencies, both composed of urban Afrikaners, crossed the culture line to the opposition. The division
of whites into parties based on language was nearly complete.
There of course continued to be some English-speaking Nationalists and many Afrikaner UP-men, but group voting patterns
had rigidified to an alarming degree.

Why, however, did this bifurcation of white society benefit
the Nationalists, who received one-fourth less votes than
their opponents? United Party strength lay in overwhelmingly
English-speaking suburban areas where Nationalists frequently
did not even put up candidates, so a large number of United

Party votes were, in effect, wasted. In rural and lower-class urban districts, Afrikaners constituted a moderate, but never overwhelming, majority. One after another of these districts gave slim margins to Nationalist candidates. Every Nationalist vote therefore had crucial weight. Last but not least, the rural constituencies usually were underpopulated. All districts had originally been quite equally apportioned, but the South Africa Act did not require redistricting until the population had risen or fallen by 15 percent. Gradual urbanization had depleted the farms and filled cities during World War II, so that, in the final analysis, many Nationalist candidates were elected by small majorities in underpopulated rural districts.

English and Afrikaans-speakers were virtually equal in number in 1904. The former were 93 percent urban, the latter 89 percent rural, but this gradually changed. The Afrikaner birthrate, even in the cities, was one-third higher than that of English-speakers. Consequently, by 1951, the Union was 41 percent English and 59 percent Afrikaner. Furthermore, a majority of both groups was now urbanized. However, industrialization had failed to modify the Afrikaners' exclusive mores. The South African factory system did not create the social and political liberalism that industrial revolutions had encouraged in West European and United States history.

The full significance of these population shifts did not become apparent until 1936. Until that time census takers merely asked people what languages they knew. Because bilingualism increased markedly (one-third of the whites could speak both languages in 1910, three-fourths in 1936), there seemed to be a growing basis for Holistic pan-white unity. However, the censuses of 1936 and 1951 also asked for the preferred language. Then, with correlated statistics drawn from school, birth and church records, the full trend toward Afrikaans became apparent. This tendency worked with the language-identification of political parties and the unique structure of electoral districts to facilitate the Nationalist victory of 1948.

Indeed, it is truly surprising that the Nationalist vote was so small. There remained a large block of Afrikaner votes that had not been tapped. However, in the elections of 1953 and 1958, the Nationalist Party made substantial inroads into this reserve of strength. By 1960 the government could be almost certain of getting an absolute majority of the popular vote. Consequently, after their first victory in 1948, Afrikaner ascendancy and Nationalist rule faced an opposition that steadily diminished in size and power.

Under Malan and his successors, South African life has been influenced in three significant ways. The Nationalists first reorganized and unified the scattered Afrikaner movements. They then began to carry out the apartheid program, and, finally, the non-Afrikaner movements started to weaken. Each of these steps requires explanation.

The Ossewabrandwag and Broederbond were immediately restored to official favor. The National Socialist "New Order" became more vociferous. The stigma on Nazism was officially canceled, and government employees were permitted—even encouraged—to join these autonomous, ultranationalist bodies. The government then took steps to keep non-Afrikaner whites to a controllable number. Dr. Theophilus Dönges introduced and carried a Citizenship Bill that eliminated British nationality. In order to acquire South African citizenship, Commonwealth subjects now had to meet the same requirements as "other aliens." Furthermore, the government could, courts notwithstanding, deny an application or revoke the naturalization papers of any immigrant. Finally, the Afrikaans-speaking movements achieved a long-sought union: in politics the National Party absorbed Havenga's Afrikaners, thus transforming the ruling coalition into a majority government. Meanwhile the unofficial social and cultural organizations, moderate and extremist alike, formed an elaborately structured new hierarchy paralleling the Nationalist Party. The Broederbond became a secret, innermost council of the most elite, reportedly exercising strict control over the leaders' every act and belief. By appealing to heritage and *Volk* consciousness, the OB, now well supervised, provided a social outlet for Nationalist masses. A Jeugbond (Youth League) was formed. Domestic propaganda originated with an Instituut vir Christelik-Nasionale Onderwys (Institute for Christian-National Education, or IVCNO), which was carefully supervised by the "Twelve Apostles" at the head of the supreme Broederbond. IVCNO in turn infiltrated the public education system in the Transvaal and the Orange Free State. School children were told to report any teachers who deviated from the IVCNO curriculum. The State, not the parents, determined the language and religion that each white child must learn. The history syllabus presented the romanticized glory of Afrikaner tradition as though it were indisputable fact. Science courses taught that God created all creatures in a predetermined hierarchy; evolution could occur, but it would always be either a mutation from original "nature" or a mixing with inferior breeds, so it was clearly evil. In other words, white superiority could be destroyed by either miscegenation or any compromise of foreordained distinctions. Furthermore, the guarantees of religious and academic freedom were removed from all university charters, though many faculties refused in practice to abridge those traditional rights.

Churches continued to be legally separate from the State. However, the Dutch Reformed denominations—to which nearly all Afrikaners belong, though some only casually—developed interrelationships that strongly supported the Nationalist movement. The Cape's original NGK, by far the largest Dutch group, had intermittently accepted moderate ideas from modern Calvinists in Scotland and the Netherlands. The NHK, the autonomous Transvaal church, usually considered itself the true synod of nationwide South African Christianity. The rigid Dopper GK, smallest of all, believed that its members were the "Chosen People" of God. Theological seminaries of the last two denominations exercised a strong influence over both the government and the NGK congregations, particularly in rural and lower-class urban areas. The smaller a sect was, the greater its proportional influence seemed to be. Churches may remain separate from the State and the predominant NGK may seem relatively moderate, but NHK or GK leaders hold a disproportionate number of high official posts and the local white congregations are strongly influenced by minority-church theology. The largest, most-quoted Dutch church therefore exerts the weakest influence, so the more rigid interpretations of apartheid have a significant role on both the top and mass levels of the reunified Nationalist movement.

After 1948, the Party was able to begin the application of apartheid. The basic concepts were based upon ideals presumably advantageous to all races. However, the assumptions, already questionable, were somewhat modified in the mill of practical politics. It is thus the application, rather than the theory, that caused the greatest problems. Each region of the country was particularly concerned with the separation of one nonwhite group: Bantu in the Transvaal, Free State and Eastern Cape, Coloreds in the West and Central Cape, or Indians in Natal.

There are nearly half a million Indians in South Africa, most of them born and living in Natal, where they are almost as numerous as the white population. Largely English-speaking, they have a living standard superior to that of India itself. Trade with the Zulus is largely under their control, though there are also many Indian plantations in the province. Attempts to repatriate them to India, initiated by Hertzog in 1939 and revived by Charles Swart for the Nationalist government, have not succeeded. Indian investment in South African business and commerce is too great, and the Hindu religion has become too eclectic, its caste structure too blurred, for reassimilation into the traditional motherland. At the same time, devoid of any reserves of their own and still distinct from all other South African cultures, they cannot be absorbed into any other group. Nevertheless, the Nationalist government continues to hope that the Indian population can be cut to an "irreducible minimum," totally separated from both white and Negro society.

The Colored population, 1,500,000 strong, constitutes the largest nonwhite block in the Western Cape. Its legal and political rights, equal to those of whites since 1853, were guaranteed in the South Africa Act by "entrenched clauses" which Britain and the Cape thought would be exceedingly difficult to repeal. These people were totally Europeanized in culture, political organization and outlook, and they held many of the skilled and semiskilled jobs in Cape commerce, industry and agriculture. Malan and his chief Cape lieutenant, Dr. Dönges, were more concerned with their threat to white purity than were the Nationalists from the provinces where other races predominated. However, the Party instigated a move to alter the constitution so that Coloreds could be set apart. Moderate apartheid advocates thought of accepting them as allies against the Bantu masses, but the government first ousted all Coloreds from the armed forces, then excluded them from the unemployment compensation system, and finally put them under the Bantu pass laws. In 1951 Parliament passed a Separate Registration Bill that placed the Coloreds on a voting roll separate from whites and gave them only a limited, indirect representation in the central legislature. Because this measure was passed by a simple majority, contrary to the constitutional process for amending an entrenched clause, the South African Supreme Court disallowed this action. The government thereupon proposed to establish a High Court of Parliament, empowered to override the Supreme Court by simple majority, but English-speaking voters began to fear that their equal rights—which were also guaranteed by an entrenched clause—might later be abolished in a similar manner. However, the established courts invalidated the High Court scheme, thus thwarting once more the basic step toward Colored apartheid.

Malan made the constitutional question a central issue in the 1953 elections. Nationalists claimed that the "entrenched clauses," ostensibly dictated by the British government, were not binding upon the sovereign South African Parliament. The Nationalists captured ninety-four seats, compared to sixty-two for the combined opposition, and increased their percentage of the popular vote to forty-six. It now became apparent that the

Nationalists might eventually control two-thirds of both houses of Parliament, which in joint session could legally amend the constitution. The Malan government therefore took elaborate steps to guarantee the passage of its entire apartheid plan.

Johannes Strijdom, the blunt-spoken and determined leader of the Transvaal Nationalists, replaced the ailing Prime Minister Malan in 1954. Next, the size of the Supreme Court was doubled, Parliament voting by simple majority rule, in order to guarantee the acceptance of all legislation. Finally, Strijdom introduced a Bill to change the structure of the Union Senate. The concept of equal representation for each province was replaced by extra seats for the more populous Cape and Transvaal, both of which were under Nationalist control. Southwest Africa, in which UN trusteeship was never recognized, had already been given Assembly and Senate seats, all held by Nationalists. Furthermore, the party that controlled the provincial government—Nationalist in all but Natal—was allowed to occupy all of that province's seats in the Union Senate. The former system of proportional representation thus disappeared, the size of the Senate nearly doubled, and the Nationalists gained control of eighty-eight percent of that body. In joint sessions of Parliament there was subsequently no difficulty in passing constitutional amendments, and the courts no longer offered an effective check on Nationalist Party programs. The constitution and all legal safeguards had therefore been reduced to the status of regular law, subject only to the standard rules of majority procedure.

In 1956 the "entrenched clause" for Colored voters was quickly repealed. The apartheid program for other races, which had already got under way, was virtually assured of Parliamentary and court approval. Indeed, the elimination of Colored voters was a step that favored the government because it weakened one of the opposition's potential sources of support.

The 9,000,000 Bantu constituted the primary object of apartheid legislation. About half of them lived on the reserves, with another 30 percent on European farms and 20 percent in urban "locations." However, half of those living on reserves actually earned their livelihoods in temporary employment from mining and from tenant farming because their own lands were overcrowded and submarginal. Three-fourths of the Bantu therefore depended upon the European agricultural and industrial economy, wherein they did most of the physical work for wages much lower than that of comparable white laborers. Nonwhite life expectancy was half that of the Europeans. (Two-thirds of the Bantu deaths are attributable to "diseases associated with malnutrition.") Cheap Bantu labor is essential for South African prosperity because the profit margin on mining and agriculture, despite the low wage scale, is smaller than that in any similar country. To grant equality would cause the price of gold to exceed the world price, and food prices, already high, would skyrocket. And, as the whites are well aware, Bantu voters on a common roll would hold an overwhelming majority at the polls.

Apartheid legislation since 1948 has attempted to systematize and extend the practical segregation embodied in early laws, particularly those of 1913 and 1936. Marriage and sexual intercourse among the races became crimes in 1949-1950. A Population Registration Act then required all people, including whites, to carry a certificate of racial identity. The racial definitions, which were based upon "appearance," "general repute and acceptance," and "the life story of every individual," depended upon the decisions of a special commission under the Minister of the Interior. Categories could be appealed, but anyone submitting a "vexatious or unfounded" petition would be fined. The third measure in 1950, a Group Areas Act, which Dönges called the "cornerstone" of apartheid categorization, restricted each race—white, Negro, Indian, Colored—to the "full" areas it already occupied. The opposition UP was willing to accept voluntary segregation, but, like most nonwhite spokesmen, did not wish to freeze the status quo forever. The strongest nonwhite doubts concerned not the principle, but the extensive decree power that the Act granted to government bureaus. Enforcement of the new measure was entrusted to Dr. Hendrik Verwoerd, Minister of Native Affairs, who in 1954 pushed an Amendment Act that gave him power to expel Africans from lands that lay inside "full" white zones. In 1956 this law was applied to non-Europeans near Johannesburg, 100,000 of whom had their houses, lands and businesses condemned by the law of eminent domain. The government granted tenancy in neat new group areas, farther from the city and thoroughly sealed off from urban land that the whites wanted to occupy.

The Malan government closed its first term of office in 1953 with the far-reaching Bantu Authorities Act, which, in short, attempted to reëstablish tribal chiefs and to start a deliberate process of African retribalization. The assumption that this could be done, despite the fact that three-fourths of the natives were dependent upon the European economy and government, was most remarkable. "Positive apartheid," Malan called it, and Verwoerd hailed it as "a restoration of the natural Native democracy" and tribal nationalism. Whites would continue to supervise the African "Bantustans," of which there would be about eight, and internal government would gradually be turned over to elective tribal councils. In practice, most of the Bantustan authorities have been Africans appointed and directed by the government. Traditional rulers who had survived the detribalization process seemed to accept the new scheme, but the partially detribalized masses demonstrated rising resentment at the lack of effective elections, the retrogressive revival of chiefly rule, and direct interference by white magistrates. Many felt that the government was imposing divisions in order to preserve white domination. The Nationalists usually attributed all such dissatisfaction to Communist meddling in the "natural" tribalism that God had given to the Africans.

The Nationalist government gained strength in the 1953 elections, partly by emphasizing the need for railway segregation laws which the courts had invalidated, and immediately proceeded to revolutionize Bantu education. Mission schools, which had always been the backbone of nonwhite training, had to sub-

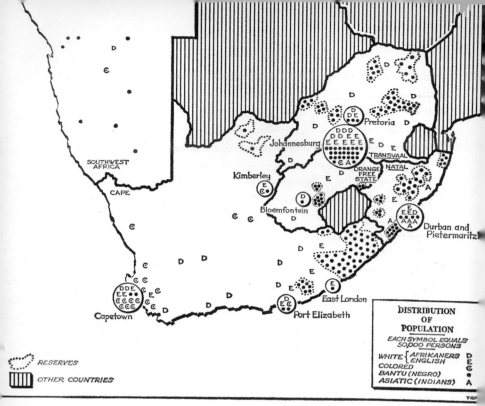

AFRIKANERS AND APARTHEID, 1960

DISTRIBUTION
OF
POPULATION

EACH SYMBOL EQUALS
50,000 PERSONS

WHITE { AFRIKANERS		D
ENGLISH		E
COLORED		C
BANTU (NEGRO)		•
ASIATIC (INDIANS)		A

mit to either State control or the supervision of "sufficiently advanced" Africans. The new curriculum was designed to revive
tribal loyalty and Bantu languages. All sides agreed that coördinated planning in the African education was long overdue, but
the Nationalists alone supported the new plan for schools geared
to cultural isolation and apartheid mentality. They stressed the
importance of mass education for the African's "rightful place
within the society to which he belongs," but the UP questioned
whether such plans suited the needs of the urbanized or Europeanized Bantu majority. However, Verwoerd dismissed the opposition as "leftist," discontinued all integrated schools and
nationalized most of the mission facilities. The Anglican Bishop
of Johannesburg, the Right Reverend R. Ambrose Reeves, de-

terminedly closed his denomination's schools, but Verwoerd retaliated by forbidding any of them to reopen.

Another act established government commissions to hear African labor grievances, which, trade unions being forbidden, had no outlet. Nationalists said that unions were not a natural adjunct of tribalism, so African trade organizations would never exist unless "left-wing agitators" imposed the idea from abroad.

In addition to other laws and regulations that were intended to create or to enforce apartheid, the government made one major addition to the separation code. The University Education Act of 1959 barred any African from attending an established institution of higher education, except for Fort Hare College, a predominantly nonwhite school that was supposed to become a model for advanced tribal training. Non-Europeans already enrolled in the older universities could finish their prescribed courses, but subsequent professional education is to meet only the requirements of de-Europeanized Bantustan life.

Nonwhite organizations—political or social—have been firmly discouraged unless they are willing to accept the Bantustan idea. Coloreds had been united in an African Peoples' Organization since 1902, but the advent of nationalism divided this body into opposing camps. The Colored People's National Union attempted to coöperate with the authorities, hoping to find a preferred place in the apartheid scheme by working with the government-appointed Colored Advisory Council. Those who considered this sycophantish, calling themselves the Anti-Colored Advisory Council Movement, tended to look toward Indians and the Bantu for alliances against white restriction.

Indians have also been divided between the nonviolent, liberal South African Indian Congress, an outgrowth of the movement Gandhi founded in 1894, and the smaller South African Indian Organization of 1951, which represents the wealthier merchants and professional men who are more eager to appease the whites. The Organization also includes the Pakistani Moslems, who feel excluded by the Hindu-dominated Congress.

Bantu Africans have had greater difficulty in organizing because they are more widely scattered, more numerous, and subject to so many types of urban locations, white tenancies, reserves and Bantustans. The strongest and oldest factor has been the South African Native Congress (soon renamed the African National Congress), which was formed in 1912 by Bantu lawyers who had studied in New York and London. Its original concern was the lack of native rights in the South Africa Act, but it became increasingly active in opposing the Land Act (1913), the pass laws, the abolition of the Cape Native franchise (1935) and the Hertzog segregation laws of 1936. When in that year the ANC decided to participate in Hertzog's unofficial Natives' Representative Council, an All-African Convention emerged to oppose such coöperation. The schism never healed, but the Congress retained a dominant position. By 1946 it had withdrawn in disillusionment from the Representative Council and concentrated on mass agitation for equal rights. The ANC protested vigorously against apartheid educational theory, demanding instead preparation for the modern world. After 1948 the Congress registered "legitimate demands" for progress by "constitutional means," and protested against Malan's "repressive policy of trusteeship, segregation and apartheid." However, in a letter to ex-Chief Albert J. Luthuli, the cautious and supple Congress President, Prime Minister Malan insisted that the differences between white and black "are permanent and not man-made." The new laws, he added, are not "oppressive and degrading," but an effort by whites to "preserve their identity as a separate community" and to "protect" the Bantu "heritage."

The ANC replied with a passive defiance campaign, timed to coincide with the 300th anniversary of the first white settlement. Tribal leaders, perhaps sponsored by the government and hoping for advantage under the retribalization scheme, formed a small, weak Bantu National Congress. The ANC, seeking equal rights within the European-controlled political system, began to work with the Indian movements. Of all Europeans, only the Communists were willing to coöperate on apparently equal terms with any of the nonwhite movements. Luthuli successfully forestalled any significant influence from that quarter, but, as the African sense of dissatisfaction and desperation grew, it became increasingly difficult to refuse the only consistent source of outside help.

By refusing to deal with the ANC, to allow trade unions, or to make provisions for nontribal development, the government had closed all channels of contact with urbanized and detribalized Africans. The moderate ANC late in 1958 began to lose strength to a more vigorous, uncompromising movement, the Pan-African Congress. The PAC, directed by Robert Sobukwe, an African who taught Bantu languages at the English-speaking Witwatersrand University, lacked both the organizational structure and the long-range patience of the older body. It aimed at the rapid achievement of a unified national state in which Africans, with full electoral rights, would far outnumber all other races. For competitive purposes, the ANC was forced to take a stronger stand on the major issues. By 1959 feelings among all nonwhites had reached a pitch that alarmed the government, which finally isolated the major African and Indian leaders and prevented them from directing their respective organizations.

This step was dangerous because, by removing the moderate and educated element, it left the African movements in untrained, inexperienced, more militant hands. The PAC called a work stoppage and encouraged Africans to burn their hated passes. The protest started as a passive-resistance campaign, but police impatience and African edginess soon led to violence. Late in March of 1960, a particularly bitter clash took place at Sharpeville, an urban "location" near Johannesburg, leaving over sixty Africans dead. Some witnesses said that demonstrating masses were shot in the back while fleeing the police; official accounts claim that Africans were attacking with stones. The anti-pass campaign, which in the long run stiffened the government's stand, quickly collapsed because the low-paid African laborers had no savings with which to buy food and supplies for an extended work stoppage.

One of the characteristics of South Africa under Nationalist rule has been the progressive division of white as well as non-white opposition. United Party strength declined steadily in three successive elections. In 1958 it still held a bare majority in the popular vote, but the government won 103 out of 156 seats —one seat short of two-thirds control. Minority parties disappeared, but only briefly. One consequence of the continued growth of Nationalist strength was an increase, following the electoral contest, in organized dissatisfaction. Some of the new parties, notably the Progressives and Liberals, promised to reverse the pattern of apartheid and to revive the development of interracial coöperation. However, no party, in or out of Parliament, promised anything resembling equality or integration, except for the semisecret Communists, whose motives were patently ulterior. All the new moderate parties were offshoots of the UP, which now was not only weakening but splitting apart. Ironically enough, the revival of liberal parties, which fragmented the opposition, served only to strengthen the Nationalist Party position.

The advocates of apartheid had worked with remarkable acumen to entrench and strengthen their political advantage. The Colored people, most of whom opposed nationalism, had been disenfranchised. The pro-Nationalist whites of Southwest Africa, an area that had virtually been annexed to the Union, were given representation in Parliament. Legislative majorities had been built by the fortuitous balance of language groups in individual constituencies, and strengthened by far-reaching constitutional revisions that gave large blocks of seats to the winners of bare pluralities. There is also no doubt that, in electoral campaigns, the Nationalist Party used the apartheid appeal astutely, stressing its humanitarian or protective theories in appropriate instances, and playing upon traditional racist fears in others. Yet equally, if not more effective, was the Nationalists' ability to take political advantage of anti-Communist sentiment.

The South African Communist Party won two seats—one in 1948 and one in 1949—in local elections among detribalized Africans at the Cape. Nationalist newspapers perceived a subversive danger, though the English-language press warned that repressive measures would only increase the Communist appeal. The government did not recognize that communism, in its early stages, would use any idea that might prove popular, as it was doing with the African rights movement. Instead, the Malan government passed a "Suppression of Communism Act," which created a State Liquidator with power to ban any organization or publication that promoted a Communist activity. The law really outlawed not only Marxism, Leninism and the like, but also any organization that "aims at bringing about any political, industrial, social or economic change . . . by unlawful acts or omissions. . . ." The government clearly believed that, but for communism, all natives would peacefully welcome the advent of apartheid.

Subsequent government rulings have put the "Communist" label on a wide variety of movements, some of them scarcely connected with Marx or Moscow. The law has therefore been described not as a ban on communism, but as a device by which Nationalists may proscribe various forms of opposition, particularly nonwhite leadership, unacceptable missionaries, and white South Africans who sympathize with any of these. The most spectacular application of this act, the so-called "Treason Trials" of 1956, involved more than 150 people of every race, including members of Parliament, Chief Luthuli, non-Dutch churchmen, and a variety of other liberal citizens. After four years of public hearings, the courts dismissed the cases for lack of evidence, but the attendant publicity had a marked effect in silencing many who might otherwise have criticized the regime.

Early Nationalist goals had included the "restoration" of an Afrikaner republic. The Party believed that the position of the British monarch, though wholly nominal, constituted a theoretical infringement of South African sovereignty and perpetuated an alien influence in the country. The dream of restoring the Trekker political tradition of the nineteenth century was however held in abeyance while the Nationalist Party worked to strengthen its hold on Parliament. Malan retired in 1954, after six years in office. Strijdom, his successor, died in office three years later and was replaced by Verwoerd. The government waited for the day when an absolute majority of the white voters would support Afrikanerdom. By 1960 the possibility had become real. First, a reduction of the voting age from twenty-one to eighteen enfranchised a younger age-group that was predominantly Afrikaner. Then came the Sharpeville incident, which caused a rise in Afrikaner alarm. Finally, an attempt on the life of Prime Minister Verwoerd—though made only by one independent English-speaking white man—sharpened the feeling of division within white society. This had already been increased by the British Prime Minister, Harold Macmillan, who on a state visit to the Union in February, 1960, had bluntly warned that "winds of change" were blowing across white Africa.

A republican referendum was called, in which, the government implied, loyal South Africans would be separated from all who held alien allegiances. The Nationalists won, 52 percent to 48—capturing a straight majority for the first time—and proclaimed a republic on May 31, 1961. Such a constitutional change required the approval of other members of the multiracial Commonwealth, who tried to press Verwoerd for a modification of the apartheid laws. After three days of tense discussion, during which Canada joined the Asian and African members in pressing the issue, Verwoerd angrily denounced discriminatory practices in those countries and accused their prime ministers of "vindictiveness." Rather than submit to such influence, which he called "alien interference," the Prime Minister, with Parliamentary approval, withdrew South Africa's application for membership, marched out of the conference, and proclaimed his country's secession from the Commonwealth. A ceremonial presidency, which Parliament gave to Charles Swart, replaced the British sovereign, though the effective government continued to be entrusted to the Verwoerd ministry. The ultimate goal of the Nationalist Party had finally been achieved, in both law and practice: the unfettered independence and sovereignty of Afrikaner Christian National civilization in the Republic of South Africa.

28

THE CLAIM TO IDENTITY

ALMOST every one of the thirty-one major nations in sub-Saharan Africa underwent a major change between 1958 and 1961. Twenty-two of them, from Senegal to Tanganyika, acquired independence. Ghana and South Africa, already independent since 1957 and 1910 respectively, changed from theoretical monarchies into republics. Constitutional revisions preparatory to independence took place in four others—Kenya, Uganda, Ruanda-Urundi and the Rhodesia-Nyasaland Federation—and the two remaining territories, both legally integrated into the Portuguese mother country, began to seethe with unrest. Only Liberia, free for more than a century, experienced little effect from the wholesale transitions.

Political, economic and social difficulties were associated in every case, though marked tension occurred in less than one-third of the countries and overt violence in only one-tenth of them. Rather than attempting suppression or direct repression, most of the former colonial powers tried to assuage Africa's rising ambitions for self-government.

In the vast region between South Africa and the Sahara, nonwhite leadership tended to fall into the hands of an anti-tribal, European-educated elite. These groups, fired with anticolonialist sentiment and often jealous of their local prestige, consciously and willingly accepted a form of the economic and political nationalism that had long motivated European politics and diplomacy. A reasonable basis for such nationalism was found within the framework of commerce and administration that the European colonial powers had established. There is doubt whether subsequent generations of leaders will be motivated by the same virulent anticolonialism and separatist nationalism, though the successors seem certain to find lasting support for national distinction among the detribalized, urbanized groups, which in most cases are increasing even faster with independence than they did under foreign rule. The present elite will have to be replaced, either from the detribalized masses or from an emerging educated class. Many of the new countries hope to make these two groups synonymous, in order to perpetuate a base upon which national unity and strength may continue to develop. Nonwhite nationalism in South Africa, increasingly stripped of sophisticated leadership by the ruling whites, is in danger of becoming demagogical or fanatical.

Racism is a motivating factor in some areas—as a mild, traditional, pragmatic definition of anticolonialist identity in West Africa, and as a specific cause célèbre in some of the multiracial trouble spots of East and Central Africa. The nucleus of racialist identity rests, in most such cases, with both the white and nonwhite groups, the fears of one stimulating those of the other, as in Kenya, the Congo, the Rhodesias and South Africa. This type of problem, which does not exist in politics north and west of the Congo River, may have been adequately resolved in Tanganyika.

Nationalism, whether black or white, has usually found its identity as much in opposition to tribalism as to colonialism. Yeoman agriculture, rather than tenuous tenancy, and urbanization have been noticeable prerequisites to nationalist independence movements, even in the former Belgian Congo. National identity usually expresses itself in terms of the demand for more education, more local control over and return from economic

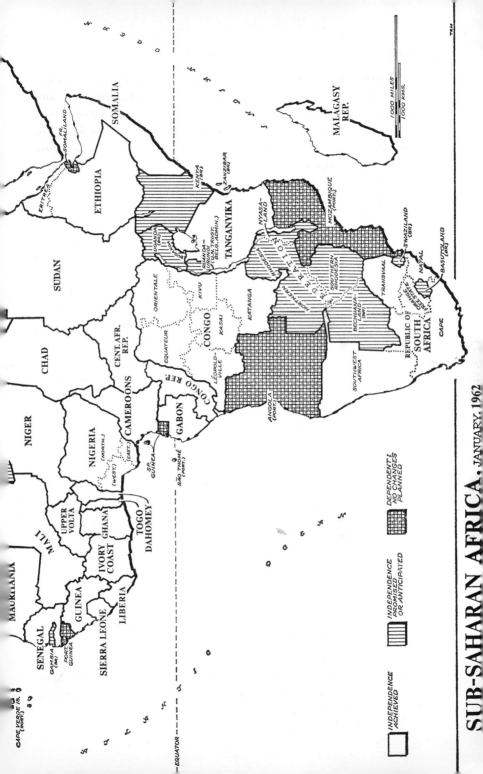

SUB-SAHARAN AFRICA, JANUARY, 1962

INDEPENDENCE ACHIEVED

INDEPENDENCE PROMISED OR ANTICIPATED

DEPENDENT; NO CHANGES PLANNED

1000 MILES
1000 KMS.

CAPE VERDE IS. (PORT.)

MAURITANIA

MALI

NIGER

CHAD

SUDAN

ETHIOPIA

FR. SOMALILAND

SOMALIA

SENEGAL

GAMBIA (BR.)

PORT. GUINEA

GUINEA

SIERRA LEONE

LIBERIA

IVORY COAST

UPPER VOLTA

GHANA

TOGO

DAHOMEY

NIGERIA (WEST) (NORTH) (EAST)

CAMEROONS

CENT. AFR. REP.

SP. GUINEA

SÃO THOMÉ (PORT.)

GABON

CONGO REP.

CONGO

ORIENTALE

EQUATEUR

LÉOPOLD-VILLE

KASAI

KIVU

KATANGA

UGANDA (BR.)

RUANDA-URUNDI (U.N. TRUST; BELG. ADMIN.)

KENYA (BR.)

ZANZIBAR (BR.)

TANGANYIKA

NYASA-LAND

MOZAMBIQUE (PORT.)

NORTHERN RHODESIA

SOUTHERN RHODESIA

FEDERATION

ANGOLA (PORT.)

SOUTHWEST AFRICA

BECHUANA-LAND (BR.)

SWAZILAND (BR.)

TRANSVAAL

ORANGE FREE STATE

NATAL

BASUTOLAND (BR.)

REPUBLIC OF SOUTH AFRICA

CAPE

MALAGASY REP.

EQUATOR

development, and the political machinery through which such goals may be attained. Foreign opposition to these wishes only stimulates reckless or desperate reactions in which the conservation of resources, balanced exploitation and the hope for integrated economic and social bases are sacrificed to frantic, perhaps totalitarian, and violent defiance. The danger of communism seems to lie in three areas: any Western action reminiscent of political or economic colonialism, which could blind nationalists to the threat of Communist subterfuge and dramatic promises; internal disunity or economic frustration, to which Communist organization could provide a tempting though false answer; and Western failure to realize that an African government's efforts to supplement a short supply of capital are not necessarily an idea dictated from Moscow.

In international diplomacy most of Africa is concerned with itself—its own independence, development and self-direction—rather than with power blocs. Much of Africa's so-called "neutralism" results less from a lack of conviction than from a belief that African nations must devote their still-limited resources to "catching up" with the world. From the African point of view, any attempt to align the continent or to divide it into blocs is a threat to the development of unfettered, viable solutions to regional problems. "Balkanism," which many non-Africans see in the plethora of new nations, is greatly feared on the continent itself. Yet, at the same time, Pan-African federalism does not seem to meet the requirements of many states who feel markedly distinct in culture and outlook from their neighbors. Experiments in economic and social coöperation, upon which any effective political coöperation would probably be based, are being made, though some of them have not proven to be fruitful. Ghana, Guinea and Mali have on paper formed a loose union, bound apparently by a common fear of colonialism or "neo-colonialism." Most of the former French possessions and trust territories have participated in a "Brazzaville Twelve," which informally coördinates the activities of still-sovereign nations. The Commonwealth may serve as a framework for some similar coöperation, particularly since the secession of South Africa has left that organization more homogeneous in ideology. Ghana has taken a lead in inter-African coöperative discussions, although President Nkrumah has not always pleased everyone by assuming that there is an extensive or permanent unanimity on nearly all major questions. African-unity overtures from Egypt and Morocco, which are white Arab states north of the desert, have been met officially with polite but noticeable reserve.

In the twentieth century sub-Saharan Africans have become aware of their own identity and concerned for their standing relative to the rest of the world. White, Negro, Asian and mixed communities have strongly asserted their claim to self-development, uniqueness and independence. Many conflicts of interest among these groups have not been resolved. Like other continents, Africa has become an amalgam, a crucible of complex forces. Africa is one thread, distinguishable yet not isolated, in the fabric of human history.

BIBLIOGRAPHY

GENERAL

Bibliographical Works

American Historical Association. *Guide to Historical Literature.* New York, 1961. Pages 78-82, 404-421, 423-426, 745-757, 760-769.
American Universities Field Staff. *A Select Bibliography: Asia, Africa, Eastern Europe, Latin America.* New York, 1960. Pages 195-253.
Conover, Helen F. (comp.). *Africa South of the Sahara, a Selected List of Writings, 1951-1956.* Washington, 1957.
————. *Introduction to Africa, a Selective Guide to Background Reading.* Washington, 1952.
————. *Research and Information on Africa: Continuing Sources.* Washington, 1954.
International African Institute. *Select Annotated Bibliography of Tropical Africa.* New York, 1956.
Mendelssohn, Sidney. *Mendelssohn's South African Bibliography.* 2 vols. London, 1910.
Porter, Dorothy (ed.). *A Catalogue of the African Collection in the Moorland Foundation, Howard University Library.* Washington, 1958.
Price, Frank W. (ed.), and Robert L. Lehman (comp.). *Africa*

(Some of the more outstanding works are starred [*])

South of the Sahara: A Selected and Annotated Bibliography of Books in the Missionary Research Library. New York, 1959.

Ragatz, Lowell J. *A Bibliography for the Study of African History in the Nineteenth and Twentieth Centuries.* Washington, 1943.

South African Public Library. *A Bibliography of African Bibliographies, Covering Territories South of the Sahara.* (3rd ed.) Capetown, 1955.

University of Cape Town. *Bibliographical Series.* Cape Town, 1941 ff.

Wieschoff, Heinrich A. *Anthropological Bibliography of Negro Africa.* New Haven, 1948.

Periodicals and Serials

*Africa. London, 1928 ff. Quarterly.

*Africa Report (formerly *Africa Special Report*). Washington, 1956 ff. Monthly.

Africa South. Capetown, London, 1956 ff. Bimonthly.

African Abstracts. London, 1950 ff. Quarterly.

African Affairs. London, 1901 ff. Quarterly.

*African Studies (formerly *Bantu Studies*). Johannesburg, 1921 ff. Quarterly.

African Studies Bulletin. New York, 1958 ff. Quarterly.

The Archives Year Book for South African History. Capetown, 1938 ff. Annually.

Archivos. Madrid, 1947 ff. Quarterly.

*Bulletin de l'Institut Français d'Afrique Noire. Dakar, 1939 ff. Irregular.

East African Studies. Nairobi, 1953 ff. Irregular.

Ethnographic Survey of Africa. London, 1950 ff. Irregular.

Études Congolaises. Léopoldville, 1961 ff. Bimonthly.

Handbook of African Languages. London, 1952 ff. Irregular.

Journal de la Société des Africanistes. Paris, 1931 ff. Irregular.

*Journal of African History. Cambridge (Eng.), 1960 ff. Semiannual.

Journal of Racial Affairs. Stellenbosch (S. Africa), 1949 ff. Quarterly.

Journal of the Historical Society of Nigeria. Ibadan, 1956 ff. Annual.

Notes Africaines. Dakar, 1939 ff. Irregular.

Nyasaland Journal. Blantyre, 1948 ff. Semiannual.

Race Relations. Johannesburg, 1933 ff. Quarterly.

Revue de l'histoire des colonies françaises. [Title varies.] Paris, 1913 ff. Quarterly.

*Rhodes-Livingstone Papers. Livingstone (N. Rhod.), 1938 ff. Semiannual.

*Survey of Race Relations in South Africa. Johannesburg, 1947 ff. Annual.

Tanganyika Notes and Records. Dar es Salaam, 1936 ff. Semiannual.

Transactions of the Historical Society for the Gold Coast and Togoland. Achimota, 1953 ff. Irregular.

Uganda Journal. London, 1934 ff. Semiannual.

United Empire. London, 1909 ff. Bimonthly.

*Zaïre. Brussels, 1947 ff. Monthly.

Anthropology, Linguistics and Prehistory

*Alimen, Henriette (A. Broderick, transl.). The Prehistory of Africa. London, 1957.

*Bascom, William R., and Melville J. Herskovits (eds.). Continuity and Change in African Cultures. Chicago, 1958.

Caton-Thompson, Gertrude. The Zimbabwe Culture, Ruins and Reactions. Oxford, 1931.

*Cole, Sonia. The Prehistory of East Africa. Harmondsworth, 1954.

Forde, Cyril D. (ed.). African Worlds: Studies in the Cosmological Ideas and Social Values of African Peoples. London, 1954.

Fortes, Meyer, and Edward E. Evans-Pritchard (eds.). African Political Systems. London, 1940.

Frobenius, Leo. "L'art africain," Cahiers d'art. (Paris, 1931). Pages 7-55.

*Greenberg, Joseph H. Studies in African Linguistic Classification. New Haven, 1955.

Leakey, L. S. B. The Stone Age Races of Kenya. London, 1935.

————. Adam's Ancestors. (4th ed.) London, 1953.

Lhote, Henri. "Peintures préhistoriques du Sahara." (Catalogue of exhibition) Paris, 1958.

*————. La découverte des fresques du Tassili. Paris, 1958.

Murdock, George Peter. Africa: Its Peoples and Their Culture History. New York, 1959.

Ottenberg, Simon and Phoebe (eds.). Cultures and Societies of Africa. New York, 1960.

Proceedings of the 1st Pan-Africanist Congress on Pre-History. Oxford, 1952.

Radcliffe-Broun, Alfred R., and Cyril D. Forde (eds.). African Systems of Kinship and Marriage. London, 1950.

Royal Anthropological Institute. Early Human Remains in East Africa. Cambridge, 1933.

Smith, Edwin W. The Golden Stool: Some Aspects of the Conflict of Cultures in Africa. (2nd ed.) London, 1927.

Tempels, Placied. *La Philosophie bantoue*. Elisabethville, 1945; Paris, 1949.

Wingert, Paul S. *The Sculpture of Negro Africa*. New York, 1950.

Arab Travelers

Al-Bakri (W. MacGuckin and Baron de Slane, transl.). *Description de l'Afrique septentrionale*. (Rev. ed.) Algiers, 1913.

Al-Idrisi. *Nuzhat al-Mushtak. De geographia universali*. Rome, 1592.

———— (Amédée Jaubert, transl.), *Géographie d'Edrisi*. 2 vols. Paris, 1836-40.

———— (R. Dozy and M. J. de Goeje, transl.). *Description de l'Afrique et de l'Espagne*. Leyden, 1866.

Al-Istakhri (M. J. de Goeje, ed.). *Masalik al-Mamalik*. Leyden, 1891-92.

Al-Masudi (B. de Meynard and P. de Courteille, transl.). *Les prairies d'or*. 9 vols. Paris, 1861-77.

Al-Omari. *Masalik el Absar*. Paris, 1927.

Al-Sadi (O. Houdas, transl.). *Documents arabes relatifs à l'histoire du Soudan: Tarikh es-Soudan*. 2 vols. Paris, 1898-1900.

Ibn Battuta (H.A.R. Gibb, transl.). *The Travels of Ibn Battuta, A.D. 1325-1354*. Cambridge (Eng.), 1958.

Ibn Haukal (Baron de Slane, transl.). *Description de l'Afrique*. Paris, 1842.

Ibn Khaldun (Paul Casanova, ed. and transl.). *Histoire des Berbères et des dynasties musulmanes de l'Afrique septentrionale*. 4 vols. Paris, 1925-56.

Leo Africanus (A. Épaulard, transl.). *Description de l'Afrique*. (New ed.) 2 vols. Paris, 1956.

Roncière, Charles de la. *La découverte de l'Afrique au Moyen Age*. 3 vols. Cairo, 1924-27.

Salil-ibn-Razik (G. P. Badger, ed. and transl.). *History of the Imams and Seyyids of Oman*. London, 1871.

Strong, A. S. (ed.). "Chronicles of Kilwa." *Journal of the Royal Asiatic Society*. N.S. XXVII, 1895.

Werner, A. (transl.). "History of Pate." *Journal of the African Society*. 1914-15. Pages 148, 278, 392.

Yaqut (F. Wüstenfeld, transl.). *Mu'jam al-Buldan*. 6 vols. Leipzig, 1866-73.

European Exploration

Axelson, Eric V. (ed.). *South African Explorers*. London, 1954.

Barros, João de. *Dos feitos que os portugueses fizerem no descubri-*

mento e conquista dos mares e terras de Oriente [1552]. (6th ed.) 4 vols. Lisbon, 1944-46.

Barth, Henry. *Travels and Discoveries in North and Central Africa, 1849-55.* 5 vols. London, 1856.

Blake, John W. (ed.). *Europeans in West Africa, 1450-1560: Documents.* 2 vols. London, 1942.

Caillé, René. *Travels Through Central Africa to Timbuctoo, and across the Great Desert, to Morocco, Performed in the Years 1824-1828.* 2 vols. London, 1830.

Central African Archives (Southern Rhodesia). *The Oppenheimer Series.* London, 1945 ff.

Clapperton, Hugh. *Journal of a Second Expedition . . . to which is Added the Journal of Richard Lander.* . . . London, 1829.

Galvão, António de. *Tratado dos describrementos* [1563]. Oporto, 1944.

Hart, Henry H. *Sea Road to the Indies.* London, 1952.

Howard, C. (ed.). *West African Explorers.* London, 1952.

Kingsley, Mary H. *Travels in West Africa.* London, 1897.

Lander, Richard L., and John Lander. *Journal of an Expedition to Explore the Course and Termination of the Niger.* 3 vols. London, 1832.

Livingstone, David. *The Last Journals of David Livingstone,* 2 vols. London, 1874.

———. *Missionary Travels and Researches in South Africa.* London, 1857.

———. *Narrative of an Expedition to the Zambezi and its Tributaries.* London, 1865.

——— (James I. Macnair, ed.). *Livingstone's Travels.* London, 1954.

——— (Isaac Shapera, ed.). *Family Letters.* 2 vols. London, 1959.

——— (Isaac Shapera, ed.). *Livingstone's Private Journals, 1851-1853.* Berkeley and Los Angeles, 1960.

Pacheco, Duarte (G. H. T. Kimble, ed. and transl.). *Esmeraldo de situ orbis.* London, 1937.

Park, Mungo. *Travels in the Interior Districts of Africa, 1795, 1796, and 1797.* (5th ed.) London, 1807.

———. *Travels in the Interior Parts of Africa.* . . . 2 vols. London, 1816.

Perham, Margery F., and Jack Simmons (eds.). *African Discovery: An Anthology of Exploration.* (2nd ed.) London, 1957.

Prestage, E. *The Portuguese Pioneers.* London, 1933.

Richards, Charles, and J. Place (eds.). *East African Explorers.* London, 1960.

Schiffers, Heinrich (Diana Pyke, transl.). *The Quest for Africa.* New York, 1958.

*Seaver, George. *David Livingstone, his Life and Letters.* London, 1957.

Selous, Frederick C. *Travel and Adventure in South-East Africa.* London, 1893.

Speke, John H. *Journal of the Discovery of the Source of the Nile.* London, 1863.

———. *What Led to the Discovery of the Source of the Nile.* London, 1864.

Stanley, Henry Morton. *How I Found Livingstone in Central Africa.* London, 1873.

———. *Through the Dark Continent.* 2 vols. New York, 1878.

———. *The Congo and the Founding of Its Free State.* 2 vols. New York, 1885.

———. *In Darkest Africa: or the Quest, Rescue and Retreat of Emin, Governor of Equatoria.* 2 vols. New York, 1890.

———. *The Autobiography of Sir Henry Morton Stanley.* New York, 1909.

Other Historical Works

Blake, John W. *European Beginnings in West Africa, 1454-1578.* London, 1937.

*Buell, Raymond L. *The Native Problem in Africa.* 2 vols. New York, 1928.

Cambridge History of the British Empire. 8 vols. Cambridge (Eng.), 1929-59.

Cornevin, Robert. *Histoire des peuples de l'Afrique noire.* Paris, 1960.

*Davidson, Basil. *Old Africa Rediscovered.* London, 1960.

Donnan, Elizabeth. *Documents Illustrative of the Slave Trade to America.* 4 vols. Washington, 1930-35.

*Elias, Taslim Olawale. *The Nature of African Customary Law.* Manchester, 1956.

*Fage, John D. *An Atlas of African History.* London, 1958.

Freyre, Gilberto (S. Putnam, transl.). *The Masters and the Slaves.* (2nd ed.) New York, 1956.

*Groves, Charles P. *The Planting of Christianity in Africa.* 4 vols. London, 1948-58.

*Hailey, William M., baron. *An African Survey: Revised 1956.* London, 1957.

————. *Native Administration in the British African Territories.* 5 vols. London, 1950-53.

Herskovits, Melville J. *The Myth of the Negro Past.* New York, 1941.

Hitti, Philip K. *History of the Arabs.* (6th ed.) London, 1956.

Horrabin, J. Frank. *An Atlas of Africa.* London, 1960.

Johnston, Harry H., baronet. *The Story of My Life.* (2nd ed.) Indianapolis, 1923.

Kimble, George H. T. *Tropical Africa.* 2 vols. New York, 1960.

Leconfield, Hugh A. Wyndham, baron. *The Atlantic and Emancipation.* London, 1937.

————. *The Atlantic and Slavery.* London, 1935.

Lugard, Frederick J. D., baron. *The Dual Mandate in British Tropical Africa.* (4th ed.) Edinburgh, 1929.

Macmillan, William M. *Africa Emergent.* Harmondsworth, 1949.

Morgan, Kenneth (ed.). *Islam—the Straight Path: Islam interpreted by Muslims.* New York, 1958.

*Oliver, Roland A. *The Missionary Factor in East Africa.* London, 1952.

*————. *Sir Harry Johnston and the Scramble for Africa.* London, 1957.

Parrinder, Geoffrey. *African Traditional Religion.* London, 1954.

*Perham, Margery F. *Lugard: the Years of Adventure, 1858-1898.* London, 1956.

*————. *Lugard: the Years of Authority, 1898-1945.* London, 1960.

Pim, Alan W., baronet. *The Financial and Economic History of the African Tropical Territories.* Oxford, 1940.

Schnee, Heinrich (ed.). *Deutsches Kolonial-Lexikon.* 3 vols. Leipzig, 1920.

Taylor, J. V. *Christianity and Politics in Africa.* Harmondsworth, 1957.

Townsend, Mary E. *European Colonial Expansion since 1871.* Philadelphia, 1941.

————. *The Rise and Fall of Germany's Colonial Empire, 1884-1918.* New York, 1930.

Westermann, Diedrich. *Geschichte Afrikas: Staatenbildungen südlich der Sahara.* Cologne, 1952.

Contemporary Affairs

Bowles, Chester. *Africa's Challenge to America.* Berkeley, 1956.

Carter, Gwendolen M. *Independence for Africa.* New York, 1960.

————, and William O. Brown (eds.). *Transition in Africa*. Boston, 1958.

*Cohen, Andrew, baronet. *British Policy in Changing Africa*. Evanston, 1959.

Decraene, Philippe. *Le panafricanisme*. Paris, 1959.

Filesi, Teobaldo. *Comunismo e nazionalismo in Africa*. Rome, 1958.

Fitzgerald, Walter. *Africa: A Social, Economic and Political Geography of Its Major Regions*. (8th ed.) London, 1955.

Great Britain. Colonial Office. *An Economic Survey of the Colonial Territories, 1951*. 7 vols. London, 1952. Vols. I-III.

Gunther, John. *Inside Africa*. New York, 1955.

Haines, Charles Grove (ed.). *Africa Today*. Baltimore, 1955.

Hance, William A. *African Economic Development*. New York, 1958.

*Hodgkin, Thomas L. *Nationalism in Colonial Africa*. London, 1956.

Meek, Charles K. *Land Law and Custom in the Colonies*. (2nd ed.) London, 1949.

Padmore, George. *Pan Africanism or Communism?* London, 1956.

Phillips, John. *Agriculture and Ecology in Africa*. London, 1959.

Sithole, Ndabaningi. *African Nationalism*. Capetown, 1959.

Stamp, Laurence Dudley. *Africa: A Study in Tropical Development*. New York, 1953.

WEST AFRICA

General

Austen, Dennis. *West Africa and the Commonwealth*. Harmondsworth, 1957.

Bovill, E. W. *Caravans of the Old Sahara*. London, 1933.

*————. *The Golden Trade of the Moors*. London, 1958.

Brasio, António. *Monumenta missionaria africana: Africa ocidental*. 4 vols. Lisbon, 1952-54.

Burns, Alan C., baronet. *Colonial Civil Servant* [autobiography]. London, 1949.

Cowan, L. Gray. *Local Government in West Africa*. New York, 1958.

Davies, Kenneth G. *The Royal African Company*. London, 1957.

De Graft-Johnson, John C. *African Glory; the Story of Vanished Negro Civilizations*. New York, 1955.

Delafosse, Maurice. *Haut-Sénégal-Niger*. 3 vols. Paris, 1912.

———— (F. Fligelman, transl.). *The Negroes of Africa; History and Culture*. Washington, 1931.

*Fage, John D. *An Introduction to the History of West Africa.* Cambridge (Eng.), 1955.

Lugard, Flora Shaw, Lady. *A Tropical Dependency: An Outline of the Ancient History of the Western Soudan with an Account of the Modern Settlement of Northern Nigeria.* London, 1906.

Martin, Eveline C. *The British West African Settlements, 1750-1821.* London, 1927.

Parrinder, Geoffrey. *West African Religion.* London, 1949.

Pedler, F. J. *West Africa.* (2nd ed.) London, 1959.

———. *Economic Geography of West Africa.* London, 1955.

*Trimingham, J. Spencer. *Islam in West Africa.* Oxford, 1959.

French (including Equatorial Africa, Togo and Cameroons)

Akindélé, Adolphe, and Cyrille Arguessy. *Contribution à l'étude de l'histoire de l'ancien royaume de Porto-Novo.* Dakar, 1953.

Boulnois, Jean, and Boubou Hama. *L'empire de Gao* [Songhai]. Paris, 1954.

Boyer, Gaston. *Un peuple de l'ouest soudanais, les Diawara. Contribution à l'histoire de Songhay.* Dakar, 1953.

Cornevin, Robert. *Histoire du Togo.* Paris, 1959.

Delavignette, Robert L. *Service africain.* Paris, 1946.

Delcourt, André. *La France et les établissements français au Sénégal entre 1713 et 1763.* Dakar, 1952.

Deschamps, Hubert. *Les méthodes et les doctrines coloniales de la France (du XVIe siècle à nos jours).* Paris, 1953.

Dia, Mamadou. *Réflexions sur l'économie de l'Afrique Noire.* Paris, 1952.

Eboué, Adolphe F. *La nouvelle politique indigène pour l'Afrique Equatoriale Française.* Paris, 1945.

Gide, André P. G. (Dorothy Bussy, transl.). *Travels in the Congo.* New York, 1929.

Gouilly, Alphonse. *L'Islam dans l'Afrique occidentale française.* Paris, 1952.

Hamon, Léo. *Introduction à l'étude des partis politiques de l'Afrique française.* Paris, 1959.

Herskovits, Melville J. *Dahomey, an Ancient West African Kingdom.* 2 vols. New York, 1938.

Le Cameroun, aspect, géographique, historique, touristique, économique et administratif du territoire. Paris, 1953.

Lembezat, Bertrand. *La France Equatoriale.* (2nd ed.) Paris, 1950.

Robert, André P. *L'évolution des coutumes de l'Ouest africain français.* Paris, 1955.

Roberts, Stephen H. *History of French Colonial Policy, 1870-1925.* 2 vols. London, 1929.

Rudin, Harry R. *Germans in the Cameroons, 1884-1914.* New Haven, 1938.

Schweitzer, Albert (Mrs. C. E. B. Russell, transl.). *African Notebook.* Bloomington, 1958.

Spitz, Georges. *L'Ouest africain français: A.O.F. et Togo.* Paris, 1947.

*Thompson, Virginia, and Richard Adloff. *French West Africa.* Stanford, 1958.

*————. *The Emerging States of French Equatorial Africa.* Stanford, 1960.

Ziéglé, Henri. *Afrique Equatoriale Française.* Paris, 1952.

Ghana (Gold Coast)

Apter, David. *The Gold Coast in Transition.* Princeton, 1955.

*Bourret, Florence M. *Ghana: The Road to Independence, 1919-1957.* London, 1960.

Busia, Kofi A. *The Position of the Chief in the Modern Political System of Ashanti.* London, 1951.

Claridge, William W. *A History of the Gold Coast and Ashanti.* 2 vols. London, 1915.

Fage, John D. *Ghana: A Historical Interpretation.* Madison, 1959.

Meyerowitz, Eva L.-R. *Akan Traditions of Origin.* London, 1952.

————. *The Sacred State of the Akan.* London, 1951.

————. *The Divine Kingship in Ghana,* London, 1960.

*Nkrumah, Kwame. *Ghana: The Autobiography of Kwame Nkrumah.* New York, 1957.

Padmore, George. *The Gold Coast Revolution.* London, 1953.

Rattray, Robert S. *Ashanti Law and Constitution.* Oxford, 1929.

————. *Ashanti* (reprint with additions). Oxford, 1956.

————. *Religion and Art in Ashanti.* Oxford, 1927.

————. *The Tribes of the Ashanti Hinterland.* 2 vols. Oxford, 1932.

Smith, Edwin W. *Aggrey of Africa: A Study in Black and White.* New York, 1929.

Timothy, Bankole. *Kwame Nkrumah.* London, 1955.

*Ward, William E. F. *History of Ghana.* (rev. 2nd ed.) London, 1958.

Wight, Martin. *The Gold Coast Legislative Council.* London, 1947.

Wolfson, Freda (ed.). *Pageant of Ghana.* London, 1958.

Nigeria

Akpan, Ntieyong U. *Epitaph to Indirect Rule.* London, 1956.

Awolowo, Obafemi. *Awo: The Autobiography of Chief Obafemi Awolowo.* Cambridge (Eng.), 1960.

———. *Path to Nigerian Freedom.* London, 1947.

Azikiwe, Nnamdi. *Economic Reconstruction of Nigeria.* Lagos, 1948.

———. *Political Blueprint of Nigeria.* Lagos, 1945.

———. *Renascent Africa.* Lagos, 1937.

Biobaku, Saburi O. *The Egba and Their Neighbours, 1842-1872.* Oxford, 1957.

*Burns, Alan C., baronet. *History of Nigeria.* (5th ed.) London, 1956.

*Coleman, James S. *Nigeria: Background to Nationalism.* Berkeley and Los Angeles, 1958.

*Dike, Kenneth O. *Trade and Politics in the Niger Delta, 1830-1885.* Oxford, 1956.

Ezera, Kalu. *Constitutional Developments in Nigeria.* Cambridge (Eng.), 1960.

Flint, J. E. *Sir George Goldie and the Making of Nigeria.* London, 1960.

*Hodgkin, Thomas (ed.). *Nigerian Perspectives: An Historical Anthology.* London, 1960.

Hogben, S. J. *The Muhammedan Emirates of Nigeria.* London, 1930.

Kingsley, Mary H. *West African Studies.* (2nd ed.) London, 1901.

Kirk-Greene, A. H. M. *Adamawa Past and Present: An Historical Approach to the Development of a Northern Cameroons Province.* London, 1958.

Krieger, Kurt. *Geschichte von Zamfara, Sokoto-Provinz, Nordnigeria.* Berlin, 1959.

Meek, Charles K. *Land Tenure and Land Administration in Nigeria and the Cameroons.* London, 1957.

———. *Law and Authority in a Nigerian Tribe.* London, 1937.

Parrinder, Geoffrey. *Religion in an African City.* London, 1953.

Perham, Margery F. *Native Administration in Nigeria.* New York, 1937.

——— (ed.). *The Economics of a Tropical Dependency.* 2 vols. London, 1946-48.

Smith, M. G. *Government in Zazzau . . . 1800 to 1950.* London, 1960.

Smythe, Hugh H. and Mabel M. *The New Nigerian Elite.* Stanford, 1960.

Talbot, Percy A. *The Peoples of Southern Nigeria: A Sketch of their History, Ethnology and Languages.* 4 vols. London, 1926.

———. *Tribes of the Niger Delta.* London, 1932.

Urvoy, Y. *Histoire de l'empire du Bornou.* Paris, 1949.

Wheare, Joan. *The Nigerian Legislative Council.* London, 1950.

Sierra Leone, Gambia and Liberia

Anderson, Robert E. *Liberia, America's African Friend.* Chapel Hill, 1952.

Banton, Michael P. *West African City: A Study of Tribal Life in Freetown.* London, 1957.

Bixler, Raymond W. *The Foreign Policy of the United States in Liberia.* New York, 1957.

*Buell, Raymond L. *Liberia: A Century of Survival, 1847-1947.* Philadelphia, 1947.

Davis, Stanley A. *This is Liberia.* New York, 1953.

Hargreaves, J. D. *Life of Sir Samuel Lewis.* London, 1959.

Huberick, Charles H. *The Political and Legislative History of Liberia.* 2 vols. New York, 1947.

Johnston, Harry H., baronet. *Liberia.* 2 vols. London, 1906.

Kup, A. Peter. *A History of Sierra Leone, 1400-1789.* Cambridge (Eng.), 1961.

Lewis, Roy. *Sierra Leone: A Modern Portrait.* London, 1954.

Southorn, Bella S. *The Gambia.* London, 1952.

Staudenraus, P. J. *The African Colonization Movement, 1816-1865.* New York, 1961.

Utting, Francis A. J. *The Story of Sierra Leone.* London, 1931.

EAST AND CENTRAL AFRICA

General (including Nyasaland, for which also see "Southern Africa: Rhodesia and Nyasaland")

Axelson, Eric V. *South-east Africa, 1488-1530.* London, 1940.

Boxer, Charles R., and Carlos de Azevedo. *Fort Jesus and the Portuguese in Mombasa, 1593-1729.* London, 1960.

*Coupland, Reginald, baronet. *East Africa and Its Invaders, from the Earliest Times to the Death of Seyyid Said in 1856.* Oxford, 1938.

*———. *The Exploitation of East Africa, 1856-1890.* London, 1939.

Davidson, Basil. *The African Awakening*. London, 1955.

Dundas, Charles, baron. *African Crossroads*. London, 1955.

Great Britain. East Africa Royal Commission. *Report*. London, 1955.

Lugard, Frederick Dealtry, baron (Margery F. Perham and Mary Bull, eds.). *The Diaries of Lord Lugard, 1889-1892*. 3 vols. London, 1959.

Marsh, Zoë A., and G. Kingsnorth. *An Introduction to the History of East Africa*. Cambridge (Eng.), 1957.

Mitchell, Philip E., baronet. *African Afterthoughts*. London, 1954.

Portuguese

*Duffy, James. *Portuguese Africa*. Cambridge (Mass.), 1959.

Egerton, F. Clement C. *Angola in Perspective*. London, 1957.

Nevinson, Henry W. *A Modern Slavery*. New York, 1906.

Oliveira Boleo, José de. *Moçambique*. Lisbon, 1951.

Belgian

Ceulemans, R. P. P. *La question arabe et le Congo (1883-1892)*. Brussels, 1959.

Cornet, René J. *Katanga*. (3rd ed.) Brussels, 1946.

Gérard-Libois, J., and B. Verhaegen. *Congo 1960*. 2 vols. and annex. Brussels, 1961.

Gilis, Charles-André. *Kimbangu: fondateur d'église*. Brussels, 1960.

Hennessy, Maurice N. *The Congo: A Brief History and Appraisal*. New York, 1961.

Johnston, Harry H., baronet. *George Grenfell and the Congo*. 2 vols. London, 1908.

Joye, Pierre, and Rosine Lewin. *Les trusts au Congo*. Brussels, 1961.

Legum, Colin. *Congo Disaster*. Harmondsworth, 1961.

Maquet, Jacques J. *Le système des relations sociales dans le Ruanda ancien*. Tervuren (Belg.), 1954.

Marvel, Tom. *The New Congo*. New York, 1948.

Morel, Edmund D. *Red Rubber: The Story of the Rubber Slave Trade Flourishing on the Congo in the Year of Grace 1906*. London, 1906.

Rwanda politique (1956-1961). Brussels, 1961.

Ryckmans, Pierre. *Dominer pour servir*. (new ed.) Brussels, 1948.

*Slade, Ruth. *The Belgian Congo: Some Recent Changes*. London, 1960.

Thompson, Robert Stanley. *Fondation de l'état indépendant du Congo*. Brussels, 1933.

544 BIBLIOGRAPHY

Van der Kerken, Georges. *La politique coloniale belge.* Antwerp, 1943.

Uganda

Gale, H. P. *Uganda and the Mill Hill Fathers.* London, 1959.
*Ingham, Kenneth. *The Making of Modern Uganda.* London, 1958.
Johnston, Harry H., baronet. *The Uganda Protectorate.* (2nd ed.) 2 vols. New York, 1904.
Low, D. A. *Religion and Society in Buganda, 1875-1900.* Kampala, 1956.
*———, and R. C. Pratt. *Buganda and British Overrule, 1900-1955.* London, 1960.
Taylor, J. V. *The Growth of the Church in Buganda.* London, 1958.

Kenya

Dilley, Marjorie R. *British Policy in Kenya Colony.* New York, 1937.
Eliot, Charles, baron. *The East African Protectorate.* London, 1905.
Farson, Negley. *Last Chance in Africa.* London, 1949.
Hill, M. F. *Permanent Way: The Story of the Kenya and Uganda Railway.* Nairobi, 1950.
Huxley, Elspeth. *White Man's Country: Lord Delamere and the Making of Kenya.* (2nd ed.) 2 vols. London, 1953.
———, and Margery F. Perham. *Race and Politics in Kenya.* (new ed.) 2 vols. London, 1953.
*Kenyatta, Jomo. *Facing Mount Kenya.* London, 1938.
*Leakey, L. S. B. *Defeating Mau Mau.* London, 1954.
*———. *Mau Mau and the Kikuyu.* London, 1952.
Leys, Norman. *Kenya.* (2nd ed.) London, 1925.
———. *The Colour Bar in East Africa.* London, 1941.
Lipscomb, J. F. *White Africans.* London, 1955.
*Wood, Susan. *Kenya: The Tensions of Progress.* London, 1960.

Tanganyika and Zanzibar

Cameron, Donald C., baronet. *My Tanganyika Service and Some Nigeria.* London, 1939.
Hollingsworth, Lawrence W. *Zanzibar under the Foreign Office, 1890-1913.* London, 1953.
Ingrams, William H. *Zanzibar, Its History and People.* London, 1931.
Leubuscher, Charlotte. *Tanganyika Territory: A Study of Economic Policy under Mandate.* London, 1944.

SOUTHERN AFRICA

General (including Rhodesia, South Africa, and dependent territories)

Ashton, Edmund H. *The Basuto.* London, 1954.
Clark, John Desmond. *The Stone Age Culture of Northern Rhodesia.* Claremont (Cape), 1950.
*————. *The Prehistory of Southern Africa.* Harmondsworth, 1959.
Jackson, Mabel V. *European Powers and Southeast Africa.* London, 1942.
Kuper, Hilda. *An African Aristocracy: Rank Among the Swazi.* London, 1947.
Millin, Sarah Gertrude. *Rhodes.* (rev. ed.) London, 1952.
Sachs, Wolf. *Black Hamlet.* London, 1937. (Reprinted as *Black Anger,* New York, 1947.
Schapera, Isaac. *The Khoïsan Peoples of South Africa.* London, 1930.
———— (ed.). *The Bantu-Speaking Tribes of South Africa.* New York, 1952.
Sillery, Anthony. *Sechele: The Story of an African Chief.* Oxford, 1954.
Smith, Prudence (ed.). *Africa in Transition.* London, 1958.
Theal, George M. *History and Ethnography of Africa South of the Zambesi.* (3rd ed.) 11 vols. London, 1888-1919.
Vedder, Heinrich. *Das alte Südwestafrika.* Berlin, 1934.
Walker, Eric Anderson. *Historical Atlas of South Africa.* Capetown, 1922.
*————. *A History of Southern Africa.* (3rd ed.) London, 1957.
Wellington, John H. *Southern Africa, a geographical study.* 2 vols. Cambridge (Eng.), 1955.
Wiid, Johannes A. *Die Rolle der Burenrepubliken in der Auswärtigen und Kolonialen Politik des Deutschen Reiches in den Jahren 1883-1900.* Nuremberg, 1927.
Williams, Basil. *Cecil Rhodes.* London, 1938.

South Africa, Republic of (General)

Bosman, D. B. *Oor die Ontstan van Afrikaans.* Capetown, 1939.
Bryant, Alfred T. *The Zulu People as they were before the White Man Came.* Pietermaritzburg, 1949.
Cory, George E. *The Rise of South Africa.* 5 vols. London, 1910-30.
Curtis, Lionel. *With Milner in South Africa.* Oxford, 1951.

Davies, Horton, and R. H. W. Shepherd (eds.). *South African Missions, 1800-1950: An Anthology.* London, 1954.

De Kiewiet, Cornelius W. *A History of South Africa, Social and Economic.* Oxford, 1941.

De Kock, Victor. *Ons Drie Eeuwe: Our Three Centuries.* Capetown, 1952.

Du Plessis, Izak D. *The Cape Malays.* (2nd ed.) Capetown, 1947.

Du Plessis, Johannes. *A History of Christian Missions in South Africa.* Lovedale (Cape), 1911.

Eybers, G. W. (ed.). *Select Constitutional Documents Illustrating South African History, 1795-1910.* London, 1918.

Gandhi, Mohandas K. *Satyagraha in South Africa.* Stanford, 1954.

Hoernlé, Reinhold F. A. *South African Native Policy and the Liberal Spirit.* Lovedale (Cape), 1939.

Hurwitz, Nathan. *Agriculture in Natal, 1860-1950.* Capetown, 1957.

Keppel-Jones, Arthur. *South Africa.* (2nd ed.) London, 1953.

MacCrone, Ian D. *Race Attitudes in South Africa.* London, 1937.

Macmillan, W. M. *Bantu, Boer and Briton.* London, 1929.

Malherbe, Ernst Gideon. *Education in South Africa (1652-1922).* Capetown, 1925.

Marais, Johannes S. *The Cape Coloured People, 1652-1937.* Johannesburg, 1957.

Milner, Alfred M., viscount (Cecil Headlam, ed.). *The Milner Papers.* 2 vols. London, 1931-33.

Mossop, E. E. (ed. and transl.). *The Journals of Brink and Rhenius.* Capetown, 1947.

Mukherji, S. B. *Indian Minority in South Africa.* New Delhi, 1959.

Neumark, Solomon Daniel. *The South African Frontier: Economic Influences, 1652-1836.* Stanford, 1957.

Palmer, Mabel. *The History of the Indians in Natal.* Capetown, 1957.

Patterson, Sheila. *Colour and Culture in South Africa.* London, 1953.

*————. *The Last Trek: A Study of the Boer People and the Afrikaner Nation.* London, 1957.

Sundkler, Bengt G. M. *Bantu Prophets in South Africa.* London, 1948.

Theal, George M. (ed.). *Records of the Cape Colony.* 36 vols. London, 1897-1905.

Van den Heever, C. M., and P. de V. Pienaar (eds.). *Kultuurgeschiedenis van die Afrikaner.* 3 vols. Capetown, 1945-47.

Van der Merwe, W. J. *The Development of Missionary Attitudes in the Dutch Reformed Church in South Africa.* Capetown, 1936.

Van Riebeeck Society. *Publications.* 37 vols. Capetown, 1918-56.

Walker, Eric Anderson. *Lord de Villiers and His Times: South Africa 1842-1914.* London, 1925.

————. *The Frontier Tradition in South Africa.* London, 1930.

Wessels, J. W. *History of Roman-Dutch Law.* Grahamstown (Cape), 1908.

Wiid, Johannes A., A. L. Geyer, and A. J. H. van der Walt. *Geskiedenis van Suid-Afrika.* 2 vols. Capetown, 1955.

Wilson, Monica. *Reaction to Conquest: Effects of Contact with Europeans on the Pondo of South Africa.* London, 1936.

South Africa, Republic of (1800-1902)

Agar-Hamilton, J. A. I. *The Native Policy of the Voortrekkers.* Capetown, 1928.

Bird, John. *The Annals of Natal.* 2 vols. Pietermaritzburg, 1888.

Bryce, James B., viscount. *Impressions of South Africa.* New York, 1897.

De Kiewiet, Cornelius W. *The Imperial Factor in South Africa.* Cambridge (Eng.), 1937.

de Wet, Christiaan Rudolf. *Three Years' War.* New York, 1902.

Fitzpatrick, J. P. *The Transvaal from Within.* New York, 1900.

Hattersley, Alan F. *Portrait of a Colony: The Story of Natal.* London, 1940.

————. *The British Settlement of Natal: A Study in Imperial Migration.* Cambridge (Eng.), 1950.

Hockly, Harold E. *The Story of the British Settlers of 1820 in South Africa.* (2nd ed.) Capetown, 1957.

Kruger, Stephanus J. Paul (A. Texeira de Mattos, transl.). *The Memoirs of Paul Kruger.* New York, 1902.

Moffat, Robert. *Missionary Labours and Scenes in Southern Africa.* London, 1842.

Mofolo, Thomas (F. H. Dutton, transl.). *Chaka the Zulu.* London, 1949.

Reitz, Deneys. *Commando: A Boer Journal of the Boer War.* (2nd ed.) London, 1945.

Reitz, F. W. *A Century of Wrong.* London, 1900.

Scholtz, J. du P. *Die Afrikaner en sy Taal, 1806-1875.* Capetown, 1939.

Smith, Edwin W. *The Life and Times of Daniel Lindley* (1801-80). New York, 1952.

Uys, C. J. *In the Era of Shepstone*. Lovedale (Cape), 1933.

Van der Horst, Sheila Terreblanche. *Native Labour in South Africa*. London, 1942.

Walker, Eric Anderson. *The Great Trek*. London, 1934.

Worsfold, W. B. *Sir Bartle Frere*. London, 1923.

South Africa, Republic of (*since 1902*)

*Carter, Gwendolen M. *The Politics of Inequality: South Africa Since 1948*. New York, 1958.

Dvorin, Eugene P. *Racial Separation in South Africa*. Chicago, 1952.

Krüger, D. W. (ed.). *South African Parties and Policies, 1910-1960: A Select Source Book*. London, 1960.

*Malan, Daniel François. *Afrikaner Volkseenheid: En My Ervarings op die Pad Daarheen*. Capetown, 1959.

Marquard, Leo. *The People and Policies of South Africa*. London, 1952.

Morris, James. *South African Winter*. London, 1958.

Newton, Arthur P. (ed.). *Select Documents Relating to the Unification of South Africa*. 2 vols. London, 1924.

Pienaar, S., and Anthony Sampson. *South Africa: Two Views of Separate Development*. London, 1960.

Pyrah, Geoffrey Barker. *Imperial Policy and South Africa: 1902-10*. Oxford, 1955.

Roskam, K. L. *Apartheid and Discrimination*. Leyden, 1961.

Smuts, Jan Christian. *Holism and Evolution*. New York, 1926.

*South Africa. Commission for the Socio-Economic Development of the Bantu Areas. [Tomlinson Commission] *Summary of the Report*. (U.G. 61/1955) Pretoria, 1956.

Thompson, Leonard M. *The Unification of South Africa, 1902-1910*. Oxford, 1960.

Rhodesia and Nyasaland (*see also "East and Central Africa: General"*)

Barnes, James. *Politics in a Changing African Society: A Political History of the Fort Jameson Ngoni*. Capetown, 1954.

*Colson, Elizabeth, and Max Gluckman (eds.). *Seven Tribes of British Central Africa*. London, 1951.

Coupland, Reginald, baronet. *Kirk on the Zambezi*. Oxford, 1928.

Davidson, James W. *The Northern Rhodesian Legislative Council*. London, 1948.

Debeham, Frank. *Nyasaland: The Land of the Lake*. London, 1955.

Epstein, Arnold L. *Politics in an Urban African Community*. Manchester, 1958.

Gann, L. H. *The Birth of a Plural Society: Northern Rhodesia under the British South Africa Company, 1894-1914.* Manchester, 1958.

*Gray, Richard. *The Two Nations.* London, 1960.

Hanna, Alexander John. *The Beginnings of Nyasaland and Northeastern Rhodesia, 1859-1895.* Oxford, 1956.

————. *The Story of the Rhodesias and Nyasaland.* London, 1960.

Johnston, Harry H., baronet. *British Central Africa.* (2nd ed.) London, 1898.

Leys, Colin. *European Politics in Southern Rhodesia.* Oxford, 1959.

*Mason, Philip. *The Birth of a Dilemma.* London, 1958.

————. *Year of Decision: Rhodesia and Nyasaland in 1960.* London, 1960.

Paver, Bertram Garrett. *His Own Oppressor.* London, 1958.

Shepperson, George, and T. Price. *Independent African: John Chilembwe and the . . . Nyasaland Native Rising of 1915.* Edinburgh, 1958.

Thompson, Cecil H., and Harry W. Woodruff. *Economic Development in Rhodesia and Nyasaland.* London, 1954.

INDEX

Mumba, Levi Z., 477
Murdock, George Peter, 15, 18
Mutesa I, 171, 194-5
Mutesa II (see Frederick Mutesa
II)
Mwami, Ruanda-Urundi, 459-62
Mwanga, 195-8
Mzilikazi, 134-5, 145, 263, 284

NAACP (see National Association
for the Advancement of Colored
People)
NCNC (see National Council of
Nigeria and the Cameroons)
NEPU (see Northern Elements Pro-
gressive Union)
NGK (see Nederlands Gerefoorme-
erde Kerk)
NHK (see Nederlands Hervoormde
Kerk)
NLM (see National Liberation
Movement)
NPC (see Northern Peoples Con-
gress)
NPP (see Northern People's Party)
NYM (see Nigerian Youth Move-
ment)
Nachtigal, Dr. Gustav, 236, 248
Nachtmaal (Nagtmaal), 122
Nairobi, 399, 415-17
Napier, Sir George, 143
Napoleon I, 128-9
Natal: Ngoni (Bantu) arrive, 115;
Republic (Boer), 144-8; British
in, 146-8; Colony (1843-1899),
263-8, 275, 281, 286, 292, 296-7;
Colony (1899-1910), 301, 304-7;
Province, Union of South Africa,
310, 495, 498-9, 506, 513, 515;
(see also Zulu)
National African Company, Ltd.,
235-6, 238
National Assembly, Uganda, 410
National Association for the Ad-
vancement of Colored People
(NAACP), 326-7, 329-30, 332,
336, 357, 419

National Church of Nigeria, 360
National Congress of British West
Africa, 339, 341, 356
National Convention, South Afri-
can, 306-7
National Council of Nigeria and the
Cameroons (NCNC), 358, 360-
3, 365
National Fusion ministry, South Af-
rica, 500-1
National Liberation Movement
(NLM), 351-3
National Socialism (Nazism), South
Africa and, 502, 504-6, 511
National Union Movement, 283,
291-3
nationalism, African non-white):
general discussion, 112-20, 525-7;
European stimulus toward, 317-
20, 322-4; and Africans studying
abroad, 334-5 (see also individual
countries)
nationalism, European: and social
Darwinism, 186-7; as factor in
imperial expansion, 167-9; in
South Africa (see Afrikaners;
Boers; British South Africans)
Nationalist Party, Union of South
Africa: (before 1932), 310, 317,
492-4, 496, 499-501; Purified,
501-6; Reunited, 506-11; (after
1949), 511-15, 517-18, 522-3
Native Affairs Commission, 496
Native Associations, Nyasaland,
474-5, 477
Native Trust and Land Act (1936),
Union of South Africa, 497, 520
Native Welfare Associations, North-
ern Rhodesia, 483
Natives Land Act, Union of South
Africa (1913), 494-5, 497, 520
Natives' Representative Council,
Union of South Africa, 520
Nazism (see National Socialism)
Ndebele (see Matabele)
Nederlands Gerefoormeerde Kerk
(NGK), 155-6, 512-13 (see also

ABOUT THE AUTHOR

DONALD LAWRENCE WIEDNER *was born in Oceanside, New York, in 1930. He attended high school in Floral Park, New York, and received his bachelor's degree from Colgate University in 1952. Dr. Wiedner did postgraduate work at Harvard, where he obtained his M.A. in 1953 and, after two years' service as lieutenant in the Navy, his Ph.D. in 1958. He has taught at the University of Michigan and at Mount Holyoke College, and is now Assistant Professor of History at the University of Alberta. Dr. Wiedner was elected to Phi Beta Kappa in 1952; he has been awarded fellowships by the Woodrow Wilson and Danforth Foundations; and in 1960 he was elected Fellow of the African Studies Association. He has published reviews in* Africa Report; A HISTORY OF AFRICA *is his first book.*